THE SAINTS AND THE STATE

The Mormon Troubles in Illinois

James Simeone

OHIO UNIVERSITY PRESS
ATHENS

Ohio University Press, Athens, Ohio 45701
ohioswallow.com

Printed in the United States of America
Ohio University Press books are printed on acid-free paper ∞ ™

31 30 29 28 27 26 25 24 23 22 21   5 4 3 2 1

Library of Congress Cataloging-in-Publication Data

Names: Simeone, James, 1960– author.
Title: The Saints and the state : the Mormon troubles in Illinois / James Simeone.
Other titles: Mormon troubles in Illinois
Description: Athens : Ohio University Press, [2021] | Series: New approaches to Midwestern studies | Includes bibliographical references and index.
Identifiers: LCCN 2020048160 (print) | LCCN 2020048161 (ebook) | ISBN 9780821424469 (hardcover) | ISBN 9780821447383 (pdf)
Subjects: LCSH: Mormons—Illinois—History—19th century. | Pioneers—Political activity—Illinois. | Nauvoo (Ill.)—History—19th century. | Illinois. Militia. Nauvoo Legion—History. | Illinois—Politics and government—To 1865. | Illinois—History—1778–1865.
Classification: LCC F550.M8 S56 2021 (print) | LCC F550.M8 (ebook) | DDC 977.3/4303—dc23
LC record available at https://lccn.loc.gov/2020048160
LC ebook record available at https://lccn.loc.gov/2020048161

To Kathi, a nonconforming individualist

Contents

Illustrations

FIGURES

TABLES

Series Editors' Preface

The Saints and the State is the fourth book in Ohio University Press's New Approaches to Midwestern Studies series and the first to appear during our tenure as series editors. It carries forward the tradition of strong monographs that tell important and sometimes underexplored aspects of midwestern history and society. In the spirit of the series, James Simeone takes an interdisciplinary approach, weaving together the histories of religion, political thought, and partisan politics to explain the tumultuous story of the Mormons' settlement in and ultimate expulsion from Illinois. Managing the tension between majority rule and minority rights within democratic governance has always proven a challenging endeavor. The expanding frontier of the early republic offered no haven from that reality, especially when questions of morality and religion were involved.

The rich narrative surrounded by probative analytical arguments tells how Jacksonian America grappled with diversity and particularly with the presence of one of America's first homegrown religious movements, Mormonism. The book offers, in part, a rethinking of how to view discrimination and violence against Mormons, which is typically ascribed to social and religious intolerance. This book does not dismiss those arguments but situates them within larger and equally salient questions of how rights-based justice requires state protection. Simeone skillfully weaves together this story, drawing some important conclusions about the role of minority rights within a republican system, namely that without a certain level of state capacity—and trust in it—enforcing fair and inclusive justice is exceedingly difficult.

Through its discussion of state capacity, *The Saints and the State* consciously engages modern political problems and offers windows into universal political challenges that remain with us today. In this case study of how youthful democracies grapple with real and imagined fears of disorder, Simeone addresses the proper ongoing relationships among justice, rights, and state power within a democratic form of government. His conclusion that legal norms are filtered through majority cultures that often drive nonliberal policy outcomes calls on readers—academics and publics alike—to rethink their assumptions about state control, majoritarianism, and the relationships between marginalized communities and political institutions. These topics are useful not only to historians but to anyone interested in studying and furthering the importance and parameters of democracy.

In grappling with such sweeping issues, *The Saints and the State* contributes to and intervenes in a growing scholarship on the nineteenth-century state. Though much of that literature to date has focused on the East Coast, Simeone extends the story of antebellum state development into the Old Northwest, offering valuable insights into the region that this series covers. By so doing, he problematizes a body of scholarship on the early republic that stresses the power of the states or the federal government in shaping the daily lives of Americans. This book convincingly argues that in the sparsely populated West, neither the state nor the national government had enough authority or power to exert influence without the use of local hierarchies and households, which in turn created challenges for groups defined as outside those localized norms. The weakness of the state prevented it from successfully enforcing supposedly neutral laws premised on equality. This, in turn, helps explain the violence that culminated in the Mormon War and the coerced removal of a religious minority from Illinois.

The Saints and the State is a provocative book, one that ultimately questions the ability of the state to operate as a neutral actor. Even in its nascent form and under Jacksonian leadership suspicious of state power, the antebellum state of Illinois created an ordered society that privileged majority morality at the expense of minority views. Simeone's melding of ideas and history suggests that achieving a modicum of fairness in a modern democracy requires appreciating disproportionate power relations and a level of individual and collective self-awareness and empathy that partisan politics too frequently prevents.

We are very pleased to welcome this thoughtful and timely history of ideas and political practice into New Approaches to Midwestern Studies.

Brian Schoen, Ohio University
Matthew E. Stanley, Albany State University

Preface

No work can speak to all audiences, but a work on democracy should try to be as inclusive as possible. I have kept modern-day settlers to Illinois in mind as I have written, believing they will find these pages especially pertinent to the issues they are facing as immigrants today. While I have thought of friends like Nazma Ali, Diego Mendez Carbajo, Ryszard Stadnik, Agbenyega "Tony" Adedze, Rabah Seffal, Carmela Ferradans, and Munib Mafazy as an audience, I have tried to speak to my students too. They are among the current generation of youth who persistently question American democracy and who just as persistently seek solutions to its contemporary troubles. I have appreciated being able to discuss the dilemmas of democracy with bright students like Casey Plach, Todd Zoellick, Amy Uden, Ryan Dyar, Zoe Bouras, Andy Baldock, Nick Valdivia, and Anthony Gunnell.

I seek a third audience in those who believe that democratic law can be fair and that democratic government can correct its biases. Those who share these aspirations should pay close attention to the fate of Governor Thomas Ford. He is the closest the story of the Mormon troubles in Illinois comes to having a hero, if a tragic one. Ford believed democratic majorities could deliver justice better than any other form of governmental authority could, but he had a blind spot. He thought the only route to fairness was through making the law general and neutral to all groups, a belief in which he persisted in face of evidence to the contrary. If law in democracies is simply used to regulate and control the harm one citizen might cause another, it could be both neutral and fair. But law is also used to enforce a societal order. It enforces civic membership based on society's ideas of inclusion and exclusion.

In Ford's time, Illinoisans pioneered the image of the independent producer and used it to determine insider and outsider status, as we still do today. The informal rules governing who is designated an independent producer are necessarily arbitrary and particular to any given societal culture. While this part of the state can never be neutral, we can work to make it fair. Ford's myopia as to the way democratic states use civil society's status order is seen in his comments on Illinois's "black laws," the set of nineteenth-century laws regulating the behavior of the state's "free Negroes, mulattoes, servants and slaves."[1] In his *History*, he remarks upon the laws' great detail and cruelty and wonders for "what purpose such severities were denounced against slaves and servants when their numbers were so few that they could not be dangerous."[2] As an antislavery man, Ford was clearly disturbed by the law's lack of fairness toward the African American minority. African Americans had done nothing to deserve their demeaned status and posed no harm. Ford thereby implies that the law's only purpose is to enforce the harm principle by minimizing dangers to private or public safety. In fact, the law also serves as a means for citizens to communicate majority worth; it is also an ordering device. It assumes that fellow citizens will not only refrain from harm and respect each other's rights but also share a worthwhile public life.

Just as the air we breathe animates our bodies, a shared societal culture vivifies what the majority seeks to do with the state. Often without realizing it, we use the law not simply to enforce the harm principle but to order society. This means that state neutrality with respect to the law is impossible and often not even desirable as an ideal. The best we can aim for is fairness. The sooner we recognize and own this fact, the more likely our democracy can approach the ideal of justice for all.

Acknowledgments

To conduct archival research over several years, one needs the support of many people. A number of scholars have offered me assistance, and my debts to the academic community are many. Librarians across the country have helped on more occasions than I am able to remember, but I especially thank Tony Heaton, Meg Miner, Thomas Mann, Debbie Hamm, Jane Ehrenhart, Cheryl Schnirring, John Hoffmann, and Bill Kemp. The staffs at the Newberry Library, the Chicago Historical Society, the Library of Congress, the New York Public Library, and the Abraham Lincoln Presidential Library have been especially helpful. The Illinois history community has been a constant source of support and inspiration. I have enjoyed conversing with Bill and Jane Ann Moore, Graham Peck, Tracy Roberts, Bill Johnson, Dave Edmunds, Stewart Winger, Sundiata Keita Cha-Jua, Dana Weiner, Mark Voss-Hubbard, Stacy Robertson, and Sam Wheeler. In Livingston County, Marty Travis graciously shared the Spence-Travis-Darnall family records with me.

I owe a special debt to Vernon Burton, who took me into the University of Illinois graduate history seminar he held in his family's living room. The seminar gave me a chance to present early versions of this work, and I benefitted from being forced to articulate the concept of the regime to a room full of skeptical historians. Vernon's knack for supporting academic orphans is only one of his many gifts. I especially appreciated his introducing me to the Association of British American Nineteenth Century Historians (BrANCH) seminars, which made it possible for me to dialogue with William Shade, Sean Wilentz, David Carwardine, Richard Blackett, Daniel Walker Howe, and John Ashworth. The Society for Historians of the Early American Republic (SHEAR) has always been open to scholars of American political development; I remember lively conversations with Donald Ratcliffe, Silvana Siddali, and

Andrew Shankman. Through SHEAR I was also able to meet Paul Finkelman, who originally invited me to contribute to an Ohio University Press series on the Midwest. I thank editors Tyler Balli and Rick Huard for the care they took ushering the manuscript through several stages of completion. Among political scientists, I have had the opportunity to think out loud with Rogers Smith, a leading light within the field of American citizenship and a champion of its worth-based approaches. None of these scholars, however generous with their time, bear any responsibility for what I have written; any errors that remain in the work are my own.

For over twenty years the social science reading group at Illinois Wesleyan University (IWU) provided me a home for scholarly debate and congenial discussion. I thank the regular participants for my continuing education, including Chris Prendergast, Diego Mendez Carbajo, Irv Epstein, William Munro, Carl Gillett, Bob Schultz, Jim Sikora, Greg Shaw, Rebecca Gearhart Mafazy, Dennie Groh, Jason Moralee, Teddy Amaloza, Paul Bushnell, Mike Weis, Sonja Fritzsche, and Brian Hatcher. The generous spirit of collegial discussion has lived on in the Dialogues across the Disciplines group, and I thank Bob Erlewine, Carolyn Nadeau, Carmela Ferradans, and Joanne Diaz for keeping the life of the mind alive on the IWU campus. Bookseller John Chandler and friends Adam Stephanides, Susan Gofstein, Bill O'Donnell, Jason Reblando, Andy Engen, Ed Donley, and Bob Scheffler continue to be an intellectual lifeline. IWU colleagues Amy Coles and Kevin Sullivan took the time to track down sources in their areas of expertise for me.

I am grateful that Richard E. Bennett inadvertently entangled me in the topic of Mormon troubles in Illinois by inviting me to present a paper on antebellum Illinois politics to his Mormon history seminar at Washington University. I thank three anonymous reviewers for Ohio University Press who encouraged my efforts and suggested improvements. And finally, I thank Kathi Zurkowski for her unfailing love and inspiration. Even her sad poems are funny.

Introduction

Settler Illinois as a Developing Democracy

The story of the Mormon troubles in Illinois is a story of failed governance. Many democratic regimes confront the problem of legitimating governance, but emerging democracies face the problem without adequate tools of enforcement. It is my contention that settler Illinois was one such developing democracy and that we can better understand the dilemmas faced by modern democratic states, both developing and developed, by carefully observing the experience of antebellum Illinois.

To study the state is to study power. Political power can be viewed as existing along a continuum that runs from pure force on one end to pure persuasion on the other. As Alexander Hamilton argued in the first *Federalist,* state power is experienced as legitimate authority if it allows for "reflection and choice"; if not, it will be marked as an illegitimate kind of "accident and force."[1] All governments seek to convert power into legitimate authority. Rule by naked force or violence is too costly. But persuasion is costly, too, as anyone who has tried to induce consensus in a large group can attest. Consequently, political systems economize on consent and aim for something short of pure persuasion. In the case of democracies, the calculus of consent centers on the majority; political power is rendered into authority first and foremost by claiming to represent the majority. Of course, being accountable to the majority of voters does not mean being accountable to all those affected by state power. In liberal democratic theory, all those outside the circle of members remain unaffiliated and potentially face the state's force without protection. Those who are unrecognized and considered outsiders by the majority frequently experience the violent, forceful side of the liberal state.

States have historically developed into democracies in waves. Although focused on their own internal affairs, nations undergoing democratization have participated in a larger contagion effect from outside their borders. Laurence Whitehead counts five waves of democratization by "contagion through proximity" since the first democracy at Athens; these waves account for seventy-six governments, a large percentage of the democracies standing today.[2] Across time the definition of democratic government has remained fairly stable. A messy, if more or less accepted definition cultivated over the years by Robert Dahl and colleagues, is as follows: democracy is a form of government that results in elected officials obtaining office through "free and fair elections . . . [in which] all adults have the right to vote [and] run for public office." Of particular importance is "freedom of expression (especially for opposition parties)." At a minimum, democracies allow the formation of political parties, which provide citizens "sources of information that are not monopolized by the government of the state, or by any other single group."[3] The focus on fairly run elections and effectively enforced rights attests to the fact that citizens experiencing democratization are preoccupied first and foremost with the internal drama of harnessing the power of the state by subjecting it to the control of what the majority considers the electorate. In settler states—states where the people have moved into a new territory—local majorities are especially preoccupied with controlling the electoral process and the granting of rights.

If they develop in a liberal direction, many democracies tie their legitimacy to respect for individual moral worth. Such respect comes in the form of protecting the rights of individuals, whether members or nonmembers. Because the definition of legitimate authority keeps evolving as the protection of rights evolves, the need to secure legitimacy is a never-ending quest in governance. But developed democracies often reach a stable order by having enough capacity for law enforcement to satisfy the majority and enough respect for rights to provide a modicum of due-process protection to minority individuals or to those considered outsiders. Much as the majority often prefers to focus on the rights of its members only, the dynamic of governance in democracies inevitably spotlights the way the state treats minorities and outsiders.

Developing democracies are that subset of democracies which have not yet cemented their legitimacy to govern because they lack either the capacity to enforce the law or the law they seek to enforce persistently lacks popular support. Under such regimes, the protection of minority rights suffers and conflicts between majorities and minorities emerge. The institutional means that regimes develop over time to impose governance during conflicts often live on, shaping institutional state structures long after the critical junctures which first brought them to life have passed. Developed democracies have survived the governance conflicts of the past by patching together solutions enabling them to persist. They are shaped and marked by past deposits of new norms, rules, and organizations. States thus carry an archeology of conflicts within their lineaments.

In the settler states of antebellum America, incapacity to enforce the law left a legacy of beleaguered sheriffs, extralegal posses, and a recurring chorus of support for "rough justice."[4] The legacy chaffed against the Jacksonian Democrats' erstwhile calls for "equal rights."[5] One institutional residue was the nearly despotic prosecutorial power bestowed on local district attorneys, a power inherited nationally by the Federal Bureau of Investigation, which burgeoned during Prohibition and metastasized during the war on drugs in the 1980s. As Marie Gottschalk has suggested, the placement of the carceral powers of the American state in its prosecutorial subdivision—as opposed to the subdivision on health and welfare—has imparted a punitive approach to incarceration ever since.[6]

The Mormons (as members of the newly renamed Church of Jesus Christ of Latter-day Saints were commonly known) threatened the legitimacy of the majority societal culture in Illinois. The troubles were deep and long lasting enough to leave a detailed historical record. The Mormons challenged the majority's normative aspirations as much as its legal order. The societal culture expected the state government to enforce law and order and also reflect the majority's social norms. The settler state was legitimated not only by effectively enforcing the law but also by protecting the norms contained in extant "stories of peoplehood."[7] Normatively, Illinois residents experienced emigrating and acclimating to the settler state as an epochal process with deep personal and collective meaning. They vied for and struggled over legitimating stories as much as they struggled to enforce the harm principle, the rule that all individuals are free to act as they will as long as their actions do no harm to other individuals or their property.

Effective governance requires trust. When trust fails, people turn to worth. It is a norm constructed in the give-and-take of civil society using the stories that the majority finds compelling. Trust was not easy to come by in frontier Illinois. To fill the gaps and bolster social cohesion, settlers told a story of a group of independent producers who came to the state to share in the adventure of land ownership and self-government. The independent-producer story was rarely articulated as such, but it could be found hovering in the collective imagination whenever the question of membership and the regulation of insider and outsider status arose. Under settler-state rules, the determination of who proved to be a worthy independent producer was delegated to local majorities. In theory, the state neutrally adjudicates worth by resolving conflicts between individuals involving harm; coercion is justified only against those who violate the harm principle. This is the deceptively simple and formal principle that, Joel Feinberg writes, "permits society to restrict the liberty of some persons in order to prevent harm to others."[8] If the Mormon troubles merely involved the misapplication of the harm principle rule to the Mormon minority, it would be unremarkable and of little import to our understanding of developing democracy. Indeed, many Illinoisans tried to frame the Mormon troubles as a matter of the sect's threat to persons and property in Hancock County, where the Mormons settled. Governor Thomas Ford's problem of governance would have been considerably simplified if this were the only issue the Mormons raised. As a judge in Ogle County, Ford had encountered and understood the activities of frontier outlaws and the communal response of "Regulators" and "Vigilant Societies" demanding "prompt and sure punishment."[9] Ford perceived that calls for action against outlaws were often motivated as much by the need to prevent harm as by the desire to project a community order patterned after a particular identity. His resistance to and denial of the identity needs of local order in the name of justice were widely unpopular.

The tension between justice and order is ancient and profound. Do the tools of contemporary scholarship bring us no closer to understanding how justice and order are traded off in developing democracies? This study was undertaken in the belief that we can move beyond these broad distinctions to grasp why calls for "prompt and sure punishment" and rough justice repeatedly prevail over equal justice under law and due process in developing democracies. We can assess the way authority is constituted in developing states by focusing on how majorities frequently privilege one societal culture and one image of the ideal citizen and by realizing that they do so as a means of solving the collective-action problems they face. In American settler states like Illinois, the ideal citizen was the independent producer; it is an image that is with Americans still. When worth is called upon to supply the basis of trust, civil society engages in a politics of identity always subject to illiberal consequences.

Majorities are used as ordering devices as well as expressions of justice. When order and justice are conflated in democratic politics, rough justice frequently appears as the devious twin of popular justice. While we can better understand majorities by their use of the state, we can also assess minority group cultures more accurately by determining how encompassing they are for their members. Minority groups predictably respond to the demands majoritarian society places on group identity by deepening the ties of their own attachment. When the minority group is a religious sect, a familiar and ungovernable process is initiated in which "the need for spirituality" overlaps dangerously with "the need to belong."[10] Mormon minority group culture frequently expressed the camaraderie and solidarity of the oppressed, and though the rite of common property they developed in Ohio was abandoned in Illinois, the religious rites invented at Nauvoo created an inward focus and group loyalty that more than compensated for the unity ensured by shared property.

Leaders in all democracies shape states into ruling regimes that can be defined as durable sets of ideas, interests, and institutions. Regimes vary greatly in their foci and capacity to deliver services. Developing democracies are those in which the demand for popular justice is strong while the state's capacity to supply it and other services is weak. The definition of developing democracy thus applies especially to emerging democracies because their state capacity is frequently weak.[11] The two-sided dynamic of strong demand for authority and weak supply gives the concept of developing democracy explanatory power. Indeed, it has been extended by Larry Diamond to apply to modern developed democracies as well. Diamond urges scholars to take at all times a "developmental view of democracy, which emerges in fragments or parts, by no fixed sequence or timetable. From such a perspective, the presence of legal opposition parties, which may compete for power, and of greater space for civil society, constitute important foundations" for understanding how democracies vary.[12] In this view, legitimacy in any democracy depends on the capacity of state and civil society institutions to deliver a regime accountable to the people. The process of state formation, however, takes time and is subject to contingency; in newly developing democracies, the authority that civil society organizations offer to help build public order runs from feeble to overwhelming. Because levels of state capacity and demands for popular justice vary widely, the degree of development in democracies, young and old, can be usefully gauged. This is so despite the overly simple notions of development that scholars sometimes employ. It is a gross inaccuracy, Charles Tilly argues, to suggest development occurs in "standard stages, each more advanced than the previous stage," or that development is synonymous with complexity and that "differentiation leads to advancement."[13]

Undoubtedly, all democracies are developing at some level; all are merely "approaching democracy" as Czechoslovakian president Václav Havel suggested in a speech before the United States Congress in 1990.[14] But as Havel pointed out, the US had by then the benefit of approaching democracy and learning from its mistakes for over two hundred years, while Czechoslovakia was just beginning its developmental journey. In emerging democratic states, leaders frequently focus on "people power" and rely on stories of worth to compensate for a lack of governing capacity. Regime services are provided on a self-help basis and thus follow majority norms with grave consequences for attitudes on toleration. For their part, minority groups can be tempted to develop oppositional cultures under which membership becomes an all-encompassing experience serving as the equivalent of self-government. Group cultures can be arrayed on a continuum, from those that fully encumber a member's duties to those which impose mostly optional duties. Other factors, such as manipulation by the elite and civil society bonds, also affect the willingness to tolerate difference, but it is variation within the continua of majority norms and minority opposition that makes achieving popular justice through workable democratic institutions and ideologies more or less likely.[15] Together, these two factors—self-help service from majorities and the degree of minority group consciousness—allow us to assess how much governing capacity a democratic regime can achieve. Governance load can be conceptually measured by adding the degree of minority group consciousness to the amount of self-help service volunteered by majorities. The higher the load, the more the state will struggle to maintain order. The greater precision with which we can chart these factors allows a more fine-grained assessment of the governance work facing all states approaching democracy.

In newly developing democracies the capacity to apply the law is uneven. Gaps in enforcement create gaps in authority. The Mormon troubles in Illinois exposed many gaps in authority, which prompted civil society actors to serve as an ordering backstop when the state's ordinary police powers failed. The case study presented here exposes where the skin of the state broke to reveal the regime's sinews and tendons. In the exposure the anatomy of the antebellum settler state is discernible, offering an opportunity to observe and mark the critical junctures in the state-formation process.[16] Scholars continue to debate the very nature and power of the antebellum American state. Points of emphasis include the common-law rules enforced by the courts, the policymaking power of the parties, the coercive instruments of state governments, and the punitive impulses of executive branches.[17] The combination of strong but discretionary national measures at the federal level, along with popular but frequently ineffective institutions at the state level, made for the kind of uneven enforcement which plagues developing democracies.[18] *The Saints and the State* seeks to contribute to the state-formation debate by explaining how the Illinois regime came to be, dissecting its powers, and detailing how its uneven authority shaped and drove the Mormon troubles.

In Illinois the Mormons had enough societal power to have their formal rights recognized, a power Joseph Smith demonstrated repeatedly in successful appeals to the writ of habeas corpus. But these victories for due process, which Governor Ford celebrated as vindications of the rule of law, only enraged the anti-Mormons and prompted them to organize extralegal civil society norms and institutions against the Mormons. In much of Hancock County and certainly in the surrounding counties, the Mormons lacked what Daniel Brinks and Sandra Botero have called the "lateral support" needed for the effective enforcement of their legal rights.[19] Two durable patterns resulted that are still evident today: a popular impatience with and devaluation of due process as a route to justice and legal fairness, and the temptation on the part of societal majorities to use the ordering strength of their numbers as lateral support to manipulate enforcement of the law and thus legal outcomes. In both patterns the reliance on extralegal force is justified in ways that sap the promise of fairness, which is often taken as a mark of legitimate democracy. The mere ordering power of the majority is taken, under a kind of category mistake, to be a sign of justice itself.

Despite their recourse to vigilante justice, the anti-Mormons, in marshaling their lateral societal support, did not justify their actions by pointing to the Mormons' unconventional religious ideas or activities. Instead they issued reports on cases of thievery, complained about violations of "normal" settlement patterns, and highlighted disreputable "antirepublican" practices. It was not religious bigotry that caused Ford's democracy to run uneven but a felt loss of local control and a stymied ability by the "old settlers" to enforce their unwritten civic status quo. The difficulty of recognizing and acknowledging this part of democratic state power is a key lesson of the story of peoplehood told here. Those from competitive or individualist political cultures are especially susceptible to denying the need for societal culture norms and background foundational beliefs in the first place. These norms and beliefs are effectively hidden from individualists' view because they are a part of the status quo, a social force individualists struggle to see as anything but a kind of neutral starting point even as they appeal to its norms to impose order.

Perhaps the most damaging consequence of the competitive view of status quo neutrality is the belief that the public interest emerges automatically from market processes or the parallel idea that the public interest is nothing more than the natural result of citizens acting in their self-interest.[20] Alexis de Tocqueville addressed the issue in *Democracy in America,* in which he famously titled one chapter "How the Americans Combat Individualism by the Doctrine of Self-Interest Rightly Understood."[21] Published in an English translation in 1839, the chapter assumed that no society can do without a commitment to civic duty or virtue, which the idea of the public interest makes obligatory. Tocqueville disarmingly conceded that self-interest rightly understood is "not at all a sublime doctrine," yet he defended it because as a matter of practice he believed it would produce the same result as a commitment to duty and the public interest.[22] Whether it does or not is debatable, but Tocqueville was correct to observe that in effect the concept of civic duty had become optional in American civil society and easily confused with individual interest. The costs of this approach were ominously displayed during the Mormon troubles when the anti-Mormons took the initiative to perform citizenship in their own interest by organizing emergency meetings, political conventions, and impromptu militia actions.

In the preface to his *History of Illinois,* Ford acknowledged that he devoted many chapters to "our very unimportant mobs and wars, and particularly the Mormon wars." He added that "small events and little men" were the only materials available to tell his story.[23] The argument here is that, small and wrapped in foundational beliefs as it is, the story of the Mormon troubles in Illinois is needed in our times. In developed democracies the state has the capacity, if not always the political will, to apply the law fairly to all. The Mormon troubles in Illinois expose the role civil society groups play in driving illiberal developments by infiltrating the state and biasing its actions, a process that affects the United States more broadly. While state capacity has been strengthened, and thus the breakdown in public order is less likely, the hidden backstop power of civil society remains potentially available today. Americans still rely on an independent-producer master narrative that continues to be enforced largely at the local level. Membership in the group of American citizens is still subject to the rules of recognition set in place and maintained by the majority's societal culture.

The story of the settler state and its civil society shadow takes many twists and turns. It is a tragedy that unfolds in a succession of missed opportunities and fateful choices. In chapter 1 we find the Illinoisans blithely ignorant of the way state and society will structure their ability to receive the Latter-day Saints. As in many cases in which agency meets structure in democracies, early Illinoisans thought fairness to individuals was and should be a matter unconnected to culture. But as Feinberg notes, the purely "formalistic" version of the harm principle provides "no guide to the proper *content* of the law."[24] Societal cultures enforced by elites in the name of the majority provide the content and thus are an undeniable part of democratic authority.[25] In chapter 2 the political dilemmas Joseph Smith's beliefs created for state residents and officials are outlined.

Here the limitations of viewing the state as simply a neutral arbiter of the harm principle are exposed.

Chapter 3 outlines the Illinois regime created by the state's Jacksonian democracy and focuses on the driving force of the Democrats' egalitarian political culture. It introduces the notion of vertical equality, an idea of equality that emphasizes the ranking and comparison of groups in society. "Egalitarians," in this sense, are people who endorse equality for their particular group; they are less interested, if at all, in the liberal notion of equal moral worth, the idea that "each citizen is entitled to equal concern and respect."[26] Illinois politics did generate a few universalist egalitarian leaders, like Democrat Thomas Ford and Whig Abraham Lincoln, but they did not control the regime or characterize the larger culture. Chapter 4 makes plain the contemporary reality of the group status order in the state and in Hancock County; it sketches the contours of the Illinois way, the settler state's majoritarian societal culture, and the place of the Mormons within that culture's status order.

Chapter 5 narrates how the Illinois regime's institutional means, namely its common-law writ of habeas corpus and militia system, structured the interaction between political leaders and the Mormon minority. There readers will encounter the recurring pattern whereby a socially marginalized minority in a developing democracy finds ways to use the law to its short-term advantage at the cost of enraging the local majority. In chapter 6 the impact of the regime's political ideology and its commitment to local control are detailed. It argues that hegemonic conceptions of toleration and freedom of religion emphasized by scholars were less important in shaping outcomes than the anti-Mormons' perception of the Mormons as a collective threat to local control. The perception underscores how anti-Mormon leaders used an individualist political culture to justify a refusal to extend inclusion and toleration to a group they saw as dangerous. The Mormons could not be trusted with power, they argued, because while they asked for toleration, they unfairly denied it to others. Chapter 7 rehearses the difficulties Governor Ford faced in trying to end the troubles by treating both sides neutrally. By willfully dismissing the politics of civic worth, he prompted the dissolution of state authority in Hancock County. The high-minded denial of his own party's identity politics cost Ford the only public things he cared for: democracy's honor and the state's "goodly" reputation.

1

. . . .

Illinois in 1839

Land of Worth and Accommodation

Quincy, Illinois, was a "city of refuge" for Mormons in 1839.[1] The refugees from Missouri reported that Quincy citizens "nobly came forward" to provide food and shelter. Latter-day Saints praised "the citizens of Quincy *en masse,* and the people of Illinois generally" in the city paper *The Argus.*[2] The *Daily Chicago American* expressed what many in the state believed: "The Mormons, having been cruelly persecuted in Missouri, are all moving to Illinois, as the home of the oppressed."[3] Later that year when the Mormons relocated to Commerce, Illinois, their leader and prophet, Joseph Smith, renamed the village Nauvoo, or "beautiful plantation" in the pidgin Hebrew he gleaned from an Ohio rabbi.[4] The name fit the isolated high plain created by a sweeping Mississippi River oxbow. Illinois was a place of refuge and beauty for many immigrants in the 1830s and 1840s.

In Governor Thomas Ford's terse estimate, Illinois was "a goodly land" where "a crowd of strangers . . . met for adventure."[5] Its fertile soil with convenient access to water and timber pulled at the agrarian dreams of many. Their dreams were captured in various narratives seeking to demonstrate the dreamers' worth and value. The narrators came from many places and circumstances, but each made a special claim to belong. The newly arrived Mormons emphasized their persecuted status. Others, too, claimed a status as exiles, driven by persecution in many forms: Native Americans forcibly removed from the East, Black people escaping from slavery, White southerners fleeing the political culture of slavery, and the poor lured away from every eastern state and from foreign lands like Ireland and Germany.[6] The Mormons joined a settler state quite comfortable with claims of persecution, with many of its people committed to open doors because of their own recent arrival. Illinois had "become a refuge for the oppressed of all nations," intoned Nathaniel Niles in a Fourth of July oration at Belleville.[7] In the best version of their dream, Illinoisans accommodated all kinds of newcomers.

In the hardscrabble version, Illinois was a land of "suckers," a people akin to the fish schooling near the shores of the Mississippi, constantly moving to find a new and better location.[8] Many Americans were in fact moving to Illinois; it was the fastest-growing state in the Union in 1840. Its population tripled between 1830 (157,445) and 1840 (476,183) and then almost doubled again by 1850 (851,470). Many of Illinois's new American immigrants in this period came from the Northeast, with New York replacing Kentucky as the state with the highest percentage of new immigrants.[9] Already in 1840 Illinois could stake a claim to being the most diverse state in the Union, and by midcentury it vied with Ohio for leadership of a new region in the nation. The West was a land of settler states filled with newcomers. Many grappled with the agricultural challenges posed by unique microclimates and varying soils. As Pennsylvania emigrant Hiram Rutherford noted, "Illenois is said by some to be the hottest, the coldest, the wettest and the driest country in the United States. Still the crops seldom fail."[10] Editor John York Sawyer advertised for the *Western Ploughboy* because a new agricultural paper was needed "particularly in Illinois, where the population is made up of emigrants from almost every State in the Union, and Kingdom in Europe."[11]

Diversity of another sort had been an Illinois strength since its days as a frontier territory. In 1818, when Illinois entered the Union, and all through its first decade, the state was typical of states that bordered southern states—filled with people from the hills and mountains of Kentucky, Georgia, Maryland, and Virginia. One-tenth of these upland southern households brought with them enslaved African Americans, many of whom became indentured servants soon after entering the putatively free state. The Illinois they came to had, until recently, been the home of numerous Native Americans from different tribes who still regularly visited the northern half of the state.[12] Illinois Territory had been a property of Virginia, claimed from the British by George Rogers Clark during the Revolution. The Old Dominion deeded it to the United States in 1782. The British had wrenched the area from French Louisiana in 1763 after the Seven Years' War. In its days as the "Pays des Illinois," the French colony was governed by free leaseholders, or *habitants,* who lived in the old villages of Cahokia, Kaskaskia, and St. Mary and farmed ribbon plots splayed perpendicularly along the Mississippi River. For half a century, they maintained their farms with slave labor, exported corn and wheat to New Orleans, shipped wine to Paris, welcomed voyagers, and traded with coureurs de bois. As an infant settler society, French Illinois cultivated peaceful relations with the Kaskaskia in the surrounding area and the Potawatomi upriver in Chicago, and they watched nervously as the fierce Shawnee migrated into western Indiana, pushed out of Ohio and Kentucky by the Americans.[13] Quebec-born Pierre Menard, the state's first lieutenant governor, was only the most prominent representative of the substantial French presence along the river system running from Chicago to below St. Louis.

After statehood, many other Europeans came to share the Illinois dream. The English created a settlement in Edwards County in 1819, German émigrés gathered around Belleville, the Swiss went to Edwardsville, Swedes to Chicago and Galesburg, and free Black people to Golconda in Pope County, Brooklyn in St. Clair County, and New Philadelphia in Pike County. Jobs on the Illinois and Michigan Canal, first dug in 1836 at Chicago, lured a new tide of Irish laborers, the first wave having already made their home near the Galena lead mines. The canal business also brought a band of religious outcasts from Norway, known locally as the "Sloopers," who established a LaSalle County town along the canal in 1834.[14] The Mormons, many of whom originated in New England, soon contributed to the mix a new flow of English immigrants, who had converted to the faith after hearing Mormon missionaries. By 1841 these exiles from the industrial boom-and-bust cycles of Manchester and Birmingham numbered over one thousand annually.[15]

ILLINOIS'S THREE TIERS: SOUTH, CENTRAL, AND NORTH

In its growth between 1830 and 1850, Illinois added two new identities: central and northern tiers laid on top of the oldest southern

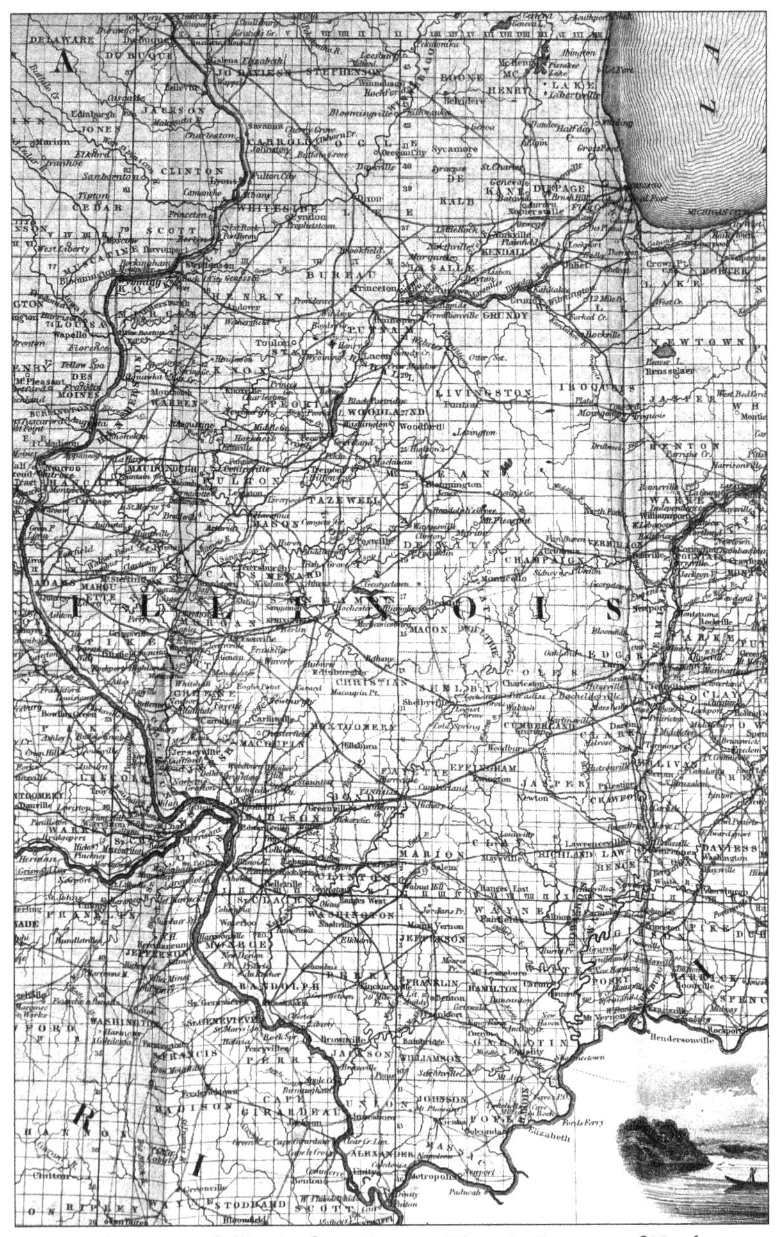

FIG. 1.1. 1844 Map of Illinois (from Brown, *History*). Courtesy of Newberry Library

layer. Each tier developed a distinct regional identity reflecting its settlement pattern. In this era Illinois became a perfect miniature of the nation's three lateral regions to the east. Northerners (especially from New England, Pennsylvania, and New York) were in the minority when they came to the southernmost tier of the area in its territorial days (1809–18). But the decade from 1830 to 1840 saw a massive influx of northerners (viz., "Easterners" or "Down Easters" as they were variously called) to the central and northern tiers.[16] They became the majority population in the northern tier and vied for the majority in the central tier. This was the era when the state capital moved north to Springfield and when Chicago grew to be the hub of northern Illinois and the state's largest city. While Galena in the northwest had more people in 1830, by 1840 Chicago had surpassed it; soon Cook and Will Counties in the northeast became the most populous in the northern tier. After 1839 Nauvoo, in the central latitude, grew so rapidly that its population exceeded those of regional centers at Quincy and Alton and likely exceeded Chicago's in 1843.[17]

Gradually, the population center was moving north. In 1830 the state had fifty-four counties, all but twenty south of Springfield; by 1850 forty-six of the state's ninety-nine counties were north of the capital. In the northern tier there was a move toward occupational diversity, for many came not to farm but to work the lead mines in Galena, to dig the Illinois and Michigan Canal, to merchandize and trade in Peoria and Chicago, or to lay tile to drain the upper Wabash River valley. These nonfarming occupations accelerated the productivity of the Illinois economy. The number of canal diggers peaked at 2,193 in August of 1838.[18] The canal waterworks, made possible by the thirty-seven-foot rise in the route, anticipated "a power at Ottawa sufficient to drive forty pairs of mill stones of four and a half feet in diameter."[19] By 1845, fifty-four million pounds of lead were annually extracted from the bluffs adjacent to Galena.[20]

Physical movement kept old neighborhoods changing and created new settlements seemingly overnight. After a few seasons most new arrivals were gone. In 1829 the United States Department of State published a report indicating that 9,220 of the "free taxable inhabitants" in Illinois were not freeholders, which led stump speakers to declaim that over one-half of the households in the state did not own their lands.[21] The agrarian dream persisted, but for most it remained a dream; the majority of suckers moved on, and fee simple land ownership remained an elusive, beckoning prize. Such mobility was characteristic of the West: in Ohio as many as

84 percent of the immigrants to the state moved on before 1850.[22] Similarly high rates likely prevailed in Illinois. Not all who settled persisted; those who did persist exerted a disproportionate influence on the communities formed in towns like Alton, Belleville, Galena, Jacksonville, Peoria, Quincy, and Vandalia.[23]

As the Illinois frontier moved north into the newer central and northern tiers, conflict with the Native populations in these areas was erased from the record or the memories were lost. William Leggett, who came to Edwardsville in 1819 and wrote many stories set on the frontier, imagined these newer tiers as empty. In "The Rifle," Leggett's protagonist states that the settlers found Illinois forests and prairies a "primeval nature . . . whose silence has not often been broke by the voice of man."[24] Despite such denials, the new state had in fact long been settled by Native Americans, and when George Rogers Clark arrived with the Virginia militia in 1778, it was still home to Illiniwek, Kickapoo, Fox, Sauk, Delaware, Ottawa, Potawatomi, and Ho-Chunk nations.

The Natives, too, viewed Illinois as a beautiful and fertile land of adventure. Those who remained contested hotly the many "treaties" made with the Americans beginning in 1804, which aimed to remove them. By the early 1830s only a scattering of Native families survived, spread thinly across the northern half of the state. Many had already left because the game that they primarily relied on had also fled. An eyewitness comparing central Illinois fauna in 1806 and 1812 noted a large change in only six years: "The beaver was gone and the buffalo and elk [had become] very scarce."[25] Hiram Rutherford records seeing a "drove of Buffaloes" passing through Independence (Champaign County) in April 1842, but this was a rare occurrence by then.[26] As a Sauk chief eulogized in 1838: "Courageous were thy youthful sports, for thou wouldst steal upon the young panther . . . and tame the prairie-wolf. . . . [But] when we returned from the hunt laden with game, when we came to our birthplace, the home of our fathers, where we worshiped the great *manitou* . . . in the beautiful prairies of Illinois . . . there we found the white man. He had burned our wigwams, and ploughed up the graves of our fathers."[27] The skirmish of 1831 and the Black Hawk War of 1832 occurred because the Sauk believed they still had the right to use the fertile bottomlands on the Rock River as a garden and summer camp. Speaking on the Iowa bluffs, a Native orator lamented: "We remonstrated with the white man to leave our cornfields, but his ears were deaf, and his heart was stone. We pled for our Fathers' graves, and the land of our birth . . .

[we] broke the pipe for friendship and peace [and fought] . . . till a traitor betrayed our chief, and numbers compelled us to yield. Brothers, Our Father in Washington has placed us on this [western] side of the Great River, and told us to make it our home."[28]

Along with the conflict over land, other social conflicts structured life in Illinois. Powerful forces created race- and class-based social statuses. The Illinois "Black Codes" of 1819 prohibited Black people from voting, testifying at trials against White people, and serving on juries.[29] Susan "Sukey" Richardson, who escaped from her notoriously cruel Randolph County master in 1842, represented one of 331 enslaved people listed in the 1840 census of the nominally free state.[30] Richardson had been indentured in 1816. Conflicts over indentured servants' status and slaveholder abuse rang out in the state's courtrooms, where attorneys such as William Underwood and Lyman Trumbull defended what rights Black people had under the law.[31] In this period Illinois remained "a society with slaves" if not a "slave society" dedicated to protecting the peculiar institution in all its dimensions.[32] Racism was so pervasive that Illinois's free Black population lived in daily fear of kidnapping. Elijah Morris of Golconda, for example, experienced home invasion, robbery, and assault and battery as well as witnessed his four children being stolen away in the night.[33] Whether in Pope County, on the border with Kentucky, or in Adams County, on the border with Missouri, the dispute over slavery drove resentment against both human-stealing southerners and damn-the-consequences abolitionists.[34] Nonetheless, the state's Underground Railroad assisted escapees not only from slave state masters but from local masters.

Racial prejudice flourished even where slavery was absent. Indeed, as Alexis de Tocqueville noted in his comparison of Kentucky and Ohio, racism frequently became more salient in slavery's absence.[35] In 1835, Frank McWorter, a freedman who had purchased his own liberty, set up New Philadelphia in Pike County as a settlement to include free Black communities. New Philadelphia struggled to attract settlers because in 1829 the state legislature passed additional racist restrictions, including the requirement that free Black individuals post a one-thousand-dollar bond to enter the state.[36] The struggles of "Free Frank," as he was known, may have convinced other free Black individuals to pioneer exclusively Black towns, as occurred at Brooklyn, Illinois.[37] Despite structural obstacles, Black pioneers fought and often obtained a piece of squatter sovereignty in Illinois, whether in separate settlements or as part of the plural mix. Anna-Lisa Cox has documented property-owning African American farmers in twenty-four counties in antebellum Illinois in as many as fifty-six settlements.[38]

The social stigma against dependent hired labor affected the lead miners working "badger holes" in Galena and the Irish canallers working on the Illinois and Michigan Canal. The Irish rioted at Chicago in 1836, 1838, and 1839 in displays of resentment against class and colonial bias. Canal bosses routinely lowered their wages in the middle of a contract. They generally treated their workers as objects to be controlled; in response canallers threw stones and punches. They destroyed property and tried to fight their way to respectability. The workers also fought each other as they reanimated grudges born in Ireland or wage conflicts first experienced on eastern canal projects. By 1847 they were united enough to strike for higher wages, asking to be treated as "white Citizens" and not "common Slave Negroes."[39] With a low status in the frontier's pecking order, the workers emphasized their racial privileges. Their need to assert a place above Black people reveals the contested nature of their status, which was called into question by many Protestants. Illinois ministers respected the agency of Black Christians more than they did the agency of Roman Catholic immigrants, whom they perceived to be mere tools of the Antichrist (i.e., the pope). Economic disparities were especially wide in the towns and cities. In 1849, 1 percent of Chicago's population held 52 percent of the taxable wealth, while 74 percent were destitute.[40]

Such class- and race-based conflicts were real enough. Organized and empowered under the Jacksonian regime, they structured all other conflicts. The political realities of two-party competition in Illinois raised all the issues we associate today with developing democracies, in which the informal power of groups serves as an ordering force in place of the state's formal power to administer the law. At the same time, it is likely that the conflict lived most consciously by the average Illinoisan was the domestic experience of getting "clear of the land office." This tense drama hung over each farm household and played out daily. The preemption system allowed settlers to squat on and improve unsurveyed land. Squatters later had the right of first refusal to purchase the land in increments of forty acres or more from the federal government over a period of years.[41] No connection was held more sacrosanct than the tie between free labor on the land and ownership; the principle that cultivation bequeathed ownership rights was valorized in both the law and public opinion. LaSalle County settler Elmer Baldwin related how his neighbors viewed preemption as a "sacred right," a prepolitical right the settlers organized to protect in "claim clubs."[42] It is indicative of how powerful this settler norm was that the Illinois legislature passed a law in 1841 shielding mortgage holders from losing their equity in foreclosed properties. The law was declared unconstitutional by the US Supreme Court for violating the clause in article 1 section 10 limiting a state's power of impairing the obligation of contracts; the court's opinion in 1843 was met by public protest in the streets of Springfield.[43]

Once newly acquired land was surveyed and a land office opened, the competition over purchase began. This set up a noticeable pattern in which new settlers focused on raising market crops and saving money. The *Western World* wrote: "The country is new. The farmers have hardly begun farming in a profitable way. They are using all the industry and economy they can, to enable them to make prompt payments."[44] Those who could not make payments might end up as suckers, serial squatters who would "skim and scratch" and leave before the land hit the market.[45] William Cullen Bryant's brothers Cyrus and Arthur came to Illinois in 1832 and settled farms in the northern tier around the town of Princeton, about eight miles from the Illinois River. Bryant described a fairly typical first-year experience in a detailed letter to his mother back in Massachusetts:

> [How Cyrus and Arthur] got to Princeton in October, chose the pleasantest of the vacant places though not quite so extensive for two as could have been wished—how they *bought two yoke of oxen,*—how one of the oxen died and another had the horn distemper—how they cut prairie hay to keep them on, which the season being late was wretched fodder wherefore they had to buy more corn—how they hauled logs and built a cabin, and brought boards from the distance of 8 miles, paying a great price for them—how they had to buy three yoke of oxen for a prairie team to break up the ground, and drag rails to the place where they were wanted—how they put in some wheat in the fall for a man in the neighborhood of which they are to have three acres for their share—how they intended to get 40 acres fenced and broken the present season and mostly planted with Indian corn, though they expect but a small crop the first year—how they bought a plow chains and wagon—how Cyrus became ragged—how he bought a pair of cowhide boots and shoes—and a little factory cotton for shirts—how they have worked early and late—how they have been obliged to pay a high price for everything—how they are out of cash—how they are in

> trouble for fear the land will come to market and find them unprovided with money to purchase it.

Bryant added a detail which captured the precariousness of a settler's first winter: "I think they will have a cold time of it this winter in the little log cabin unless it is much repaired. The doors are composed of small pieces of split wood and are about as serviceable in keeping out the cold as an old flour barrel would be."[46]

Settler narratives like these created unity out of the diversity of the immigrant backgrounds. No matter your origins, you adapted to the land and climate. Most settlers viewed the prairie land as a pasture commons. As one experienced in "prairie farming" told readers in 1837: "The best purpose to which the prairie lands can be applied is that of grazing. An almost infinite number of cattle can be raised on them as they are without an inclosure."[47] Instead of enclosing livestock in pens, as most immigrants had done back east, they needed to enclose crops; by right of custom, animals ran free and their owners were not liable for the damages caused by grazing neighbors' crops. The state supreme court made this custom the law of the land in a landmark 1848 case.[48] The strenuousness of settling an uncultivated land marked all settler narratives. Whether southerner or Yankee, Native or naturalized, the experience was harrowing. While Alma Stevens stressed to her sister-in-law back in Connecticut that her Fairfield, Illinois, settlement was "a very healthy place indeed," she related that it could also be very dangerous. She recounted how the settlers had buried seven persons in their graveyard in a little over eighteen months.[49] Elmer Baldwin counted twenty-five people who drowned trying to ford the Vermillion River on a ten-mile stretch near his LaSalle County home before the first bridge over the river was built in the late 1840s.[50]

Narratives of trial emerged and were repeated. Valentine Martin Darnall came to Illinois in 1828 from Kentucky in a caravan of his neighbors from Boone County, Kentucky. They walked through Indiana, likely entering Illinois at Danville and following the Ottawa Trace, an Indian trail, to present-day Livingston County. Darnall, having spied many potential homesteads on the way, returned to Kentucky and in 1830 emigrated to Illinois with his wife, Rachel, and four children. They settled in Indian Grove, a mixed timber and prairie plot just east of Indian Creek that had been abandoned the year before by the Kickapoo. The family arrived on October 27, and by the first of November Valentine had built a log cabin with help from "the settlement at Mackinaw . . . the only tool used being an axe, for he had no saw."[51] Darnall left for Mackinaw "to procure a supply of meat for his family" just before the "Great Snow" of December and January 1830–31.[52] He had promised Rachel he would return before dark but spent the next three days stuck at the settlement, basically an Indian village on the Mackinaw River eight miles away. "The fall of snow was phenomenal. . . . In a dead calm, it fell to the depth of four feet. This was followed by a drizzling rain, which soon turned to sleet. Then the weather became intensely cold, and the whole face of the country was covered with a sheet of ice."[53] When Darnall finally did try for home on the morning of the fourth day, "it was a perilous undertaking, and at times, seemed useless to proceed." He was "without guide or compass," and "the horse would sink to his saddle-girths in the snow." But man and horse persevered, and "just as the sun was setting, he espied the smoke curling from the chimney of his little cabin." Rachel "had dressed herself in a pair of her husband's trousers, to better enable her to get through the snow, and had cleared it away from the calf and sheep pens. . . . [She] succeeded in getting . . . three young claves into the cabin by the fire to prevent their freezing." It was two months before they could return to Mackinaw for supplies. Luckily, Valentine spied "four wild hogs that he had been trying for some time to tame. They were so hungry that they followed him. . . . Two found their way into his scanty larder during the Winter."[54]

Rachel Darnall was hardy. She made it through much adversity, whether due to the climate or hostile Indians. Besides the Great Snow, in 1835 rain flooded the fields and high water remained long into the summer, while in 1837 a "great drouth" prevailed.[55] As for their relationships with Native Americans, her father had been held captive for three years back in Kentucky, where her and her family's frontier experiences may be taken as common. Yet in Livingston County the Darnalls were on good terms with the Ottawa chief Shabbona, who lived and camped near Indian Grove all during the 1830s. He was one of 630 Native Americans living at nearby Oliver's Grove when the 1830 census was taken.[56] As neighbors they would "go on hunting and fishing trips," during which "the Indians stored part of their provisions" at the Darnall homestead. The Natives taught Valentine how to tap the maple trees in the bush surrounding Timber Creek. Rachel once asked a friendly Kickapoo chief what would happen if war broke out between the settlers and the Indians: Would "he and his tribesmen . . . kill them if an uprising should occur? . . . The old Chief is said to have replied, 'Oh, yes, but we kill 'em quick,' meaning that they would not be tortured."[57]

Mixed Native and White communities of this sort existed throughout the state's northern half in the frontier period, a development that in the Chicago of the 1820s included intermarriage among a group of American, French, and Native families who dominated its multiracial society. In the 1830s one of Chicago's favorite citywide competitions featured the risky maneuvers Native American divers executed from the pontoon bridge over the Chicago River at Lake and Randolph Streets.[58] While frontier pluralism could be elegant, it was more often unruly, as Thomas Ford could attest. He served as the state's attorney and later as a circuit judge in northern Illinois from 1830 until he was elected governor in 1842. He presided over the convoluted court case that settled Mark Beaubien's land grants in Chicago. The locals found Judge Ford a walking contradiction: despite his "small and scrawny figure," he faced down many "organized bands of rogues engaged in murders, robberies, horse stealing, and in making and passing counterfeit money."[59]

Ford was a classic sucker himself. Before the age of twenty-five, he had lived in rural Pennsylvania; rural Illinois; Lexington, Kentucky; rural Indiana; St. Louis, Missouri; and Galena, Illinois. He knew the frontier could be a dangerous place; for him it was already as much about loss as gain. When Ford was three years old, his father left their frontier home for a stroll and never returned; he was presumed to have been waylaid on the road, but by whom was never discovered. Ford knew many individuals whose hard work enabled a town or family to succeed before they moved on or died unheralded. He observed whole settlements where the people worked constantly and lost all sense of weekly surcease: "Labor through the week to them is a drudgery; and . . . performed with surliness and grudging."[60] As the scholar Henry Clyde Hubbart notes, "There was a wastage of human life in building-up these agrarian communities, analogous to that in the rising factory system of the East."[61] But narratives of pluralism, disorder, and loss tended to be muffled and submerged, their place taken by stories of individualism and the successful agrarian dream. In places like Missouri and Illinois, John Mack Faragher argues, "by 1850, memories of ethnic cooperation [between Native and settler populations] . . . were all but forgotten," replaced by a "rhetoric of exclusion" under which "rude, fierce, and contemptuous [settlers] daily encroached upon the hunting-ground of the Indians."[62]

As the daily interaction with Indians suggests, this was the era of the cowboy in the old Middle West. The cowboy's job was to drive cattle to market. The southern latitude of Illinois had always looked south to the New Orleans market; the new central and northern tiers looked to Chicago. The settlement of central Illinois took place before the Illinois and Michigan Canal connected the city to the Illinois River, a project that would not be completed until 1848. In lieu of a completed canal, farmers walked their produce to Chicago. Central Illinois settlers endured the Panic of 1837 only to be confronted with the years of depression and dearth of new emigrants which followed. Over the previous five years, "the farmers of Illinois had never seen more prosperous times. . . . Wheat was about two dollars a bushel; corn and oats, one dollar to one dollar and a half. . . . All newcomers were consumers not producers, for the first year or two."[63] But by 1838 eastern money dried up and there was little available locally to pay off the land office. Settled farmers responded by getting together to drive large herds of their hogs to Chicago for sale, "agreeing to feed the hogs at night by turns, each in succession returning to his home for a load of corn . . . and thus, by relieving each other, accomplished what would otherwise have been an impossible task." The journey typically took ten to twelve days of travel over "unbroken prairie. . . . There was not at that time even an Indian trail leading from that point to Chicago."[64] Chicago was a particular lure for farmers because its prices for foodstuffs like wheat were "greater than paid in other places in the west." Farmers came from as far as two hundred miles away: "In every direction, the [roads could] be traced in the distance by the long lines of 'Prairie Schooners' [covered wagons] numbering from five to fifty, and even eighty, in a single company."[65]

Darnall family members drove turkeys to Chicago, first walking them through tar and feathers to make boots for their feet, which would otherwise have been shredded on the hundred-mile journey. By 1839 "cattle kings" Isaac and Absalom Funk of McLean devised the idea of creating pens to hold hogs and cattle in the city to fatten them before slaughter. Thus the Chicago stockyards were born. The stockyards transformed Illinois farms into a national corncrib and converted subsistence and local-market farmers into capitalists. But turkey boys running birds in tar-and-feather boots had as yet little understanding of how their actions were contributing to the transformation of "locally oriented, household-based economies" into "market-dedicated farming."[66] The subsistence-surplus market farming practiced by William Cullen Bryant's brothers and the Darnalls would persist for another hundred years.[67]

The steamboat was another way to travel to the new world of central Illinois. When William Cullen Bryant visited his brothers in 1832, he began his river travel at Cincinnati, taking one boat down the Ohio River and up the Mississippi to St. Louis, Missouri; another to Alton, Illinois; and a third up the Illinois River to Naples, Illinois, where he hired a wagon to make the final journey to Jacksonville. Eliza Farnham, who came in the spring of 1836, traveled a similar route but disembarked at Pokerton, eventually joining her sister's family near Tremont (Tazewell County).

Farnham celebrated the prairie for its beauty and fertility but also for its freedom: "Social and physical freedom exist here in their most enlarged forms . . . freedom from want . . . freedom from social trammels; freedom from the struggles of emulation founded in vanity, or other vitiated desires. . . . The combined effect of all these [give] the widest freedom of thought and action . . . inspiring each individual."[68] Many women settlers celebrated their social freedom and made the most of the meager civic opportunities the unorganized state of society opened to them. In 1838 women in Putnam County's Female Anti-Slavery Society expressed their agency by organizing a "free produce" society, an early kind of community-supported agriculture dedicated to buying foodstuffs produced solely by free labor.[69] Four years later, among the Mormons, Sarah Melissa Granger Kimball and Emma Smith organized the Female Relief Society of Nauvoo to raise funds for building the temple and to help Mormon families in emergencies and extraordinary circumstances.[70]

Independence, security, and social freedom fueled the Illinois dream, but they were not the whole of it. The dream of religious freedom lured and burdened many seeking to combine sacred and civic duties. When the Covenanters, who professed Reformed Presbyterianism, came to Randolph County during the territorial era, they withdrew from the public realm. They were antislavery by religious principle, and they expressed disapprobation of worldly ways by asking to be freed from them, such as by not voting or serving on juries. Later a new kind of antislavery opinion percolated up among the Covenanters and received reinforcement from newcomer groups. When the Yankees first arrived in Illinois, *abolition* was still a dirty word everywhere in the state. Antislavery stalwarts like George Churchill and Hooper Warren (from Troy and Edwardsville, Madison County, respectively) led lonely lives as vilified outsiders. The murder of abolitionist editor Elijah Lovejoy in Alton in 1837 confirmed the pattern of abuse. But soon isolated antislavery advocates in places like Bureau, Putnam, and Peoria Counties began to find each other, and leaders like Benjamin Lundy, Owen Lovejoy, and Mary Davis commenced publishing newspapers, forming political parties, and establishing antislavery societies. By the 1840s, Lundy's *Genius of Universal Emancipation,* Lovejoy's Liberty Party, and Davis and other "liberty Women" were promoting antislavery in northern Illinois, albeit as a tiny minority.[71] The itinerant Black abolitionist William Paul Quinn and freedman Erasmus Green used the African Methodist Episcopal (AME) Church to anchor the Rocky Fork settlement in Madison County, a seminal Underground Railroad site.[72] Sites along the Underground Railroad thrived in many counties, including at least Adams, Cook, DuPage, Fulton, Kane, Knox, Madison, Pike, Pope, Randolph, St. Clair, and Woodford; these almost invariably relied on religious abolitionists to aid their efforts.[73]

Religious variety added another layer of diversity to the state. Many early settlers came in groups of families tied to Baptist churches back in Kentucky or Virginia, establishing new congregations in neighborhoods scattered along the rivers and bottomlands. Others who came were unaffiliated or became "freethinkers," members of an informal club that always welcomed members in Illinois, as it did everywhere else in the West. Organized debate societies often explored skeptical themes, as did the Peoria Lyceum in 1841 when it wondered, "Is the Mosaic account of creation in accordance with reason and philosophy?" The Galena Young Man's Society asked, "Has ambition caused more evil to the human family than superstition?"[74] Particularly freethinking in orientation was the Illinois bar, which the *Sangamo Journal* believed was composed of "men of talents, industry, and influence [who] too often slake their thirst at the fountain of [religious] infidelity."[75] It was also true that many who came without religious affiliation joined groups like the Baptists and Methodists after they settled. Methodism especially attracted those White settlers who had left their homes in the South to get away from the institution of slavery; it also appealed to German Protestants.[76] Not every Methodist in Illinois was antislavery, but the vast majority of them were. Methodist networks played a key role in the constitutional struggle to prevent Illinois from becoming a slave state in the early 1820s.[77] By 1850 every county in the state contained at least one Methodist church. Other religious groups formed identifiable centers of activity in particular towns: Regular (antimission) Baptists at Palestine and Lebanon; "Presbygationalists" at Jacksonville and Galesburg; Catholics at Cahokia, Galena, and Belleville; and Episcopalians at Chicago and Grand Detour. Following an older territorial pattern of religious settlement, several religious groups established congregations scattered along rivers and creeks. These groups included Friends of Humanity Baptists in Monroe County; Missionary Baptists in Madison and Morgan Counties; Disciples of Christ in McLean, Wabash, Lawrence, and Crawford Counties; and Cumberland Presbyterians in Champaign, Menard, and Sangamon Counties.

Joseph Smith brought a band of two hundred Latter-day Saints to Illinois in May 1834. They came on foot amid a thousand-mile march from Kirtland, Ohio, en route to western Missouri, where the Mormon settlement in Jackson County was imperiled. The band, called Zion's Camp by Smith, was basically a paramilitary troop on a mission to protect their fellow saints from mob violence. In Illinois, Smith walked at the head of the irregulars along with his mastiff, Major. While passing through Putnam County in Illinois, they stayed near a Mormon family who was housing young Hosea Stout, a Kentucky transplant who had been raised by Shakers and who had been proselytized in 1833 by a visiting Mormon elder. Stout was so taken by Smith and the camp that, as he later recalled, "it was all I could do to refrain from going" with them that day.[78] Stout had a lifelong interest in military endeavors. Standing at six feet six in his bare feet, he had recently returned from militia service in the Black Hawk War. He joined the Mormons in Caldwell County, Missouri, where he served in the paramilitary Danite Band. In 1840, when he moved to Nauvoo, he was named a second lieutenant of the Nauvoo Legion and later became the city's chief of police.

The Mormon presence contributed to Illinois's increasing pluralism in the 1830s. Among the older residents, the reality of difference led to a predictable reaction in favor of unity. One uniting factor was the promotion of immigration. Local boosters could refer to a tradition of accommodating newcomers as old as Roger Williams's openness to antinomians and George Washington's embrace of Quaker pacifists. William Cullen Bryant, when stranded in the Illinois country, found himself a stranger without shelter but felt welcomed: "Every house on a great road in this country is a public house and nobody hesitates to entertain a traveler or accept his money."[79] In 1834 the citizens of Vandalia issued a memorial "to invite the Polish exiles to visit our state and to locate their lands in Illinois (should Congress make them a grant)."[80] Congress did not issue the grant, but the offer is evidence that boosters considered the state a global village.

Four years later, Gustave Koerner publicly queried Congressman John Reynolds (of the First Congressional District) on his opinion of the Society of Native Americans, a group newly organized in Illinoistown to resist immigrants. Koerner wrote on behalf of "several of my fellow German countrymen who have made this country their home for themselves and their children *forever.*" Reynolds replied in the pages of the *Belleville Representative*. He "encouraged the emigration of respectable people from all parts of the earth. . . . Our State Constitution and laws are liberal to emigrants, and in my opinion, the same is just and proper."[81] The congressman was likely referring to the alien suffrage provision under the 1818 constitution, which extended the right to vote to any White male who resided in the state for at least six months. This policy received broad support because it had worked in practice, as a Will County lyceum orator reflected in 1842: "It would form some justification for exclusions or limitation were any political dangers to be apprehended, but experience has settled that question. The foreigner settled on our soil . . . loves the institutions which enable him to stand erect as a free man. . . . Almost every man who comes here becomes a producer."[82] How long did it take the foreigner to naturalize? Koerner advocated keeping the nation's existing five-year naturalization period. Congressman Zadok Casey, whose parents were born in Ireland, might have favored a longer term; he seconded a bill to extend the period from five years to as many as fourteen or twenty-one. Many Democrats wanted to reset it back to two years, the length prescribed by Thomas Jefferson in 1790. But Casey's committee, which in the end failed to change the term, was less confident about admitting foreigners; its report pointedly observed that one-half of the paupers and three-quarters of the convicts in the Sing Sing prison in Ossining, New York, were foreign born.[83]

The mere fact that a nativist group had formed indicates that at least some in Illinois felt threatened by the constant flow of immigrants who—in Ford's terms—pursued adventure among strangers. Chicagoan Caroline Palmer Clarke reported that "the great influx of strangers" to her town in 1835 made "society . . . perfectly unorganized and unsettled."[84] Unsettling change and pluralism led some to try and organize civil society, those public sphere attachments independent of government, to create overarching associations. They hoped these associations would bridge the gap between the state and family and stabilize public and private arenas of authority. For example, local Sunday schools, regardless of affiliation, were often supported with contributions from all the Protestant denominations in town. Such efforts were publicly praised, as in Edwardsville on July 4, 1831, at a ceremony dedicated to the fiftieth anniversary of the Sunday school movement. Baptist, Presbyterian, and Methodist Sabbatarians cooperated to produce the event. Nationally, Sabbatarians had failed in 1830 to pass a federal law to stop the mail on Sunday. Locally, however, they were able to get a law passed in 1829 to penalize "Sabbath breaking."[85] They now gathered in Madison County to defend the patriotism of Sunday school. Missionary Baptist Rev. George Stacey addressed the crowd and argued that the movement connected "religion and common education together, as one of the main pillars of the nation." "National morality," he asserted, cannot "prevail in exclusion of religious principles. . . . [The] infidels of our day [were wrong] to introduce a mode of instruction which is to receive no aid from religion, [under which] the Sabbath would be trodden under foot, the Bible profaned."[86]

Protestant unity regarding Sunday schools belied deep disagreements about the relations between grace and effort as well as those between church and state. A Fourth of July celebration at Galena in 1835 was organized by the Sabbatarians and the address made by Reverend Tullige, an Episcopalian. He was proud of the town's Sunday school pupils, who were being "raised up to become ambassadors of the cross in heathen as well as in Christian lands."[87] But public endorsement of religion could lead to contestation and discord. Most mainstream Christians agreed that religion could improve society; the issue was which denomination should lead the improving. But leaders of dissenting sects saw motives of worldly gain and corruption in these efforts at social control. And in fact, High Church Protestants like Lyman Beecher openly strategized about how to reassert control over the "laboring classes" when they became "contaminated" by forces such as intemperance.[88]

Scholars have spilled much ink to disprove this social control thesis, but in their efforts to right a wrong they miss the point. Reformed Protestants had neither the numbers nor the totalizing influence needed to exert effective control over American society in the Jacksonian era, nor could the reformers yet be described simply as a self-interested group.[89] The reformers aimed at "social improvement," not social control; the goal was the public spirited one of improving society not the self-interested one of asserting a privileged group status.[90] But, motives aside, the political power of the resentment the reformers precipitated needs to be acknowledged. The mainline ministers' approach was a punitive one: they could not point out what in society needed correcting without heaping scorn on the "error-prone" members of dissenting groups. Dissenters responded by arguing that the reformers were as worldly as the society they aimed to correct—and frequently more corrupt. A typical rejection of mainstream reform is seen in the response of Joseph Smith's wife Emma to the Washingtonian temperance movement when she asserted that "the Washingtonian Benevolent Society . . . [was] one of the most corrupt institutions of the day."[91] The tensions created by the efforts to exert social control were serious enough to generate enduring divisions in Illinois. Separate missionary and antimission Baptist associations formed in 1832 after a decade of division over the question of paying ministers and sending them abroad.[92] Old School Presbyterians rejected the 1801 union between Presbyterians and Congregationalists and split from the New School group over doctrinal issues in 1838.[93]

Among the Reformed denominations, generally there was enough unity to allow a closing of ranks against infidelity and fraud. Unfortunately for members of the group founded in 1830 as the Church of Christ and in 1838 renamed The Church of Jesus Christ of Latter-day Saints, the average pious Illinoisan, Reformed or dissenting, was predisposed to place "the Mormon creed" in the column of "imposition" and fraud. One early notice of the Mormons in an Illinois newspaper, an excerpted selection in the *Illinois Advocate* of July 1, 1831, cited the sect's "wicked and corrupt" leaders, who controlled their followers ("deluded creatures") by means of a buried text "written in mysterious characters upon golden plates." Thus was the sect of the "Golden Bible" introduced to many Illinois readers.[94] The buried text written on golden plates was the Book of Mormon, which early convert Martin Harris claimed "would settle all religious controversies and speedily bring on the millennium."[95] Distrust of the new sect was not remarkable given such pat views asserting immense authority.

The tendency to frame Mormon leaders as wicked and their followers as deluded was reinforced when Latter-day Saints began proselytizing as they passed through Illinois on the way to Missouri. In 1833, Parley Pratt stopped in St. Clair County to preach and debate with ministers of other denominations. Pratt was headed to the Zion—declared the church's new home by Joseph Smith in 1831—located on the western Missouri frontier, where several tribes of Native Americans had been settled by the federal government. The Mormons relished theological debates and often had success converting listeners, as Pratt reported after his Illinois visit. Mormons attempted to attract followers throughout the state, and evidence suggests their efforts were effective. As noted, Illinoisan Hosea Stout was converted in 1834 by a Mormon group that included Joseph Smith himself. In another case, "a man named King from Indiana" on his way to Missouri succeeded in converting John D. Lee in Fayette County in 1837.[96] Stout and Lee, like Parley Pratt and Brigham Young before them, became committed recruits and remained with the church for decades. But success in these local competitions for adherents only deepened the sense among others that the Latter-day Saints were a threat.

The Mormons' experiences in Missouri were fraught with conflict and violence. Although Mormons aimed for unsettled areas, like the lands below the Missouri River near Independence, wherever they settled, their mushrooming numbers induced suspicion. Their concentration in one area helped them achieve majority status so suddenly that they inevitably challenged the authority of the first settlers. Being northerners and following a revelation to settle Zion amid the Indians, they engendered suspicion among Missouri's mostly southern inhabitants. During the summer of 1833, after a group of free Black people joined the Mormon settlement, a mob forced the community to emigrate once again, this time north of the Missouri River in the newly annexed Platte Country. Then in the spring of 1838, Smith, who had been living in Ohio for several years with another branch of the church, decided it was time to leave Ohio; he and over five thousand Mormons from Kirtland joined their fellows at Far West in Missouri. Here, too, mobs harassed them. Conflict between the Missouri settlers and the newcomers reached a climax in October 1838 with the atrocity at Hawn's Mill, where fifteen Mormons were wounded and seventeen cornered and gunned down in cold blood.[97] Smith and other leaders surrendered and were imprisoned in Liberty Jail. They directed the remainder of the community to flee to Illinois, despite the wintry conditions. Walking through the snow in the winter of 1839, the Mormons were considered pitiable refugees, a mistreated, mobbed, and massacred people. Religious leaders in Illinois urged all with a conscience to give them shelter.

The closing of religious ranks worked to the Mormons' advantage when they escaped to Quincy and other towns and settlements in west-central Illinois. But the quest and capacity for unity in public purpose would later haunt them. Illinoisans were "liberal to emigrants," as Congressman Reynolds observed, but their constitution and laws only sketched out the broadest direction on how to manage refugees or naturalize migrants. The constitution endorsed alien voting and sought to protect individuals in the right "to worship Almighty God according to the dictates of their own consciences."[98] But as was typical in American constitutional language, the phraseology was general and was intended to avoid conflict and hide different purposes. Constitutional language is "incompletely theorized" in precisely this way on purpose.[99] The First Amendment, for example, proclaims that Congress should "make no law . . . respecting an establishment of religion," a principle that could be endorsed by widely differing groups, such as those committed to limiting the power of the federal government (e.g., Anti-Federalists), those who believed that religion was corrupted by state support (e.g., Baptists and Methodists), and even by those who doubted revealed religion altogether (e.g., freethinkers).

As pluralistic as Illinois seemed, its constitution also relied on what political theorist Will Kymlicka calls a "societal culture . . . a culture which provides members with meaningful ways of life across the full range of human activity."[100] Such cultures invariably include the set of beliefs and purposes needed to provide specificity and guidance to tailor general and incomplete constitutional principles to meet specific majoritarian preferences.[101] A collection of individuals settling for adventure are not a true society until they agree on what constitutes good and bad ways of living. Societal cultures rely on particular biases of the majority group to fill out the ordering rules needed to provide guidance in implementing general liberal principles.

THE ILLINOIS WAY: A SETTLER SOCIETAL CULTURE

Because these rules and the guidance they provide are shaped by cultural bias, a focus on political culture is crucial for understanding how the Mormons were received in Illinois. Societal cultures are political, constructed out of extant materials, which in Illinois were dominated by multiple subvarieties of individualism and egalitarianism. Some individualists are tempted to think either they do not need a societal culture or all Americans share one version. But crises expose the fallacy of the first premise because traditional understandings of foundational beliefs fail to provide sufficient guidance, and the second premise ignores the way leaders in democratic settings creatively mix political cultures at the regional and local levels to get elected.

Culture clash over foundational beliefs was especially apparent in Illinois, where the institutional political setting built during the Jacksonian era was very competitive. At first, party competition is likely to quash ideological extremes, but the move to the middle dictated by the pursuit of the median voter loses its hold when newcomers challenge the status quo as the Mormons did. Scholars looking at Illinois during this period have in fact been attracted to the one-culture thesis. After all, the state overwhelmingly supported Andrew Jackson for the presidency, and Jacksonian democracy in Illinois has been portrayed as preoccupied with increasing personal freedom and promoting individualism.[102] Yet group identity and status structured political life in Illinois in important ways during the period.

One explanation for the persistence of both individualist and egalitarian subcultures is that the rise of individualism led people to seek comfort in egalitarian groups. Scholars generally emphasize the search for community as a trope for understanding the way religion functions in capitalist societies, a theme also present in the portrayals of less explicitly religious groups in America such as abolitionists, the Anti-Masons, the Owenites, and even the

Fourierists.[103] The focus on self-governing communities led to a "republican synthesis" of the founding and antebellum eras, one in which Americans of all stripes used a broad rhetoric of virtue and corruption to emphasize the theme of "civic obligation."[104] Many scholars view the Mormons themselves through a republican lens, portraying them as a group of egalitarian yeomen who came together to seek shelter from social chaos and personal confusion in an era of increasing religious diversity, geographical mobility, division of labor, and loss of deference.[105] Others, in slightly different ways, have made the search for republican community a key to the Jacksonian era as a whole.[106]

The focus on religious, ethnic, and regional groups as sources of community has been instructive; it reminds us that groups serve individuals by fulfilling their separate and shared purposes. But the comforting dimension of communal life is only one aspect of the impact of groups on society, and many have argued that the focus on Mormons as the "socially disinherited" seeking shelter from a capitalistic America is overstated.[107] In this debate, the political dimension of group life is sometimes lost. It should not be forgotten that individuals not only seek out groups for meaning; they also live in and experience the world through groups. Groups, and the pecking order they precipitate, are means as well as ends, causes as well as effects. Furthermore, there were limits to Illinois's individualistic and pluralist community of accommodation. Illinois was not simply a community of individuals. It was also a state, a self-governing power. Some communities and groups might be formed solely by acts of choice and voluntary membership, but states are communities which claim to be authoritative within their domains, and their authority will be applied whether one is a member or not. It is a mistake, as Ira Katznelson notes, to view the state simply as "a civic association . . . no more than one such association among many."[108] States are not themselves pluralistic about membership; they claim ultimate obedience and absolute priority. When the state is used as a tool to enforce group status, the individualist ideal of a rule of law treating all persons neutrally is severely tested because group loyalties create biases in favor of groups in the majority coalition and distrust toward the groups in the minority. Those considered nonmembers altogether (e.g., Native Americans) are even more subject to indiscriminate state power. As Illinois's economic and transportation networks grew, party competition and political debate melded ideology to generate what might be called the Illinois way, the settler state's societal culture, which specified individual worth and clarified governmental purpose.

Liberal states limit the power of government through written social contracts in the form of constitutions; at the same time, democratic states authorize government power through unwritten social contracts in the form of societal cultures. Because liberals emphasize above all the use of rights to protect individuals within a private sphere under their own control, the details that inform duties and civic norms in the public sphere are left open to negotiation among the members. Negotiation over public law and policy in democratic states is conducted in the name of the majority electorate. Democratic majorities form their own societal identities, most commonly by means of political parties. Thus the story of the Mormon troubles in Illinois is not a legalistic tale of the violation of the constitutional contract between an abstracted individual and the state. Nor is it a simple story of how either individuals or the state failed to enforce the civil law in the name of the "higher law" of popular sovereignty.[109] Civic orders are built around pictures of the ideal citizen. The majority uses the state to enforce its narrative of the ideal citizen and the surrounding status order. The standard view that American society in the 1830s was predominantly individualistic ignores the constitutive role—the status-ordering role—group life played in suggesting to adherents an idealized civic narrative. In turn, this narrative was used to enforce the status order. Competitive individualism itself is a subculture, one among several others that vied for predominance. The Mormon and anti-Mormon group majorities which congealed in certain counties during the era promoted competing civic narratives that exerted independent force as causes of events. Examining these causes leads inescapably to the conclusion that group conflict, structured by majority call and minority response, created the polarization that drove the troubles.

For this reason, an important building block in any explanation of how democracy and toleration were configured in Ford's goodly land of adventurers is the variable of group allegiance. To perceive this allegiance clearly, we must unpack the variety and nature of groups in the state. Here the individualistic narrative of accommodation obscures more than it illuminates. It is fair to say that Illinoisans experienced daily life as individuals and family members. The individual and the family were indeed the basic units of meaning and analysis. But these narrow designations and close ties mainly shaped the private sphere, a zone liberal democracies hope to rope off from the public sphere and often from public power. By contrast, it is in the public sphere where much of the power of democracy operates and where toleration is manifested, if at all. It is at the public sphere level of societal culture that majorities and minorities operate. What is needed is a theory that recognizes both narrow and wide group affiliations and which can make sense of the competition among varying conceptions of worth. Wide affiliations necessarily involve deeper public commitments to specific background assumptions and foundational beliefs designated simply as "societal culture" by Kymlicka. These often-unspoken assumptions and beliefs are the political equivalent of public folklore.[110] Like folk norms but politically constituted, they give adherents guidance "central to group identity." As folk historian Robert Toll emphasizes, they tell people "who they [are] and how to live with their neighbors."[111]

An alternative to viewing the American nation as containing a single political culture is to see its politics as essentially a competition among adherents of multiple cultures whose details are sorted out at the local level. In Illinois the competition eventually further divided the common settler societal culture into three distinct regional cultures, one dominant in each of the three tiers of settlement. Daniel Elazar has championed the multiple-cultures approach, one he developed, not coincidentally, by using Illinois as a test case. His research was primarily focused on twentieth-century midsize towns, "Cities of the Prairie," whose cultures he showed were shaped by patterns of migration and settlement begun in the early nineteenth century.[112] He emphasized the three-tiered "geohistorical" context that had shaped the three distinct political cultures that he and his associates demonstrated acted as powerful independent variables.[113] Indeed, a recent study found Elazar's three political culture variables strongly correlate with an array of different policy outcomes at the state level.[114]

Political culture is a broad concept containing many values, but Elazar narrowed his focus by defining his three cultures according to one key dimension: the attitude toward the ends of government. This dimension fixes "limits" and imparts "subliminal direction" to how actors view the role of government in the political system.[115] Each of the three tiers produced a distinct view of government's purpose: what Elazar called the moralistic, traditionalistic, and individualistic.[116] The northern tier contained mainly moralists, people who sought to commit the state to broad, public-spirited, ultimately prescriptive goals; government at any level was to actively enforce morally correct behavior. The southern tier also viewed government as a means to order society, but among the traditionalists the goal was keeping earlier or slowly emerging social hierarchies in place. The middle tier produced individualists. In Elazar's conception they were the product of attempting to mix the northern and southern tiers' views and failing to make the two mesh. They developed a pragmatic, laissez-faire view toward government, believing themselves free to negotiate both traditional order and moralistic duty. They felt empowered to improvise their own understanding of societal purposes at the local level.

The individualist political culture was on display in the reception of the Mormons at Quincy. Its adherents created a narrative of accommodation for refugees as individuals. Thomas Ford believed the bias was especially prominent in the earliest generation of settlers, those who came before 1830: "The people were, most of them, pioneers and adventurers, who came to a new country hoping to get a living with more ease than they had been accustomed to, or to better their condition as to property. . . . So that government made no encroachment on liberty, they inquired no further into its true aim and object."[117] But as the decades wore on, this approach was far from the only understanding of the purpose of Illinois. More accurately, Elazar's three subcultures vied for influence in shaping the Illinois way, a collective understanding of community purpose and individual worth.

The diversity of conceptions of community purpose is frequently exposed in travel narratives. Travelers encounter people from different parts of the country and highlight the differences they encounter. During her trip from Chicago to Alton in the summer of 1841, Eliza R. Steele had time to observe many fellow passengers and recent arrivals. A walk along the Illinois River at Peoria took her to a cottage of recent arrivals. The family "had removed from Pennsylvania," where the man had employment and the family was happy. Steele asked them why, then, they emigrated. The wife replied: "Oh, he had heard of the West, where every one is sure to get rich, and so he came." Steele commented: "Most of the emigrants we have met could give us no better reason for removing than this woman."[118] Steele, who grew up in New Jersey, made it plain that she considered the answer superficial. She took the reader through an elaborate scientific, nationalist, and religious explanation of why she thought so.

Steele demonstrated a clear understanding of evolution as a scientific fact. Her analysis contained a mythic, geological view of the New World. The mastodon's bones and coal found in the ground made the Illinois soil rich; this was the buried meaning or hidden potential gift Illinois represented to those who could recognize it. The Indians, the first humans to take possession of the land, had "misused their gift," because they did not cultivate but fired the prairies. Indeed, their word for *prairie* was *fire*. But "the almighty . . . in his wisdom, foresaw the time would come, when the exhausted soil, and crumbling institutions . . . of the Old World, would require a new field for its overgrown population." Thus a new wave of humans came to populate the rich prairies. Realizing the divine plan and manifest destiny required a proper understanding of the civic duties of citizens, an understanding, as Steele made clear, that she believed many of the self-directed immigrants in central Illinois lacked. She concluded ominously:

> When I see them on their march . . . they remind me of the Hebrews. . . . May these travelers study the eventful journey of the Palestine emigrants, and shun those errors by which they were driven forth from its fair fields. The Hebrews were told, if they would only obey their heavenly leader "ye shall eat your bread to the full and dwell in the land safely. . . ." What magnificent promises! And how powerful the promiser! Oh that these [Illinois] people would lay these words to heart, and consider well the Hebrews fate![119]

Steele, who was attended on the trip by Violette, an enslaved person, later visited the Monticello Female Seminary in Alton and observed that its "disinterestedness shone out in bold relief from the selfish and reckless value of fortune which we had beheld in our pilgrimage." She was relieved that such public interestedness existed "when we reflect how much the destiny of our nation depends on the next generation."[120] Displaying a commitment to the public interest is the sine qua non of moralist political culture. It matters that government have an ultimate purpose to which it is dedicated—in Steele's case a national contract with God—precisely because without it individual actions devolve too readily into mere selfishness. Losing that larger public purpose is tantamount to losing one's republican soul. It is a foundational belief with a rich history and strong societal support in New England reaching back to the Puritans. They expressed multiple iterations of eschatological pacts with God that, beginning with John Winthrop's lay sermon aboard the *Arabella* (1630) and the Halfway Covenant (1662), sacralized the New England community as whole. Descendants of the nonseparating Protestants settling the New World in the seventeenth century, the Puritans felt a need to make themselves and their secular neighbors a model "city upon a hill."[121]

Despite a broad secularizing trend and a focus on personal religious experience ushered in with the First Great Awakening in the eighteenth century, Yankee citizens in the nineteenth century still believed they had, along with an individual covenant of grace, a collective national covenant.[122] Secular northern writers did not hesitate to use America's God-given public purpose to spur further political reform, as Herman Melville did in the effort to remove the traditional mode of punishment—flogging—from the US navy codebook. He wrote in *White-Jacket* (1850): "We Americans are the peculiar chosen people—the Israel of our time; we bear the ark of the liberties of the world. . . . We should, if possible, prove a teacher to posterity, instead of being the pupil of bygone generations."[123] Scholar David Greenstone explicates that the Yankees retained a foundational belief that Americans had "a collective, corporate role to play in secular history . . . [which] role had to be judged by the transhistorical standards of God's providential plan rather than by the standards of worldly success alone." By the nineteenth century, dedication to the public interest on the grounds of individual civic duty had become a foundational belief among Yankees, embodying what Elazar calls the moralistic political culture and Greenstone refers to as "the New England conscience."[124]

It is interesting to compare Steele's narrative of worth with that of the Mormons. They, too, had a moralistic background story, and theirs also featured the Native Americans and a divine purpose for a people immigrating to North America. As early as September of 1830, Joseph Smith had received a revelation directing his scribe Oliver Cowdery to take a "journey among the Lamanites," who lived "on the borders."[125] *Lamanites* is a term that comes from the Book of Mormon, which features two main groups: Lamanites and

Nephites. These two tribes descend from a band of ancient Jews who broke away from Jerusalem, built a ship, and traveled to "the promised land" in North America. Over time the families and followers of two warring brothers, Nephi and Laman, become separate peoples. The Nephites remain true to the divine way; their story is told by Mormon in the book carrying his name. But the Lamanites fall away, becoming a "wild, and ferocious, and bloodthirsty people . . . dwelling in tents . . . with a short skin girdle about their loins and their heads shaven; and their skill was in the bow."[126] As historian Richard Bushman puts it, "Modern readers of the Book of Mormon assumed that the American Indians were descendants of the Lamanites."[127]

Redeeming the Native Americans in Missouri and thus redeeming the American national covenant with God was the larger public purpose the Mormon church aimed for in its first eight years. Like Steele's Hebrews, the Nephites' divine promise echoes the language of the Old Testament: "That inasmuch as those whom the Lord God shall bring out of the land of Jerusalem shall keep his commandments, they shall prosper upon the face of this land, and they shall be kept from all other nations, that they may possess this land unto themselves."[128] On a mission from God, the Mormons must be classified as moralistic; indeed their justification, grounded in a revelation so recent and particular to the Americans, was more urgent and exclusive than even the New England Puritans. But like the separating Pilgrims of Virginia, their desire to live apart from the world often took the sting out of their moralism because they applied their vision to themselves first and foremost as a separate chosen people. Finding separation within the confines of the United States proved difficult for the Mormons, whether they lived under a communal property regime, as in Ohio; on the far western frontier, as in Missouri; or in their own city-state, as in Illinois. During the summer of 1844, when Joseph Smith announced his run for the US presidency, the premise of separatism was in part abandoned for a potential effort at leading a national redemption. But Mormon millennialist terms and this-world theocracy exposed the church and its leader to scorn from all three cultures in the state.

In the cultural triad, moralists typically conflict with traditionalists. Moralists pursue new societal forms or reforms that clash with the status quo. A classic case of culture clash occurred in Missouri and Illinois between antebellum moralists and traditionalists over the issue of slavery. A few antislavery comments by W. W. Phelps, editor of the Mormon newspaper *Evening and the Morning Star,* were enough for his press to be destroyed in Missouri.[129] Illinois had its proslavery traditionalists as well. These lived mainly in the southern tier, and their perspective can be represented by John Reynolds of St. Clair County, the congressman who championed immigrant rights and had previously been elected governor. Reynolds grew up in Illinois and, like many of his peers, espoused a particularist variety of egalitarianism that, in a democratic setting, was indistinguishable from traditionalism. As governor he acted precipitously to initiate a war with Black Hawk to signal his support of the settlers and antagonism toward the Natives. As was the case with immigration policy, he strove to make Illinois safe for poor White people everywhere.

Reynolds made his premises explicit in *"The Balm of Gilead": An Inquiry into the Right of American Slavery,* which he published just before the Civil War. Informed by the latest views on evolution and utilitarian philosophy, Reynolds articulated a case for defending the status quo. Like Steele, he followed the emerging scientific consensus that species evolved over time and had, in some cases, become extinct, an idea that had, before 1830, seemed an affront to God's creation. Citing *Vestiges of the Natural History of Creation* (1844), by Robert Chambers, who Darwin credited with preparing the public mind for his natural selection theory, Reynolds explained that "all the facts of geological research go to establish the progressive order of creation . . . [and] that all animals and vegetables were created at a single instant is an absurdity."[130] Humans also evolved from a multitude of races to a few, with "the probable extermination of the weaker nations and races." The "wisdom of God in creating them cannot be scanned" since "each race was created not only with different powers of intellect, but in a defined and limited sphere . . . and they cannot ascend over or mount higher by any improvement, than the point designated by the Creator."[131]

Here Reynolds's traditionalism became apparent, and he proceeded to extend it. Despite the apparent purposelessness of evolution, God intended the White race, conveniently Reynolds's own race, to be the ruling race. Here Reynolds reached for another rationalist innovation, Jeremy Bentham's utilitarianism. He offered a summation: "Any habit, custom, or practice amongst men, that produces happiness, must be just, moral and virtuous."[132] He further elaborated: "The black races are created with less *crania* than the Caucasian races" which establishes the fact "that the negro races possess not the mental power to make a living for themselves in a cold climate."[133] He continued: "The black races of the United States . . . enjoy more happiness than is enjoyed in Africa by the blacks, who are as free as the air they breathe."[134] Reynolds added that antislavery adherents, because they are "fanatics for universal freedom" and moralizers, did not realize this.[135] Traditionalism here defended a very particular image of "the people" and their purpose. Traditionalism was not individualistic in any relevant sense of the word, though in its effort to avoid the dismemberment of the Union, it echoed the pragmatic stance of individualist culture. Reynolds's allegiance to the group of poor Whites, a group derisively called "the white folks" in Illinois, informed the background assumptions and foundational beliefs of his defense of the status quo.[136]

While the hierarchical assumptions embedded in Reynolds's traditionalism were perhaps the most obvious obstacle to an inclusive pluralism in Illinois, they were by no means the only one. Moralizers and individualists often had their own reasons to exclude. Moreover, all the evidence suggests we err if we try to explain any policy outcome in the American state using only one subculture or if we try to demonize one culture as singularly intolerant. The political psychology literature on threat detects a special link between "rational-actor" (individualist) perspectives and intolerance, which shows individualistic culture should bear some responsibility for bigotry.[137] Subcultures persist in democratic regimes because they have functional aspects as well as negative drawbacks. When Illinois's leaders worked to fashion an electoral majority, they borrowed elements from all three cultures. The Democratic Party was a transnational entity synthesizing elements of the country's political cultures into a coherent political ideology; in Illinois the reigning Jacksonian Democrats tenuously tied together an amalgam of the state's political cultures to shape the Illinois way into a workable settler societal culture. When in the end the Mormons failed the regime's inclusion test, it was administered at the local level using a culturally composite civic narrative.

These considerations set up several overarching questions. If Illinoisans were so pluralistic, if they believed so earnestly in their land's claims of accommodation, why were the Mormons excluded?

Why did the Mormons fail the test when so many other groups passed? The explanation proffered here begins with an understanding of the complex nature of antebellum state power. It was a power whose constitutional form was crafted of national principles, whose political substance was built of regional societal cultures, and whose actual force was often the result of implementation by local majorities. The key institutional glue holding federal, state, and local together was the political party. After 1835 the national Democratic and Whig Parties had competitive outposts in every state in the union; the parties were the only entities in American society that reached simultaneously for the highest ideals of the nation while marshaling foot soldiers in nearly every county in the land.[138] At the broadest level, the Mormons were excluded because both parties in Illinois came to reject them. But the opposition began at the local level—despite significant efforts by both the state's Democrats and Whigs to court their favor.

The result was predictable given a state authority that combined national party ideology and local control. The composite nature of the Illinois state can be better understood by referring to the current debate over antebellum state building.[139] Although the American state looked "scrawny" compared to its European counterparts, it was still able to effectively unite the nation with an expansive postal delivery system, defend its borders with strategically placed military posts, and undergird an open market by negotiating rules for an international trading regime.[140] But as Stephen Skowronek reminds us, "State formation is seldom about more or less authority and almost always about the kind and location of authority."[141] The question is not whether the people have power but rather which people and where. When the federal state was weak, as it was in its control over slavery, it was because of the carefully guarded counterinterests of the southern slaveholders, who demanded that slave policy be controlled in the states.[142] Similarly, a set of countervailing interests demanding local control over settler membership limited the capacity of the Illinois state to protect the Mormons.

In Illinois, accommodation of the Mormons was tied to worth, and worth was determined using the materials at hand, as in the Illinois reception of Native Americans. While the Illinoisans expressed a stance of open pluralism with their claim of "settling a wilderness," in fact, Michael Witgen argues, "they were engaged in a struggle to convert Native homelands into American homesteads."

The resulting "settler states" were shaped as much by the inclusive "ideology of the American state as a republic" as by the exclusive force "of the republic as a colonial power."[143] Under these circumstances individual Native Americans might be befriended and recognized as equals, but background assumptions (such as that they did not optimize the land's production) deemed the Indigenous people unworthy as a nation to govern the land. Following similar unwritten biases, African Americans in Illinois were excluded because they were deemed incapable of being an independent self-governing people. Both Natives and African Americans were subjected to biased tests of civic worth hidden in the exercise of state power. The Native Americans were deemed independent, but not producers. Like the African Americans, the Mormons were deemed producers, but not independent.

How were these biases brought to bear against the Mormons? Why were they singled out when other religious groups, such as the Methodists or the Catholics, were seemingly spared? How were group biases organized at the state level, and how did they operate at the local level? If we are to understand why the Mormon troubles occurred in Illinois, we must first grasp how group allegiance worked among the Mormons and how it worked more generally in the state and then parse how group allegiance was constructed in Hancock County. To paraphrase Max Weber, in Illinois, and perhaps in all developing democracies, authority operates at the group level: groups live in civil society, a house of status; their stories of worth organize the state, a house of power.[144] The next three chapters offer different perspectives on group allegiance. Chapter 2 takes the perspective of the Mormon refugees, chapter 3 adopts the perspective of the elites who organized the Jacksonian regime and shaped its narratives of membership, and chapter 4 inhabits the perspective of the group members in Illinois who lived the narratives and controlled the rules of recognition by which inclusion and exclusion were settled at the local level.

2

Joseph Smith and the New Politics of Belief

We have seen how Illinoisans viewed the Mormons, but how did the Mormons view themselves? Indeed, who were the Mormons? To answer that question, we must begin with an understanding of their charismatic founder and prophet. Who was Joseph Smith? This was a question on the tongue of every Illinoisan by 1840. Other questions followed in rapid succession. Did the Mormons live together in one city to protect themselves from the Missourians? Would they be pooling their property as they had in Ohio? Above all, did Smith and the Mormons share the settler beliefs widely endorsed in the Sucker State? Seeking answers to these questions in 1840 required, as it does today, a reflection on the nature of belief itself. Beliefs are claims about the world people hold to be true. As scholar R. F. Atkinson writes, "Our beliefs may be false, but having them is holding them as true."[1] People held as true that nations had destinies, that publics had purposes, and that races had rankings. Beliefs come fast and furious when the freedom of conscience, a generative wellspring of expression, is enjoyed by individuals in an open society. However, a necessary consequence of this freedom is that diversity of belief becomes an ineradicable condition of life in liberal democracies. There is no accounting for tastes or beliefs, but the liberal state must try because beliefs lead to actions, and actions can harm others and violate their rights.

Tolerating the beliefs of some while respecting the rights of others is a difficult balance to strike. When contested facts, charismatic leadership, and communal settlement are added to the mix, balancing the equation can become impossible. Such proved to be the case during the Mormon troubles in Illinois. Foundational community beliefs, the combustible fuel spurring so many individual actions in liberal democracies, were scrutinized and put to the test of majoritarian politics as Illinoisans grappled with the toleration/rights equation.

Smith was born in 1805 to a struggling farm family in Vermont. The Smiths moved several times during Joseph's youth, but he came of age just outside the bustling commercial canal town of Palmyra in northern New York State. By all accounts, he was a searching youth who felt confused and threatened by the religious pluralism of the boomtown. Smith also felt uncomfortable with the religious uncertainty within his own family. His mother tried many different faiths and finally joined a Presbyterian congregation, while his father continued to frown upon so many neighbors "getting religion" at camp meetings. As the Mormon founder later put it in the official church history:

> There was in the place where we lived an unusual excitement on the subject of religion . . . and great multitudes united themselves to the different religious parties. . . . Some were contending for the Methodist faith, some for the Presbyterian, and some for the Baptist, . . . yet when the converts began to file off, some to one party and some to another, it was seen that the seemingly good feelings of both the priests and the converts were more pretended than real; for a scene of great confusion and bad feeling ensued; priest contending against priest, and convert against convert; so that all their good feelings one for another, if they ever had any, were entirely lost in a strife of words and a contest about opinions.[2]

The future revelator espoused a strong distaste for the role excited feeling played in religious rivalry and condemned its frequently divisive results. Scholars see in these views—which simultaneously appeared elsewhere, not solely with the origins of Mormonism—a determined "flight from American pluralism."[3]

For the youthful Smith, the religious and the magical were merged; together they had enough power to dispel all confusion and doubt. At age fourteen he reported seeing an angel in a vision. On a job digging a well at age seventeen, he found a "peepstone," which he "occasionally looked at to determine where hidden treasures in the bowls of the earth were."[4] Seeing visions and searching for buried treasure were fairly common in rural New York; the whole Smith family enjoyed and were known for their digging. Joseph himself had a local reputation as a "digger," and contemporaries remembered him as a person "of whom we had often heard as a fortune teller."[5] His strong imagination was fascinated by the mounds left in the area by Indigenous peoples. As his mother reported, "He would describe the ancient inhabitants of this continent, their dress, mode of travelling, and the animals upon which they rode. . . . This he would do with as much ease, seemingly, as if he had spent his whole life with them."[6] This early capacity to authoritatively see and know firsthand solved the pluralism problem for Smith and later for his followers.

The family was deeply committed to the Protestant Dissenter tradition, as was the whole of upstate New York. The area later was famously known as the "Burned-Over District" because of the repeated flames of religious feeling sweeping it during the Second Great Awakening, which began with the Cane Ridge, Kentucky, revival meeting in 1801. When Smith reported to the family that he had been visited by the angel Moroni and directed to unearth the golden plates on which a new Christian testament was written, the news was exciting but not so out of the ordinary as to be unbelievable. In a public letter to Chicago editor John Wentworth published across the state, the prophet later explained how he responded to the visions and the plates. Over the next two years, he used "a curious instrument . . . which consisted of two transparent stones set in a rim on a bow fastened to a breastplate" and later other peepstones to translate the mysterious golden plates, dictating in a trance the contents of what would be published in March of 1830 as the Book of Mormon.[7] His wife Emma later recounted: "Joseph Smith could neither write nor dictate a well-ordered letter . . . [yet he] would dictate to me for hour after hour; and when returning after meals, or interruptions, he would at once begin where he left

FIG. 2.1. Joseph Smith (from Gregg, *History of Hancock County*). Courtesy of Newberry Library

off, without either seeing the manuscript or having any portion of it read to him."[8]

What Illinoisans knew as the "Golden Bible" begins, "I, Nephi, having been born of goodly parents . . . make a record in the language of my father, which consists of the learning of the Jews and the language of the Egyptians." Nephi proceeds to relate how his father, Lehi, was spoken to in a dream by God, who told him and the Jews to leave Jerusalem before the city was destroyed, before "many [were] carried away captive into Babylon."[9] Lehi's family and followers travel by ship to North America six hundred years before the time of Jesus Christ. They divide into two peoples, the industrious, virtuous, and White-skinned people of Nephi, who "did till the land, and raise all manner of grain," and the idle, corrupt, and dark-skinned Lamanites, who "became wild, and ferocious."[10] The two peoples fight perpetually for centuries. Their enmity was so great that not even the visitation of Jesus Christ, first in vocal form and then as a "Man descending out of heaven . . . clothed in a white robe," to them in North America could end their fighting or reunite them.[11] Eventually, the Lamanites succeed in subduing the Nephites. Through all of this, beginning with Nephi, many Nephite leaders keep a record of their people, transmitting the records from one generation to another. These transmissions end with Moroni, son of Mormon, who buries a record of what had transpired on American soil centuries before the first Pilgrims ever landed on its shores.

The prophet, surrounded by his chief supporters organized as Elders, and later as the "Twelve Apostles," now began a series of public "Thus saith the Lord" revelations. Parley Pratt, who witnessed many of them, related that Smith spoke "each sentence . . . slowly and very distinctly, with a pause between each, sufficiently long for it to be recorded, by an ordinary writer in long hand."[12] The early revelations, published in 1833 as the Book of Commandments and two years later as Doctrine and Covenants, linked the new church to the plotline of "Moroni, whom I have sent unto you to reveal the Book of Mormon [which contains] the fulness of my everlasting gospel," and the saints to the characters therein: "You shall become even as Nephi of old, who journeyed from Jerusalem in the wilderness."[13] The revelations made it abundantly clear that the last days before yet another coming of Christ were near ("It is the eleventh hour, and the last time that I shall call laborers into my vineyard"); that the existing churches in America had failed Christ;

and that a new church was needed to usher in the Millennium ("I will establish a church by your hand," one that was "to declare my gospel unto a crooked and perverse generation").[14] It was to redeem this epic lost cause, to right this sacred wrong, that the Mormons committed themselves. Under this commitment Smith would knit all believers together into a new community.

This higher commitment had brought them low many times, and now brought them exhausted and vilified to the banks of the Mississippi. If Illinoisans were surprised by these unlikely refugees at the western border, they were more surprised when Smith drew out the larger meaning of the Mormon story for his Illinois readers in the pages of the *Times and Seasons:*

> We are informed by these records [the Book of Mormon] that America in ancient times has been inhabited by two distinct races of people. . . . The book also tells us that our Saviour made his appearance on this continent after his resurrection, and that he planted the gospel here in all its fullness, and richness, and power, and blessing; that they had apostles, prophets, pastors, teachers, and evangelists; the same order, the same priesthood, the same ordinances, gifts, powers, and blessing, as was enjoyed on the eastern continent, that the people were cut off in consequence of their transgressions, that the last of their prophets who existed among them was commanded to write an abridgment of their prophecies, history, etc., and hide it up in the earth, and that it should come forth and be united with the bible for the accomplishment of the purposes of God in the last days.[15]

For many, the idea that America was the site of biblical events and that the Indians were part of those events was no doubt the most interesting, although not unprecedented, part of the Mormon story.[16] As Elias Higbee and Parley Pratt later noted in their address to the public in Washington, DC, "The ancient events of America now stand revealed in the broad light of history, as far back, at least, as the first peopling of the continent after the Flood."[17] But ecclesiastically, this commentary was pregnant with many other implications: pragmatically, Smith was not simply claiming to be a prophet himself but was adding new material to "be united with the bible"; substantively, he was joining biblical times with the contemporary era in a seamless whole. By claiming that the two were continuous in terms of the production of prophets and miracles among the laity, Smith in one stroke did away with the need for a separate church hierarchy while he added to the Mormon laity a host of "gifts" and "powers" the existing Christian hierarchy itself did not claim.

Given the dramatic nature of Joseph Smith's claims, it is remarkable that so many people believed them. The extant evidence suggests that despite some initial doubts, most of his family believed the plates and the things he saw in the peepstones were real and that the translation was the direct word of God. Historian Richard Bushman argues that this reception should shape how scholars view the episode. He writes, "Since the people who knew Joseph best treated the plates as fact, a skeptical analysis lacks evidence."[18] But if many who knew Smith were ready to take what he said as real, others were skeptical and many others incredulous. Martin Harris, to whom Smith dictated part of the Book of Mormon, was a believer; he agreed to mortgage his farm to raise three thousand dollars to have five hundred copies printed. Lucy Harris, Martin's wife, was skeptical, so much so that she likely stole part of the unpublished manuscript. When her husband and Smith could not find the manuscript, she told Smith bluntly, "If this be a divine communication, the same being who revealed it to you can easily replace it."[19]

Doubt and disbelief of Smith's claims was common in Illinois. Eudocia Baldwin, a Hancock County native who visited the Smith family in the Nauvoo Mansion just as it opened in the summer of 1843, related how after dinner "some Egyptian mummies were exhibited for a small sum" by Joseph's mother, Lucy Mack Smith, "a trim looking old lady in black silk gown and white cap and kerchief." Lucy "gave [them] a detailed account of [the Egyptian] lives and doing three thousand years before." Baldwin said, "Upon my asking her how she obtained all this information, she replied in a severely virtuose tone and a manner calculated to repress all doubt and further question: 'My son Joseph Smith has recently received a revelation from the Lord in regard to these people and times and *he* has told all these things to *me*.'"[20] Baldwin reported that she and her group were not persuaded by what amounted to an argument grounded solely on Joseph's authority.

Disbelief frequently led to efforts to disprove. Smith's beliefs often extended, as they did with the mummies, beyond his own personal religious experiences to claims about the world. And as

Baldwin's response indicates, many in Illinois reacted to his empirical claims by doubting and trying to disprove them. By declaring such claims discredited, opponents argued the case for tolerating the Mormons was unjustified. This was the tack taken by Thomas Gregg, editor of the *Warsaw Messenger*. In the fall of 1843, Gregg shared with his readers a story of the visit English divinity professor Henry Caswell made to Smith at Nauvoo. Upon arriving in town, Caswell casually showed a Nauvoo shopkeeper a relic he had brought with him: a six-hundred-year-old Greek Psalter. But Caswell cannily declined to disclose that he knew its provenance. The shopkeeper brought him to Smith, who took a quick look at the book and immediately declared in the presence of his followers that it was "a dictionary of Egyptian hieroglyphics." As Gregg told the tale: "The brethren present were greatly astonished at this exhibition of their Prophet's power of revealing hidden things. After their exaltation had somewhat subsided, the Professor coolly told them that their Prophet was a base impostor! and that the book before them was but a plain Greek Psalter! . . . Joe 'stepped out.' . . . Such is the manner in which this arrant knave imposes upon his followers! And such is the manner in which his knavery is sometimes exposed! Yet, strange that people continue to believe him!"[21] Caswell went away disgusted with "the iniquity" of Smith's "imposture" and felt duty bound to publish his findings because "Mormonism needs but to be seen in its true light to be hated."[22]

Baldwin's, Gregg's, and Caswell's responses highlight several problems with Bushman's suggestion that the validity of religious beliefs is properly assessed by the believer's personal acquaintances or by what amounts to an appeal to community standards. While some beliefs are wholly personal, many reach into the empirical world and are subject to other evidentiary standards, such as expertise or the experimental method. The above anecdotes can stand in for a host of others in which Joseph Smith was simply factually incorrect about his beliefs. But the detection of empirical falsehood does not go very far for a variety of reasons. One is that the Mormons were careful to distinguish between Joseph the infallible prophet and Joseph the fallible man. When Caswell revealed his certain knowledge of the Psalter to his Mormon doctor companion, he replied: "Sometimes Mr. Smith speaks as a mere man. If he gave a wrong opinion respecting the book, he spoke as a mere man."[23] Another reason is that the factually refutable part of any one belief is often quite minimal. A final contextual reason is perhaps most powerful: once polarization gets to the point that individuals aim to entrap members of an opposed group, the evidentiary process of determining fact from fiction becomes intractable. Given Caswell's canny behavior, he was marked early on as an "anti-Mormon" by the Latter-day Saints, and the Mormon paper *Times and Seasons* later published an account of Caswell's visit that questioned his veracity on grounds of his use of deception and an interest in self-promotion.[24]

The Caswell episode highlights a second problem with Bushman's standard. It offers little guidance to situations in which community opinion is divided about a given belief. That problem is difficult enough when mere factual beliefs are involved, but when the beliefs involved exist in a complex mix of facts, norms, and aspirations, the problem is unresolvable. Furthermore, in many such cases the beliefs involved can be described as foundational. Examples include wide-ranging beliefs like "The United States is a special country" and more simple but still community-shaping beliefs like "Alcohol is good for you." Such beliefs are nearly impervious to "correction" because they cross multiple knowledge domains, making them all but untestable. Thus, they remain essentially contested.[25] But given that shared political and religious beliefs are foundational to all cultures, how should democracies deal with disagreement over these kinds of beliefs? Justifying and legitimating an answer to this question is something a liberal polity must negotiate if it seeks to produce a constitutional democracy in a multicultural setting.

FOUNDATIONAL BELIEFS AND LIBERAL TOLERATION

The way early American leaders framed religious beliefs opened up a wide space for these beliefs by greatly discounting their dangerous consequences or the problem of disagreement. Thomas Jefferson put it disarmingly in his *Notes on the State of Virginia* (1787): "It does me no injury for my neighbor to say there are twenty gods, or no god. It neither picks my pocket nor breaks my leg."[26] This American stance does not reduce to a vanishing zero the cases in which the state needs to act to control a disputable belief, but it makes recourse to state authority much less frequent. Jefferson's approach fit the broad outlines of the European liberal tradition, which aimed to limit governmental power in order to protect what Jefferson called the individual rights of "life, liberty, and the pursuit of happiness." One of the liberal tradition's purposes was to minimize the political problem of assessing other people's beliefs by narrowing the scope or the range of cases under which the problem might arise. Liberals like Jefferson focused on the harm principle, the idea, as J. S. Mill had it, that "the only purpose for which power can rightfully be exercised over any member of a civilized community, against his will, is to prevent harm to others."[27]

By the mid-nineteenth century Mill was distinguishing between "the part of a person's life which concerns only himself, and that which concerns others," between self-regarding and other-regarding actions, in an effort to strike a balance between tolerating a wide variety of potentially destabilizing beliefs and keeping the social order intact.[28] Individuals were free to believe what they might and indeed to act at will if only they themselves were affected. Mill's distinction created a "private sphere," or zone of unmitigated personal freedom, apiece with liberalism's general strategy of sealing off each individual's concerns from broader societal purposes and government intervention. American settlers in the West experienced a private sphere of freedom as a practical matter. They exited the East and moved on to more elbow room. As the 1820s wore on, they nudged the nation to endorse a broad notion of freedom of religion under the new political regime set up by Andrew Jackson and the emerging Democratic Party.

The change ushered in by the expansion of private sphere freedoms needs to be underscored. Before the American and French Revolutions, which nurtured classical liberal ideals, control over foundational political and religious beliefs was firmly in the hands of the state, an established church, or some combination of both. The history of the seventeenth and eighteenth centuries is replete with stories of the cruel suppression of belief. Repression rests on the simplest response to the politics of belief because it denies the right of individual belief altogether. Early protoliberals such as the Englishman Thomas Hobbes followed this approach; he did not recognize a freedom of expression or a right of public "opinions and doctrines" in any individuals other than those holding the sovereign power.[29]

Even a proper liberal like John Locke rejected the idea that beliefs should be tolerated for their own sake or to protect the rights or dignity of believers; he rested his case for toleration on the need to limit state power. He argued that government means should reach only to "outward" actions. The need to protect the public safety justified the use of force to prevent harm, and only for this purpose might actions inspired by religious belief be regulated. The use of coercion was wholly inappropriate in the case of the internal world of belief. Thus, Locke reasoned, magistrates who used "outward force" in an attempt to control individual belief acted irrationally by committing a category mistake or, more damningly, were improperly motivated by "power and empire" rather than by the spirit of Christian "charity, meekness, and good-will."[30]

The politics of belief was made anew and became conceptually more difficult because of the importance liberals increasingly placed on the individual capacity to freely choose and rationally debate. The focus on individual autonomy, or the freedom to endorse, communicate, alter, or reject rational beliefs, makes modern societies across the board more open to new beliefs than are traditional societies of all kinds.[31] But such moderns are also more skeptical of certain kinds of belief on account of their disreputable sources; they are not focused simply on their potentially dangerous consequences. Since their earliest days in Greece, Western philosophers aimed to liberate people from fear of the unknown, from uncritical support of the conventional status quo, and from the coercion of authority figures—common sources of belief in traditional societies. Those operating under any of these assumptions were not thought to be fully free or rational, and their beliefs were not thought respectable by the liberal polity.

By making individual autonomy an ideal, Immanuel Kant ushered in a reformed version of liberalism.[32] He urged individuals to "dare to know," to leave behind beliefs founded on convention alone, and to "use their own minds."[33] The development of autonomy as an ideal legitimates pluralism not simply as a factual matter—promoting a diversity of religious beliefs—but normatively by implying that diversity not only exists but can be a good thing. Toleration moves from being a dubious virtue (because it potentially imperils the rights of others or undermines autonomy) to a thing right in itself. It opens the door to the celebration of "the varieties of religious experience" as expressions of the full panoply of "human consciousness," as it did in the late nineteenth century for William James.[34]

People advocating daring beliefs added a new layer to the civic assessment of others' beliefs. They made fellow citizens engage in a kind of meta-assessment about the probability of other people's beliefs being disreputable in origin as well as potentially dangerous in consequence. Beliefs assessed as fear driven, coerced, or factually false could be disrespected on the grounds of disreputable source. As we have seen, however, factual falsity, while a clear guide to detecting erring belief, is often inconclusive where beliefs are not simply empirical but mixed with norms and aspirations at a foundational level. Thus those judging beliefs often have to leave truth and falsehood behind and move to the context in which the belief originates. From the perspective of governance, it is not the truth or falsity of beliefs themselves that a government or other individuals must parse but the probability of a belief originating in illiberal grounds such as fear or coercion. How communities decide to categorize a belief—rational and respectable or irrational and unrespectable—will determine whether members holding the belief are tolerated and treated as equals.

The need to assess the nature and tendency of other people's beliefs adds a novel dimension to public life. In the case of outlier beliefs, it adds a pragmatic reason for nonintervention by the state because the beliefs of others can arguably be characterized as less threatening to the tangible aspects of social order, such as life, liberty, and property. If this stance is taken, pluralism is endorsed and the need for persecution is avoided; an irrational attempt at control is replaced with the state acting rationally to protect individual rights and a social good. Thus are pragmatic agreements that avoid recourse to a common set of beliefs made more legitimate and respectable. The use of incompletely theorized agreements becomes a preferred route to compromise, such as the US Constitution's ban on Congress establishing a religion discussed in chapter 1.[35] The pragmatic policy of agreeing to disagree was the aspect of American pluralism that Joseph Smith found threatening because it countenanced and normalized in fellow Americans beliefs that he considered, if not physically injurious, theologically wrong and in some cases evil. It is a supreme irony that the Mormons in many cases benefited from a political development they deplored.

A pragmatic stance toward the beliefs of all members is perhaps especially attractive to those who defend an individualist culture. Individualists see pragmatism as a way of avoiding what they find problematic in competing societal cultures—for example, the status quo of the traditionalists or the proselytizing of the moralizers. Some individualists may in fact claim all beliefs are relative and none are more reasonable or more virtuous than others, but many individualists are motivated not by an absolute skepticism (a claim that is internally inconsistent and ultimately indefensible) but by an effort to "disencumber" the political agenda from potentially explosive or unresolvable differences.[36] If this kind of defensive individualism succeeds, space is freed up on the political agenda for issues that can be negotiated, and traditionalists and moralizers will have fewer opportunities to focus political debate on either the tacit status quo or other nonnegotiable, if principled, beliefs.

An intriguing example of the individualist disencumbering strategy can be found in one of the nation's greatest politicians, Abraham Lincoln. As an Illinois Whig, Lincoln worked to redirect his party away from its moralistic use of "denunciations against dram-sellers" as a "system of tactics" in its role in the temperance movement. In his February 22, 1842, address before the Washington Temperance Society in Springfield, he compared the ineffective moralizing strategy of the first temperance cause, led by hectoring Second Great Awakening preachers, with the success of the Washingtonians, who were recovering alcoholics. The denunciations were both "impolitic and unjust" because for decades "universal public opinion not only tolerated [alcohol manufacturing, merchandizing, and consumption], but recognized and adopted its use." This predominant opinion mattered because "the universal sense of mankind, on any subject, is an argument or at least an influence not easily overcome. . . . And men ought not, in justice, to be denounced for yielding to it . . . where they are backed by interest, fixed habits, or burning appetites."[37] Here the deployment of a belief about beliefs assessment is not relativistic and skeptical but pragmatic. While it is impossible to read these words without thinking of how they foreshadowed Lincoln's treatment of the national slavery issue and antislavery tactics generally, they should also be read for the message they sent their intended audience—the leaders of the Whig Party in Illinois.

Nationally, and in the state, the Whigs had Evangelical and conservative party wings, both of which were tempted to dismiss public opinion outright. They rejected out of hand what they saw as irrational beliefs about the benefits of alcohol or the need to drop the property qualification for White male voters. But Lincoln asked them to resist the temptation to belittle what they saw as the mere "enthusiasm of a popular cause" or the fleeting "influence of fashion." In doing so, they would reject what had become in both cases majority public opinion.[38] As we shall see, an emerging generation of Whig leaders in Illinois worked strenuously to disenthrall their party from the stance of social control (moralistic or traditional) and to cajole it to embrace the settlers' egalitarian rhetoric or to at least adopt an individualist stance of governmental nonintervention. Lincoln was trying to persuade his party that its beliefs on temperance were as a matter of fact losing votes and as a matter of belief not compelling. He urged that the party adjust its tactics and stance. With an acceptance of the new political-regime norm resting on a belief in the political equality of all White men (whether or not they owned property), the party might pass into law policies it sought on other more pressing issues. But its influence on the temperance concern would come not on conservative and traditionalist grounds (holding property ownership as more important than political equality) or for evangelical and moral perfectionist reasons (holding drinkers as inherently sinful or unfree) but on the individualist grounds of pragmatism (reasoning with the intemperate and the propertyless on the negotiable terms of their own beliefs). Indeed, Lincoln magnanimously refused to condemn alcoholics on moral grounds because, as he argued incisively, many excessive drinkers were, he believed, more morally commendable than nondrinkers: "The demon of intemperance ever seems to have delighted in sucking the blood of genius and of generosity."[39]

In Illinois's developing democracy, a government in which the capacity of state institutions to enforce the law was still tentative, the focus on the resolving power of public opinion was advocated by the Democrats as well. They urged that the majority had the authority to make the final determination when beliefs irredeemably conflicted. For example, William Leggett, who spent his early adult years in Illinois and became a leading Democratic Party editor in New York City, began his new paper in 1836 by endorsing "the political maxim that the majority have the right to govern." This claim was posited by Leggett as a maxim, an unargued assertion. It was premised on the politically contested but factual belief that "the majority have the capacity to govern." But Leggett held that American societal culture should embrace it as a foundational belief.

By midcentury this belief was widely accepted by traditionalists and moralists alike, though one that remained often in the background as an assumption, akin to what Oliver Wendell Holmes Jr. later called "a fighting faith."[40] Deference to the majority was implicit in Eliza Steele's moralistic exhortations, for example, about how western immigrants should behave; she scolded and chastised them—an unlikely form of persuasion—but she never questioned their authority to determine the course of the nation. Similarly, John Reynolds couched his traditionalist claims about the benefits of slavery in terms of the good of the greatest number—a rough surrogate for majority public opinion.

The movement toward pragmatic toleration made conditions in Illinois ripe for a welcoming response to the Mormon refugees. But there was another liberal premise contained in American thinking at the time that endangered the Mormons. This was the concept of the undivided sovereign. The inviolate private sphere and the harm principle are prime examples of the way liberals try to limit the power the state can exert over members of the polity by dividing that power into pieces. The range of sovereign state power in liberal hands is subject to what liberal theorist Jean-Jacques Rousseau calls the "conjuring acts of our political theorists . . . a sleight of hand worthy of a carnival."[41] Nevertheless, if the range of sovereign power is thus cut into innumerable pieces and limited, its depth remains unfathomable. The sovereignty of any state, the Frenchman observed, is by definition indivisible and without bottom. This was the orthodoxy of his and the subsequent generation. He went on to draw the same conclusion Hobbes had: the power of any sovereign is unlimited.

The unlimited depth of sovereign power was a line of liberal thought tied to international affairs, the external relations liberal states had with other states. It was a line of reasoning which Benjamin Franklin famously commented made him "quite sick."[42] Franklin was politically and temperamentally liberal; he had fought the British Parliament, which had claimed "external" sovereignty over the American colonists as a matter of agreed international legal doctrine.[43] He fought against the idea when it emerged in the Constitutional Convention, but it survived as part and parcel of liberal conjuring. The liberal trick has, Rousseau notes, two parts: it first divides the sovereign power into so many pieces that it appears to disappear; it then puts all the loosely related pieces back together again in a way that allows the state enough uncontested authority to ensure a functional society. The US Constitution, with its prominent recognition of the separation of powers (creating three distinct branches of the national government) and federalism (the division of authority between the national and state governments), errs on the side of limitation to the detriment of functionality. Ever since the Constitution's ratification, visitors to the United States have remarked on the nation's internal sense of "statelessness."

The social contract theory of Hobbes and Locke made this illiberal external treatment possible, and even encouraged it. They had inherited the concept of the unlimited sovereign, and while they used the social contract to limit the power of government within the nation-state, they allowed the sovereigns they created to maintain near unlimited power in operating outside the nation-state. Such unlimited power was justified on the grounds of a right of self-defense, a natural right all entities retained in the state of nature. Governments might be removed from the state of nature and limited by one people's social contract, but toward all others, the government remained in a state of nature. Both Hobbes and Locke imagined settlers outside the state with power to take uncultivated land from nonmembers while leaving the sovereign with unlimited authority over the naturalization of members. The United States Constitution similarly granted Congress plenary power over the rules of national membership, which it exercised fully in the Naturalization Act of 1790.[44]

Given the general tenor of liberal doubts about the power of the state vis-à-vis members and given the universal language most liberals adopt, the liberal indifference to the state's absolute power vis-à-vis nonmembers is striking and added to the stakes of the determination of membership status. Liberals relegated the acceptance of outsiders' beliefs to a mere internal matter to be settled among the members of civil society. Another nineteenth-century liberal, G. W. F. Hegel, worried that societal culture would not be sufficiently disinterested in its recognition of outsiders' beliefs and rights.[45] The liberal state was tethered to preventing harm in the name of the public good, but that good would now in important ways be defined and applied by civil society (e.g., private sphere) actors and applied to outsiders.

This weakness in liberal thought was expressed by American liberals whenever they applied their ideas to nonmembers. As open and tolerant as leaders like Benjamin Franklin and Thomas Jefferson could be toward fellow citizens, they were notoriously illiberal toward groups they considered outsiders, such as the Moravians or the Native Americans. Jefferson, in his second inaugural address, referred simply to how "the stream of overwhelming population" had displaced "the hunter's state," a kind of civil society fait accompli. The president recognized only the limits of "humanity" whereby the Native Americans should be encouraged to take up "that industry which alone can enable them to maintain their place in [settler society]."[46] It would be left to future generations to puzzle over how the self-governing power recognized in colonies of settlers would be limited when applied to nonmembers living as a group among them. The delegation of the recognition of outsiders to civil society greatly restricted the scope of the belief problem because it was seen as a wholly internal and individual matter. It made it possible for settler states to ignore the equally fundamental differences among beliefs that arose within their societal cultures because they were not matters for state action.

In frontier settler states like Illinois, federalism authorized de jure zones of independent operation from the national government. De facto, the Illinois state needed to draw on the power of civil society groups in order simply to enforce the law. This self-help version of popular sovereignty had roots in the colonies' assertion of self-government against the British Parliament.[47] But federalism, as a liberal strategy limiting state power, backfired in some cases of protecting individual rights; having to share sovereignty allowed powerful local groups to bias the societal culture, which resulted in widespread illiberal treatment of marginal groups viewed as nonmembers, including the Mormons.

CRITICAL JUNCTURES: IMPOSTERS, FOLLOWERS, AND THE NAUVOO LEGION

Illinoisans who opposed toleration of the Mormons would from time to time refer to what they considered outrageous and unwarranted beliefs of Joseph Smith. They exhorted their fellow Illinoisans to exclude him and mark him as a nonmember simply on the ground of the irrationality of his beliefs. But as we have seen, this was a move the Whigs had frequent recourse to, and it was a source of their unpopularity as diagnosed by Lincoln, one of their own. Perhaps because of the unpopularity of prescription, it was much more common to find those opposed to the Mormons attempting to demonstrate that the saints disdained the majority opinion of "the gentiles" (church members' term for non-Mormons) or that they felt empowered to harm the gentiles with impunity. An example of both claims being frequently repeated can be found in the Whig organ, the *Sangamo Journal,* after its party had been twice jilted at the polls by the Mormons in the spring and fall of 1842. The *Journal* prominently featured a review of the tell-all book written by John C. Bennett after he left Nauvoo as an apostate. Bennett's *The History of the Saints* listed all the crimes committed by Mormons over the last two years in Illinois and Iowa that had been entered into the public records of the "neighboring circuit courts." These included seven specific cases, though "Bennett says that hundreds of other incidents of the same character could be detailed." But, the Whig editor intimated, Bennett went further by claiming the prophet's attitude toward gentiles was worse than the cases of murder, horse stealing, robbery, and theft: "Joe is notoriously profane, but he says God will not notice him in *cursing the damned Gentiles!*"[48] The paper's implication was obvious: if he cursed the gentiles, how could he respect their authority or refrain from harming them when he could act with impunity?

After ridiculing Smith and his followers, the Whig editor arrived at the same question we have asked: How did the prophet succeed in getting so many to believe him? Or, as the editor put it, how could "a Ruffian Prophet . . . such a vulgar, low minded fellow as Joe Smith" secure "unlimited control over some thirty thousand human beings . . . despite . . . their own knowledge of his baseness?" He had no answer other than to compare Smith's popularity to the "success of Jemima Wilkinson or the Matthias' humbug." But the analogy does not hold, and it is worth a careful examination to demonstrate why. Wilkinson was a Quaker who in 1776 proclaimed herself to be "the Christ" upon a near-death recovery from typhoid fever. Becoming a "genderless spirit" and the "Universal friend," Wilkinson preached in the Burned-Over District of western New York for over twenty years and, like Smith, claimed to receive revelations from God and to perform miracles.[49] But unlike Smith, Wilkinson never developed a large following—a poorly timed attempt to walk on water may have been her undoing—and she died largely forgotten in 1819.[50]

Richard Matthews of Matthias fame also declared himself to be a god. An orphaned carpenter journeyman, he moralized against drink and prostitution on the mean streets of New York City until visions and violent fits and financial ruin brought him to Rochester and the Burned-Over District. He, too, had prophecies fail; further, misogyny and resentment of reformed preacher Charles Finney's version of evangelism (which was open to gender equality) drove him to madness. In this condition, alone and seeing only his own truth—and the devil everywhere else—Matthias made his way to Kirtland, Ohio, in 1835 to the Mormons and rival prophet Joseph Smith. As Paul Johnson and Sean Wilentz relate in *The Kingdom of Matthias,* the two prophets eyed each other testily. But Joseph Smith characteristically agreed to hear him out and let him preach before dismissing him from the city, declaring that "my God told me that his God is the Devil." Smith later recorded in his diary, "I for once cast out the Devil in bodily shape and I believe a murderer."[51]

Matthias had come to Kirtland a broken man, a prophet turned tyrant, although along the way he converted and befriended the freed slave Isabella Van Wagenen, later known to all as Sojourner Truth. By the end of their tale, Johnson and Wilentz compare Matthias to other megalomaniacs, including modern-day cult leaders like Jim Jones and David Koresh.[52] These people used their personal charisma for short-term power over a small group of followers. Bennett portrayed Joseph Smith this way in his exposé, as a "power-mad charlatan."[53] But as others have noted, his accusation is really a case of projection; it is Bennett who, Aaron Burr–like, is revealing himself, "revealing his own feverish dreams."[54] Matthias and Bennett fit perfectly the "confidence man" impostor. This was a trope familiar to the nineteenth century and reproduced in fiction so effectively and chillingly by Herman Melville in *The Confidence-Man.* This person is the mysterious stranger and master of disguises who suddenly appears in a community or on a steamboat, fleeces his victims, and disappears. But Joseph Smith did none of this. We need to look elsewhere to evaluate his beliefs and explain his hold over his followers.

How then should we understand Joseph Smith's unique ability not only to attract so many followers but also to keep their support? Perhaps the best clue to Smith's unique power came, improbably enough, from another desperate drifter. Joseph Jackson left a coherent and detailed eye-witness testimony of his encounter with Smith.

By his own account, in March 1843 he migrated to Nauvoo in straits of poverty and desperation; he confessed to being driven by curiosity to see firsthand "the thieving Mormons." He had heard so many complaints and remarkable claims about the Mormons as he worked in and around Carthage that he decided to see Joseph Smith for himself. He introduced himself as a "fugitive from Macon City, Georgia," who needed "protection." Jackson reported Smith's reaction: "This seemed to tickle his fancy wonderfully." After Jackson admitted that "he was a desperate man," they discussed what Jackson could do to earn his keep, and Smith suggested that "he would make any man rich, who would be unto him as was Joab to David." Joab was the Old Testament commander of King David's army.

Jackson offered to go to Missouri and "release O. P. Rockwell," the Mormon imprisoned in Missouri accused of attempting to assassinate Governor Lilburn Boggs. According to Jackson, they proceeded to discuss not only freeing Rockwell but murdering Boggs. He then makes an interesting observation: "He [Smith] then commenced an argument, to make me believe that he was right and lawful in the sight of God. . . . I then remarked that as to his religion, I cared nothing about it, for I did not believe in the supremacy of God." Jackson added:

> I was utterly astonished to see this man concoct the most hellish plans for murder and revenge, and yet, with pertinacity insist that it was right in the sight of God. . . . All this was done with an air of sanctimonious gravity, and with a look of innocence that would almost make one believe that the Prophet really thought, that he was acting under the command of heaven. . . . And here lay the whole secret of Joe Smith's success. He had a singularly unmeaning countenance. . . . He had so long practiced duplicity that there was scarcely a compunctious feeling left in his bosom.[55]

Mormon writers discount Jackson's account, which is not surprising given that he was an admitted drifter, accused the Mormon leader of accessory to murder, and later admitted a planned attempt to murder the prophet himself. Bushman claims he was offered a job "as a real estate clerk when he arrived destitute in Nauvoo" but then turned sour when Hyrum Smith's daughter turned away his romantic offers.[56] Mormon writers often refuse to credit any characterizations coming from the pen of apostates like Jackson,

Bennett, and John D. Lee. But firsthand accounts like Jackson's contain directness and details that cannot be ignored. Smith's guileless candor was quite unlike the typical confidence man or megalomaniac. If this affectless stance of Smith unnerved and amazed men like Bennett and Jackson, it may have added a layer of believability to Mormon adherents.

The straightforward, knowing aspect of Smith's character has been identified by Harold Bloom as similar to Gnosticism. The Gnostics emphasized a direct experience with God. Bloom sees this emphasis on the surety of belief arising from personal experience as characteristic of many disparate strains of American evangelical religion, including traditions as theologically diverse as the Southern Baptists, the Seventh-day Adventists, the Jehovah's Witnesses, and the Christian Scientists.[57] Bloom's observation is important for the toleration equation if simply because surety of belief rooted in individual experience makes the belief-about-belief meta-assessment all the more difficult. Belief rooted in individual experience also made the Mormon approach more compelling to many. As Wallace Stegner has emphasized, according to Mormon theology, the miracles were still coming; individual experience was brought immediately and face-to-face with God. What made Smith's Mormonism so attractive? "Fresher news, later dope," Stegner hypothesized. As he wrote: "The Mormons . . . had one thing that no other religion could offer. God had spoken to them, not two thousand years ago away off in Asia Minor, but yesterday, the day before."[58]

But the focus on individual experience should not be allowed to obscure another crucial aspect of Smith's belief: its story of peoplehood. At Nauvoo, Smith produced a series of astounding theological innovations. The defense of plural marriage, the articulation of human godhood, and claims of a multiple-universe heaven—all these have for obvious reasons received the lion's share of attention. But these were doctrines either open to a very few or focused on subtle theological details ungraspable or irrelevant to many. From the perspective of the average Mormon follower, Smith's doctrine on the baptism of the dead, announced at Nauvoo in September 1840, not long after his own father's funeral, was likely the most important and compelling of Smith's Illinois-born beliefs. Through baptism of the dead, members of one's family who had passed away but who never experienced or acceded to Mormonism could, through the refiner's fire of the temple ordinances, be welded into heaven. It applied to the family level the grandiose notion of Americans as a lost tribe of Israel and a chosen people. The narrative fit with the followers' sense of what should be, a sense that was created by the setting of their lived experience. His story line of national unity and meaningful collective redemption fit their everyday family life. Joseph Smith's followers found his character believable enough, but the content of his prophecy, in particular the grounded cultural resonance of baptisms of the dead, was a second and perhaps more profound secret to his success. It was a recipe that founders like Moses, Solon, and Luther had used before him.[59]

If the problem of toleration in liberal democracies were as simple as creating a fair implementation of the harm principle under a neutral rule of law, it would be hard enough to solve. But the human spirit produces people like Joseph Smith, whose gift of prophecy, as Joseph Jackson testified, went all the way down into his bones. And when Smith looked into himself, he produced a message that resonated with thousands of similarly situated followers. Perhaps we can understand the unique believability of the prophet's beliefs, both to himself and to his followers, by thinking of them in terms of first- and second-order preferences.[60] Humans in general have the capacity to ask for "not simply what [they] desire but also what [they] want to desire."[61] Smith and his followers had a second-order preference for America to be a certain kind of place and they wanted to be a certain kind of people; they would embrace whatever first-order or immediate preferences they needed to adopt in order to make that happen, even if inconvenient, albeit with the occasional backslide. Here community belief was the product of both experience and will in a way that was recursive and self-supporting.

As real as national narratives are and as compelling as group life becomes in democracies, many will want to return to the question of the seeming unreality of Mormon beliefs. Can a mere majority or fervent minority belief turn a fiction into a fact? Isn't there a reality check built into the system? The answer seems to be it depends on how far embedded in the societal culture the fiction or fact is. As we have seen in the cases of Eliza Steele and John Reynolds, advocates for competing majority narratives and their underlying cultural assumptions frequently turn to natural science for an alternative approach to testing the truth of hypotheses—namely empirical investigation. But, as with Steele and Reynolds, geology and biology, while a crucial crutch, are mixed with other values to produce a potent mix of knowledge and belief.

Numerous cases from the past and present can be produced in which actors claim divine inspiration of one kind or another. From this set, investigation frequently uncovers that the vast majority are faulty in one way or another. A weeping icon proves to be a matter of condensation, stigmata the result of hands unused to field work. But what about cases in which the evidence is mixed or uncertain? How might the belief-about-beliefs meta-assessment proceed in such cases? One approach scientists developed to evaluate uncertain or mixed evidentiary claims is the use of statistical probability. Multiple observations of any given claim can be plotted on a curve and, following a rule of accepting two standard deviations from the mean set of observations (known as the 95 percent rule), verifiable patterns confirmed. Joseph Smith repeatedly made use of observational evidence to defend the authenticity of his claims. Three and then eight witnesses were brought forward to sign testimonials that the golden plates were real. But the testimonials were not persuasive to outsiders like Governor Thomas Ford, who learned from "men who were once in [Smith's] confidence" the process the prophet used to get the testaments. Smith would tell the witnesses that they needed to prepare, because the tablets could only be "spiritually discerned." When they looked and reported seeing nothing, he sent them off to pray, saying "O ye of little faith . . . down on your knees." And Ford reported the next time they looked, "they were persuaded that they saw the plates."[62] As Fawn Brodie puts it, the witnesses were "not conspirators but victims of Joseph's unconscious but positive talent for hypnosis."[63]

Ford approached Smith's claim of being a seer, prophet, and revelator with precisely the detachment required for an unbiased probabilistic assessment. In his first meeting with Joseph Smith in 1842, and not for the last time in his travails with the Mormons, he gathered the evidence and weighed it carefully. In the case of the golden tablets, unlike with the cases of horse stealing or murder, he concluded in his *History of Illinois* that Smith's claims were "absurd" and a "delusion."[64] Given his own admitted biases—Ford told Smith directly in 1842 that he was "no religionist"—it is hard to fault his logic.[65] Indeed, as Smith himself observed in 1844: "I don't blame anyone for not believing my history. If I had not experienced what I have, I would not have believed it myself."[66] Using reasoning that followed from the logic of all probabilistic claims, Ford had to concede that his own conclusions were merely probabilistic and not verifiable.[67]

These considerations open the issue to a broader level upon which are exposed some of the more intractable challenges facing democratic toleration. Simple reductionist resolutions are insufficient.[68] Historians Leonard Arrington and Davis Bitton try one such simple approach when they note that "Smith's account of the origin of the Book of Mormon has, of course, never been acceptable to nonbelievers. But finding a creditable alternative explanation has been difficult."[69] Bushman, continuing in this vein, states that "explanations [that] keep the story within the realm of the ordinary . . . require considerable fabrication themselves."[70] This simple resolution creates in many minds a false equivalence. For many would resist it with a similarly simplistic counterreduction: the claim that Smith invented the Book of Mormon is not a considerable fabrication because it is an explanation supported by straightforward, if sympathetic reasoning, namely that Smith, as a youth of immense sensitivity and imagination, was driven by need and induced by a trance state to an act of hypnotic creativity and invention. What need? There were many: the need to escape from poverty and pluralism; the need to unite his family and all Mormon families to redeem their worth; and the need to redeem the special worth of the American nation. To address each level of need by knitting a story in which an exiled family band becomes a warring tribe and then a new nation was to tie old and new together in a way that brilliantly pointed to a future of purpose.[71]

The trouble with this kind of functionalist explanation, reducing beliefs to needs and desires, is that it applies to the explainer as well, whereupon it will be argued that the skeptic has "needs" too, and an endless reductio ad absurdum begins. Instead of this back-and-forth, a more plausible approach is to recognize that the empirical facts that justify foundational beliefs of worth are mixed with norms and aspirations in ways that make foundational claims essentially contested. Consider, for instance, the famous foundational claim made by Locke in his *Letter Concerning Toleration:* "Nobody is born a member of any church."[72] While this can be asserted as an empirically true claim, its use in many contexts is normative. It is at once empirical and normative, claiming that as a matter of fact no one is so born and no one *should be.*

Such foundational beliefs litter the ground in American politics and, in the 1830s, were far from being unique to the Mormons; indeed, groups such as the Democrats, the Whigs, the Unitarians, the abolitionists, the Quakers, the Shakers, the Masons, and the Anti-Masons all constituted their communities and shared forms of life around distinctive background assumptions that they committed to faith. A plethora of belief communities was common under the new politics of democratic toleration and religious pluralism. When a belief community is fit to a setting which reinforces its biases, complete with political and economic institutions, it can become entrenched. The problem for a pluralistic, liberal democratic order is not in acknowledging that groups are committed to separate and inconsistent foundational beliefs but in determining which subset of such beliefs are pathological in the sense that they lead to harm to either group members or the larger community.

Rousseau acknowledged the new political reality religious diversity created in republics as early as 1762, when *The Social Contract* was published. On the one hand, monotheism made toleration of religious pluralism extremely problematic, since "it is impossible to live in peace with people who one thinks are damned."[73] Philosopher Ernest Gellner puts the problem in its broadest form: "The idea of the Management of the universe practicing cognitive favouritism and nepotism among its own creation—which is what the idea of Revelation means—is morally repugnant in a society whose tacit entrenched constitution proclaims equal and symmetrical access to truth."[74] On the other hand, new religions, and thus new political conflicts and manifestations of intolerance, are in principle an ever-present possibility. Rousseau argues that all lasting political orders are based on religion, but not all religiously based political orders are lasting. Lasting orders are those announced in extraordinary times by a "legislator" gifted with a certain kind of reason. As he elaborates:

> It is this sublime reason, which transcends the grasp of ordinary men, which decisions the legislator puts in the mouth of the immortals in order to compel by divine authority those whom human prudence could not move. But not everybody is capable of making the gods speak or of being believed when he proclaims himself their interpreter. The great soul of the legislator is the true miracle that should prove his mission. Any man can engrave stone tables, buy an oracle, or

> feign a secret intercourse with some divinity, or train a bird to talk in his ear, or find crude methods of imposing his beliefs upon the people. He who knows no more than this may perchance assemble a troupe of lunatics, but he will never found an empire and his extravagant work will soon die with him. Pointless sleights-of-hand form a fleeting connection; only wisdom can make it lasting. The Judaic Law, which still exists, and that of the child of Ishmael, which has ruled half the world for ten centuries, still proclaim today the great men who enunciated them. And while pride-ridden philosophy or the blind spirit of factionalism sees in them nothing but lucky impostors, the true political theoretician admires in their institutions that great and powerful genius which presides over establishments that endure.[75]

Many will be unwilling to relinquish what they see as the truth for expediency, and they have ample license to perpetuate the hoary debate between philosophy and religion that reaches back at least to the Greek philosopher Heraclitus. Both sides claim the truth. But for those willing to put their pride aside, two of the points Rousseau makes are crucial. The first is that religious founders are in some sense saved by their followers. Brodie used the idea to conclude *No Man Knows My History:* "There was a great hunger in his people, and they accepted him for what he set himself up to be. They believed the best of him and thereby caused him to give his best."[76] The second is that republican state authorities are of necessity put in the position of determining whether new religions will prove "durable" or "ephemeral." This is an empirical matter that requires weighing evidence and probabilities; the matter of "lasting establishments" can only be proven over time or judged based on the degree of conflict and harm they produce. Implicit here is the idea that beliefs should be judged by the societal culture's own standards. For a first cut, liberal states use the harm principle, a rough-and-ready tool, especially as promulgated by one as adept at rhetoric as Thomas Jefferson. But when contestation arises, constitutional democracies will either cling to the image of neutrality as a guarantee of fairness, however impossible it is to achieve in practice, or delegate the job of ultimately defining the societal culture to civil society majorities.

Ford tried to make a neutral evidentiary and probabilistic assessment of Mormon belief and actions in Illinois. In his 1844 report to the Illinois General Assembly, he summed up a list of reported Mormon and anti-Mormon actions dating back to 1839: "Upon the whole, if one half of these reports had been true, the Mormon community must have been the most intolerable collection of rogues ever assembled, or, if one half of them were false, they were the most maligned and abused."[77] Ford implies that both statements are true. Indeed, it was just this evenhanded judicial stance of Ford's that so enraged the Mormons and the "old settlers" of Hancock County. Yet Rousseau's pragmatic logic forces upon political authority the pose of the judge. But in judging, governing authorities must of necessity examine and independently assess the credibility of the religious claims being made. In this case, the state had to judge the saints—precisely what Smith's cosmology would not allow. By putting ourselves in Ford's shoes, we begin to understand the true difficulties of democratic toleration.

Smith's personality was such that he likely was fully convinced that his dictation was divinely inspired, even if, as Brodie surmised, "it is doubtful . . . he ever escaped the memory of the conscious artifice that went into the Book of Mormon." Yet as she noted, contrary to her own assumption, Smith did not seem to have been burdened by the weight of falsehood. Where "a persisting consciousness of guilt over the cunning and deception with which his prophetic career was launched would have eventually destroyed" others, Smith appeared to thrive and revel in his prophecies.[78] His personality was not, as Ford reported, "dark and gloomy" but frequently "full of levity."[79] Prophecy sustained him, and he continued as a seer and revelator until he died. Even in the darkest times of the mid-1830s, when Smith's prophecies failed—for example, when he was wrong about the "anti-banking" notes being redeemed for gold in Kirtland, Ohio, or about Zion's Camp redeeming the Mormons in Missouri—the vast majority of his followers never abandoned their prophet, nor did they abandon the world they built together from his prophecies.[80] Their legislator had great soul, as Rousseau would have put it; as Smith's followers would have put it, miracles are what you make of them.

Take another prominent example of Mormon outlier belief turned to practice: polygyny. That Joseph Smith practiced plural marriage at Nauvoo is a fact despite its denial for years by the Utah church and its denial to this day by the offshoot Emma Smith authorized, the Community of Christ (formerly, the Reorganized Church of Jesus Christ of Latter Day Saints), with headquarters in

Independence, Missouri. Facts can be true or false. Foundational beliefs are partly empirical and objective and partly normative and subjective; like the events surrounding miracles, much about foundational beliefs is empirically and objectively verifiable. But how people treat them, how they experience them, how they understand them, determines their significance; it is what in philosopher R. G. Collingwood's terms makes history the story of human action and not a mere collection of the facts or events.[81] In society, if not in the laboratory or classroom, this subjective and idealist component is so much more important than the objective and empirical. What Smith meant by plural marriage made real the foundational belief of "sealing" for eternal life. For Smith and the Mormons who left Nauvoo for Utah, it laid, as Brigham Young recalled, "the foundations for worlds and for angels and for Gods."[82] Ford expressed an astute understanding of foundational belief when he dismissed charges of plural marriage against Smith and the Mormons as irrelevant because such were "enjoyed in some mystical and spiritual mode."[83]

The divine inspiration behind the Book of Mormon and all the revelations that followed were for the Mormons foundational beliefs. It is noteworthy that the Mormons participated in the pervasive culture of empiricism that most Americans, religious and nonreligious alike, shared. It would not have been obvious to a contemporary like Ford that the Mormons posed a special threat because they dangerously lowered the level of credulity in American society as a whole.[84] Empiricism, a school dedicated to so-called common sense, holds that all valid knowledge is grounded on empirical evidence. It is a school to which a majority of Americans belonged and perhaps still belong. As the *Southern Literary Messenger* asserted in 1844, "The American people have the reputation of being a very sensible people."[85] *Sensible* can mean *prudent,* but in the nineteenth century it also meant *empirical,* a disposition preferring to base belief on evidence from the senses. This was the school of thought assumed by the Mormons, who treated a revelation as a matter to be proven. Indeed, one of the Mormon complaints with American religious pluralism, and the numerous Christian sects that thrived under it, was "the thousand and one twistifications by which . . . prophecies are spiritualized into everything and nothing."[86] Like good American empiricists, the Mormons pointed to the discovery of caverns near prehistoric burial mounds in New York as "evidence that the Book of Mormon is true . . . [since] the discovery was not made until two years after the Book . . . was published."[87]

The existence of great Indigenous civilizations in North America was still debated at the time. But skeptics like Charles Ballance of Peoria noted that bones were not sufficient evidence; many mounds contained bones. He claimed to have won a challenge when a hill that was affirmed to be a natural, nonhuman formation was found to contain bones after being dug up on the spot. Mormons believed that the evidence supporting their own specialness was ample. They pointed to the church's rapidly increasing membership at home and abroad as further evidence of their truth. Was it not "a marvel and a wonder," they asked, that the Mormon religion had spread so fast, "especially since the men who were engaged in preaching this doctrine were men of no influence, being the poor, illiterate, and despised ones of the earth?"[88] Critics like Disciples of Christ founder Alexander Campbell pointed to the way the Book of Mormon addressed "every error and almost every truth" discussed in the theological and political disputes of the day—this was evidence to him that it was a cheap pastiche dreamed up and willed into existence by Smith.[89] But to Mormon readers the same evidence was read differently: "The text's ability to engage and clarify contemporary debates was a crucial feature of its inspired nature."[90]

Brodie praises Smith's "great dramatic talent." His was an "imagination . . . as untrammeled as the whole West." While she catalogs the many frauds of the era, her point is not that Mormonism is a "pathetic petty deception" like so many others but the product of "an audacious and original mind."[91] Joseph Smith's audacity was part of his humanity. It makes him a fitting subject for the study of political development, for if liberal democracies have no place for the imaginative and the credulous, they will be greatly impoverished and unworkable in the world. Smith and his community of believers, for all their unexpected ideas and practices, were well within the realm of the human norm to be expected in any democratic society. In this regard, even the Mormon practice of polygamy, often presented as the outer bound of tolerable Mormon practice, did not present a unique challenge to Illinois democracy. A criminal indictment could have been presented to a grand jury by authorities outside of Hancock County if Smith and his selected followers were simply imposters who used the cover of religion to pursue sexual desires. But such an indictment was never brought, though some women, such as Martha Brotherton, refused advances, exercised the exit option, and published their refusal.[92] As historian Lawrence Foster argues persuasively, the view of Smith as an "oversexed individual" who used religion to "rationalize his amorous propensities . . . is too simple." Foster writes: "Available evidence shows that Smith began formulating polygamous beliefs at least as early as 1831, ten years before any significant attempts to introduce the practice can be identified. Why did he wait so long if all he was after was personal sexual gratification? At the very least, his actions suggest that if it was a rationalization, it was a very complex one indeed."[93]

While it was frequently noted at the time that "fanatical" Mormon religious beliefs were a primary driver of the Mormon troubles in Illinois, the claim must be examined with care. Illinois, because of its pluralism, developed leaders who tended to be embracive when it came to religions. The typical view during the campaigning summer of 1842 was articulated by Jarvis Jackson in his stump speech as candidate for state senator in the southern tier of the state: "Mormons! Mormons!! There is a great cry about Mormons among all the grades of politicians. Well now gentlemen what I have to say on this subject is that I know nothing about it. But I would say this much that the constitution of this State and the United States [grants] every man the privilege of worshiping as he pleases." For Jackson the rub was not religion per se but the privileges of membership, which all members shared on an equal basis. If the Mormons asked for greater privileges, Jackson was not a supporter, something he made clear by concluding, "Now if the Mormons have any other right, have any other charter or exclusive privileges I would be among the first to oppose such charters."[94]

The charter Jackson had in mind was the Nauvoo city charter. Smith knew about the Democrats commitment to "equal rights." In his own way he was committed to them too. But his egalitarianism was particular to the Mormon group because he believed he had found in the Mormon way a special solution to the American dream and an alternative civic narrative. Thus, when an equal rights social contract ran up against his commitment to Mormon specialness, he was determined to ignore the former. He would prevail over the majority's commitment to religious pluralism, if he could. Imprisoned in Missouri, he came to Illinois with a plan to shield and separate himself and his followers from all majorities, local or national.

With John C. Bennett as his aide de camp, he sought militia and habeas corpus powers as part of the Nauvoo city charter. The Mormon militia, called the Nauvoo Legion, was one result. The Democrats, under Stephen A. Douglas, were willing to offer these concessions in exchange for electoral support, which Smith cheerfully offered: "Douglass is a *Master Spirit* and *his friends are our friends.*"[95] He also announced support for the Democratic candidate for governor, although the Mormons continued to vote for other Whig candidates, as indeed they had since escaping from the hated Democrats of Missouri and being rescued at Quincy by so many Illinois Whigs.

The Democrats also tacitly approved Smith's riding about the state protected by the Danites, a remnant of the personal bodyguard from Missouri who wore conspicuous white uniforms.[96] Entering the partisan fray was not unprecedented for a religious group in Illinois, but the writs, the Nauvoo Legion, and the Danites would need to be used discreetly to avoid invidious comparison. Beginning in 1841, such discretion was not possible once agents from Missouri crossed the border and repeatedly issued warrants for Smith's arrest. The charge was accessory to attempted homicide. The victim was the former governor of Missouri. Smith would need his special habeas corpus powers multiple times, and each successive use raised the anti-Mormon temperature until it reached a fever pitch. It was not Mormon religious belief but Mormons' political maneuvering and use of "special privileges" that led to the assassination of Smith and his brother and to expulsion.

During the summer of 1842, Smith put the Nauvoo Legion to personal use, issuing public orders as mayor of Nauvoo for the legion to post a nightly watch to guard him and the city. When these orders were published, the Whig papers reacted with alarm. Simeon Francis, editor of Springfield's *Sangamo Journal,* observed: "From these official notices, it would appear that the Mormons have a government entity of their own—an army of their own—portions of which are detached on requisition of the mayor of Nauvoo, when he pleases to make a requisition upon the commanding officer for their services—This is indeed a curious state of things—A *Christian* society in Illinois keeping up a military organization for their own particular purposes! What would be thought if the Baptists, Methodists, Presbyterians, or Episcopalians of the state" did the same?[97]

Smith, an astute observer of American democratic practice, had built himself a miniature version of the Illinois state with his own pivotal control over key functions; his effort marked the first of many crucial junctures in the progression of the troubles. He patterned many of his church's structures after institutions he found among the states where he lived. He created a surrogate political party by restoring the Levitical "Aaronic Priesthood"—the ancient Christian practice under which every male member became an agent of the church—while reserving the ultimate power to set policy at the top.[98] The parallel to the Democratic Party was not missed. He fostered Mormons' own civil society institutions, such as the Female Relief Society and the grand lodge of Masons, after whose elaborate rituals, degrees, and orders he patterned membership in the church.[99] He had his own First Presidency and his own bicameral congress in the Quorum of the Twelve Apostles and the Council of Fifty. The Nauvoo Legion, with its special uniforms and parade routes, paralleled the many independent volunteer militia companies that Illinois law encouraged, such as the Quincy Riflemen and Hancock County's own Carthage Greys.[100]

While some of these forms appeared republican enough, the purposes behind them aimed for a new synthesis. If they used many of the same words and phrases, they demonstrated how differences at the level of foundational beliefs could lead to differences in principle. Smith and the Mormons mainly desired to be left alone, but there were some premises of American democracy, as it had evolved by 1840, that they did not accept. Most prominently, they did not believe in a strict separation of church and state and a freedom of the press unleashed from libel laws. As historian Klaus Hansen has argued, "the spiritual and the temporal" were always inextricably linked in the Mormon worldview. Smith's millennialist impulse led him as early as 1829 to claim that he was restoring "the kingdom of God" on earth.[101] Mormons spoke of constitutions, rights, parties, and minorities, but in all these cases they substituted their own meanings and tied them to the alternative, otherworldly ends they were called to serve. When the Mormons spoke of the separation of church and state, they meant that their true church should be free from government interference long enough to convert the rest of the country by proselytizing. Smith's repeated emphasis on the "freedom of conscience" carried the same asymmetrical, particularist meaning.[102] As nebulous as his descriptions of the Mormon "political kingdom" could be—for Smith needed to obscure great differences in meaning even if the words were the same—in the end he made clear his purpose was a worldly caliphate, a real governing power that could not exist except in conflict with the state created by the unconverted American people. Perhaps because he spent so much time on otherworldly revelations, he missed the obvious danger of competing directly with the regime the Democrats and Whigs had put in place.

By his own logic, Smith was redeeming America. Government by men in these last days was corrupt and futile, for it aimed at dividing men. In contrast, the "government of God" created harmony, redeemed "the blood of the oppressed," and aimed to "promote the universal good, of the universal world . . . to establish peace and good will among men." The idea had special resonance in 1842, when the country was entering its sixth year of depression and stagnation. No one could gainsay Smith's evidence of present ruin: "Our nation, which possesses greater resources than any other, is rent from center to circumference, with party strife, political intrigue, and sectional interest; our counsellors are panic struck, our legislators are astonished, and our senators are confounded; our merchants are paralyzed, our tradesmen disheartened, our mechanics out of employ, and our poor crying for bread. Our banks are broken, our credit ruined, and our states overwhelmed in debt." It was time for a change, time to let God steer the ship. What was needed was "a theodemocracy": "the world has had a fair trial for six thousand years; the Lord will try the seventh thousand himself."[103]

The chiliastic logic of the last days drove him to seek political support outside Hancock County and in the nation as a whole. On January 29, 1844, at a meeting of the Quorum of the Twelve Apostles, he made this purpose plain and public by announcing his candidacy for the US presidency.[104] He would teach not only Illinois but all of America how special the nation was and how it ought to run its government. Mormon historians discount the importance of this moment in the Illinois saga, but this is a mistake; another critical juncture had been broached. The *History of the Church* quotes Smith to the effect that the presidential ploy was worth doing simply to avoid being the plaything of two-party competition.[105] An official church history states that "the Mormons . . . steered a middle course" by nominating their prophet for the office.[106] Bushman, too, seems indifferent as he summarizes scholars' debate about Smith's purpose in running for president.[107] Certainly, Smith himself was already looking past the presidency and his perch in Illinois. He had made plans to colonize the West, to leave Nauvoo, which was no longer *the* Zion but a Zion. There would be Zions all over the US: "The whole of America is Zion."[108] His followers would soon also populate the nation's West. His Council of Fifty included gentiles and was making its own plans to reach "the summit of all earthly powers."[109] Here it should be stressed with Rousseau that the Mormon prophet did not "just" have visions and institutions and rituals; he also had the sweat and sinew of fifteen thousand men, women, and children living at Nauvoo and a similar number scattered about the country and England. The followers completed the vision, made the beliefs real, and provided the community of interpreters needed to keep the whole together.

The decision to run for president, whether it was passive, aggressive, or both, was catastrophic for the Mormons in Illinois. By this move, Smith lost his last hold on the state's political establishment. Mormon rivalries with Illinois's Protestant clergy and with the old settlers of Hancock County might have been mitigated by these political elites had he maintained their support. Now he made apparent to all that the state government had lost control. For the leaders of the local anti-Mormon movement, this was the signal they had awaited. They immediately began plotting to take advantage of any opportunity, any spark, to bring a conflagration down on Smith and his people. With the Mormons' explicit rejection of the authority of both parties in the state, a de facto proclamation of political independence, the anti-Mormons determined to seek expulsion. Thus began the "wolf hunts" in rural Hancock County, the paramilitary sweeps through the countryside that were the proximate cause of removal.[110]

By defying local and state rules of political standing, the Mormons displayed their defiance of Jacksonian Democrats, the only rivals in the state whose numbers they could not best.[111] Smith was assassinated before the presidential poll could take place, but the outcome begs the question of why he decided to run in the first place. To understand how Smith got to the point that running for the highest office in the land made sense, we need to look at the Illinois context. What was the Illinois way, the authority Smith was standing up to and rejecting? What were its operating assumptions, its social contract, and its foundational beliefs about the ends of life? Ultimately, it was the conflict over these beliefs and ends, over matters of worth and standing, that led to an irrevocable conflict.

Understanding how rules of standing were made binding in Illinois will clarify the moves and countermoves the Mormons and their opponents executed. Membership in Illinois had written and unwritten rules. Inclusion and exclusion were structured by state laws like the Black Codes and the 1818 Illinois Constitution clause allowing the alien vote. But as we have seen, the liberal polity also counted on membership rules set in place by unwritten norms contained in civil society standards. The role of citizens in developing and acting on these norms was and still is, as scholars Will Kymlicka and Wayne Norman observe, an important function "on which the health and stability of modern democracy depends."[112] Implicit narratives of worth, made explicit daily in city and settlement interactions, conveyed models of civic standing, platforms from which citizens were authorized to act. The authority to enforce the polity's formal and informal rules was the core of what westerners like Douglas meant by "popular sovereignty."[113] In practice it was rule by the local gentry, those model citizens whose standing and popularity gave them authority.

Under the Jacksonian regime, the key test ensuring inclusion in the circle of worthies was how a group negotiated, or failed to negotiate, local majoritarian government. The generous offer of refuge and accommodation was extended to all independent producers under these implicit terms. The offer did not apply to all as the universal liberal version promised; strings of social standing, de jure and de facto, were attached. Both the Illinois majority and the Mormon minority were organized around rules of worth that are surprising and little understood. We must reconstruct the Illinois regime, an operable, self-consistent set of ideas, interests, and institutions, in order to map the breakdown of toleration and order that Mormon beliefs and actions caused. Placing the regime in context will take us into the heart of the two-party system that organized political power in the American nation.

3

Saints and Suckers in the Settler State

"Settlers, Freemen, Citizens of Illinois, will you vote for one who will drive you away from your farms and claims? Answer on the first of August. Vote against Martin Van Buren who stigmatizes you as *trespassers* and *intruders*." So argued the Whig Young Men's Association in the pages of *Voice of the People*, a short-lived Chicago newspaper published in the summer of 1838.[1] In January of that year President Van Buren had indicated that the preemption bill he would sign in the coming year would be his last. He hoped the whole preemption policy would be revised "to remove as far as practicable, the causes which produce intrusion on the public lands." Van Buren saw the squatters in Illinois as a willful local minority; he aligned himself with the authority of the government embodying the national public interest. But he was a much better party builder than rhetorician. His careless use of a noun, *intrusion*, was opening enough for the western Whigs in Illinois to register their allegiance with squatter sovereignty and to stand against the "aristocratic land officers."[2] This parody of egalitarian rhetoric was more typical of the Democratic Party of the previous twelve years.

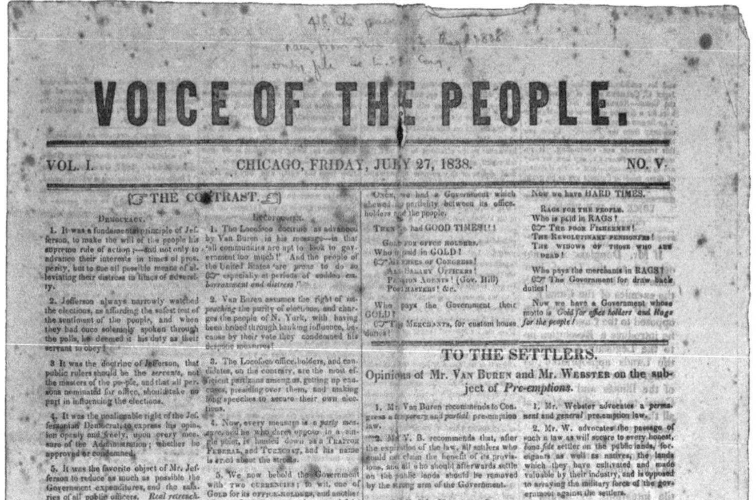

VOICE OF THE PEOPLE.

VOL. I. CHICAGO, FRIDAY, JULY 27, 1838. NO. V.

THE CONTRAST.

Democracy.

1. It was a fundamental principle of Jefferson, to make the will of the people his supreme rule of action;—and not only to advance their interests in times of prosperity, but to use all possible means of alleviating their distress in times of adversity.

2. Jefferson always narrowly watched the elections, as affording the safest test of the sentiment of the people, and when they had once solemnly spoken through the polls, he deemed it his duty as their servant to obey!

3. It was the doctrine of Jefferson, that public rulers should be the *servants*, not the masters of the people, and that all persons nominated for office, should take no part in influencing the elections.

4. It was the inalienable right of the Jeffersonian Democrat, to express his opinion openly and freely, upon every measure of the Administration; whether he approved or condemned.

5. It was the favorite object of Mr. Jefferson to reduce as much as possible the Government expenditures, and the salaries of all public officers. *Real retrench-*

Locofocoism.

1. The Locofoco doctrine as advanced by Van Buren in his message—is that 'all communities are apt to look to government too much!' And the people of the United States 'are *prone* to do so especially at periods of sudden *embarrassment and distress!*'

2. Van Buren assumes the right of *impeaching* the purity of elections, and charges the people of N. York, with having been bribed through banking influence, because by their vote they condemned his despotic measures!

3. The Locofoco office-holders, and candidates, on the contrary, are the most efficient partizans among us, getting up caucuses, presiding over them, and making long speeches to secure their own elections.

4. Now, every measure is a *party measure*, and he who dares oppose in a single point, is hunted down as a TRAITOR FEDERAL, and TURNCOAT, and his name is cried about the streets.

5. We now behold the Government with TWO CURRENCIES; to wit, one of GOLD for its OFFICE-HOLDERS, and another

ONCE, we had a Government which shewed no partiality between its office-holders and the people.

THEN we had GOOD TIMES!!!

GOLD FOR OFFICE HOLDERS.
Who is paid in GOLD!
MEMBERS OF CONGRESS!
ALL SALARY OFFICERS!
PENSION AGENTS! (Gov. Hill)
POSTMASTERS! &c.

Who pays the Government their GOLD?
The MERCHANTS, for custom house duties!

Now we have HARD TIMES.

RAGS FOR THE PEOPLE.
Who is paid in RAGS?
THE POOR FISHERMEN!
THE REVOLUTIONARY PENSIONERS!
THE WIDOWS OF THOSE WHO ARE DEAD!

Who pays the merchants in RAGS?
The Government for draw back duties!

Now we have a Government whose motto is *Gold for office holders and Rags for the people!*

TO THE SETTLERS.

Opinions of Mr. VAN BUREN and Mr. WEBSTER on the subject of *Pre-emptions.*

1. Mr. Van Buren recommends to Congress a *temporary* and *partial* pre-emption law.

2. Mr. V. B. recommends that, after the expiration of the law, all settlers who could not claim the benefit of its provisions, and all who should afterwards settle on the public lands should be removed by the strong arm of the Government.

1. Mr. Webster advocates a *permanent* and *general* pre-emption law.

2. Mr. W. advocates the passage of such a law as will secure to every honest, *bona fide* settler on the public lands, foreigners as well as natives, the lands which they have cultivated and made valuable by their industry, and is opposed to arraying the military force of the government against the settlers.

FIG. 3.1. *Voice of the People* (partial front page). Courtesy of Newberry Library

Imitation, the Democrats might have said, was a form of flattery, the sincerest way to entrench a regime.

Still, the ideal of democratic inclusion had taken a hit. Easy as it was for Illinoisans in 1839 to assert generalities of accommodation and toleration, the new party system structuring the Jacksonian regime soon frustrated these aspirations and vaunted universal claims. By 1840 Illinois party politics had not only matured; they were already overripe. The Whigs had become a competitive opposition organization committed to sacrificing all to the goal of delivering a majority at the polls. If the Whig Party was ever to leave a mark on the polyglot mix that was the Illinois way, it needed to win a few statewide elections. Whig candidate Cyrus Edwards came close: he won 49 percent of the vote in the race for governor in 1838.[3] The party now saw in the Mormons a prize to be seized by the victorious in party warfare.

The young Whigs went on to ridicule the gall of a "Dictator—telling the sovereign people that they must take care of themselves! That they must not expect too much of the government!—whose sole business it is to take care of itself and its officeholders."[4] Here the Whigs adopted the Democrats' populist stance of the resentful and excluded outsider. The Whigs had argued repeatedly throughout the 1830s that they cared more for the quality of democracy than for "the democracy of numbers," as the *Sangamo Journal* had put it.[5] But a focus on quality was a tough sell in the West, where the old settlers were on alert for controlling and patronizing behavior on the part of the new settlers from the East. As Governor Thomas Ford put it, "The latest comers [to the state] were forever uttering sarcasms and slighting remarks of the State and the people . . . to show themselves off as something superior to others."[6] To counteract the old image of their party, the young Whigs worked hard to portray themselves as a party dedicated to improving the lot of the average laborer. They railed against Van Buren and his merry band of "Locofocos," the nickname of the radical antibank wing in the Democratic Party. In the Whig view, the Locofocos had created the current depression, which had followed the Panic of 1837.

The importance of a consolidated two-party system to the story of the Mormon troubles is perhaps not obvious. It requires a step back to consider what a state is and why its various incarnations matter. The antebellum American state, the rudiments of which are still with us, has been particularly beguiling. Solving the "historical enigma" of the American sense of statelessness has engaged scholars of many stripes since Alexis de Tocqueville first introduced the puzzle in *Democracy in America*.[7] Was the antebellum state a powerful institution that made a difference or a mere cipher, a receptacle for forces playing out elsewhere? We will gain some purchase on an answer by observing the actions of one of its opponents, Joseph Smith. But first we need to consider the purposes of the liberal state.

INDEPENDENT PRODUCERS AND REGIME SERVICES

Several key distinctions structure how the state is conceptualized from a liberal perspective. The dominant tradition within liberalism views the state as an instrument.[8] It is a tool for securing rights and property in a demarcated private sphere while leading collective action in the public sphere. In the private sphere, citizens pursue their own ends and identities. Liberals tend to emphasize private sphere freedoms and to minimize the civic ideals encumbering individual duty. In practice, however, the citizen in the public sphere is shaped by broader purposes, and civic standing is influenced by both public duties and private power. Those public duties liberal theory does address are tied to empowering individuals. In John Rawls's version, for example, well-ordered liberal societies feature states tasked by a consensual theory of justice to protect individual rights and to redistribute wealth so far as to provide individual equality of opportunity.[9]

As many have noted, putting the liberal state in a generalized form obfuscates its function. It downplays the state's leading role as a membership organization, an association that sits at the head of all social groups and orders them. Liberal writers prefer to think in terms of "individual" and "state" categories and to "bracket as much as possible membership questions."[10] Yet particular membership criteria are central to the actual lived experience of American citizens.[11] Those commandeering the antebellum American state used membership rules to express and police civic ideals. Embedded in the background assumptions of these ideals in Illinois were foundational beliefs about what made settlers worthy. As political scientist Rogers M. Smith argues, American civic ideals are retailed in the political arena as "stories of peoplehood" that convey specific foundational beliefs in narrative form.[12] These civic narratives knit state and civil society together into a cohesive societal culture. Will Kymlicka emphasizes how societal cultures justify majority choices about what a good life is and how under liberal norms immigrants are expected to conform in order to be recognized as full members.[13]

To see how Illinois's state and its societal culture operated, the liberal view of the state must be supplemented with Aristotle's concept of the regime. The regime was for Aristotle a constituent subset of the state; it was the set of governing institutions that pursue the public good from either a monarchical, aristocratic, or democratic perspective depending on the regime in question.[14] In political scientist E. E. Schattschneider's terms, the regime imparts a particular "mobilization of bias" to the state.[15] It moves some issues to the top of the political agenda and relegates others to the bottom. The very existence of regimes within a state thus unsettles the liberal assumption of status quo neutrality, the belief that states can be neutral with respect to the public good and that private sphere relations can be unencumbered by public sphere duties, collective action problems, or power asymmetry.[16] Creating a new regime is an act of power precisely because it sets the state's constitutive agenda in a gambit to make or remake a people's identity. Regimes are combinations of discrete ideas, institutions, and policies that durably and nonneutrally shape the way the public sphere will encumber the private sphere. Regimes create commitments to a constitutive public good that is nonneutral for members.

The Jacksonian regime did impart a bias to American politics. Over time it created a shift in American ideology, undergirded by durable changes in institutions, that shaped the policies of the antebellum era. Culturally, its ideology prioritized a particularist variety of egalitarianism, its key institutions were the two-party duopoly and local control over the militia, and its prominent policies were decentralized economic development, national Indian removal, budgets funded by tariffs and public land sales, and the separation of church and state.[17] The regime's egalitarian ideology and its localist institutions require careful scrutiny. Localism is especially important in the Illinois iteration given its frontier society. Unlike Europe's "nineteenth-century constitutional states," such as Great Britain, France, and Prussia, which had long occupied their territory, the United States authorized a settler societal culture located on newly controlled lands.[18] Across an arc of frontier spanning Illinois, Missouri, Arkansas, Mississippi, and Alabama, the sprawling antebellum American state empowered self-governing departments, each only a few decades old. Combining a settler context with an egalitarian culture and localist institutions, the Illinois department created the distinct pattern of authority many observers experienced as an absence of power or as a missing "sense of the state."[19]

Let us consider the regime's egalitarian culture first. Illinois's political culture was a subspecies of the liberal tradition. Illinois elites conceived civic identity as "in principle an equal, nonparticularistic capacity."[20] When the Mormons came to Illinois in the early spring of 1839 as refugees from Missouri, they were welcomed as citizens on such universalist terms and in a spirit of religious toleration. Indeed, the residents of Quincy and Adams County welcomed them as useful additions to a local economy which had been in deep depression for three years and where immigration had otherwise halted. What meager resources the civil society of the day could muster were offered to the refugees as succor.[21] But as Desmond King notes, while "liberalism is defended as an inclusive doctrine . . . historically membership has in fact been restrictive," and the Mormon reception was no different.[22]

To see why, we must descend into the civic narrative the regime expressed. Illinois's constitution of 1818 restricted voting to "white male inhabitants" and militia membership to "free male able-bodied persons (negroes, mulattoes, and Indians, excepted)."[23] Background assumptions, bracketed in this way or remaining unarticulated, eliminated women, Negroes, and Indians from the circle of full citizens. Exclusion of Native Americans was the most pressing concern for the American settlers, and the claims justifying it had ramifications for other excluded groups. The Illinois Territory was described by ordinary Americans either as uninhabited or as inhabited by a people unworthy of the space. Native Americans in Illinois fought the War of 1812, the Winnebago outbreak of 1827, and the Black Hawk skirmish of 1831, and the war of 1832 to resist White encroachment on their lands and protest management of their tribal interests. To counter Indian resistance, Illinois men answered the call by the thousands to serve as militia volunteers: 963 from the Illinois Territory in 1812, 1,400 in 1831, and 1,694 in 1832.[24]

In the Jacksonian civic narrative, the Native Americans failed as members because they did not practice agriculture; they were hunters and gatherers, not cultivators. In the legal jargon developed out of the "doctrine of discovery," Native Americans merely had "occupancy" or usage rights to the land, whereas cultivators had access to full ownership (including the right to buy and sell) under fee simple tenure.[25] The preference for cultivators has a long history in the liberal tradition going back to Thomas More's *Utopia* and John Locke's *Second Treatise on Government*. The rationale was that cultivation added to the natural productivity of the land. Cultivators did not just use the land but produced a surplus for the community; they were worthy members, as was suggested by their appearance on the currency of the day. The social worth of cultivators provided justification for aggressive actions taken on the ground. Land was extorted from the Natives in Illinois and the territory cleared in a series of treaties executed from 1795 to 1833.[26]

The producerism bias was openly asserted in Illinois. It also could be found hovering just beneath the surface of many civic claims. One example is found in Representative William Lee D. Ewing's 1831 claim that American settlers were justified in taking the Indians' land without consent or treaty: "If we think it is right for free people of other countries to pull down tyrants who seek to keep them in ignorance and servitude, is it not equally right in us to refuse the Indian the privilege of perpetuating the reign of darkness and barbarism over the fairest portions of our continent? . . . I see no reason why . . . we should permit them to occupy the land which they will not cultivate, to the exclusion of a race of

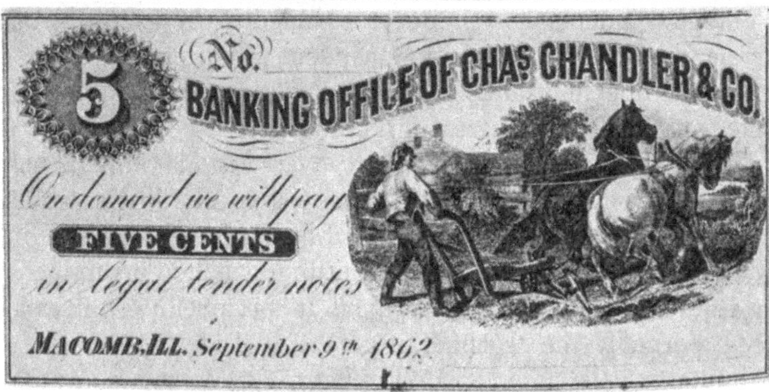

FIG. 3.2A AND FIG. 3.2B. Plowboy images on Illinois currency (from Fred R. Marckhoff, "Currency and Banking in Illinois before 1865," *Journal of Illinois State Historical Society* 52, no. 3 [Autumn 1959]: 365–418). Courtesy of Newberry Library

industrious farmers."[27] Ewing's claim depends on several conflations and misrecognitions: if people have a right to rebel, it is only against rulers tyrannizing them directly; and the Native Americans did in fact work the land in Illinois by harvesting animals, growing crops, and tapping maple trees.

The racial bias of Ewing's words is also worth noting: the producerist justification covering his errors of fact and logic is urged explicitly in terms of a racialized American farmer. The use of racial claims to mask and justify misrecognition errors is a common pattern. Scholars Nancy Fraser and Linda Gordon explain that race was used to justify a shift in the relations established by colonialism: "In earlier usage colonials were dependent because they had been conquered; in nineteenth-century imperialist culture, they were conquered because they were dependent. . . . Racism helped transform dependency as political subjection into dependency as psychology and forged enduring links between the discourse of dependency and racial oppression."[28] The membership bias of the Jacksonian regime is also highlighted in Ewing's emphasis on tyranny. This was the traditional idea of independence: "He who is controlled by another is a slave."[29] Only free agents were considered full members; such were not dependent on others and therefore not open to the manipulation of consent liberals took as a surrogate for slavery. Thus those made ineligible for full membership were wives controlled by husbands, enslaved people dominated by masters, and leaseholders under the thumb of a landlord. The biases meant the membership standard of being an independent producer excluded many. Even if we take the standard as valid, many independent producers were unfairly denied membership status given how the regime norms were interpreted and applied in various Illinois locales.[30]

The illiberal rendering of an already exclusionary liberal narrative raises the question of how accurate it is to call Illinois's political culture egalitarian in any way. Liberal theory has formally defined egalitarianism as an ideology committing its adherents to increasing political and social equality *for all*. It is implicitly a universalist creed. Formally, the "egalitarian general-will ideology" applies to all humans; it is, as political scientist C. B. Macpherson puts it, true to "the humanistic values which liberal democracy has always claimed."[31] But this formal definition must be modified in the settler state setting, and in the same manner Macpherson argues, it should be adjusted in anticolonial settings. For in the routine practice of majorities (as opposed to aspiration or occasional practice), American egalitarianism through much of the nineteenth century was a political culture promoting equality first and foremost for a particular group or subset of society. This reality conforms to social anthropologist Mary Douglas's theory of culture, which ties lived settings to expressed cosmology.[32] The lived setting of Jacksonian egalitarians was very much as a group subaltern to the American elite represented by the Federalist Party.

TABLE 3.1. DOUGLAS'S FOUR CULTURES

	HIGH GROUP	LOW GROUP
HIGH GRID	Hierarchical	Fatalist
LOW GRID	Egalitarian	Individualist

Adapted from *Natural Symbols*, 59

Douglas's theory elucidates the illiberal potential in egalitarian culture. She describes four distinct cultural types—hierarchical, individualist, egalitarian, and fatalist—arrayed in a grid-group matrix. The grid axis measures high and low degrees of societal order; the group axis measures high and low degrees of group integration. Hierarchical cultures endorse a high degree of ranking along with intensive integration within the group, while individualist cultures combine fluid systems of societal ordering with a low degree of group integration. Egalitarian cultures combine high degrees of group integration with low or fluid societal ordering, while fatalist cultures combine high degrees of societal ordering and low group integration. In Douglas's theory egalitarians are people who voice dissent in hierarchical settings. They correspondingly often seek integration in a group as an alternative source of order and security. The grid-group theory offers a way to conceptualize people like the Jacksonians, who appear to be uniformly individualistic because they fear and dissent from Federalist hierarchy but who often exhibit a strong sense of group identification and attachment. Some Jacksonian egalitarians did seek to deracinate the group of worthy dissenters and present a universal, humanist opposition. But many had a particularist image of independent producers—the group of White male farmers—with whom they associated and identified.

Douglas's theory has many virtues. It overlaps with Daniel Elazar's schema of traditionalistic, moralistic, and individualistic attitudes toward government. Because Douglas's theory is tied generally to group and societal order settings, it can be elaborated to interpret a broader range of attitudes, including important cosmologies of God and nature. In addition, Douglas adapted her theory to situations in which group settings and societal orders are mixed. It can be modified to describe unique hybrids which reflect partially overlapping settings and combined cosmologies, as was the case in antebellum America. In the search for votes, parties built agreements across subcultures to produce tentative consensus. They also manufactured hard lines of difference to further entrench disagreements which, while they reinforced winning cleavages, rearranged how people lived and viewed themselves. In practice, majorities built new subcultures and used regimes to entrench new societal cultures.

How did egalitarian political practice in American settler states come to diverge so radically from the universalist aspiration? Douglas would answer that the New World setting differed from the Old

World, where egalitarian political culture first formed. Liberal egalitarianism first achieved political saliency as a distinct prodemocracy movement in working-class England, where class interests were defined as universally applicable to all class members and implicitly for all people. According to Macpherson, the early nineteenth-century egalitarians who led England's first prodemocracy political movements were activists for whom "democracy was never entirely or essentially a class thing. For them it had always been not just a way of freeing themselves from oppression, but of freeing the whole of humanity, of permitting the realization of the humanity of all men."[33] But in its settler setting, egalitarianism in the early nineteenth century often took a herrenvolk, or master race, form, the masters being the White male heads of households whose interests took priority.[34] Because of this starting point in settler societies, the racial group is primary in a way it is not in societies with class-based views of equality. American egalitarians took a vertical view of equality, which emphasized the fate of a favored group in a societal culture's pecking order.[35]

The particular image the Jacksonian regime idealized was the White settler family. Most settlers were squatters, and most of them were members of the subaltern "white folks," as recently arrived southern Appalachian immigrants were termed.[36] By 1840 those who had not moved on or passed away had become, in the thousands, freeholders, "gentlemen of property and standing" who upheld regime norms and the law in their counties.[37] The majority Jacksonians in Illinois still considered themselves advocates of inclusion because they emphasized their state was open to all worthy settlers, squatters included. The constitution extended voting rights to all twenty-one-year-old White men who were "actual residents" of the state, a residence requirement allowing alien suffrage which would be considered liberal in its reformed definition today. The offices of governor and lieutenant governor were limited to those men who had been citizens of the United States for thirty years, although in a multicultural gesture an exception was made for Louis Menard, a Frenchman born in Kaskaskia who served as the first lieutenant governor.[38] With its combination of alien voting and myopic independent producerism, the Illinois regime's egalitarianism mixed liberal and illiberal elements.

A crucial element of the Jacksonian regime in places like Illinois was local control over society by means of the county-level legal order.

Such government has been termed a "state of courts and parties," but it should be stressed that those two institutions were (except on appeal and in convention) radically decentralized.[39] Circuit-riding judges, county sheriffs, justices of the peace, and constables were routinely the only criminal law enforcement officials over miles of territory, and these few often relied on gentlemen of property and standing or an informal posse of them to keep order.[40] The collective action problem of keeping the peace was solved by civil society chipping in when and where the state lacked the resources to secure, as in Max Weber's formal definition of state function, "the monopoly of the legitimate use of physical force within a given territory."[41] Voting was done orally and in public (viva voce) from 1829 through 1848, which, even with election judges and constables, allowed local norms more sway. In this way societal organizations like claim societies, road crews, and county militias became incorporated into the regime order. These extralegal or loosely legal enforcement institutions provided the regime with unpaid protection services. They also allowed local majorities' interests to shape the enforcement of the law.

By substituting private power for public authority, the American state characteristically moved away from the universal, voluntarist, and contract-based abstraction posited in liberal theory. The move, a key legacy of the antebellum state, became so ingrained in later American state building that political scientist Grant McConnell labels it "the orthodoxy."[42] McConnell ties the tradition back to the Virginia agrarians John Taylor and Thomas Jefferson. They made a fetish of "local autonomy," arguing that local government was more natural, responsive, and rational.[43] Local autonomy simultaneously replaced the larger state, which created a sense of statelessness and opened the door to idiosyncratic exercises of local power. One of the most influential political philosophers of the twentieth century, Hannah Arendt, emphasizes the virtuous aspects of Jefferson's "ward republic" ideal, which allowed local majorities "the power to act on their own."[44] While McConnell emphasizes that these local actors authorized by the regime were likely to deviate from the public interest—to become "corrupt" under Aristotle's theory—Arendt rhapsodizes about their agency as the lost treasure of the revolutionary tradition.

The potentially illiberal abuses arising from substituting local initiative for centralized control were well understood in Illinois at the time. But as Ford ruefully recognized in his *History,* both the power and its abuse were written into the very fabric of the Jacksonian regime. It is worth quoting his reflection in full:

> The general sentiment in favor of martial law and the disorders calling it forth are fearful evidences of a falling away from the true principles of liberty. Ever since Gen. Jackson on some great occasions, when the fate of half the country was at stake, *"took the responsibility,"* the country has swarmed with a tribe of small statesmen who seem to think that the true secret of government is to set it aside and resort to mere force upon the occurrence of the smallest difficulties. It may be well enough on great occasions to have one great Jackson; but on every small occasion no one can imagine the danger of having a multitude of little Jacksons. Jackson's example is to be admired rather than imitated; and the first may be done easier and safer than the last.[45]

One implication of Ford's observation is that state authority is susceptible to being displaced and directly hijacked by class interests within society.

This view was part of a critique of liberal states by the emerging communist movement in Europe. Just two years before Ford's words were published in 1854, Karl Marx believed he had exposed the contradictory logic within all bourgeois liberal states. He argued that the executive branch of the liberal state could be described accurately as the executive committee of the ruling class, a claim he thought applied as well to "pure republican" versions of government. Marx hammered the point home with a rhetorical question: "When you play the fiddle at the top of the state, what else is to be expected but that those down below dance?"[46] Resorting to force to uphold the harm principle is a feature of all but failed states. But Marx's dancing implies directing individuals to further some republican purpose in the public sphere, an authority that local self-help implicitly replaced and to some extent denied. At such moments, even Marx's liberals in denial—that is, liberals without a "sense of the state"—must acknowledge they are wielding power. Political theorist William Galston reminds liberals that "public and private domains are linked in a complex web of reciprocal impact and dependence," which means that local control will impart a bias to the state. But the realization that private and public spheres cannot be easily disentangled often comes too late or never at all.[47]

The regime services provided on a self-help basis by Illinoisan heads of households at the local level solved a collective action problem the settler community faced. Like many liberals, Illinoisans were focused on their private sphere goals and not on the public sphere sacrifices needed to carry them out. They wanted collective security, but they did not have the time or the resources to build the state capacity needed to pay for and deliver it.[48] Still, when they or their sons resorted to supplying protection services on demand as volunteers, they benefitted from the resulting civic platform. For example, the "citizen soldiers" of the Black Hawk War of 1832 were publicly commended in the General Assembly for having "volunteered their services in the cause of their country."[49] At the same time, such volunteers often biased public authority in favor of majoritarian interests—whether through the election of militia officers or the willingness to man posse ventures. Of course, as James Madison in his Federalist phase was at pains to point out, even if these interests are truly representative of local majorities, they do not represent the interests of national majorities, let alone the public interest.[50] But as Anti-Federalist writers like Melancton Smith believed, in the short term these interests had an appearance of republican accountability to all the "substantial yeomanry" and had a whiff of "great virtue."[51]

Indeed, rule by the volunteer yeomanry provides an empirical explanation of the missing "sense of the state" experienced by citizens in large swaths of the antebellum United States. Local actors "taking the responsibility," repeated endlessly across the nation, plausibly account for the perception of statelessness. If American citizens in the majority believed the state was not alien or overbearing, it was because in many ways these local actors, when acting alone—even more so when organized into majorities by the parties—took over the responsibilities of and *were* the state. Here was a classic case of a developing democracy failing to deliver the rule of law. The popular demand for justice overwhelmed the state's official capacities to deliver it, and civil society took up where government institutions left off.

Whatever the benefits which accrued to the local majorities under this scheme, the costs to the excluded were real. No matter how much Native Americans farmed, or African Americans purchased land, or women organized, they were not recognized as independent producers by Jacksonian majorities. They were in fact "misrecognized," as Hegel had it. Following his metaphysical dialectic between human consciousness and the world, Hegel viewed rights to external things like property as part of an "inner act of will that says something is mine [but which] must also become recognizable by others."[52] As we have seen, liberal orders imagined the state's sovereign powers over nonmembers to be unlimited. Liberal theorists from Hobbes to Locke left the power of recognizing nonmembers to civil society, the public part of the nation beyond the family but not including the state. Hegel worried, correctly as it turned out, that private power would warp the articulation of the public's interest in supplying inclusive property protection and extending civic membership universally.[53]

The Mormons were treated as a liminal case, accepted on probationary terms; they were eventually expelled by Hancock County's old settlers, who counted the Mormon reputation for thievery against their productivity and feared their political dependence on the prophet Joseph Smith. The Mormons, a majority in both Nauvoo and Hancock County by 1842, had created their own local majority. Under the rules of the Jacksonian regime, they had the authority to adjust the rules of membership to suit their biases, but in exercising this power, they conflicted with the first wave of settlers, who had arrived just ten years earlier.

Smith's response to the American state took an intriguing turn when he led his people to Illinois. Having been arrested and convicted as an imposter in New York State, tarred and feathered as a bankrupt in Ohio, and jailed in Missouri for six months, where his people were mobbed and massacred, he arrived in Illinois as a refugee with a specific plan in mind. Remarkably, he planned to build his own protective network to rival the American state, and perhaps more remarkably, he proceeded to execute and realize his plan.[54] Unlike in Missouri, he would work within the law and build according to regime norms. In Illinois he, too, would "[take] the responsibility," join the "tribe of small statesmen," and become one of the "little Jacksons." Smith's powers of observation and imitation were acute; his expectation that the state could be made to bend to his conception of popular justice was as strong as any Democrat. The city-state he created in Nauvoo imitated the Jacksonian regime to the point of replicating its particularist and localist biases. But in turning to the Mormon creation, it is first necessary to flesh out the details of the regime Smith imitated. With the maturation of the Whig Party into a loyal opposition, all the dynamics characteristic of a party duopoly were set in place.

ILLINOIS PARTIES IN THE JACKSONIAN REGIME

President Andrew Jackson was committed to ending the federal government's reliance on the Bank of the United States (BUS), the formidable Philadelphia institution which held the government's debt. Jackson saw the BUS as a threat to the republic because of its exclusive power over the currency. There were no United States bills at the time; the federal greenback had yet to be invented. Americans used specie (gold and silver coins) or bank notes as currency. BUS president Nicholas Biddle had built his bank's paper into a stable and respected currency through prudent control over state-regulated banks, an oversight its charter allowed. Jackson's veto of the bill rechartering the BUS in 1832 was only his first sally against an institution he viewed as a "monster of corruption."[55] By the summer of 1836, he and Congress had managed to extinguish the federal debt, which the BUS had been created to hold. Jackson next announced his Specie Circular, a policy that aimed at limiting speculation in public lands. It contained two rules designed to replace the currency-regulating powers of the BUS: Jackson directed the Treasury to disallow the use of small bills to pay ordinary federal fees and taxes, and he required the land offices around the country to accept only gold and silver specie as payment for public lands. Jackson had previously adopted a policy of distributing the unspent surplus from federal revenue back to the states. The overall goal of these three policies was to keep the national circulation of money flowing by returning what was drained from the South and West by trade or land payments to Philadelphia and New York. While rational on paper, the rules created turbulence in the money supply: shortages and excesses developed in all the wrong places. In practice, the new rules damaged the value of many regional currencies by weakening confidence in the system on which the whole nation relied.

The BUS lived on under Nicholas Biddle, now rechartered as a state bank in Pennsylvania, and though its power over the money supply ended, Biddle's power continued, and even increased, as he suddenly pursued an easy money policy.[56] Jackson's removal of federal deposits from the BUS in 1833 spurred demand for gold and silver, but there was enough specie available in the system in 1834 to avoid a panic.[57] After that, however, British and Chinese interests began selling gold and silver for their own purposes, with the result that Mexican silver pooled in the United States; this allowed a credit basis for other regional banks to follow Biddle's lead and issue loans for more purchases of public lands. The flood of easy money drove a speculative, inflationary spiral. External factors caused the influx of silver, and as economic historian Peter Temin argues, "It would not be too misleading to say that the Opium War was more closely connected to the American inflation than the Bank War between Jackson and Biddle."[58]

But in politics correlation is more important than causation. The *Chicago American* had no doubt in November 1836 that the economy was being upset by Jackson's policy, which presidential hopeful Van Buren vowed to continue. The editor condemned "this mammoth system of *experiment* that is constantly keeping the country . . . suffering for money [and] our enterprising businessmen breaking for the necessary accommodation of means, when our treasury is running over."[59] Eventually, a run on the eastern banks did develop in the winter of 1837, and their specie calls on the regional banks led to a credit crunch nationally. Banks that were overextended soon failed, and states like Illinois, where there were relatively few banks, experienced a shortage of specie. After the New York banks suspended payments, the State Bank of Illinois followed suit on May 24, 1837, and the economic shutdown became universal. Now began the demise of the numerous "paper towns," existing only in speculators' imaginations, in Illinois and throughout the West. In the spring of 1836, the sale of 375 town lots in Chicago funded construction of the Illinois and Michigan Canal to the amount of $1,355,755. But planned sales in towns such as Lockport, Peru, and Ottawa for even one-tenth the Chicago amount would soon be unthinkable as the land bubble burst.[60]

When Van Buren took office, the country was in the middle of its greatest economic crisis to date. Yet he continued to implement the Democrats' plan of attack on the BUS. He promoted his subtreasury bill, which would distribute surplus federal revenues to the states and deposit operating surpluses in "pet" banks across the country. The goal was to create what the Democrats called an independent banking system, one separate from the state but still responsive to government regulation.[61] Having multiple banks control the money supply instead of one bank (which was therefore a monopoly) was less threatening because it did not create special privileges and thus was in line with "equal rights," but it was also less effective at controlling inflationary pressures caused by reckless lending. To the Whigs, Van Buren's policy was Locofoco inspired for sure. The bill was stalled in Congress for two years by a coalition of Whigs and Democratic conservatives, a group including two of Illinois's three members. It eventually passed both houses and was signed into law on July 4, 1840.[62] Did this two-year effort act as a last blow to the system, deepening the depression by unhinging currency stability, or did the large, sudden influx of silver from England and China start an inflationary bubble that was destined to burst? Scholars still debate the issue, but it is fair to say, as the Whigs argued, that the government at best created unnecessary market turbulence and at worst used its power to punish enemies (e.g., the BUS) and reward friends (e.g., banks in New York).[63] In the eastern part of Illinois along the Wabash River, the slogan in 1840 was "We will have General [William Henry] Harrison, or general Ruin."[64]

In this context it is not surprising to find the young Whigs of Chicago jumping at the chance to frame their party as the one more focused on settler interests. They quoted Daniel Webster, who had visited the Old Northwest and Chicago in 1836 and, like all Whigs, emphasized the quality of the settlers there: "They have the character of Frontiersmen; they are hardy, adventurous, and enterprising. . . . They appear to me to be industrious and laborious."[65] These words, coming from the Boston Brahmin who was eyeing a run for the presidency, indicate how central the settler state image was to Illinois. They underscore how crucial the ideology of the independent producer was to both sides of the political debate in Illinois, a place where the Mormons now sought refuge. They also indicate the power of the narrative. It was the Democratic Party which stood pat and engaged in "mocking the sufferings of the people," Whig representative John Todd Stuart declared in Congress, not the Whigs, their so-called aristocratic opponents.[66]

By these rhetorical moves, the Whigs were signaling that they were willing to compete under the premises of the Jacksonian regime. They would no longer attack the extension of suffrage to those without property qualifications and stand as a loose-knit group issuing noble but electorally ineffective antiparty sentiments. The shift was significant since, as historian Gerald Leonard has argued, the antiparty tradition opposing all self-interested "factions" in a republic committed to the public good had been deeply entrenched nationally and in Illinois.[67] The Whigs went so far in 1839 as to nominate their candidates in a convention. Even a strong party Democrat like Ford doubted the propriety of the convention's nomination of candidates "without the organization of little township democracies . . . [which would allow] the people themselves to govern." Lacking this, he wrote, "the convention system is a most admirable contrivance to enable active leaders to govern without much responsibility to the people."[68] But for Ford, a devotee of the theory of responsible government, the new regime, with its two-party competition, was a good thing. It enabled policy differences to be aired, and party discipline allowed the majority to rule; voters could then hold the majority party responsible for its policies at the next election. Ford expected the dissenting minority to "compel the majority to take the undivided responsibility of government. By this means there will always be a party to expose the faults and blunders of our rulers, and the majority will be more careful what they do."[69]

Accountability to the electorate and trust in government are potential results of two-party competition, but they are far from automatic and take time to become ingrained. Party members think in terms of the next election cycle. The only issues by which the Whigs could distinguish themselves before the Panic of 1837 were Henry Clay's American System of tariffs protecting domestic manufacturers and paying for internal improvements, and the constitutional issue Clay called "the alarming growth of the executive power."[70] The American System was a federal government policy perceived as largely irrelevant to the frontier economy; federal subsidies for projects like the Illinois and Michigan Canal (connecting the Illinois River and Lake Michigan) came in land grants, not tariff revenue. As for the constitutional issue, as long as the economy was booming and the trusted Jackson in office, it failed to generate much interest. Whigs in Illinois instead attacked the Democrats' commitment to party patronage. Removal from office based on partisan considerations, known as "proscription," was unpopular, and the Whig press made plausible claims that party loyalty hurt the quality of governance in the state. The political removal of an effective Indian agent in northern Illinois, for example, was said to be the immediate cause of the expensive Black Hawk War earlier in the decade.[71]

Joseph Duncan won a seat in Congress as a supporter of Andrew Jackson in 1826, but by 1831 he was alienated from the party Van Buren was building in Illinois. In 1834 he ran on an antiparty platform and won the governor's office. By this time most of his policy positions were aligned with the national Whigs. Duncan supported a state bank and argued that internal improvements at the state level should be led by the private sector and conducted by "individual enterprise."[72] But his victory actually hurt the Illinois Whigs in the long run, for it was achieved without the hard work of organizing supporters in each county. At the same time, it pushed the Democrats into the realization that they needed to develop a statewide party organization. The Democrats had an advantage in building a county-based institution because they could rely on the existing networks that US senator Elias Kent Kane had been tending for the national organization ever since his alliance with Van Buren in 1827.[73] Emerging party leaders such as Stephen A. Douglas, Ebenezer Peck, and Adam Snyder proceeded to organize the Democrats around slates of state and federal nominees beginning in 1835.

Lost for all time are the individual deals at the county level smoothing the road to party regularity for the Democrats, but the surviving poll books for Fayette, Green, and Sangamon Counties recording the viva voce voting indicate a remarkable shift, beginning with 1836 elections, toward mass party slate voting.[74] By 1838 the Democrats were united in holding state nominating conventions for offices like governor; from that point on, the opposition press called their conventions "the slaughter pen."[75] The Whigs continued to use the more informal caucus method, except for 1839, when the emergency conditions led to the use of a convention. They went back to the less controllable but more open caucus in 1842 and continued with it despite the persuasive argument that such relinquishing of control was foolhardy. The Whigs were also behind in the mechanics of voter turnout. Lincoln, in an oft-quoted statement, argued in 1840 that the party still needed to "organize the whole state, so that every Whig can be brought to the polls, . . . [to] make a perfect list of voters and ascertain with certainty for whom they will vote."[76] Lincoln also penned a committee report in the spring of 1843 in which he first used the biblical injunction that "a house divided against itself cannot stand." The house was the Whig Party.[77] The Whigs engaged in a harmful public debate over convention nomination, but Duncan and his supporters stood their antiparty ground. In Gerald Leonard's account, antipartyism remained a strong undercurrent among the Illinois Whigs until the end of their days.[78] Indeed, it can be said to have remained a perennial force in Illinois politics into the twentieth century, reemerging in the 1880s among the Republicans and again in the 1920s among the Progressives.[79]

Duncan's victory in 1834 gave force to the claim that taking a stand above party was best for popularity, for policy, and for governing effectiveness. But Whigs had trouble demonstrating the claim on popularity grounds alone. They were hurt locally by the patrician social position of national leaders like Henry Clay, Daniel Webster, and, after 1832, John C. Calhoun. These "big men" were committed to a hierarchical culture that lauded order and condemned disorder. Their commitment created easy fodder for the Democratic press, who denounced their opponents as "aristocratic egoists" who believed that "poverty and vice go hand in hand," that "emigrants are men whose wants if not their vices have sent them from other states," that "the poor . . . covet and [wish to] share the plunder of the rich," and that "laborers would be [best] as subservient to the will of their employers as [are] persons of color."[80] Mostly believing this rhetoric, the laboring part of Illinois society voted for the Democrats. They voiced their resistance to any sacrifice for the good of the whole under the guidance of a hectoring and patronizing leadership. They proved their civic worth by working as competent producers and serving in the militia when needed. They disdained any public interest not expressed through a narrowly understood settler self-interest.

In central and northern Illinois, Whig members were frequently found at the forefront of efforts to promote the public interest in its disembodied Madisonian form, such as reforming public spaces like town squares and schoolyards. Whig papers regularly published Sabbatarian arguments, which urged tighter regulations on grog shops and discouraged "the depreciation of the Christian Sabbath." The *Warsaw Signal* complained that the laws of the town charter were not being enforced on "a large number of boys playing at ball . . . from Sabbath to Sabbath . . . to the great annoyance of peaceable and order-loving citizens."[81] The Whig's *Northwestern Gazetteer and Galena Advertiser* ran story after story worrying about the twenty grog shops in town, of which "one half or more [sold] spirits on Sunday."[82]

But the Whigs, too, ended up turning claims for the public interest into particularist promotions, in their case the promotion of mainline Protestantism. One letter in the *Peoria Register* issued a wholesale Sabbatarian attack on "foreigners" by asking, "Must they be tolerated?" The letter observed that "a majority of them" keep or patronize "grog shops," "respect not the Christian Sabbath, . . . [and] promote neither popular education nor the public morals."[83] Duncan's 1843 letter addressing the dangers of the convention system used the "cringing of ambitious office seekers at the feet of the Mormon Prophet" as a key antiparty argument. In a telltale sign of Protestant particularism, however, he finished by forcefully attacking what he considered a more dangerous menace, the Roman Catholic Church: "another large and powerful church in this country, whose faith in its head is also superior to their political opinions; and [whose head is making] . . . extensive arrangements . . . to send millions of his subjects to this country."[84] Whigs like Duncan were liberals, but the polity he defended locally was not universal but Protestant and ranked by class; Catholics sat at the bottom of both hierarchies. The independent producers the Whigs imagined and were willing to recognize were a particular subset of all producers in Illinois.

Governor Duncan was admired by Democrats like Ford, who said the old Whig combined "genteel . . . deportment . . . [with] a moral courage to adhering to his convictions which is rarely met with." The concession was easy to make because Duncan undermined the organizational strength of his own party (thus advantaging the Democrats) and because his courage was seen as a rare exception.[85] Young Whigs in Illinois like John J. Hardin and Abraham Lincoln sought to remodel the party by replacing deportment with principle and the urge for social control with a stance of accommodation. Desperate for popular policy positions, they compromised with the Democrats on key local issues, such as the state bank and internal improvement.[86] They supported the Illinois and Michigan Canal project, which had near unanimous support in the central and northern sections of the state. The Internal Improvement

Act of 1837 (which included funding for the Illinois and Michigan Canal) had bipartisan support. But the Whig endorsement meant Whigs failed to play the checking role Ford assigned the opposition in a democracy. Lincoln's vote for the disastrous Internal Improvements Act in 1837 was in part dictated by two Whig conventions, one in Sangamon County and one statewide, which for the first time had nominated candidates for the party and at the same time authorized them to "vote for a general system of internal improvement."[87] These young, western Whigs were determined to indicate their democratic bona fides, to demonstrate they would take instruction from the people. Lincoln's temperance address at the Second Presbyterian Church in Springfield endorsed the Washingtonian approach to temperance because it was led by former alcoholics, not hectoring ministers. He rejected the condemning patrician stance. It was "impolitic," but, in a stinging rebuke of evangelical practice, it was also "unjust" because it coldheartedly "turned adrift, and damned without remedy" the drunkard, a stance a "generous man could not adopt."[88]

Both parties emphasized "generous" persuasion for a basic reason: Springfield lacked the power to control behavior through any other means. The police power, the power to enforce law and order, is one of the key measures of any state's capacity to govern. Lack of state control over the police power was a distinctive feature of the Jacksonian regime in Illinois; it was characteristic of all American settler states and is common to developing democracies in general. Justices of the peace, sheriffs, and constables exercised the police powers in the cities and counties. Except for its administration of the mail, the federal government was a distant presence. The national government nominally controlled the public lands, but local claim clubs exerted real oversight by monitoring the auctions at which newly surveyed lands went up for sale. Thomas Ford explained, "By a conventional law of each neighborhood the settlers all pledged to protect each other in the amount of their respective claims."[89]

The only statewide body with effective powers was the judiciary. Yet dramatic as the courtroom could be, its battles operated indoors after the real politics had been negotiated outdoors, whether through contentious negotiation or physical blows. The power vacuum opened by the lack of effective state control exacerbated the widespread collective action problem. Order and security are public goods. Unlike private goods, they are to no one's benefit solely to supply, are free for all to enjoy, and are no one's special responsibility to maintain. In developed liberal societies, public goods like national defense and street cleaning are overseen by government. Enforcing the harm principle and supplying public goods are the two principal grounds upon which the liberal state justifies its presence. Developing societies adopt a variety of means for securing public goods. Sometimes the law specifies the specific duties of private actors, as in Illinois, where the law required residents to spend five days annually fixing the public roads. But scofflaws tended to be rife, and compliance was difficult to monitor. Thus, in developing democracies like Illinois, public goods such as passable roads and safe frontiers often go unsupplied. The Democratic Party's solution was to fill the power vacuum with the self-appointed authority of local volunteers. By executing the police powers themselves, as participants in an Indian war, a lynch mob of "regulators," or a "wolf hunt," local men increased their social standing and imparted their own bias to the political authority of the Jacksonian regime. Political scientist Mancur Olson claims that such "selective incentives" plug the holes free riders create in collective action whenever public goods are supplied.[90] Of course, these incentives also sap the strength of the state and leave its authority impoverished when official capacity is needed to build a canal, organize a state bank, or capture a counterfeiter.

Privatizing these regime services offered short-term private incentives to men vying for social distinction but raised long-term public costs for state governance. Many Democrats seemed unconcerned about having to pay the costs in the future. The one Illinois Democrat who openly acknowledged the real costs of the privatizing approach was Thomas Ford. As governor he had to deal with the numerous extralegal and informal authorities who filled in for the state when order was needed. When he was a circuit-riding state judge, Ford had sometimes deferred to local majorities, as in the 1841 trial of the Ogle County Regulators, who had publicly executed two members of the notorious Driscoll gang. These "Ogle County lynchers," as the *Rockford Star* called them, had half their men fire blanks and the other half live ammunition at the two captured men. One hundred and eleven regulators were indicted and brought into Judge Ford's courtroom. In his charge to the jury, Ford "gave the opinion that it was impossible for a hundred and eleven men" to be held legally responsible for the killing. "Without even leaving their seats," the jury returned the verdict of not guilty.[91] In giving the charge, Ford may have considered he was following the precedent set in 1836 by a St. Louis judge who instructed a jury that murder occurred when one or two killed, but when "congregated thousands . . . [kill,] the case transcends your jurisdiction—is beyond the reach of human law."[92] Ford generally stood firm against the localist tide in other Ogle County cases, and political observers attribute his losing the popular vote there in 1842 to this controlling stance.[93]

The Whigs believed in regularizing these informal regime services and turning them into formal law. They often found themselves in the local minority; this was the political subtext of their advocacy of "the rule of law." Thus, Lincoln preferred to define "popular sovereignty" as a matter of individual rights—"each man shall do precisely as he pleases with himself"—whereas Douglas took an expansive approach, allowing the consensus of gentlemen of property and standing to overrule even national authority, as in his Kansas-Nebraska Act.[94] Enough young men saw a duty and incentive in volunteering for the Black Hawk War for numerous companies to form. The state also offered the benefits of civic membership to immigrant workers in exchange for laboring on dangerous and backbreaking work like canal digging; Illinois was too impecunious to offer compensation in wages alone. Resident producers would not likely have contracted to dig the canal, but the state had access to an international labor market supplied mainly by Irishmen and, through its subcontractors, exploited the diggers ruthlessly. State statistics are unreliable for obvious reasons, but unofficial reports suggest that deaths from disease (cholera and ague) and exhaustion topped a thousand workers in 1838 alone.[95]

Inclusive and exclusive membership rules were thus manipulated for state and societal purposes. Both parties used the story of independent producers democratically to expand the circle of ethical worth, with each party emphasizing different parts of the narrative. But they also used it willfully to exclude. The exclusion of Native Americans illustrates the pattern. In Illinois, Indians were denied, contrary to fact, the status of cultivators and thereby denied entry to the club of laboring producers. They were deemed hunters and gatherers who "scorned" labor, as in the following stanzas of the poem "Dubuque":

> The untutored SAUK, who scorns laborious toil,
> Now mourns the loss of once his native soil.
> In exile forc'd by some superior hand,
> He finds a home in some more foreign land;
> The graves where once his warlike fathers lay,
> The whiteman's plow is sweeping fast away;
> He turns but seldom to review the place,
> Where ample plenty once supplied his race;
> Revenge, half-smothered in his bosom burns
> The whiteman's art, and all his race, he spurns;
> If heaven bequeathed the earth's surface to the white,
> To rob the red man then, is doing right;
> If nations plunder nations of their soil,
> The deed is justified by want of spoil.
> No matter whether man or bird or beast,
> The strongest party triumphs o'er the least.
> Since then is tis so, we will again revert,
> To Dubuque village and its rights assert.[96]

Here the unwritten rule is that only cultivation in the European style counts as valid producing. All other styles of food production, perhaps gathering wild varieties or landrace-selection agriculture, are considered a wasteful use of the land. European-style cultivation, the "whiteman's art," is justified by production, by its "spoil." As if sensing that the justification is not conclusive enough, the author of "Dubuque" reaches for a broader support in the fact that "whether man or bird or beast, the strongest party triumphs." Want of justification often led American writers to strain for some sign of Manifest Destiny, some additional support for a foundational belief. In an impromptu statement on July 4, 1836, at the opening of the Illinois and Michigan Canal, Judge Theophilus W. Smith asserted that Illinois's White settlers should be absolved for the sin of near genocide of Native Americans. He observed: "The philanthropist perceives the moral power of a chain of causes so interwoven with the existence of this unfortunate race of human beings, that he is left with the consciousness of the melancholy reflection, that the germ of the Red Man's rapid extinction owes its origins to the laws of nature, and a culmination of causes beyond the control of human action."[97]

Fixing on the simple image of the plowman allowed the general ethical claim regarding the worth of independent producers to be particularized. From the plowman's needs a whole governing regime, an interlocking set of interests, institutions, and policies, was developed. The state's internal improvements plan was one such policy; its county-based militia system was a counterpart institution. Atop it all sat the competitive party duopoly, in which the authority of one or the other party mobilized bias and allowed the distribution of discrete interests which made the regime run. Normal politics, the use of power to compete for scarce resources within a given regime, could now proceed. If the hidden presence of government power in such a system led to a sense of "statelessness," as Tocqueville reported, it is not surprising; as Ford bluntly stated, "It has appeared to me at times that there is very little power in the government in this country except that which pertains to the leadership of the party in the majority . . . [which] is greater than the legal power of office conferred by the Constitution."[98]

Many, though not all, Democratic leaders also used their particular version of the independent producer story to exclude African Americans, enslaved or free, whom they willfully denied independence by legal definition and through the Black Codes. Many Whig leaders like Lincoln were willing to include free Black people and women, and abolitionists included enslaved people. But Whigs generally were more ready than Democrats to exclude Catholics. While Whigs like Joseph Duncan stopped short of proscribing membership on the basis of religion, by accusing "the Van Buren office holders of forming a coalition with . . . the Mormon and Catholic Churches" and emphasizing Van Buren's efforts to recruit the pope's "subjects in the U.S.," Duncan clearly suggested that members of these churches could not act independently.[99] Local Illinois majorities of both parties used the independent-producer story to attach particular group members to the national club of worthies and to exclude other groups in the state from the privileges of membership.

For both parties, the whole narrative of the independent producer was gendered. Republican virtue, the mark of the true citizen, who sacrificed individual interest for the larger public good, was open only to independent male agents, as is suggested by the word *virtue*'s root *vir,* Latin for *man.* Athenians and Romans, civic models from the past, were male citizen-soldiers. This usage was reinforced by the militia, to which only men were admitted, and by political contestation, in which only men vied and voted. Under this version of the story, the "manly" contributions of Illinois pioneer women like Rachel Darnall and Eliza Farnham (documented in chapter 1) were pushed to the background and conveniently forgotten. Why did narratives of worth or regime stories have to be narrowly uniform? Tocqueville believed it was because democratic peoples had a taste for equality that led to a proclivity for simplicity and uniformity: egalitarians "like to picture a great nation in which every citizen resembles one set type."[100] Here Tocqueville provided an alternative to Macpherson's explanation of the universal in egalitarianism: uniformity exerts a force, but at the level of form, not substance. The mechanism Tocqueville imagined is not a normative aspiration but the need for party elites to present a simple picture, the need to communicate with the nineteenth-century masses using a convenient "set type," an image or verbal shorthand.

While the two parties often cooperated in excluding outsiders like women who did not fit the uniform picture, the Whig Party was much more open to female citizenship. Democrats only infrequently argued that "sneering" at a woman who "works for a living" should be considered improper "on republican soil."[101] But both parties agreed on the exclusion of Black men from the picture of the ideal citizen. The extremely tight race for the presidency in 1840 prompted newspapers on both sides to use racist claims to lure poor Whites with the promises of what W. E. B. DuBois called "a sort of public and psychological wage" of race privilege.[102] The *Belleville Advocate* claimed that while "Harrison is said to be *benevolent* . . . in his feelings toward the blacks . . . he has no bowels of compassion for the poor white man."[103] Similarly, the *Sangamo Journal* noted that Van Buren's "toleration of negroes" went so far that he supported African American suffrage and jury duty; the Whig paper asked, "Are you willing to have your dearest rights made dependent on the testimony of a Negro?"[104]

Duopolistic competition was very hard on minorities when both parties decided to exclude them from the circle of independent producers. But it also created opportunities for negotiation. For, as should be clear, and contrary to Tocqueville's view, there is no inherent bias in democratic peoples for this or that set image of members; official, lawful inclusion and exclusion is a matter of negotiation, and elites manipulate the rules of membership to suit their immediate needs. The Mormons exerted pressure on both elites and the masses. Joseph Smith's representatives secured favorable terms for the Nauvoo charters, and his people's strenuous efforts to build up the town of Nauvoo in so short a time was evidence to many Illinoisans of their status as hard-working producers. Many reported surprise and praise for the number of houses built in the first year—claimed to be over three hundred.[105] But Mormon identity also suffered from drawbacks. Many Hancock residents presented allegations of horse stealing and other shady dealings, claims hard to substantiate given the proximity of the frontier across the river in Iowa Territory, where thieves found cover.[106] More important was Mormons' primary allegiance to an alternative group, the saints, and ultimately an alternative state, the theodemocracy of Joseph Smith's "political kingdom," which made it difficult for them to demonstrate their allegiance to the set type of worthiness currently framed under the Illinois way.

If we think of a political regime as a tool and recognize that tools are designed for specific purposes, we gain a better understanding of the political context the Mormons faced. Illinois was part of a federal union of states, and its party system was a creature of the system created at the national level. No one was more responsible for transforming the party system into a functioning tool than Martin Van Buren, who almost single-handedly resurrected the old Republican-Federalist party cleavage when it threatened to disappear under James Monroe's nonpartisanship. Van Buren would have heartily agreed with the political science adage that "stability in political communities cannot be assumed; it must be achieved."[107] His clear goal was to stabilize the republic by preventing the issue of slavery from dividing it. Van Buren, in his *Autobiography*, explained his horror at "the Missouri Agitation," which he viewed not as a humane effort to limit slavery but a "political and partisan" effort to discredit the Jeffersonian view of the South in order to resuscitate buried Federalist dreams of increasing the powers of the national government.[108]

Van Buren promoted the informal "balance rule," whereby the Senate would always contain equal numbers of free- and slave-state members.[109] This was the key to the stability the Missouri Compromise brought. As one contemporary noted in 1820: "Many of the members openly avow their intention: They say they have now an equality in the Senate, eleven slave holding, and eleven free states, and they are determined not to bring in a free state without bringing in at the same time a slave state to preserve the balance."[110] Van Buren worked hard to reunite the old Jeffersonian coalition of southern planters and mid-Atlantic workingmen, a rural and urban coalition which, reunited by Jackson, kept the slavery issue off the national agenda for the next quarter century. Balance on slavery created stability but also biased the system in favor of the contention between national versus state power. In Illinois the Mormons encountered a duopoly that was stable but fiercely contentious and far from hegemonic.

Stability in democracy is necessary because establishing the political trust that makes government legitimate is a long-term proposition. Since any electorate's trust is so slow to develop—and is even retarded by a weak opposition—only two stratagems remain in the arsenal of legitimizing state authority: force and worth. As Ford put it, "Either moral or physical force must be used for the purposes of government."[111] When the state is decentralized as it was in Illinois, a disciplined use of force is effective only for external threats because any internal division requiring force will likely also divide the local militias. Even with external threats, the state militia was of questionable use, as was proven during the Black Hawk War. Thus, Illinois politicians focused on the one tool remaining: the moral power of worth. As political scientist Rogers M. Smith argues, worth stories are compounded of economic, political, and ethical materials, and they are fashioned in pure or mixed combinations.[112] The independent-producer story is a case in point. It has economic aspects in that Illinois membership was frequently tied to the benefit of increasing one's wealth, a claim that sought to contrast the state with specific eastern and other midwestern states. It had political aspects: the Mormons were told that joining the Illinois community would make them freer than they were in Missouri. And Illinois's independent producers considered themselves to have distinct ethical worth because their hard work produced surplus and shelter from tyranny for others. Such selective incentives belied the universalist rationale for entering a just social contract, but they succeeded in attracting potential members and giving citizens reasons to join the particular deal on offer in Illinois: come to the prairie state for the adventure, stay to build a refuge from tyranny.

Volunteering may not be an effective means of advancing organizational goals, but it is a wonderful method for displaying worth. For this reason, the militia was significant not for use but for show: for its capacity to make worth visible. The militia, symbolically powerful, was a means of enforcing the locally understood rules of membership in the club of independent producers. As it turns out, it was honored mainly in the breach. Units were as unorganized and undisciplined as the government records documenting them.[113] None of the mandatory state militia units participated in the Black Hawk War. Instead, Governor John Reynolds had to count mainly on 600 citizen-soldiers from especially formed volunteer units in June of 1831 and 1,600 in May of 1832. These dedicated recruits tended to be more committed and trainable.[114] Be that as it may, each of the 126,606 militiamen listed in the 1845 census knew that militia status counted in the currency of social standing.[115]

While the Whigs and Democrats cooperated on internal improvements, they found in alien suffrage and judicial reorganization issues they could competitively retail in local markets as issues of worth. Adam Snyder of Belleville, born in Pennsylvania of German immigrant parents and a Pennsylvania Dutch speaker, courted the alien vote in St. Clair County as a Democratic Party organizer and congressman. With about a quarter of Snyder's first district votes coming from St. Clair County alone, the German electorate paved the way for his congressional victory in 1836.[116] The growth of the alien vote along the Illinois and Michigan Canal route in Cook, LaSalle, and Will Counties captured both parties' attention. Democrat Thomas Carlin, son of Irish immigrants, won the governor's race in 1838 over his Whig opponent by only 926 votes out of 60,370 cast.[117] The Democratic majority in the above three counties was 1,696 votes in 1838, whereas in 1834 Duncan had carried them by 182 votes. The huge increase was attributed to the Democrats' control over the alien vote in the canal neighborhoods.[118]

In 1839 the state was shaken by a political revolution of sorts when the Whigs orchestrated a legal challenge to the alien voting privilege. The Whigs had the text of the constitution of 1818 against them as well as precedents from other states, but their tortuous reasoning was upheld in an arranged case by Whig judge Dan Stone at Galena.[119] Anticipating the appeal to the state supreme court, Snyder introduced in the General Assembly a judicial reorganization bill that would allow the current democratic majority in the legislature to pack the court before the appeal was heard.[120] The party line votes on this arguably unconstitutional law entrenched animosity between the parties for the next decade. Together with Snyder, Stephen A. Douglas ensured that those "tender-footed" Democrats who could not follow their leadership were denied party support at future elections.[121]

MR. SMITH BUILDS HIS DREAM STATE

Thus matters stood in 1839 when Joseph Smith crossed the Mississippi River to enter Illinois as a refugee. Ideologically, the Illinoisans' commitment to the independent producer had not changed since Smith's first visit in 1834. The democracy was still open to the lure of popular justice, inviting the people to make the state their own. But institutionally, the landscape had been transformed. Now a mature regime setting of party organization and competition reached all things. A state bank and internal improvements laws, intended to guide economic development, were both bankrupted by improvident management, the national suspension of specie payments, and the burst of the land bubble. Thus, economically, the state was also transformed. A frown of depression replaced the smiling face of prosperity. By 1839 it was veering dangerously toward repudiation of its debts. All the more reason then for the state's political parties to compete for Mormon votes in Hancock County, which sat at the center of its western border, the one region of the state where immigration was booming.

If Illinois had changed since Smith's 1834 visit, becoming more cautious economically and more organized and competitive politically, so, too, had Smith: he was cagier and more methodical. The prophet had learned much and changed much over the past five years. He had just emerged from six months in the prison in Liberty, Missouri, where, despite the primitive conditions, he had time to reflect on his past course. To build "beautiful" Nauvoo and secure the Mormons' safety, Smith realized he needed to apply all the lessons he had learned in previous entanglements with the American state. The Mormons' settlement pattern in Missouri, ranging over three counties, left the group vulnerable to local majorities. The Mormons would return to the urban strategy they followed in Kirtland, Ohio, but Smith now renounced the communal sharing of property which led to anti-banking notes, internal division, and financial ruin. In Illinois he would need to erect a different kind of city using the old laws in a new way. More than ever focused on his theological journey, the remarkably resourceful Smith would use whatever materials Illinois had available. Mormon institutions in this way became at once utterly familiar and utterly foreign to the Illinoisans, similar in form but different in purpose from anything the suckers had built.

To assess the success of Smith's handicraft, it is useful to gauge his progress from that Missouri jail cell to three years later, in December of 1842, when he agreed to stand trial in Springfield, Illinois, on charges brought in Missouri. He arrived in the capital flanked by a small horse guard of "forty of his best soldiers" from the Nauvoo Legion, the Mormon militia that had been authorized by the General Assembly two years earlier.[122] It was an entrance Machiavelli could place next to Pope Julius's march into enemy Perugia with nothing but his crimson robes and a retinue of cardinals.[123] Fortune favors the brave—especially in state building—and both cases of brio ended in success. Julius left Perugia with his choice of prince in place, and Smith left Springfield a free man. Federal judge Nathaniel Pope granted his petition for a writ of habeas corpus and thereby quashed the process for his arrest.

Smith relied on the legal counsel of the newly elected governor, Thomas Ford, who believed the extradition request from Missouri was illegal. The fact that Smith consulted with the governor and trusted the system enough to give himself up indicates how well things had gone in Illinois for the Mormons in the brief time since they emigrated. With well-placed friends among both the Whigs and the Democrats, they had obtained in the fall of 1840 enough favor from the Illinois legislature to write a city charter for Nauvoo that delegated many privileges of local autonomy in elaborate detail. Mormon success was assured by the support of Hancock's senator, Sidney H. Little, who sponsored the legislation, as well as by the advice from other prominent Whigs, such as Edward D. Baker and Cyrus Walker. They also had the support of St. Clair County senator Adam Snyder, who chaired the legal affairs subcommittee, in which the charter details were negotiated.[124] The Democrat Snyder would run for governor in 1842 and had the support of party leader Stephen A. Douglas. In a letter to his followers in December of 1841, the prophet had commended Douglas to his followers as a "master spirit" in Illinois politics. As a result of this elite backing, Nauvoo's municipal court was granted the power to issue writs of habeas corpus and the city the power to record its own deeds; Nauvoo was granted powers to charter a university, a militia, a joint stock corporation, a railroad, and even a canal.[125] The Mormons' miniature state would copy the original down to sponsorship of its own internal improvements plan.

Smith was not on hand to lobby for these rights of local government on behalf of the Mormons; he was in Washington, DC, making his case for reparations from Missouri. Instead, the Mormon point man was John C. Bennett. If Harold Hill was the midwestern music man, Bennett was its confidence man of universities and militias. Prior to coming to Nauvoo and hitching his star to the Latter-day Saints, he had chartered universities in Ohio and Indiana and had created a militia outfit in eastern Illinois called the Invincible Dragoons and Flying Artillery.[126] Bennett proposed a two-mile canal be dug along Main Street to make Nauvoo a bona fide Mississippi River port town; the several millraces proposed would have given it a water power comparable to what the state was planning for the Illinois and Michigan Canal at Lockport. While Bennett certainly initiated the Mormon connections in the legislature, Smith and his brothers Hyrum and William learned they could get all they needed from the General Assembly simply by asking. The practice of using charters to endow municipalities with their own governing autonomy was already an established pattern. But generous powers of self-government would also be the Mormons' undoing among the suckers.

Already in the summer of 1840, the prophet was busy correcting the reputation for lawlessness the Mormons had earned in Missouri. He encouraged those able-bodied men among his followers to join the standing militia in Hancock County, the Fifty-Ninth Regiment. In fact, membership was mandatory by state law for all such men between the ages of eighteen and forty-five.[127] Once Bennett's militia charter was passed, these men were shifted to the volunteer unit, the Nauvoo Legion. Since Joseph Smith was elected lieutenant general of the legion, it solved two problems at once: it allowed the Mormons to protect themselves while also allowing them to operate within the law. This law-abiding approach would correct the abuses of the Danites, the secret Mormon militia in Missouri loosely authorized by Smith. Provoked by the Danites at several frontier skirmishes, the Missourians used a state militia of 2,500 men to drive the Mormons out of their state. Ensconced at Nauvoo, and with his own legally constituted army, Smith made plans to finish off his city-state with the Nauvoo Mansion as a kind of White House and the temple as a kind of national cathedral.

In these early days, Smith and the Mormons had no need to fight the state in Illinois because they were welcomed to have their own piece of it. The saints voted almost the straight Whig ticket in November of 1840, taking their cue from Smith, who at the time

FIG. 3.4. Nauvoo temple (from Gregg, *History of Hancock County*). Courtesy of Newberry Library

was in Washington denouncing President Van Buren for failing to provide restitution for the Missouri crimes. But the Democrats would not be left behind. The very next month, when the Mormons petitioned the General Assembly for their charters, Snyder and Douglas demonstrated their determination to win the Mormon vote. Over the ensuing two years, there followed a spiraling series of special favors administered by the parties, attended in each case with Mormon electoral support. The Mormons cheered each time an arrest request from Missouri—Smith was suspected of an assassination attempt on Governor Boggs—was granted a new habeas petition by a Whig or Democratic judge.

There was one crucial drawback: Mormons came to be perceived by both parties as a voting bloc; indeed, the election returns proved they had so acted. The result was disastrous because the local gentlemen of property and standing were immediately threatened. The first sign of trouble came in May 1841. The local Whigs in Hancock County felt they needed to separate from the state Whigs, who were actively courting the Mormons, because they feared the Mormons would prevail in the late-summer county commissioner race. There were three candidates running—a Whig, a Democrat, and one whose only qualification was "the fact of his being a Mormon"—and they warned that without action the last would win simply by reason of his identity.[128]

After the Whig vote in 1840, Douglas counterattacked. He personally oversaw one of Smith's habeas proceedings as a circuit judge; he also appointed Bennett the master in chancery, which made him the chief legal clerk of Hancock County. Bennett later served as the mayor of Nauvoo and a commander of the Nauvoo Legion until he irrevocably broke with Smith and the Mormons in May of 1841. But Bennett's presence damaged the group's reputation before he left. His personality grated. While he took great comfort in the protection afforded by his adopted group, his claim to a position of authority over the whole county and the shelter of a distinct and separate group in the community touched a structural nerve. By the summer of 1841, Bennett was gone, exposed as a charlatan, but the fuse had been lit. A crucial turning point had been reached. All that was needed was an explosive incident, and Smith provided that himself in June of 1844. As mayor he executed a nuisance order on the *Nauvoo Expositor,* a paper issued by several apostates. Then he allowed his followers to smash its printing press in the street. He was endorsing mobocracy, pushing imitation to the limit.

The lesson of how Jacksonian regime leaders responded when they perceived a threat to their local authority was not one Smith should have had to learn. He had experienced rough justice first-hand in Ohio and Missouri. Perhaps he thought he saw a precedent he could follow in the way Elijah Lovejoy and the abolitionists were treated in the nearby town of Alton in 1837. A mob shut down Lovejoy's newspaper three times before it killed him and overpowered the town's abolitionists. The prophet may have been seduced, given how easily the political elite in Illinois manipulated its followers, into believing that the followers did not matter. Perhaps he hoped his legal writ and his legal militia would save him and his people. But the power of local majorities, the power of mobocracy, in the end was greater. On June 27, 1844, he and his brother Hyrum were assassinated by a mob in the jail of the Hancock County town of Carthage. The Carthage Greys, a militia of the old settlers of Hancock detailed to guard the jail, watched impassively while an angry mob stormed the premises and executed the Smith brothers while Governor Ford was away.

The parallel treatment of the abolitionists and the Mormons raises a useful comparative question. Did a common motivation drive both the antiabolitionists and anti-Mormons? The answer is yes. In both cases regime defenders stepped up to enforce their prerogatives. There is much evidence to support this conclusion. To start with, one trait the Mormons and abolitionists shared was that they were both considered separate communal groups by the Illinoisans. In the case of Hancock County, as social historian Susan Sessions Rugh demonstrates, even Mormons outside Nauvoo in rural areas like Fountain Green Township were perceived as separate. The Mormon town of Macedonia was by the spring of 1846 a "Deserted Village" in large part, as the anti-Mormon *Nauvoo Eagle* had it, because of "that trait in the Mormon character, which enables them to concentrate their energies and form communities of their own. In a locality of this kind, they mingle but little with the world."[129] But as Rugh argues, the sense of separation was a recent development because several strong kin and trading ties had previously existed between the Mormons and the old settlers in Fountain Green.

Being perceived as different does not mean you will be attacked. Why were both groups attacked? Why was Lovejoy mobbed?

Leonard L. Richards develops an answer that resonates with the biases structuring the regime. Richards points out that the men in antiabolitionist mobs were not drifters or marginal figures but prominent members of the community.[130] The same holds for the anti-Mormon groups. Often the very members of the mob committing the violence voiced their commitment to law and order. If they were vigilantes, they were "establishment" vigilantes whose general aim was "to defend the existing order."[131] Such impromptu groupings were a known extralegal convention on the northern Illinois frontier; like the Ogle County Regulators, the anti-Mormons formed to deliver what they viewed as regime services.

Defenders of the status quo ante in Hancock County included an anti-Mormon group formed in the spring of 1845. Rugh quotes a public statement titled "To the Democrats of the State of Illinois," printed in the *Warsaw Signal* on May 14, 1845, in which the Democrats of the county announced that their opposition to the Mormons was not premised on "party considerations. . . . [These had] nothing to do with the actions of the old citizens." Instead they acted from "the necessary defense of their own constitutional rights . . . without which opposition and defense, the people of Hancock would be unworthy [of] the name of American citizens."[132] Rugh notes that the Democrats' statement was significant for another reason: it was signed by men who originated from southern states. Before this, it was mainly Whigs and immigrants from the northern states who had opposed the Mormons. When the Mormons continued their bloc voting in the fall of 1844 after their leaders were assassinated, "the campaign to remove the Mormons" grew more united in Hancock County. It proceeded under a new north-south coalition, the one portended by the May 1845 statement. The gentlemen of property and standing from both parties were now united.

On the national level, Richards's carefully laid case shows that antiabolitionist violence peaked not in 1831, when William Lloyd Garrison began publishing *The Liberator,* but three years later, when the abolitionists switched tactics and began organizing in addition to publishing. With the creation of the New England Anti-Slavery Society in 1832, the abolitionists began organizing against their rival in the field of reform, the American Colonization Society. From the start, Garrison and the abolitionists defended inclusion of free Black people in the political order and urged freeing enslaved African Americans. They thus violated an unspoken consensus that the class of civically worthy "producers" should be limited to Whites, but their opposition was seen as hapless until it began questioning the priority and standing of American Colonization Society members in locales across the nation. At that point, the abolitionists violated a more basic commitment of the societal culture by questioning the authority of local majorities to control the definition of civic worth.

Like the abolitionists, the Mormons in Hancock County violated the localist code by persisting in their bloc voting after the united voice of the old citizens condemned it. Rugh quotes a Protestant minister who argued the Mormons lacked republican independence; their bloc voting demonstrated that "under Mormon government a *manly independence* is an *unpardonable crime*."[133] Furthermore, after several warnings, including the assassination of their leader turned presidential candidate, the Mormons returned to bloc voting. Many locals considered this perverse. A campaign in the local papers to stigmatize the Mormons as thieves culminated in the spring and summer of 1845. Amid claims that they were stealing from non-Mormons, the Mormons in Nauvoo put up and supported a local slate in the fall of 1845. They succeeded in electing the polarizing sheriff Jacob Backenstos, but the election was another example of a minority in a developing democracy with little lateral support grasping a short-term gain at the long-term cost of enraging the majority.[134]

At first Brigham Young believed the Mormons had an advantage locally. He wrote in his diary: "The mobocrats begin to tremble and make preparations to leave this country and we pray the Lord to speed their flight."[135] But the feeling was short lived. Rugh demonstrates that the proximate cause of the Mormon decision to leave Illinois en masse came on September 3, 1845, when an anti-Mormon meeting in rural Hancock County was disrupted by gunshot and the assembled group went on rampage. Trust had dwindled so far that "they presumed the shots to be an attack on them, and in retaliation they set fire to the cabins of Mormons at Morley's Settlement nearby. Before they were finished, the whole village lay in ashes, over one hundred houses."[136] The continued burning and several murders decided Young on the necessity of leaving. Rugh concludes, "The Anti-Mormons had come upon a winning strategy, because the rural Mormon towns were vulnerable to attack in a way that Nauvoo was not."[137]

But even Smith's city-state, with its own set of institutions, was no protection for the Mormons after September 1845. They had become in fact as well as perception a separate people. In addition to their spatial separation, they increasingly emphasized their separate story of peoplehood. They had their own "Golden Bible" and an elaborate set of revelations proving that they, and all those who joined their group, were special. Here, too, the Mormons, in adopting a variety of particularist egalitarianism, which after all they shared with the Illinois majority, only exacerbated the conflict. Particularists are marked by a forthright bias in favor of one group in the societal culture's pecking order. Joseph Smith never hid his bias in favor of the Mormons. He openly preferred them and concerned himself with their worth and salvation over all other groups. But in asserting his power to prefer a subset of independent producers among the set of Illinois settlers, he violated the rule of deferring to the preferences of the "original settlers."

Scholars debate the extent to which the Mormons came to view themselves as not only religiously distinct from the mass of Americans but politically distinct as well. Mention of the "kingdom of God" was not unique in the millennial tradition of nineteenth-century American Christianity. But the Mormons were unique in emphasizing the continuity between the kingdom set up in Christ's time and the present "latter days," in which the saints had lost none of their miraculous powers. Most denominations claimed that the kingdom would reemerge after the "end times." Mormons not only believed that the end times were near but that the "political kingdom" would appear before the end.[138] The Latter-day Saints were thus special in two ways: they believed the kingdom was imminent for all Americans and it would be led in real time by Joseph Smith in the name of all Americans. When Smith ran for president in 1844, it was not only to make the whole United States safe for Mormons; it was to make the United States wholly Mormon. He would Mormonize America rather than Americanize the Mormons. Like Andrew Jackson's, Smith's will to promote his favored group knew no bounds. They were even more his own creation than the Democrats were Jackson's.

While the antebellum American state has been seen as feckless, Smith had no doubts about its power and capacity for self-defense. As the leader of a marginalized religious group, he was induced to get a state of his own. In liberal pluralist theory, the state appears as "merely one association among many to which individuals belong and owe loyalty."[139] In practice, the state's "house of power" orders all other associations and loyalties. The Jacksonian Democrats developed a regime to keep these preferences in place. With time, these preferences acquired the patina of the status quo ante, however unjust and arbitrary they were in fact. County-level groups of self-appointed authorities applied and misapplied the enforcement of membership norms based on an independent-producer civic narrative. The informal nature of these groups, sporadically contributing regime services, led to the sense of an absent state reported by Tocqueville and others.

The state's absence lived on in the minds of the Illinoisans. They welcomed the Mormons in 1839 to Illinois as individuals and, were they polled, would likely have said they rejected the Mormons in 1845 as individuals. They would have said that in 1839 a land of religious toleration welcomed a marginalized sect to join a new state on terms of economic productivity and individual freedom and that in 1845 the sect was chased out for violating individual rights like freedom of the press, harboring thieves, and voting not as individuals but as a bloc. But these violations of liberal rights are mere symptoms of the real reasons behind the Mormon troubles. In the end, expulsion came because the Mormons challenged the Illinois way, the old settlers' claim to rule and recognize independent-producer worth on their own terms.

The Illinoisans followed a particular civic narrative which specified foundational beliefs about what constituted virtuous producing and how to achieve virtuous independence. For better or worse, liberal individualists always downplay the encumbering purposes driving their public sphere goals. Individualists are so focused on the reciprocity their version of equality requires that they tend to miss the trust-inducing cues held in place by any particular status quo. For their part, egalitarians are so focused on their own group worth that they often misrecognize that of others. Despite this collective myopia, the American antebellum state was no cipher; it was a powerful tool for enforcing local group preferences, and both individualists and egalitarians used it. The structure of the settler state displaced the aspiration of universal accommodation and inclusion despite what its participants sometimes intended. The rule of gentlemen was neither gentle nor inconsequential. As Joseph Smith and the Mormons knew, it was ruthlessly enforced and frequently illiberal.

4

Nauvoo Prophecies in the Hancock Status Order

While still in Liberty Jail on March 20, 1839, Joseph Smith wrote a letter to an estimated 4,800 Mormons living temporarily in and around Quincy, Illinois.[1] He urged them to head for the large tract of land that was offered for sale by the shifty Isaac Galland and was fifty miles north in Hancock County. Still palpable was the trauma of the Missouri battles and expulsion following Governor Lilburn Boggs's "extermination" order enforced by an active militia of 2,500 men. But by now the Mormons had become an extremely resilient group. They were a self-described "people . . . of untiring industry and perseverance," and their resentment toward the Missourians became a "fire shut up in the bones."[2] It fueled a remarkable resurrection in Nauvoo. All during 1839 and 1840, strong feelings were apparent in Mormon public statements, in their documented personal and property losses, and in their continued clashes with people across the Mississippi River.

Hancock County was a recently organized part of Illinois. The town of Warsaw and the county seat of Carthage had been settled for a decade, but the northwestern corner of the country, along the river and adjacent to Montrose, Iowa, remained largely unsettled and was known to be lawless. It was in this wild area just above the Des Moines Rapids that Galland's city of Commerce was platted. Raw conditions were no great obstacle for the Mormons. They previously chose Far West, Missouri, to be closer to several resettled Native American tribes who they had hoped to convert. Indeed, frontier conditions suited the saints' desire to live separate from "the world," which they saw as damned to its "last days." They were willing to accept hardships and rough neighborhoods if it meant locating a home at a discount; in their desperate straits, all Smith and the Mormons could afford was land with dubious title in a frontier area. The 1838 Missouri War had replicated the Ohio experience but with more violence; it confirmed the Mormons' need to live apart and under rules they could control.

Smith was furious with how the Missourians had treated his people, and once safe in Illinois he embarked on a trip to Washington, DC, to seek redress from President Martin Van Buren and Congress for the group. Restless soul that he was he also sought to turn anger into action, to focus not on the past but the future. In "a long conversation" with Smith, the *Quincy Whig* editors found the Mormon prophet remarkably "divested of all malicious thought and feeling toward his relentless persecutors."[3] The *Times and Seasons,* the new Mormon paper at Commerce, urged the faithful to "not breathe vengeance upon your oppressors but leave the case in the hands of God."[4] Smith's followers read a mixed message in other pronouncements. When hard-pressed in Missouri, Smith had endorsed an eventual recourse to violence after failure in three attempts to "lift a standard of peace."[5] Later in Illinois, in more intimate and unguarded moments, Smith vented his anger and rage at all outsiders. In July of 1840 he prophesied that "the time shall be when these Saints shall ride proudly over the mountains of Missouri and no Gentile dog nor Missouri dog shall dare lift a tongue against them, but will lick up the dust from beneath their feet."[6] It is not surprising that the faithful faced the future with a backward glance.

A month before Smith reached Quincy in April of 1839, emerging leader Brigham Young held a conference in the city counseling the saints "to unite together as much as possible." Branches of the church were soon established in Adams, Fayette, McDonough, Pike, Sangamon, and likely other counties in Illinois.[7] Young and his cohorts also excommunicated several of the key apostates in the Missouri trials. These included John Corrill, Sampson Avard, and Reed Peck, men who had given public testimony against the Mormons as former members of the Danites, the secret paramilitary society which had defended the group from attack. The Danites would later be reconstituted in Nauvoo as a personal bodyguard for Smith in September of 1840 in response to the first of many Missouri warrants seeking Illinois's cooperation in the prophet's arrest.[8] The most notorious Danite was Porter Rockwell, who was suspected of attempting to assassinate Boggs and who later shot and killed the anti-Mormon Frank Worrell. But Rockwell, a rough-and-tumble gunslinger, was a personal favorite of Smith.

At Commerce—soon to be renamed Nauvoo—the Mormons were greeted with a long sickly season. The thousand acres selected adjacent to the Mississippi River and one of its bluffs were untamed, mosquito infested, and miasmatic. The area had not been inhabited since "the Sac and Fox Indians established a large agricultural village" there in the eighteenth century.[9] The terrain sloped upwards and flatted out on the bluff above, but even the settlers on the flat prairie above found the land swampy, the water unhealthy, and fever and ague prevalent. Most camped in makeshift tents and wagons or set up temporary quarters in an abandoned War of 1812 barracks across the river at Montrose, Iowa. All were still traumatized by the forced march from their homes through the winter weather and haunted by episodes like the massacre at Hawn's Mill. One young boy was among the seventeen Mormons slaughtered in cold blood after they had surrendered.

Smith would have no success in the nation's capital. He was disgusted with Van Buren's frank refusal. Recourse was to be pursued through the courts under the US Constitution, the president told him; he added that any special aid would cost the Democrats votes in Missouri. Richard Young, the Illinois senator who presented their petition for redress to Congress, advised them to work through the courts. Young publicly raised money for the group and offered to lend the church more funds if need be; Sidney Rigdon, later Smith's vice presidential running mate, thought the group should accept Young's offer and head back to Kirtland.[10] But on his return in March of 1840, the prophet cemented Nauvoo in Latter-day Saint history by beginning a series of new revelations that would revolutionize Mormon theology.

Determined to seek restitution and get his people settled, Smith was at the same time already beginning a new spiritual phase. In June and July of 1840, he was openly searching for guidance. Historian Richard Bushman emphasizes how important his father's conversion to the church was: "Joseph showed more emotion at his father's baptism . . . than at any other time of his life."[11] But his people's exposure and the sickly conditions were taking their toll. By the fall, his father and many of his people were dying in front of him. He needed refuge and sought it in revelation. Having used "considerable exertion to commence a settlement and place of gathering for the saints," he now wished the "Constituted Authorities of the Church" would endorse his work and relieve him of immediate financial responsibility so that he could turn to "the Spiritual Welfare of the Saints . . . commence the work of translating the ejyptian records . . . and . . . wait upon the Lord for . . . revelations."[12] The Egyptian records, later translated as the Book of Abraham, were scrolls purchased from a manuscript dealer in Ohio and believed to be sacred.[13] Smith began to focus on a persistent and troubling question: What of those family members who fell sick and died before they had converted to the church? A natural consequence of Mormon separateness from the world and their expectation of the apocalypse looming in these last days, the question plagued every true believer and touched every family, including the prophet's own. His dear brother Alvin had died before the Book of Mormon was published.[14]

The new round of prophecies began with the sickness of the prophet's father. He emphasized that when loved ones fell sick and died, it was a physical, not a spiritual, weakness. It was not a sign of a fallen state, because "all flesh is subject to suffer." Smith told his followers, "Still many of the saints will escape—for the just shall live by faith—yet many of the righteous shall fall a prey to disease to pestilence by reason of the weakness of the flesh and yet be saved in the kingdom of God."[15] Then, during a funeral sermon on August 15, 1840, Smith first announced a new revelation and prophecy: baptism for the dead. As Bushman argues, the doctrine of baptism for the dead took on a life of its own at Nauvoo, and "within weeks, baptisms were being performed in the Mississippi River." Bushman estimates that over six thousand baptisms were held throughout 1841; no other rite had proven so popular. Smith sent a letter to explain the new development to the apostles in England: "The Saints have the privilege of being baptized, for those of their relatives who are dead, who they believe would have embraced the gospel if they had been privileged with hearing it."[16] Living individuals could in effect "act in proxy for the deceased," and, in line with other theological strains emerging at this time, being baptized would allow "the dead to progress in the afterlife."[17] Baptism records were to be carefully kept for their "sealing and binding power" as granted by the priesthood.[18]

He elaborated upon verses 5–6 of the fourth book of Malachi in the Hebrew Bible:

> [For] the earth will be smitten with a curse unless there is a welding link of some kind or other between the fathers and the children, upon some subject or other—and behold what is that subject? It is the baptism for the dead. For we without them cannot be made perfect; neither can they without us be made perfect. . . . Behold, the great day of the Lord is at hand; and who can abide the day of his coming, and who can stand when he appeareth? For he is like a refiner's fire, and like fuller's soap; and he shall sit as a refiner and purifier. . . . Let us, therefore, as a church and a people, and as Latter-day Saints, offer unto the Lord an offering in righteousness; and let us present in his holy temple, when it is finished, a book containing the records of our dead, which shall be worthy of all acceptation.[19]

The new doctrine would keep Smith and his people spiritually preoccupied for the remainder of their time at Nauvoo. Purgatory for the dead and a role for the priesthood in sealing and caring for a saving "welding link" would unfold in due course. In the meantime, the pace of temporal matters was quickening. Amid the busy details of laying out town lots and acting as treasurer for the church, Smith received two letters from a stranger that would begin a tempestuous rise and fall the likes of which the Mormon church had never seen. The writer was John C. Bennett, soon to be mayor of the newly incorporated city of Nauvoo and the person who would replace Sidney Rigdon as the church's public "mouthpiece."[20]

By November of 1840, Bennett was acting as Smith's proxy in Springfield as he ushered charters for Nauvoo, its university, and militia through the General Assembly. In the July 27 letter, Bennett stated his "deliberate advice . . . to concentrate all of your church at one point. If Hancock County with Commerce for its commercial Emporium is to be that point, well,—fix upon it."[21] This confirmed Smith's own inclination, and while it set the group on a dangerous course—it could be exhibit A in confirmation of Thomas Ford's claim that the Mormons were "ever disposed to follow the worst advice they could get"—it was perhaps an obvious choice.[22] But such temporal matters seemed far from central. In the next few months the prophet accelerated the pace of his revelations. The Nauvoo prophecies had the urgency of the last days.

The revelations on sealing the dead had the prophet looking both outward and inside the Mormon community. Casting his gaze outward, he decided to restart the Seventies, the missionary organization within the church. He would soon send to Jerusalem and England some of his most trusted advisers, including Brigham Young. The world needed to be put on notice; the restoration was at hand. The United States, too, needed to be warned. In a July 19 sermon, as Smith related the importance of building up Zion, he described the coming end-time in America, that "this Nation will be on the very verge of crumbling to pieces and tumbling to the ground and when the constitution is on the brink of ruin, [the Mormon] people will be the staff upon which the Nation shall lean and they shall bear the constitution away from the very verge of destruction."[23]

Looking inward, Smith decided to follow Bennett's advice on the gathering. From the newly named town of Nauvoo in August 1840, he issued a letter to the "Saints Scattered Abroad" asking them to make every effort to come home to help build the temple: "The work which has to be accomplished in the last days is one of vast importance. . . . The work of the gathering spoken of in the Scriptures will be necessary to bring about the glories of the last dispensation."[24] The gathering directive was tied to the baptism for the dead in a "revelation given to Joseph the Seer" dated January 19, 1841: "The children of Israel were commanded to build a house in the land of promise; and so are the saints in the last days . . . wherein those ordinances may be revealed which have been hid for ages, even their anointings and washings and *baptisms of the dead.*"[25]

As enthusiasm for the baptism rite reached a frenzy, Smith and the Council of the Twelve Apostles abruptly announced in December of 1841 that no new baptisms would take place until a new temple was built. Historians note how the Mormons were held together by the perceived threat of persecution from the outside.[26]

A common route to group consolidation, scholars observe, comes through negation; the group unites by determining what it is not. But the positive side of group ideology should not be overlooked. Its tangible outlet for the Mormons in this period was the building of the temple, a great intrinsic motivator that captured the imagination of the rank-and-file believer. The motivation survived the death of the founder, explaining one of the more remarkable outcomes in the Mormon experience in Illinois: when the Smith brothers were assassinated, Illinoisans expected Nauvoo to explode in a spasm of vengeance. It did not happen; nor did the community implode. Given how the Mormons followed their prophet's every move, the expectations of explosion and implosion were reasonable. But there was quiet. Most of the apostles were abroad, and residents remained focused on a goal that united them even more than the living prophet—the temple rites for sealing and recording the dead.

THE HIDDEN LIFE OF GROUPS

The Mormon case indicates how centrally group belief, ritual, and setting can frame the societal outlook shared by members. The importance of group life in American politics has been generally underemphasized because scholars, following the comparative method, have been led to overemphasize differences between American and European political development. They have focused on the Jacksonians' comparatively "atomistic" culture of individualism.[27] But this misses the elemental and formative role groups played at the time in ordering American societal culture, a role made salient in a developing democracy in which individuals vied and competed to find a place in a civil society ranked by group status. Looking toward the members, we recognize that groups provide individuals with the succor of solidarity. Looking toward civil society, it is equally clear that group attachment and allegiance structure individual rank and set status.

One individual allegiance stands out among all others: the allegiance of the citizen to the government. As Max Weber argued, the state stands at the center of the political regime; the "house of power" orders the law, the economy, and civil society.[28] The power of the state therefore structures the social action taking place in the societal culture. For liberals, the legitimacy of the state is judged by how fairly it treats individuals and groups; especially when religious groups are involved, fairness is assessed based on how neutral the state's policies are.[29] Citizens use the state as a platform on which to perform their civic roles as agents in the drama of self-government.

While how the state affects group life is often noted, the reverse has been too frequently ignored. Interest groups are studied for how they influence the state's policies but very little for how they constitute state authority. In fact, group life shapes the state itself: no state can govern very long—act with authority or execute the use of force—without the support of the dominant groups in society. In democratic societies those who control the state are elected based on compelling civic narratives. Explicit stories of peoplehood require an image of the ideal member, for which political leaders borrow, mix, and match from traits endorsed by the dominant groups. These stories reflect the status beliefs dominant in society, however much the liberal state may occlude this reliance with claims of universality and neutrality. Liberal societal cultures reflect the vertical pecking order imagined or reordered by their constituent groups. As groups rally, they often shift regime narratives in favorable directions. In twentieth-century America, political scientist Christopher Baylor argues, first civil rights groups and then Christian evangelical groups decisively turned regime narratives in their own favor.[30] In the case of a liberal settler state such as Illinois, dominant groups like White male farmers not only supplied the scripts for justifying state authority but also provided the bodies and arms to enforce the law. According to the 1818 constitution and at the direction of the governor, regime services were rendered directly by citizen-soldiers who, "in time of war or public danger," were put into action by means of their militias.[31]

Ordered informally by the private sphere, the state operated formally to reinforce the social order. De jure rules marked the boundaries of formal membership. Militias were to be drawn from among "all free male able-bodied persons (Negroes, mulattoes, and Indians excepted) resident of the state, between the age of 18 and 45 years." The same group was authorized to elect all officers below the rank of general.[32] The multiple exclusions and inclusions here are worthy of note. It is perhaps not surprising that free women would be excluded, given the ready justification that republican mothers had duties enough in the private sphere. Indians also could be excluded on the grounds that governments in Illinois from the territorial days up to the present had battled several Indigenous nations over the land. The exclusion of free Negroes and mulattoes was more biased and particularist from a liberal perspective, especially since in river cities like Alton, Shawneetown, Peoria, and Springfield, such persons had played and continued to play a prominent role in civic life. In Chicago, Native Americans told an early settler named Kinzie that "the first white man who settled here was a Negro."[33] The inclusion of all resident White males of the appropriate age in the militia muster roles is perhaps most surprising. Not requiring citizenship exemplified the usual deference extended to White settlers. As we have seen, the constitution further enhanced the status of mere residents by extending to them the suffrage right generally extended only to citizens. The authority of the majority of local residents was further enhanced by the power to elect officers. According to his biographer William Herndon, Abraham Lincoln "prized . . . being elected captain [during his Black Hawk War militia service] . . . and the distinction it gave him more than any which in after years fell to his lot."[34]

Standing behind civil society's informal ordering was the foundational belief in popular sovereignty. This belief was forcefully expressed in the 1818 constitution: "All power is inherent in the people; and all free governments are founded on their authority."[35] A tacit background assumption was that local majorities would determine and police who "the people" in each county would be. Civil society's pecking order supplied the de facto rules which empowered majorities. Mormon memoirs of the 1830s and 1840s show how Illinois's societal rules were enforced and reinforced at the local level whenever outsiders contested their boundaries. Two remarkably candid memoirs by John Doyle Lee and George Washington Bean, both Illinoisans who converted to Mormonism, detail the specific burdens of an outsider identity. They provide telling evidence of the status order that existed in Illinois prior to the Mormon arrival and suggest how locals ascribed a place for the new group within the existing order.

John D. Lee was raised Catholic in Kaskaskia in Randolph County, Illinois. He evidently grew up speaking French and struggled in English. As he related, "The children at school called me *Gumbo,* and teased me so much that I became disgusted with the French language."[36] English, not French, was the de facto language of the majority in Illinois and the nation. But most Protestants offered a de jure toleration of Catholicism. The constitution required this by specifying that "all men have a natural and indefeasible right to worship Almighty God according to the dictates of their own consciences."[37]

A different element of the status order was exposed by Bean, who grew up in Adams County, Illinois. He and his two siblings attended a one-room schoolhouse taught by a Mormon that they shared in 1839 with an adult Mormon pupil, Alexander Williams, who was exiled from Missouri and learning to read and write. Having been raised in Tennessee, "among the darkies," as Bean wrote, Williams's pronunciation was open to teasing because it was marked by a group attachment considered low in the pecking order.[38] The Tennessean's desire to learn and perseverance only endeared him to the Bean children; Williams's simple honesty and integrity eventually won the whole family to the Mormon faith. In this example, the outsider is accommodated by a conversion of the insiders. But teasing at school again made transparent the larger reality of civil society's pecking order and its enforcement in a group ranking constituted of ascribed identities.

To make sense of this hidden life of groups, we need a broader theory of culture than the government-focused model produced by Daniel Elazar. The societal level of political culture can be more carefully cataloged through the framework devised by symbolic anthropologist Mary Douglas. Observing how group settings affect individuals and how individuals consequently use ideas "as symbols of the relation between parts of society," she investigates culture generally and cosmology in particular.[39] She argues that different shared institutional settings lead individuals to different overall shared conceptions of the meaning of life. This idea—that social settings shape individual meaning systems—was a structural lesson she learned from Émile Durkheim, who applied it broadly to topics like religion, suicide, and modernization. Douglas's four subcultures are tied to four distinct settings: if you live in a hierarchical society and accept a pecking order of groups, one culture and cosmology follows—a hierarchical culture; if you are part of a dissenting group, an outsiders' worldview or an egalitarian culture makes sense; if you live and thrive in a competitive, atomistic social setting, yet a third cosmology—an individualist culture—appeals; and finally, if you live in a highly ordered and regimented society but have no control over your personal identification and little voice to contest your group ranking, you likely follow a fourth worldview—fatalism.[40]

Douglas's matrix (see page 86) has allowed researchers to map the cultural perspectives of four distinct political cultures in America: the liberal, the republican, the ascriptive, and the marginalized.[41] Each of the four is associated with one of Douglas's subcultures. Liberal political ideas and structures follow the individualist culture; republican political ideas and structures follow the egalitarian culture; ascriptive ideas and structures conform to the worldview imposed by the hierarchical culture; and the response to having an identity written on or ascribed to your group, if repeatedly and widely enforced, is fatalism and marginalization. Douglas's theory offers scholars a rich toolbox for analyzing how people in democracies experience the transition to increasingly mobile societies and market economies with an accelerating division of labor.

The upshot of Douglas's theory is that no one liberal societal culture stands as a transcendent, inevitable end point for all developing democracies. Egalitarians and their group dimension complicate the transition storyline; the social order does not simply shift from hierarchy to individualism. A focus on ascriptive culture and the fatalist response to it captures those political plots where group hierarchies are entrenched, reinforced, succumbed to, or resisted. When the power of group dynamics is taken into account, the status order and the uses to which it can be put by the political regime are brought from the background to the forefront of political analysis. We realize that emerging and developing societal cultures retain robust opportunities to make allegiance to a group the primary focus of an individual's political life.[42] Evidence for this is found in the Mormon case, in which an organic product of the American setting became a racialized "other" over the course of the late nineteenth century.[43] Attention to the context of group hierarchy challenges the too easy assumption that "the realization of the European secular nation-state" is an automatic, "necessary stage in Universal History."[44] More accurately, nudging a democratic regime toward fairness with respect to outsider group status is a matter of resistance and contestation conditioned by one abstracted story of peoplehood that dominates the majority societal culture. And because group life is so variable, so are the approaches to fairness in variable societal cultures.

Douglas's theory contains obvious parallels to Elazar's typology. Elazar focuses solely on how different cultures view government; he is less concerned than Douglas with the full spectrum of human cultural variation. Still there is great overlap between Elazar's traditionalistic culture and Douglas's hierarchical culture and between Elazar's individualistic culture and Douglas's individualist culture. Where they diverge is in Elazar's moralists, who combine Douglas's individualist and hierarchal cultures. It might be said that moralizers are simply individualists who feel empowered to correct in public those they consider their social inferiors; they are competitive individualists who stand with the majority culture and so do not feel the need to compromise.

Similarly, the severe group competition and fluid group pecking order in the United States also modified the egalitarian culture Douglas outlines. American egalitarians, when influenced by rationalist values and competitive settings, often espoused universalist varieties of egalitarianism, but they could also be influenced by traditional values or hierarchical settings, in which case they tended to revert back to group loyalty and emphasize their particularism. The former (universalist egalitarians) Elazar labels individualist and the latter (particularist egalitarians) traditionalists because of their view toward government. Thus, egalitarians disappear in Elazar's schema, perhaps because they pervade American societal culture overall. The strength of Douglas's model is not only its focus on egalitarians but also its ability to conceptualize variance.[45] Political cultures are tied to settings, and since settings evolve, the cultures evolve. Political actors and individuals live in groups, whose cultures are the modular building blocks of societal culture; group cultural cosmologies are constantly being creatively cut and spliced by party leaders and political retailers, behind which stands an implicit status order. The prize of regime power and the pressure of competition produce the great subcultural mixing and matching the American political system developed.

Bean's *Autobiography* details the Illinois status order. His account must be handled with care because it was penned long after the events he describes took place, but his inclusion of offhand comments and responses in unguarded moments offer a glimpse of how group prejudices and categories were understood at the time. Bean was a retired farmer in Utah by the time he got around to dictating his narrative. He was a child "noted for having a good memory," and his perception of the world was filtered through the prejudices he had absorbed.[46] A typical Adams County boy in many ways, he was born in 1831 to a Methodist father from Kentucky and a Presbyterian mother from Missouri. He tells of the many hardships the forced evacuation from Nauvoo caused his family, including the deaths of his sister and grandmother. His perspective also suggests that the Mormon experience could lead one to a broader tolerance of outsider groups. In the course of publishing the memoir, his daughter observed, "Our father always contended that the lack of wisdom on the part of the 'whites' caused all the trouble with the Indians."[47]

Bean's narrative is especially interesting because it recalls how his family members who had strong ties to other religious denominations perceived Mormons. He recounts the Mormons' expulsion from Missouri and notes that "the city of Quincy and Adams County, generally, became the temporary lodging place for many of that persecuted people."[48] His father had just built two new cabins at the time of the expulsion, and his family ended up hosting three Mormon refugee families. The idea that the Mormons were considered as a separate group, a distinct "people"—and one with connotations of impurity—is made clear by the moment when it was discovered that refugee George Gee, who was teaching the school the Bean children attended, had a wife whose cousin was Joseph Smith: "I recollect the shock it gave us when it leaked out [about his wife]. . . . What a risk of contamination we were in!"[49]

Bean playfully winks at unspoken ascriptive assumptions among his own parents, who likely derided Mormonism as a contagion. He discloses that he possessed "a religious turn of mind" and reports he was wholly persuaded by the doctrine he heard the Mormons preach in those early days.[50] The Mormon Tennessean mentioned above, Alexander Williams, grew up poor and desired to use his time in Illinois to become literate. Attending the local school with the Beans, he won the children over "with the spirit of the true gospel [which] he gently exercised . . . in his associations with us."[51] When Williams debated a Methodist preacher before a large audience at the Bean home around 1840, the family and three others were converted. Bean simply comments that the debate "resulted in a victory for truth," although "the people generally ignored the Gospel in its simplicity and plainness as given by Elder Williams and only those four families were converted."[52]

Bean's memoir provides a window into the world of worth he learned as an Illinois child and teen. A whole social pecking order is laid out. The Methodists and the Presbyterians were "popular" churches. Their ministers expressed "determined opposition" to the Mormons and expected to defeat Elder Williams in the debate using "larger words and learned sayings."[53] Mormon "simplicity and plainness" was attractive to some. Bean proceeds to catalog more distinctions. Because of his African American vernacular, Williams's grammar lessons were "very awkward."[54] In the nearby village of Mendon lived another distinct group, "settlers of the old Puritan type from New England states whose descendants [*sic*] . . . burned witches two hundred years before." Their town was a stop on the Underground Railroad and created tension with the "exasperated Missourians" from across the river. "By association with these people," Bean had his first "glimpse of runaway Negroes, peeping out from Deacon Stillman's barn [loft], or neighbor Fowler's cellar." The conversational fatalism of the escaped slaves contrasted with their active spirit of resistance. The anarchic, lawbreaking individualism of "the Puritans" combined with their prescriptive moralism, a combination, he concluded, that represented "the real original abolitionist spirit."[55]

Bean's narrative is one of toleration and accommodation by conversion—in this case of a majority religious family by individuals from a competing minority religious group. Eventually, the whole Bean family moved to Golden's Point, which was five miles below Nauvoo. Membership in the new group apparently made life in Adams County difficult and relocation to Hancock County imperative: "The mobocratic spirit prevailed to some extent [in 1841]. . . . Members of the church were advised to gather there [Nauvoo] and assist in the building of the temple."[56] Bean's story is one of group distance and attachment; it suggests that any telling of the Nauvoo prophecies and the anti-Mormon response should also emphasize the role of group life. But by highlighting its predominant liberal political culture, many scholars would have us view Illinois as a land of individualists. Clearly, the Illinois where Bean lived was not that place. While many state laws and institutions were formally liberal, an egalitarian attachment to groups was an independent social force that responded to and sometimes resisted ascriptive rules. As with the militia membership rules, the category of "individuals" the state would recognize was determined by particularist social norms. Those not recognized as worthy independent producers, those marked as outsiders whose agency was not recognized, had to navigate the local setting in search of doled-out accommodations.

For individuals, group setting similarly shapes how they experience and think about the state and society. The independent causal impact of group setting on individual thought and action indicates that while individuals form and shape groups, groups shape and form individuals as well; the causal arrow points in both directions. People living in a group setting become deeply committed to their proximal group and express a shared view of the world which emerges from and is reinforced by the group setting. Even groups committed by principle to a broad inclusion, like Bean's abolitionists, have their purview shaped by proximity; the Adams County abolitionists assisted runaway slaves from nearby Missouri counties. Ethically, a proximity of need blocks or diminishes recognition of the intensity of need urged elsewhere. The needs of strangers are often misrecognized, and even when recognition grows as groups mix pluralistically, as they did in frontier villages like Chicago in the 1820s or New Philadelphia for much of the nineteenth century, misrecognition frequently reappears when neighborhood boundaries develop.[57] In the case of a religious group like the Mormons, who sought to live separately from society, the impact of the communal group setting on individual commitment could be all-encompassing. Defense of the threatened group became defense of self.

MAKING SENSE OF MORMON SEPARATENESS

One of the confusing aspects of the story of Mormonism is the sect's complex combination of separating and integrating impulses. The logic of Christian separatism and denominationalism was explored in the 1920s by theologian H. Richard Niebuhr. He argued that the impulse toward sectarianism was set in motion as soon as Christians were directed by the Gospels to "permeate [the world] with the spirit of divine love."[58] Entering the world with the goal of changing it, simultaneously holding themselves to the otherworldly value of loving the poor while having to negotiate with the powers that be, meant that Christians were forced to compromise with the world from the start. Beginning with the Protestant Reformation, the pattern of dissenting groups forming and breaking off from their too-worldly Christian counterparts was repeated endlessly. Separatism was thus driven by the desire to distinguish an emerging reform group from both other Christians and the thoroughly corrupt world. Dissenters famously viewed themselves as specially authorized by God to lead the world to salvation, thus inviting a quarrel with other Christians as well as the larger society. During the early years of the Second Great Awakening, a succession of reform groups emerged—Shakers, Baptists, Methodists, Cumberland Presbyterians, Disciples of Christ—each auditioning a plan under which the church and the world would be restored. Some, like the Shakers and the Mormons, pursued the path of keeping separate from the world and other Christians in shared-property settlements and towns. Niebuhr notes that many such groups burned up in a fever of "utopianism, religious impressionism, and emotional mobility." The Mormons, unique among the separatists of the era, emphasized the rationality of their religion and their shared covenant with the nation; in Niebuhr's narrative, they were the "one . . . [separatist] group . . . under able leadership . . . able to survive . . . and form a really distinct and important denomination."[59]

The conflicting roles of separating from and guiding the world stemmed from the first days of Puritanism in America. As historian Perry Miller was at pains to point out, the first cohort of American divines in New England considered themselves sent on an "errand into the wilderness," not to set up a new church but to reform and lead the old one from which they came. They viewed themselves precisely as a nonseparating group, a branch of "Nonseparating Congregationalism."[60] The English Puritans from which these divines sprang had thoroughly reinterpreted the notion of the "covenant of grace" with God. It became very close to a rational proposition, carrying "the frontiers of reason to the very boundaries of faith." Miller put it this way: "They were careful to point out that regeneration cannot come by the intellect without the inspiration of grace, at the same time adding that the road to grace is also the highway of knowledge."[61] Thus the Puritans did not see themselves as separating from the English church and starting a new Protestant tradition so much as properly interpreting and redeeming the old one. In legal scholar John Witte Jr.'s summary, the American Puritans took a large step toward integrating with the mainstream: they emphasized not only the rationality of God's will but their duty to engage with the nation and lead it. They viewed "the political covenant . . . as a tri-party agreement between God, the civil ruler, and the people."[62] From this followed all the language of a national covenant and a shining city upon a hill.

The pattern of seeking leadership and hence needing to engage with worldly status was repeated endlessly in New England Puritanism, as was the predictable pattern of rebellion and separation which it spurred. The First Great Awakening, in the eighteenth century, has been described as a movement dissenting and in many cases separating from the mainstream form of "congregationalism . . . [which had become] the New England version of the English Establishment."[63] By the beginning of the nineteenth century, New England Christians had regrouped under a "Standing order" which aimed to lead the nation under a united Calvinist front.[64] Against this order the winds of democratization and disestablishment blew so strongly they broke the mold. The Mormons participated in this later rebellious, egalitarian movement while retaining the ideal of a national covenant and thus reaffirming God's special calling for the American nation. But where most redeeming millennialists were pessimistic about the future, Mormons retained an optimistic stance. Corrupt as the American world had been (the Book of Mormon relates the genocide of the once-believing Nephites) and corrupt as it had become in their own day, they retained the nonseparating hope that American Protestantism could be redeemed—indeed "Zion could be built only in the United Sates"—if it could be brought into the Mormon fold.[65]

In Illinois, Joseph Smith was able to get enough separation from American societal culture to institutionalize among his followers an alternative cosmology. In this sense the physical gathering and independent functioning of Nauvoo influenced Mormon separatism. The Mormons were not just utopian dreamers; they took advantage of the unsettled West to create, in historian Arthur Bestor's terms, a "patent-office model of society"—that is, they built a working model of their reform vision and tried to act out how their society would do things differently.[66] But if the Missouri and Illinois frontiers provided an opening for realizing their ideal, the act of living apart from the larger society emboldened the model's development. "The very separateness of the Mormon group," according to scholar of sociology and religious studies Thomas O'Dea, "removed them still further from the inhibitions that discouraged innovation in the general society."[67] According to this view, Smith's creative synthesis, once completed, spurred him on from a critique of the corrupt gentiles to an effort to master and control them. The final steps in this process came in the winter of

1844, when he formally announced his run for the US presidency, a campaign he had already hinted at as early as June of 1841.[68] It is only with hindsight that we see that this very act, necessary from the group's inner logic, left him and the saints unaffiliated with any party, unrepresented and thus unprotected in their struggle for toleration and accommodation. In the view of some settlers, the Mormons were a competitive and aggressive force vying to exert their own control over the Hancock County status order.

Mormon efforts to integrate often took the form of efforts to control. By crafting a unique national narrative, the Latter-day Saints attempted to integrate and to discipline the independent-producer story so important to Jacksonian America. The basic outlines of the Book of Mormon story highlight the Mormon belief that producerism plays a role in creating worth. Nephi's story frames the Lamanites (i.e., the Native Americans) as one among many once-chosen cultivator people who had fallen from the chosen path, a storyline the Mormon text reproduces endlessly.[69] As the basic narrative structure of the millennial jeremiad holds, once-chosen people who fell could repent, return to earlier ways, and repair their status.[70] The Native Americans, like the saints themselves, were eligible for redemption. At Far West, Missouri, just adjacent to the area across the frontier where President Andrew Jackson had resettled several Native American tribes, the Mormons opened a mission to work with the remnants of the fallen Lamanites. At Nauvoo, Smith sent letters to four separate tribal leaders to invite them to an "ancient of days" ceremony for the new "kingdom" he was organizing in June of 1842.[71] During the covert ceremony, Smith was crowned king and the Council of Fifty, an organizational unit within the church, named his court. Although the kingdom revelation was promulgated on April 7, 1842, in a nod to the Illinois way the prophet did not publicly organize the Council of Fifty until 1844 because he recognized that it was, as historian Klaus Hansen argues, antirepublican "political dynamite."[72]

As extraordinary as the role played by Native Americans in Mormon eschatology is, the saints' own commitment to producerism suggests a basic similarity with the typical Jacksonian view of the Indians. In the view put forward by Illinois governor William Lee D. Ewing, American settlers were justified in taking the Indians' land without consent or treaty.[73] For Ewing, as for most Illinoisans, worth in the community and claim to the land came via cultivation. In the Mormon story, seen by some as "unduly solicitous of the lowly Indian," the Native Americans could redeem their worth if they returned to the cultivation practices they once abandoned according to Mormon scripture.[74] A similar pluralist and inclusive approach is apparent in the Darnall family's relations with the Kickapoo in Livingston County and the mixed-race social life of frontier Chicago and New Philadelphia (see chapter 1). Once outsider groups signaled acceptance of the majority norm of cultivation as a route to worth, they could be accepted as insiders. As with the Jacksonian story of peoplehood, White cultivators in the Mormon story were valorized by their opposition to Indians, who had mere "occupancy" rights to the land, or by their efforts to convert hunter-gatherers to cultivation.

The area of civic worth that blocked Mormon inclusion was independence, as Mormons repeatedly failed the independence standard in tests administered and graded by locals. In Missouri it was not the Mormon attitude toward enslaved people and Indians that caused the problem, though it made conflict more likely by laying a foundation of mistrust; it was the Mormons' lack of deference to majority public opinion, whatever their views about those groups. Missouri governor Daniel Dunklin wrote during an early stage of the troubles in Missouri:

> Our neighbors accuse your people of holding illicit communication with the Indians, and of being opposed to slavery. You deny. Whether the charge or your denial is true, I cannot tell. The fact exists and your neighbors seem to believe it is true; and . . . unless you can, by your conduct and arguments, convince them of your innocence . . . the consequences will be the same. . . . If you cannot do this, all I can say to you is that in this Republic, the *vox populi* is the *vox dei*.[75]

In the governor's view, neighborhood opinion—thus his emphasis on "convinc[ing] them"—was the ultimate authority in a democracy. Historian Steven Harper argues cogently that Smith and the Mormons supplanted the authority of the people with the ultimate authority of revelation from God. Divinity replaced democracy.[76] Here was a foundational difference.

Still, it should not be overlooked how similar the particularist biases of the Mormon and the American Christian God were. The Mormon strategy of "universalizing the particular," of moving from the specifics of their particular case and generalizing them as natural and commonsensical for all, was a move shared by other denominations in the state, such as the antimission Baptists and the Christians (Disciples of Christ) who followed Alexander Campbell.[77] Mormons never stopped trying to persuade their neighbors that their god was an American republican and thus safe for democracy.[78] From this vantage point, divinity and democracy were one and the same. But in the end the effort failed, mainly because all but the dissenters within the Mormons proved tone-deaf to local definitions of independence within the Hancock status order. By repeatedly fielding Mormon candidates in local elections, for example, they were held to have failed to acknowledge the old settlers' rules of social and political recognition.

That at times the Mormons did offer a nod of deference to local majority belief—despite their group views—indicates that at some level they registered majority attitudes. They recognized that when their divergent beliefs were institutionalized and translated into actions, they needed to be kept out of view or at least out of conflict with majority practice. In the spring of 1839, Lyman Wight, president of a Missouri "stake"—the Mormon word for a branch of the church—wrote a letter to the *Quincy Whig* lambasting "not only the Democrats of Missouri, but all Democrats generally." Smith immediately interceded and wrote a counter letter apologizing to the Democrats of Quincy, many of whom were assisting refugees. He added, "We profess no authority [in party matters]. . . . It is not doing our cause justice to make a political question of it."[79] This stance, practical and true as far as it went, was evasive. Smith was able to disclaim authority only because God had ultimate control over the timing of the end-time. Still, as far as the Mormons could tell, both the Democrats and the Whigs were damned. Both organizations repeatedly failed to endorse Mormon prophecies and warnings about the last days. Papering over differences with rhetoric or emphasizing shared stories of producerism allowed an appearance of convergence. This is precisely the benefit of political rhetoric to all pragmatic thinkers interested in political compromise. But such incompletely theorized convergence in the liberal policy reached only to the means of life; hidden beneath in the Mormon case was a profound divergence over ends.

We can understand how deep the divergence was by looking more carefully at the details of Mormon theology and how it informed the Mormon leadership's worldview. The cosmic endpoint of their producerism was a spiritual goal, godhood. Here God created worth through a national covenant; worth was not earned through any worldly achievement, status, or civic identity.[80] One of Smith's prophecies, given as early as 1833, focused on "the light of truth," a kind of preexisting "intelligence" that God shares and which constitutes the "spirit" in man.[81] The saints were to access this intelligent truth not by their own free reason but by obedience to the truth revealed in the Bible and in Joseph Smith's revelations. Step-by-step revealed intelligence uncovered a pathway to immortality. On July 12, 1843, he announced a new revelation on the "plurality of wives," which specified how "if a man marry a wife . . . by the new and everlasting covenant, and it is sealed unto them by the Holy Spirit . . . [they] shall come forth in the first resurrection . . . [and] then shall they be gods, because they have no end."[82] Finally, there came the astounding King Follett sermon. It is not clear how many Mormon followers mastered all the details of "the bits and pieces of the Nauvoo metaphysical doctrines" summarized in this audacious sermon of April 1844, but the new whole was startling. "Joseph redefined the nature of God," Bushman posits. "God had a body and so should every [heavenly] person. . . . God's work was to organize the matter that had always existed. . . . God built earths and heavens as an artisan makes cabinets or houses and gave them to His children to use."[83]

While clearly much of the doctrine was new, the focus on the spiritual potential within each person bore a family resemblance to the perfectionism of Charles Grandison Finney, the most popular American preacher from the North's Burned-Over District, and Finney was echoing Immanuel Kant's reformed liberal celebration of the potential for autonomy within all people. But whereas Finney emphasized attaining moral independence and voluntary discipline by using reason to promote beneficence, Smith emphasized producing spiritual perfection through access to God's "intelligence."[84] "By using the word 'intelligence,'" Bushman concludes, "rather than 'reason' . . . Joseph's revelations bound the free intelligence to God rather than setting it free to reason for itself." While this theological move "combined the moral being of the Bible with the reasoning individual of the Enlightenment," it resulted in drastically different stances toward the world and life's ends. The "test of one's humanity" was not the degree of independent thought but the acceptance and cultivation of "the light coming from God."[85]

TABLE 4.1. GREENSTONE'S NINE DECLENSIONS OF PURITANISM

	AFFIRM RATIONALITY	AFFIRM RATIONALITY AND PIETY	AFFIRM PIETY
AFFIRM DUTIES TO POLITY	Colonial patriots	Halfway Covenant Presbyterians	Evangelistic nationalists
AFFIRM POLITY AND GRACE	Democratic nationalists	New England way	Evangelical reformers
AFFIRM INDIVIDUAL DUTY	Secular anarchists	Separating Protestants	Quakers

Adapted from *The Lincoln Persuasion*, 269

The faith/reason continuum is a telling way to situate the Mormons in the American religious firmament. In the matrix created by political scientist J. David Greenstone, Protestants in America can be found holding one of three positions on the conversion process—favoring piety, favoring rationality, or favoring some combination of both. Greenstone also highlights an additional continuum of the American Protestant worldview that proves crucial to political practice: whether individual and national covenants are made with God. Since on both continua groups can adopt a both-and outlook, not simply an either-or view, Greenstone produces a nine-frame matrix. In the both-and position on the piety/rationality dimension, for example, one could locate John Leland, the Baptist minister who presented Thomas Jefferson with a "Mammoth Cheese" in honor of his stand on the separation of church and state. Leland, who preached throughout New England in the 1820s and whose views may well have influenced Smith, argued that both faith and reason were needed for salvation.[86] It was a view shared by the Mormons, who, falling in the middle of the faith/reason continuum, occupied a median position on this dimension.

On the covenant dimension, the Mormons again occupy a median spot—arguing for both individual (or family-based) covenants with God and a national covenant, although one the American gentiles were in danger of losing unless they repented soon. In an often-told story capturing both of these dimensions, Smith and former Campbellite Sidney Rigdon reported in 1838 that "daily and hourly they were asked by all classes of people . . . will everybody be damned but the Mormons?" Smith's answer was straightforward: "Yes, and a great portion of them, unless they repent and work righteousness."[87] The median placement on Greenstone's model, essentially occupying the same theological space as the seventeenth-century Presbyterians and the Puritans of the Halfway Covenant, suggests just how average many aspects of Mormon theology were.[88] Average as they were, it should not be denied that damning your neighbors to hell is unpopular and extremely annoying. When the Jehovah's Witnesses adopted a similar stance in the late 1930s, they elicited similar consternation and violence from their neighbors. As philosopher Zechariah Chafee summarizes, such sects are "distinguished by great religious zeal and an astounding power of annoyance."[89]

Illinois shared in the Jacksonian regime's reordering of the federal government's policy priorities on the public role of religion. In the national Sabbatarian debate, Democratic senator Richard Mentor Johnson prevailed in Congress using arguments about the need to steer clear of religious controversy and to avoid bias in religious policy.[90] While many stood firm with the claim that the United States was "a Christian nation," a widespread "democratization" was taking place in which many of the assumptions of the American Protestant establishment were being contested by a disestablishment movement led in the North by "religious enthusiasts" like Baptist Elias Smith.[91] He challenged his followers to embrace a true liberty of conscience: "Many are *republicans* as to *government,* and yet are but half republicans, being in matters of religion still bound to a catechism, creed, covenant or superstitious priest."[92] The Mormons saw themselves as a part of this large antiestablishment movement. Joseph Smith never tired of denouncing the "priests" of other denominations, and his response was to make every man eligible to be a priest or elder in the Mormon "order of Aaron." All these actions were indeed signs of a political regime change which, for many in the established order, meant "that a spiritual free-for-all had replaced a cosmic order."[93]

In response, religious denominations of the "Standing Order" of Congregationalists and Presbyterians fought back. Lyman Beecher, for one, started a crusade to reform a nation fallen away from Jesus Christ. This was the start of a new theology of activism, birthing many civic reform movements grouped under the Second Great Awakening—temperance and antislavery most prominent among them. In addition to these movements, a new space had opened up for out-groups like the Methodists and Baptists to proselytize. In this development, the Methodists and Baptists ended up with quite different views of the degree to which simple membership in larger units like the nation and the human race made salvation possible. In Warsaw on June 7, 1841, a dialogue between two preachers summarized the Baptist-Methodist disagreement by posing three debate questions: Did Jesus Christ die for all men? Is salvation provided for all men? And is final apostasy possible? The Baptists answered "no, no, no"; the Methodists, "yes, yes, yes."[94] Methodists and some missionary Baptist reformers like Elias Smith found great traction with an Arminian, or salvation through works, doctrine. The Methodists' first two yeses were inclusive, but the last meant that faith alone was not enough for salvation. Calvinist Baptists in the antimission camp and groups like the Mormons reasserted the old foreordination position. The Baptists' last no meant that faith or election by God alone was necessary and sufficient for salvation. The Baptist view, reduced to a mere logical conclusion, as theologians are loath to do, amounted to antinomianism. Joseph Smith himself tried to revise against that conclusion by authorizing members in the church with temple rites to secure baptism for the dead. In-groups like the Unitarians did their own revising, arguing for a "yes, yes, no" position in which Jesus showed the way for all humans to achieve a divine perfection and offered unlimited mercy for the inevitable failures along the way.

It is in this context that the appeal to the socially marginalized and the competitive advantages of Mormon millennialism can be understood.[95] Both Joseph Smith and Charles Finney were committed to Christian millennialism—a theme taken from the book of Daniel in the Old Testament and the book of Revelation in the New Testament in which Jesus Christ would return to the earth and rule with the saved for one thousand years. This way of reading the Bible began with those ancient Jews who read God's election not simply as "a moral responsibility . . . to show justice and mercy in their dealings with all men" but as a literal call to rule the fallen world. As historian Norman Cohn puts it, "Precisely because they were so utterly certain of being the Chosen People, Jews tended to react to peril, oppression and hardship by phantasies of total triumph and boundless prosperity which Yahweh, out of his omnipotence, would bestow upon his Elect in the fullness of time."[96] However, a significant tension ran down the center of this tradition, a division between what scholars call "Apocalypticism," whose followers subscribed to an immediate or very near apocalypse, and those believing in a more distant endgame. The "restoration impulse" or belief in the end-time, what today we call millennialism, ran the gamut from a short-term premillennial view to a long-term postmillennial view, a continuum that can be traced back to St. Augustine.[97] He interpreted the book of Revelation to mean that the end-time referred to was metaphorical, a view replaced by successive waves of Protestant theology culminating in a broadly shared, more immediate view. The Mormons vacillated at times but tended to err on the side of immediacy. Joseph Smith at one point noted that "45 years" would be enough to wrap up the drama.[98]

Literary scholar Sacvan Bercovitch emphasizes that starting with the Puritans and continuing to today, American Protestants have nationalized the redemptive covenant God made with the elect. Sermons urging the elect to persevere among the fallen were early on extended to refer to a national covenant. Over time, the jeremiads exhorting people to repent became American in scope.[99] America was the "redeemer nation," a claim that few cared to controvert and which secularists like Herman Melville embraced.[100] In Illinois this led to a consensus among the leading sects that God was not only an American but also a democrat. Differences could be finessed over when the end would come and whether the world would first have to be redeemed through worldly reform (postmillennialism) or whether corruption would cause the end, after which God would intervene (premillennialism). The force of the broader consensus was such that national redemption could fit many different sects—from the Fourth of July oration by a Catholic priest in Galena, who enjoined his audience to remember their "duty to expand [benevolence] among those with whom [they were] particularly united in one society," to Smith's sermon explaining baptism for the dead.[101]

Given the predominance of the Calvinist tradition in American Protestantism, millennial themes had become a kind of religious lingua franca. But as the protests of the Standing Order made clear, when the nation entered the nineteenth century this shared "cosmos" began to crumble into several different persuasions. The Unitarians cast off predestination on the supposition that it was unreasonable to assume God would create a whole set of humans only to have them forever cast off into hell. Finney came to the same conclusion by focusing not on reason but on sentiment;

caring for others and helping them self-govern was a sign of personal salvation. As he put it, "All sin consists in selfishness; and all holiness or virtue in disinterested benevolence. . . . To the universal reformation of the world [the saints] stand committed."[102] In both cases a postmillennial approach developed wherein the end of days would begin only after the Christians finally improved the world enough for Christ to take over. Lyman Beecher doubted the staying power of this kind of Arminian salvation through works driven by individual sentiment; he emphasized the nation as the millennial unit and America's "cosmic drama," which would be won by public reformation. But the texts the American Bible Society distributed with Beecher's approval spurred Sabbatarian, temperance, and antislavery reform movements, which were inspired by many merely whipped up by emotion at one of Finney's revival meetings. Of course, these reform movements could also be urged on secular grounds, as we saw in the case of Lincoln's endorsement of the Washingtonians in a speech delivered in the Second Presbyterian Church in Springfield.

The social gap between secular Whigs like Lincoln and evangelicals like Finney was much narrower than the gap between pre- and postmillennialists. Lincoln could endorse the Washingtonians, whom Finney and Beecher praised on religious grounds, while the prophet's wife Emma Smith decreed the group to be irredeemably corrupt. Arrayed against reform-minded postmillennialists like Finney and Beecher stood the Disciples of Christ, led by Ohioan Alexander Campbell, and the antimission Baptists, led by Illinoisan Daniel Parker. Among these groups, the last days were read to be literally near at hand, as the Jews in olden times had claimed. For the antimission Baptists, this meant that all contemporary religious forms were corrupt; the goal was the "restoration" of the pure and simple forms of the first Christians. This was a very attractive stance for a society steeped in classical republicanism, with its emphasis on the purity and simplicity of the sacrifice needed for independence and on time as a worldly entangler and corrupter of virtue.[103] To the literalist premillennialists, the allegorical turn in Bible reading, so favored by postmillennialists like Finney and Beecher, was precisely the problem. This literalist strain was attractive to many left behind in the increasingly literate and rapidly mobilizing nation. But in a new regime endorsing open competition among religious sects, the Mormons had developed a flawless strategy for winning the battles to convert the masses by claiming to do Campbell and Parker one better. As Parley Pratt related in his *Autobiography,* when he first encountered the Mormons in Ohio, he rejoiced that he "had now found men on earth commissioned to preach, baptize, ordain to the ministry, etc" and was "determined to obey the fulness of the gospel without delay."[104] The ancient gospel was restored not on the authority of success in a petty denominational debate but on the authority of God's word in the Book of Mormon.

The idea that Mormons had "the truth," the literal truth with no "twistifications," was palpable in early Mormon discourse.[105] It mattered that they could establish a lineal connection to the biblical past. This was apparent in Smith's desperate prison-cell letters to Isaac Galland and in the Doctrine and Covenants listing the exact ages and deeds of Adam and his heirs down to the present-day appearance of the angel Moroni and Smith's prophecies. It was crucial to Pratt that the Mormons could claim, as "it was plain the Baptists could not . . . the apostolic office by succession, in a regular, unbroken chain from the Apostles of old."[106] It also seemed important to Pratt that the Book of Mormon was prefaced by "the testimony of several witnesses in relation to the manner of its being found and translated."[107] While many were not persuaded by an emphasis on literal fact, scholar Terryl L. Givens argues that it is precisely this guarantee of "provenance," a literal linking of the saints directly to Adam and his inheritance, which made the doctrine attractive to many others.[108] It added a degree of certainty to salvation that was compelling to people in unstable worldly circumstances and for whom the "thousand and one twistifications" of reformed Protestantism sounded a false note. Indeed, Tocqueville had warned of the attraction of such doctrines to all people who had lost their provenance living in "democracy . . . which makes every man forget his ancestors . . . hides his descendants, and separates his contemporaries from him."[109] Just as the everyman sucker headed to Illinois searching for the main chance at fee simple independence, so the saints came to Illinois for the main chance at fee simple salvation.

Yet it was their certainty that blinded the Mormons to much hostile public opinion among the "original settlers" in Hancock County. Their pursuit of the truth, their purchase on God's "knowledge," made everything else lose focus. However the Mormons might have copied and shared the forms of republicanism in militia laws, Masonic rites, and guarantees like freedom of the press, they missed the signs of worth their fellow local citizens invested in these forms. The new politics of belief spawned by a world of sectarian pluralism resulted in a wonderful diversity of religious disestablishment running the spectrum of neo-Kantian believers from anarchist abolitionists to communitarian Shakers; but for most of these groups, the ends of life were fixed; the goal was redemption of the national covenant. The Mormons took an opposite tack: they joined the nation by sharing its organizational means and forms—presidents, councils, teachers—but their end truth, set down by the Book of Mormon and other prophecies, was so particular to their calling as a people—even as an American people—that it overshadowed any organizational family resemblance.

If not outside of the traditional norm, the Mormons were, like the antimission Baptists, at least out of step with their most influential peers. Could they be labeled outliers merely because they reasserted the Puritan view that the good citizen was damned to hell? The Puritan divine Thomas Hooker had condemned "the civil man" who was "outwardly just, temperate, chaste, carefull to follow worldly businesse . . . [who] will not hurt so much as his neighbours dog . . . [who] pays every man his own; [is] no drunkard, adulterer, or quarreler; [and] loves to live peaceably and quietly among his neighbours."[110] The Mormons and the Puritans agreed that good morality was not the same thing as good religion, and "salvation was unattainable by good behavior."[111] Or were the Mormons outliers because they taught that even those "saved" in other Protestant denominations would not receive "fulness in the eternal world"?[112] The antimission Baptists, one of the most prominent sects in Illinois in the 1820s and 1830s, took an even more extreme stand in the version of their creed authored by Daniel Parker. His "Two Seed" doctrine elaborated that the seed of Cain and the seed of Abel, one of Satan and the other of Christ, were indelibly part of the world. The Two Seed doctrine was rejected by free will Baptists and Methodists but helped power the antimission movement, which had over forty-five thousand adherents, mainly in the Wabash Valley, between Illinois and Indiana, by the 1840s.[113] The doctrine divided the world into two camps, those purely good and those purely evil, one group intrinsically motivated by love and the other solely motived by self-interest and gain. Mormons at this time were also strongly dualist, though during times when they were accepted by outsiders, their emphasis on the immediate and general damnation of the gentiles could become quite muffled.[114] Despite these short-term aberrations during good times, most scholars place them in the premillennialist camp.[115] This should simply tell us that, especially among the poor and unschooled, the Mormons' premillennial "flight from pluralism," far from distinguishing them, actually indicated their place in the mainstream.[116]

But making sense of Mormon separateness is one thing; making sense of Joseph Smith is another. There are times when Smith was pushed by the need to retain group members' loyalty—or by misrecognition of who the real group was—to revise his theology. Here is the influence of group life as an independent variable. When a group attempts to make its own civic narrative and governing regime, it needs to plan broadly. It may have been easy to dismiss the unrepentant to hell, but what about the friends and family of the Mormons who did not believe? Smith had an answer: "One dies and is buried, having never heard the Gospel of reconciliation; to the other the message of salvation is sent, he hears and embraces it, and is made the heir of eternal life. Shall the one become the partaker of glory and the other be consigned to hopeless perdition? Is there no chance for his escape? Sectarianism answers 'none.' Such an idea is worse than atheism."[117] But Mormonism had the doctrine of baptism for the dead. Here Smith opened up a unique theology of inclusion that was typical of egalitarians looking inward—equality for all members.

Smith must have known he had hit organizational gold when he first articulated the baptism for the dead prophecy. As noted, the rite created an incentive for finishing the temple project. But as Smith looked outward, as a member of the American people, the Lamanite story did the work of repressing doubts about greed, hiding in the shadows the sin of the American settlers taking land from the Indigenous people in the first place. Here was the classic case of a failed attempt to universalize the particular. A similar refusal to acknowledge the flawed masculine justification of male control over the family came in the theological defense of plural marriage. As newcomer Udney Hay Jacob put in a document published at Nauvoo in 1842, "Adam was enslaved by the woman, not by the serpent in the first instance."[118] Here was a biblical way to justify the unequal authority of men and women in the otherwise egalitarian group. The conception of the feminine as inherently weak and sinful occludes the grasping shadow side of masculinity asserting its priority. Scholars following Mary Douglas's idea of egalitarianism call this the subculture's "dark side."[119]

THE MORMONS CHALLENGE SETTLER CONVENTIONS

If there is any truism in liberal democratic politics, it is that while differences over ends can be negotiated or papered over with broad rhetoric, conflicts at the institutional level are sticky and hard to avoid. Political ideals and theology are easy to manipulate; the consequences of actions in institutional settings are not. They are more glaring and real because so often they cannot be avoided. How then did it happen on the ground and in fact? How did the Mormons fail to adjust to the local setting? Almost two hundred years later we are interested in these questions because their answers uncover patterns in political development and critical junctures we can note and hopefully avoid in the future. There were many junctures in the local response to the Mormon presence and the Mormon reaction, but let us consider two early ones: the Mormon threat to the local convention of cooperating with outsiders to arrest thieves, which culminated in the Tully kidnapping of July 7, 1840, and the Mormon rejection of the local convention on proper settlement patterns.

The Tully affair was the first in which the Mormons were seen as posing a challenge to local convention on vigilantism. Four Mormons who were collecting firewood in the bottomlands near the Mississippi River were accused of stealing goods consigned to Wilson and Stewart Tully of Missouri by a group of Missourians who had armed themselves and come over to reclaim the goods.[120] The four Mormons were abducted, taken across the river to the Missouri side, and severely beaten. The Missourians had learned that a hidden cache of stolen goods had been uncovered nearby and "attributed all these thefts to the Mormons, and coming across four of them . . . forcibly and without warrant . . . tied them up to trees, stripped and beat them in a most shameful and cruel manner."[121] The Mormons thought they were being chastised and humiliated simply for being Mormon. They were tried and found guilty simply because of association and being in the wrong place at the wrong time.

This is the usual fate of members of subaltern castes who happen to be found by a vigilante group out for revenge. Later in the fall of the same year, a similar outbreak occurred on the Iowa side of the river in Dubuque: "A worthless character having stated that he had lost a quantity of clothing, the theft was charged upon an inoffensive Negro man named Nat. The Negro denied the charge. A mob assembled and publically tied him up on the landing before the town, and administered no less than 300 lashes on his bare back."[122] After several extorted confessions, Nat died. Episodes like these were far from uncommon in newly settled areas—as all frontier Iowa was at the time. Order was supplied as a public good by volunteers, and those without connections to local majority groups were subject to the whims of vigilante justice.

Perhaps the heart of this lawless zone was Montrose, Iowa, across the Mississippi River from Nauvoo, and already by 1840 long considered a town of desperados. There were three dangerous rapids over an eleven-mile run on the main river from just south of Montrose all the way to Keokuk, a place Iowa sheriff Hawkins Taylor called "a men wrecker town." The whole stretch of the river was populated by workers freighting cargo and passengers along the portage. The workers experienced brief periods of intense employment followed by long idle hours, not a recipe for inculcating steady habits. Sheriff Taylor remembered that "among their number was the worst class of men to be found, murderers and gamblers and thieves of every class. Some of them had belonged to Murral's Clan of desperadoes."[123] Another clan in the area, "the old Brown gang of bandits," who specialized in counterfeiting, later executed an especially brazen robbery and attempted murder of Colonel George Davenport at Rock Island in the middle of the day on the Fourth of July 1845.[124]

Thomas Ford, before he became governor, worked as a state's attorney and later as a circuit riding supreme court judge taking appeals throughout the northern third of the state. He recalled that Isaac Galland, the man who sold the Mormons their land at Commerce, ran in 1834 for the Hancock County General Assembly seat without hiding the fact that "he had in the early part of his life been a notorious horse thief and counterfeiter, belonging to the Massac gang." He was no "pretender to integrity . . . [as] it was useless to deny the charge." Ford made clear that he was not surprised that the Mormons had migrated to Hancock County. It was marked by its river "wrecker" reputation: "Having passed my whole life on the frontiers, on the outer edge of the settlements, I have frequently seen that a few first settlers would fix the character of a settlement for good or bad for many years. . . . Rogues will find each other and so will honest men."[125] It should be noted that Ford himself had been tempted by lawlessness to reciprocate with vigilantism of the local majoritarian variety. In a famous case over which he presided as circuit judge in Ogle County, "Judge Ford declared from the bench, in reference to threats which had been made against himself by the accomplices of certain horse thieves and counterfeiters, that if his family were molested . . . he would upon his return assemble his friends and take summary vengeance."[126]

But why did Ford put the Mormons in the category of horse thieves? The fact is petty theft was a bad habit the Mormons brought with them from Missouri. Evidence for this comes from many sources but especially from within the anti-Mormon camp. Thomas Gregg, for example, claimed that "no sooner had these people [the Mormons] settled amongst us than they commenced those petty acts of stealing and other depredations upon property which were charged against them everywhere, and which were so annoying to their neighbors and provocative of hostility."[127] It is not surprising that Gregg, who later became a leading anti-Mormon, would make this claim. But several third-party observers confirmed the suspicion. The editor of the *Western World* at Warsaw reported the following in July of 1840: "During the winter and last spring various petty thefts were perpetuated in various parts of the county which many persons attributed to the Mormons they having lately come into the county and suffering under the odium of similar conduct in Missouri. With what justice these charges were made we know not, and do not know that there is any evidence to substantiate them. We merely state the facts as a matter of history."[128]

Another confirmation comes from Sheriff Taylor. He believed the Mormons took advantage of the power of their numbers in Nauvoo to avoid paying for stock and grain they pilfered from nearby communities outside the city. His recollection was recorded in a memoir written at the end of his life:

> Nauvoo . . . in everything but . . . religion and moral practices, was a model city. The homes were all painted, there was no idling, no profanity or drunkenness, but they held that they were chosen people of the Lord, that all things belonged to the Lord. . . . Each man was required to work every tenth day on the temple or pay for the hire of a substitute. Besides this, several hundred men were hired to work on the temple. These men had to be fed. To do this, they lived on the Smith

> [stolen] cattle, sheep, and grain of all kinds. . . . The people had no remedy. The Mormons were the majority in the county and had all the officers of importance. If a writ was taken out, the officer was whittled out of the city. The process of whittling out an officer was as follows: a great tall man by the name of [Hosea] Stout was the captain of the Whittling society, and he had about a dozen assistants. They all had great bowie knives and would get a long piece of pine board and get up close to the officer and pretend to be cutting the pine board, but would cut over it and cut near the officer. In the meantime, small boys would get tin pans, old bells, and all sorts of things to make a noise with and surround the officer. No one would touch or say a word to him, but the noise drowned all that he would say. The result was that he would get out of the city as soon as possible and never come back again. The Mormons would send teams out, load [them] with what they found and take it before the eyes of the owner.

The accuracy of Taylor's account in many particulars can be confirmed. He added that he believed he was "the only officer that ever took a prisoner from Nauvoo without being whittled out, but the Mormons were anxious to keep on good terms with the people of Iowa, while they were at war with Missouri and Illinois."[129] Fifty years later, settler Forest Walker conducted oral histories of surviving settlers in rural Hancock County and published them in the local paper. The story told by Pontoosuc Township resident William McAuly of his father is typical:

> My father had two fine young horses taken off of the prairie west of our house (as everybody turned their stock out to graze in those days), and we hunted for them in the timber and in the bottom lands, but could not hear of them. They were gone for good. Father was inclined to sympathize—as nearly everybody, at the time, did—with the Mormons; as they told some rough tales of how they had been run out of the slave state by the people who lived over in Missouri. . . . At the time the two horses went missing, he would not lay the taking of them to the Saints. At another time—perhaps a year afterwards—he had a fine young horse stolen, and the thief, in making for Nauvoo, kept well into the timber, and getting down well into Appanoose Township, he ran

> into some anti-Mormons. Among them was Alexander Martin, who knew the horse and wanted to know why he was riding Mr. McAuly's horse. "I got him up in Poutoosuc, and I am taking him to Nauvoo." "Well, that is not yours, and you must get down and let me have him, and I will take him back home." "I guess you'll not get the horse: I've got it now and propose to keep it. The Lord told me where it was, and sent me after it. I received orders from the church to go and get him."

In the end, the horse was returned, and William added: "We were always satisfied after that that the Mormons got the other two horses." Walker summarized that "from that hour . . . Mr. McAuly, with his son William, gave much of their time and aid toward getting rid of their troublesome neighbors."[130]

A Mormon insider perspective that dovetails with these remembrances is provided by John D. Lee. Living on Luck Creek in Fayette County, Illinois, in 1837, Lee invited a Mormon elder to preach at his house. In that same year his second daughter and only living child died of scarlet fever, and Lee noted: "The night she laid a corpse, I finished reading the Book of Mormon. I never closed my eyes in sleep from the time I commenced until I finished the book. . . . By careful examination I found that it was in strict accord with the Bible and the gospel therein contained." Lee was a believer in rational religion. When he later traveled to Missouri in June of 1838 to join the saints, his traveling companion from Illinois wanted to go immediately to a "prayer and testimony meeting" where there might be speaking in tongues and the feeling of the spirit. Lee did not attend. He related the following about why he chose not to do so: "I want no signs; I believe the gospel they preach on principle and reason, not upon signs—its consistency is all I ask. All I want are natural logical and reasonable arguments, to make up my mind from."[131] Lee was pleased with his new fellow converts: "The motives of the people who composed my neighborhood were pure; they were all sincere in their devotions and tried to square their actions through life by the golden rule. . . . I was proud to be associate with such an honorable people."[132]

But he soon found that not all Mormons acted honorably. Lee recalled observing the Mormon practice of stealing from the gentiles soon after the war in Missouri broke out: "The burning of houses, farms, stacks of grain was generally indulged in by each party. Lawlessness prevailed and pillage was the rule." Sometimes, Lee believed, the behavior was justified. As he remembered, "The Prophet, Joseph Smith, said it was a civil war; that by the rules of war each party was justified in spoiling his enemy. [But t]his opened the door to the evil disposed, and the men of former quiet became perfect demons in their efforts to spoil and waste away the enemies of the Church." He was stunned to learn that "the first moment when the restrictions of the Church were withdrawn, the most devout men in our community acted like they had served a lifetime in evil, and were natural born thieves." He later decided that "the men who stole then were really not honest, for I spotted every man that I knew to steal during the troubles in Missouri and Illinois, and I have found that they never really were converted, were never true Saints."[133]

After a season as a missionary, Lee settled with his family at Nauvoo and recalled Smith's April 1840 sermon against thievery. "We are no longer at war, you must stop stealing."[134] Lee's comments on this sermon are intriguing:

> The Prophet talked to us plainly, and fully instructed us in our duty and gave the long-faced hypocrites such a lecture that much good was done. I had at that time learned to dread a religious fanatic, and I was pleased to hear the Prophet lay down the law to them. A fanatic is always dangerous but a religious fanatic is to be dreaded by all men—there is no reason in one of them. I cannot understand how men will blindly follow fanatical teachers. I always demanded a reason for my belief, and hope I will never become a victim of fanaticism.[135]

Lee would likely have ascribed the practice of the Mormon horse thief in Pontoosuc Township to fanaticism. Nothing in Mormon doctrine claimed, for example, that God would tell you where feral horses could be found or that enemies' bullets could not harm you. Lee ascribed those beliefs to irrational folk additions or conceits of power-loving Mormons like Sidney Rigdon.[136]

But Lee himself was not immune to the boost he got when, as a member of the Danites, he saw the secret "sign or token of distress" from one in the know. During those times Lee felt "like Sampson." He wrote, "I felt the power of God nerve my arm for the fray." Another time "a single black bird came to us apparently in great distress." He ignored it the first two times it came—but prayed for it to return a third time if it was a true sign, and it did, and so he obeyed the message he thought it brought.[137] So by "fanaticism" Lee did not mean belief in the power of the group or the intervention of God in the ordinary course of nature but the belief that such power and intervention could be commandeered to suit personal interest. The word *fanaticism* was used frequently in Illinois at this day, but it could take on a variety of meanings. In 1842, Lincoln defined a "fanatic" as a person who "desires a union of Church and State" in his temperance address to the Washingtonians at Springfield.[138] By this definition the Mormons crossed the threshold of fanaticism the day Smith announced his run for president, but the line was crossed locally as soon as the first Mormon thief was protected by city government. The problem fanaticism caused locally was explained in the Missouri context by the editor of the *New Era* at St. Louis: "With [the Mormons] as with other deluded fanatics, a crime committed for the good of the church is a glorious act, and the greatest evidence of zeal for religion consists in their efforts to protect Mormon believers from the persecutions of the Gentiles."[139]

The Tully affair brought the issue of stealing into the newspapers and out to the public at large. The Mormons responded publicly. On December 1, 1841, the Mormon paper *Times and Seasons* published an editorial commending "the very energetic measures taken by our citizens to suppress thieving." In the same edition, Hyrum Smith published an affidavit condemning as a falsehood the idea, maliciously instilled "in the minds of good and worthy citizens in the state of Illinois, . . . that the First Presidency, and others in authority and high standing [in the Church of Jesus Christ of Latter-day Saints] do sanction and approbate the members of said church from stealing property from those who do not belong to said church."[140] On their public face, the Mormons wore the countenance of a people committed to equal justice under the law.

It was a commitment many Hancock County residents also believed. Thomas Sharp, for example, the new editor of the *Western World,* initially adopted a welcoming stance toward the Mormons. In January of 1841 he reported that Bennett had returned from Springfield triumphantly with his three "liberal" charters and noted the prophet's call to gather at Nauvoo. He included the "proclamation by the presidents of the church" that the Nauvoo Legion would "enable [Mormons] to show [their] attachment to the state and nation as a people." Sharp then added:

> Whatever may be thought of the tenets of their sect, it is certainly a spectacle to witness the moral power which in so short a period they have exerted. . . . Their converts are continually flocking to this new city. What might be the ultimate result will be impossible to divine. But a few years ago the Mormons were regarded as a set of thieves . . . but now that their numbers are concentrating, they begin to assume, at least in this state, a political and moral importance possessed by no other denomination.[141]

Already present in these comments, however, was an issue Sharp would soon be unable to ignore: the problem of "numbers . . . concentrating." Although only twenty-two when he came to Warsaw in 1840 as a newly certified attorney from Pennsylvania, Sharp had a systematic—some would say obsessive—mind that had uncovered a flaw in the Mormon foundation, a problem of which thievery was just a symptom. This was the very separateness of the Mormons as a religious community. A charitable view of the increased acts of stealing and their relation to Nauvoo was that the Mormons had a quality control problem; not all their converts had been properly converted, as Lee would have it. Instead of emphasizing the need for better group regulation, however, Sharp quickly focused on a structural problem, one that needed a structural solution. The Mormons claimed "the protection due to other [religious] denominations," but unlike in other religions, they mix "politics and religion." Here was an asymmetry an individualist like Sharp could not brook; it was unfairly one-sided and so undermined trust. The Mormons could not have it both ways, especially when the prophet could "command them to settle where he please[d]."[142]

Although he likely did not know it, Sharp was echoing a longstanding Illinois convention. The writer James Hall, previously a Democratic editor and Illinois state treasurer, had opined on this view more than a decade earlier in the pages of his popular *Illinois Monthly Magazine*. He had engaged in a debate on the topic of group immigration back in 1831, well before any of the Mormon conflicts began. He focused on the earlier tension created in the state by New Englanders who had settled communally, which diverged from the upland southern tradition of mixed settlements, an Illinois convention since the earliest American immigrants. He believed it was right for newcomers to defer to the norms and practices existing in their chosen state. He argued:

> When a company of people . . . set down in a country in such a way as to excite unpleasant feelings in those around them, they will not be apt to exert any salutary influence on their neighbors. There is an appearance of arrogance in the conduct of those who settle in the heart of a civilized community of their own countrymen, but yet in a new country to them, and bring with them their *own society*, their *own mechanics*, their *own customs*, and affect a kind of independence of the civil community already organized.[143]

Hall, who also wrote fiction, was almost certainly not thinking of the Mormons when he wrote this. He was thinking about northern immigrants and others like the English who settled in colonies. His ideal was what we would call today the melting pot or assimilationist model of immigration. He explained the experiences behind his reasoning:

> When such persons come in societies, they associate too much with each other, and too little with the other residents of the country, and thus deprive themselves of the opportunity of profiting by the example of the older settlers. The very object of forming a society of this description is that its members shall mutually aid each other in their business, and form a circle of the purposes of social intercourse. In this manner they preserve their own language, and instead of having their prejudices and customs worn off by collision with the people of the country, they keep alive these very customs and prejudices, by the countenance and encouragement which they afford to each other, and even feel a pride in retaining this distinctive character. Their settlement gets a name—it is called *the Dutch*, or *the English settlement*. . . . We wish to see them come to Illinois, with a manly confidence in us, and with the feelings, not of New Englanders, or Pennsylvanians, but as Americans.[144]

Here the power of "the older settlers" at the local level was justified on grounds of national identity. The norms of civic worth should be set by the local majority, Hall implied; they should be accepted implicitly by new immigrants because the local variant of civil society replicates in particular form the national narrative of worth and belonging. The Yankees were less tolerated because they lived in settlements—separately as it were. Of course, many small settlements were not frowned upon and partisan attachment could play a role in recognition. Benjamin Mills, editor of the *Northwestern Gazetteer and Galena Advertiser,* praised a "colony of fifty families from New England and New York" for their "moral and intellectual worth." He approved their group settlement "along a beautiful tract of 25 sections . . . near the Mackinaw River in the County of Tazewell."[145] But here Mills demonstrated his Whig dissent from the dominant Democratic majority, which he no doubt hoped would soon be overturned.

As the autobiography of George Washington Bean makes clear, the abolitionists and Mormons were both perceived as distinct communities and noted for their separate settlements. Just as he predicted, they were viewed by Illinoisans as being distinct from "the older settlers" in part because they lived separately and were "Down Easters." Sharp's argument that the Mormons were not properly deferring to majority belief was picked up in the Whig papers. On January 21, 1841, for example, the editor of the *Sangamo Journal* wrote: "Mr S[mith] is supposed by his followers to be a Prophet of the Most High God. Whether he is or not, is no matter of dispute at present; but as such Prophet, he is held in the highest veneration by his followers." Thus, when he announced how he would vote, they all followed suit. "We have no objection that they should act individually and independently, as their conscience dictates . . . [but parroting the vote of their leader is] perversive of the privileges of a citizen."[146]

This first local flare-up against the Mormons continued to rage until the influence of the statewide parties interceded. The Whigs were poised to win back Mormon support and wanted to quiet the anti-Mormon voice. By January of 1843, Sharp was induced to put his pen down and pick up farming. The new editors of the *Warsaw Signal* explicitly aimed to make the paper a party organ. Smith, and certainly his brother William Smith, editor of *The Wasp,* misjudged this as a retreat of local power altogether. In fact many Whig Party members were quite worried about the Mormon influence. The party's conflict with the sect dated back to early 1840, when, as Thomas Gregg notes, Joseph Smith got the Whigs to remove

Martin Hopkins of Fountain Green and replace him with Dr. John F. Charles on the Whig slate of local candidates. Candidate nomination was the lynchpin of party control of government. The Whigs could not allow such interference to continue, yet a second intervention transpired in the August 1840 election for president. Smith wanted to vote for his friend James Ralston as a presidential elector, even though he represented Van Buren and the Mormons had come out for Harrison. A third case of meddling occurred when the Whigs nominated a representative to the Iowa legislature in 1840.[147] Thus, while in the summer of 1839 Smith was saying publicly that the sect did not meddle in politics, three counter instances appearing so soon after his claim argued for the opposite conclusion.

Smith's maneuvers and the group settlement pattern indicated that the Mormons were flouting the regime rules on deference to local majorities. It might be asked: Were the rules worthy of following? Abstractly considered, the rules could be considered legitimate from a liberal democratic point of view. Theorists often distinguish between the claims immigrants can make on a polity as opposed to national minorities or conquered peoples. The latter are part of the social contract by force, while the former join by choice. Thus it is argued, immigrants should in some measure defer and conform to the social culture laid down by the state they are voluntarily joining.[148] But were the norms laid down by the state or by the nation, or were they mere local convention?[149] And were the Mormons immigrants? Were they not closer to refugees or a conquered people on the move, forced into Illinois, and thus with some justification resisting practices the current majority party asked them to follow?

Perhaps the Whigs acknowledged this point. In any case, they were desperate for votes in Illinois; Hancock County was one of their few strongholds. In addition, as we have seen, they knew Van Buren was unpopular due to the great depression and that after twelve years of Democratic rule, they were grasping for a victory. Now the party was gearing up for running Henry Clay in 1844. The next election cycle would be crucial. It is an indication of how serious matters were becoming in Hancock that the January 1843 intervention by party leaders did not last until the end of the year, let alone until the next national election. By November 1843, Thomas Sharp, now a confirmed anti-Mormon, was back at the helm of the *Signal*.

The resistance to Sharp on the Mormon side is perhaps less difficult to parse. Their falling out with Sharp began as early as

May 19, 1841, when he put into the *Warsaw Signal* for the first time a few criticisms of their group. He scolded Stephen A. Douglas for appointing John C. Bennett to the Hancock County office of master in chancery. Sharp observed that Bennett had a reputation of "evil report," adding that he "advocates a creed in which no one believes he has any faith." Another column questioned the new English immigrants' satisfaction with life at Nauvoo. A final editorial announced his intention "to oppose the concentration of political power in a religious body."[150] A week later, Smith erupted in anger. The *Signal* published a caustic letter in which he denounced the paper as a "filthy sheet . . . calculated to pollute me."[151] Given that Sharp was at this point still somewhat friendly—his comments were arguably respectful and restrained, and not aimed at the prophet personally—Smith's response is something of a puzzle. The "Report of the First Presidency" on the church's general conference held just a month earlier, in April, was one of "unfeigned pleasure."[152] Outwardly, the church was doing well. Why then the caustic reaction to Sharp in so short a time?

Mormon cosmology and the group's isolated setting at Nauvoo provide a context for understanding Smith's reaction. We should not miss the reference to pollution. Mary Douglas notes that "pollutions are used as analogies for expressing a general view of the social order." Given the Mormons' "ideal order of society," Smith marked Sharp as a danger and transgressor.[153] Sharp, in fact, was no longer a stranger to the Mormon world. He had been welcomed to Nauvoo on one of its most joyous and solemn occasions—the laying of the temple cornerstone. His editorials afterward were thus out of place and in disorder, the mark of one who returned doubt and disbelief when offered friendship and loyalty. The saints had even extended special favors to Sharp. At the April 6 celebration, Joseph's brother William Smith emphasized in *The Wasp* that "a generous and polite invitation was given by Gen. Joseph Smith for the stranger to dine at his table." Sharp was offered a place in the circle of concern and worth, the position of an honorary outsider. But, inexplicably, "he treated our kindness with mockery."[154] The Mormons, as egalitarians focused on worth, did not miss this expression of disrespect. From that point on, William Smith and the Mormons would see in Sharp nothing but a "dirty culprit" whose noxious paper was a "Signal of war."[155]

5

Performing Citizenship in the House of Power

The outcomes of the Mormon troubles in Illinois have been well documented. Church prophet and patriarch Joseph and Hyrum Smith were assassinated on June 27, 1844, while awaiting trial in Carthage Jail, and their followers were forced into exile from Nauvoo in the spring of 1846. They were spurred to leave by organized anti-Mormon arson attacks on Mormon communities in rural Hancock County. The troubles persisted past the mass exodus and into the fall of 1846. After the assassinations, political order dissolved and there followed a period of extreme group polarization which frequently broke into violence. Before hostilities ceased, at least ten men had been killed, either in combat or via homicide; a chaotic trial of the assassination conspirators resulted in jury nullification; a Mormon military march on Carthage turned it into a ghost town; and the battle of Nauvoo terrified the nearly deserted city. Overall, the state militia was called out five times to impose order in Hancock County. In September of 1846 a peace "treaty" was signed, but calm was not restored until October, when Governor Thomas Ford entered the county with a final group of volunteers to protect Nauvoo's non-Mormon "new citizens" from rabid anti-Mormons.

What accounts for so massive a breakdown in governance? How did the civil order in Hancock County fray to the point that all possibility of reconciliation was considered hopeless? In fact, the path to civic breakdown is observable and traceable. The conditions of possibility in Illinois were not unique at either the cultural or institutional level. The basic contours of these conditions—weak state capacity, strong demand for popular justice, local majority control, entrenched group particularism, and a disappointed expectation of state neutrality—are endemic to many developing democracies today. For these reasons the Mormon troubles remain relevant. Their pattern of low trust in state institutions and high correlative group consciousness raise an ominous precedent to be avoided. Common conditions produce repeatable patterns and predictable critical junctures. This chapter catalogs the progress of these patterns and junctures in the story of Joseph Smith and the writ of habeas corpus. His repeated legal success with the writ generated distrust and drove most Illinoisans to deprecate Mormon worth. Smith habitually used his military power and the Nauvoo Legion militia in ways that Hancock's old settlers viewed as a direct threat. As both sides performed their perceived civic duties, state authority dissipated while the house of power swelled with local actors who "took the responsibility."[1] Performing citizenship increasingly meant grabbing state power to serve the interests of one side or the other.

THE UNWIELDY COMMON-LAW STATE

To make sense of the habeas corpus episodes, it is necessary to see that, from the Mormon perspective, the Missouri War had never really ended.[2] In fact, Missouri governors continued to pursue the arrest of Joseph Smith and other Mormons in Illinois until the summer of 1843, and independent incursions from bands of Missourians into Hancock County persisted well into 1844. Smith had escaped Missouri custody in April 1839, perhaps with the tacit support of handlers who were moving him for a trial date. In the fall of 1840 he was still "a fugitive from justice and could expect writs to be served on him without warning."[3] The sense of danger was experienced by the whole community. "The Missourians seem determined not to let us alone," Martha Hay wrote to her relatives back east in 1843. "They keep kidnapping our people."[4] Given this sense of threat, appeals for the protection of due process were likely to be repeated.

The first habeas episode originally passed with little more than a brief ministerial act calling forth an even briefer newspaper notice. On September 1, 1840, Missouri governor Lilburn W. Boggs initiated a first extradition request for Smith and five other Mormons on charges of treason stemming from their conflict with the state's militias in 1838.[5] Illinois governor Thomas Carlin sent a sheriff to Nauvoo to locate and arrest Smith and the others listed on the warrant. But as the *Times and Seasons* disingenuously reported, the accused happened to be "gone from home, and the Sheriff returned . . . without them."[6]

A second sheriff, this one accompanied by a posse, took a different tack. The goal was to catch the prophet outside his city. On June 5, 1841, Smith had just visited Governor Carlin at his home in Quincy and had made it to Heberlin's Hotel on Bear Creek, about twenty miles southeast of Nauvoo, when Adams County sheriff Thomas King apprehended and took him back to Quincy on the authority of the original warrant. After his arrest, Smith directly sued for a writ of habeas corpus. This request was granted on the streets of Quincy by Charles A. Warren, the Adams County master in chancery. Stephen A. Douglas, Democratic Party leader and recently appointed state supreme court justice, also happened to be in town on his circuit riding duties. Douglas, who was friendly toward Smith and the Mormons at this time, suggested that Smith be allowed to present the writ before him as presiding judge at Monmouth, in nearby Warren County. When Smith appeared before Judge Douglas in Monmouth, his writ of habeas corpus petition was granted on the grounds that the warrant for arrest from Missouri was inoperable because it had been returned once and had not been renewed for a second use. With Smith thus freed on a technicality and so many powerful Democrats in the vicinity, the Whig *Sangamo Journal* cried foul: the Springfield paper believed that a "corrupt bargain" had been struck between the Mormons and Democrats with legal protection traded for votes in next year's gubernatorial race.[7]

A common-law tool like the writ of habeas corpus is a narrowly focused instrument. The writ asks an executive or police officer to bring or "have the body" before the issuing court to supply a legal justification for holding the body. It is a check on prosecutors and police who might be tempted otherwise to make arrests without "probable cause," the constitutional threshold for searches and seizures. In Illinois the exact standard was "the truth or probability of the charge."[8] If that threshold was not met, the accused was allowed to go free and could not be held in jail. In the case of a federal judge hearing and granting a habeas petition, the writ effectively quashed all state-level action. A habeas hearing did not provide a decision on the merits of the case; it assessed an indictment's legality for purposes of pre-trial holding. But in situations in which a prisoner with friendly local options would, without a writ, be sent to an alternative, hostile venue, such as Smith certainly would have faced in Missouri, it was not a stretch to view a successful habeas proceeding leading to discharge as a powerful means of evading the merits of the indictment and the law altogether. Indeed, jurist Dallin H. Oaks cites evidence that Joseph Smith viewed the habeas proceedings as a substitute for a trial on the merits.[9]

A second habeas episode, in August of 1842, was presented to the public not as a matter of party politics but of Mormon infighting. It was unlike the first case in that this time the writ was requested before and issued by the Nauvoo Municipal Court. Smith viewed the new arrest warrant as driven by the enmity of John C. Bennett, former Nauvoo mayor and newly minted anti-Mormon. As early as the summer of 1841, the Mormons knew of Bennett's habitual adultery. A public accusation at that time led Bennett to stage a suicide attempt. But disagreements were patched up, and Bennett remained mayor of Nauvoo, major general of the Nauvoo Legion, candidate for the Illinois General Assembly, and an officer in the local Masonic hall until early May, when he was reprimanded for keeping a brothel. At the same time, the prophet believed that a Nauvoo Legion battle exercise staged by Bennett was part of a plot to have him killed. After multiple accusations and recriminations, Bennett left Nauvoo for good on June 21, 1842. He went to Springfield to write a series of articles later published in the *Sangamo Journal* attacking Smith and the Mormons. He soon became infamous statewide as an arch Mormon apostate. Among the points he raised against the group was his belief that Smith had ordered Governor Boggs's assassination through the Danites, the secret paramilitary group developed during the Missouri War. In Illinois the Danites had been reduced to the prophet's bodyguard—though a stylish one wearing white uniforms with red sashes.[10] Now Bennett was attempting to bring the Danites and Mormon violence back into the limelight by prodding the Missouri governor to issue a new arrest warrant on the new ground of attempted murder.

With whatever prompting, Missouri's new governor, Thomas Reynolds, issued a new extradition request on the attempted murder charges in the Boggs case. Reynolds sent the request to the Illinois governor, Carlin, who granted extradition, issued a warrant for arrest, and sent Sheriff King a second time to arrest Smith, this time at Nauvoo. King did so on August 8. But before he could leave town with his prisoner, King was presented with a writ of habeas corpus issued from the Nauvoo Municipal Court. The Nauvoo charter granted this power. Smith was freed pending a review in the local court he controlled. Within the hour, Smith and King attended the city court and the prophet's petition was heard and granted. Thomas Sharp asked in an editorial, "What do you think of this barefaced defiance of our laws?" His piece was reprinted with support by Simeon Francis, the editor of the *Sangamo Journal*.[11] In a follow-up editorial reviewing Smith's celebratory speech at Nauvoo after the incident, Francis derided the powerlessness of the Democrats and their state: "Poor loco foco ridden state! An outlaw almost within the hearing of the Governor, ridicules the authorities of the state, as unable to execute the laws of the state on his person! Huzza for Illinois!"[12]

One of Governor Carlin's last acts in the fall of 1842 was to issue a two-hundred-dollar reward for delivering Smith and Danite Porter Rockwell to Sheriff King at Quincy. The reward went unredeemed. Smith "secreted himself in swamps" or remained in his city-state, where it would have been nearly impossible to take him by force.[13] The Missouri governor's request for extradition was still outstanding when Illinois's newly elected governor, Thomas Ford, was sworn in to office. Ford received the Mormon vote, but on his own assessment he considered their presence in the state a challenge.[14] He speculated in his *History*, "Scattered through the country, they might have lived in peace like other religious sects, but they insisted on their right to congregate in one great city."[15] Ford's inaugural address on December 8, 1842, made note of the "great deal" of attention "the charters granted to the people of Nauvoo" had created. He urged the General Assembly to take up legislation so "that those charters should be modified so as to give the inhabitants of Nauvoo no greater privileges than those enjoyed by others of our fellow citizens."[16] But the legislature, dominated by the same Democratic leaders who had authorized the charters in the first place, now took up the cause of a complete repeal of the charters. With the help of a persuasive speech by the prophet's brother Representative William Smith on December 9 and many Whig votes, Ford, who was in favor of modifying the charters, was able to beat back the repeal vote. Charter repeal would have left the largest city in the state without the power to order its affairs. But the issue of modification remained unresolved.[17]

Ford immediately sought a strategy to resolve altogether the problem of the Missouri extradition warrants that continued to be pressed on him to sign. As it happened, a delegation of Mormons was visiting Springfield to oversee another legal matter with Justin Butterfield, the respected United States attorney then attending the federal court session in the state capital. Butterfield was charged with collecting money the Mormons owed the US Army, which they had used to pay for the steamboat *Nauvoo*. The boat was destroyed in an accident, and Joseph Smith, who had signed to secure the loan and who was eligible for bankruptcy proceedings under the new law the Whigs in Congress had just passed, would be unable to complete the proceedings until his security for the boat was cleared.[18] While Butterfield never resolved the bankruptcy problem, he did suggest a solution to the Missouri warrant issue, which Ford later accepted. The Mormon delegation also met with Douglas, who advised them to ask Ford to repeal Carlin's warrant. Butterfield suggested a different approach, one that questioned the legal merits of the warrant.[19] This led to the third habeas episode.

As an attorney and judge, Ford had his own reasons to doubt the validity of the second Missouri warrant for attempted murder. This was because the crime alleged against Smith, accessory to murder, if it did take place at all, had to take place in Missouri in May of 1842, by which date the prophet lived in Illinois and had not been to Missouri for over three years. Butterfield suggested a meeting between the Mormon delegation and the governor. At the meeting, Ford acknowledged the extradition warrant Carlin made was illegal but doubted his authority as a subsequent governor to overrule and revoke it. He agreed to quiz the members of the Illinois Supreme Court, who were gathered in Springfield at the time, to learn their opinion of the matter. Ford did so the next day and immediately wrote to Joseph Smith via the Mormons in town on December 17, 1842, explaining that while he and a few court members doubted his power to rescind Carlin's order, they unanimously agreed with Butterfield's assessment that the Missouri warrant was invalid. Ford concluded, "I can only advise that you submit to the laws and have a judicial investigation of your rights."[20] The Mormon delegation then showed the letter to Butterfield, who added his own letter to Smith to confirm the soundness of the legal opinion and strategy. Upon reading both letters back in Nauvoo, Joseph Smith agreed to the plan. As it turned out, they could not locate the original Missouri warrant from King, and Ford had to issue a duplicate arrest warrant for Smith, which he "placed . . . in the hands of the sheriff of Sangamon County."[21] After Smith came to Springfield and allowed himself to be arrested, he could directly obtain a federal habeas writ from Judge Nathaniel Pope and have the warrant reviewed in Pope's federal circuit court. Smith was taking no chances; before leaving, he had himself arrested by Nauvoo constable Wilson Law. He would come into Springfield under the cover of his own law.[22]

As previously noted, the prophet made a dramatic entrance to the state capital. He was arrested and tried according to plan. On January 5, Pope read his ruling from the bench. He argued that the petition should be granted and Smith discharged. The arrest warrant hinged on Smith being in Missouri as an accessory to the assassination attempt on Boggs, but no evidence was produced that he was there; instead, all the affidavits supplied affirmed his residence in Illinois on May 6, 1842, the day of the attempt. Thus, "as it is not charged that the crime was committed by Smith in Missouri, the governor of Illinois could not cause him to be removed to that state, unless it can be maintained that the state of Missouri can entertain jurisdiction of crimes committed in other states."[23] The burden of Pope's legal opinion was to show that such a broad reach by one state on the sovereign capacity of another was unconstitutional. He followed closely the line of reasoning laid out by Butterfield as Smith's attorney. A Whig with a strong sense of ceremony, Butterfield made the most of his moment in the courtroom, packed with the "distinguished ladies of Springfield," including Mary Todd Lincoln.[24] He was reported to have begun, "It is a momentous occasion in my life to appear before the Pope—he made an appropriate bow to the judge—in defense of a prophet of God—a bow to Joseph—in the presence of all these angels—a last deep bow to the ladies."[25]

After his release, Smith returned in triumph to Nauvoo with his freedom now carrying the Illinois regime's stamp of approval. He threw a big party at the recently opened Nauvoo Mansion. Mormon poet Eliza R. Snow memorialized the event in her poem "Jubilee Song":

> That deed,—that time we celebrate;
> So rife with liberty,
> When the official Pow'rs of state
> Pronounc'd the Prophet free.
> Protection's wreath again will bloom,
> Reviv'd by Thomas Ford;
> Which under Carlin had become
> Like Jonah's wither'd gourd.
> And while we give our feelings scope
> And gratitude award,
> To Edwards, Butterfield and Pope,
> We'll not forget the Lord.[26]

The Mormons would always put the Lord first, but the otherwise bipartisan spirit rang true, for while it was Ford, a Democratic governor, who had arranged the test case, it was the Whig attorney Butterfield who had provided the reasoning and the Whig judge Pope who had delivered the opinion. Even more, by making a federal case out of it, the third writ added the authority of the national government to the guarantee of Smith's freedom.

All in all, Ford could be forgiven for believing the vexing Missouri interference problem had been fixed. But it was not to be. A third warrant for arrest came to him from Missouri governor Thomas Reynolds on June 17, 1843; this warrant, reverting to the first charge of treason, asked Ford to enforce the extradition request by calling out the militia. Ford refused to do the latter, but he did issue the arrest warrant "reluctantly," according to his friend and agent Mason Brayman. Ford felt obligated "in pursuance of the constitution of the United States" to issue the arrest warrant; he handed it to Harmon Wilson, the Hancock County deputy sheriff from Carthage who agreed to assist the Missouri sheriff.[27] Within the week, on June 23, 1843, Smith was arrested in northern Illinois by the sheriff from Missouri, Joseph Reynolds. The prophet and his wife were visiting her sister Elizabeth Wasson and her husband, Benjamin, on the Rock River near Dixon, about 170 miles northeast of Nauvoo. He believed his whereabouts were secret; he later issued a church complaint against Sidney Rigdon, believing that Rigdon had tipped off the Missourians.[28] It is unclear whether Rigdon did inform, but the new warrant was surely driven by another Mormon on the outs—John C. Bennett.[29] The warrant revived the old charge of treason committed by Smith when he was in Missouri and thus was "a writ no Illinois court could touch."[30] Politically, the timing could not have been worse for Ford; it was little more than a month before the very competitive Sixth Congressional District seat election. In a district dominated by Nauvoo, the prominent Whig candidate Cyrus Walker would square off against Democrat Joseph P. Hoge.

The story of Smith's arrest at Dixon on June 23 is a thrilling one. It is indicative of the strong and effective support Mormon followers gave their leader. News of Ford's signing of a new arrest warrant was quickly gathered in Nauvoo, and in a few short hours Hyrum Smith had raised over three hundred volunteers at the Masonic hall committed to mounting a rescue party.[31] Time was of the essence, but the rescuers did not know the route the captors would take southwest to Missouri, so they split into three groups, fanning out to cover the Mississippi, Rock, and Illinois River routes. In the meantime, two Mormons from Springfield road day and night to try to reach Dixon before the sheriff and deputy arrived at the Wassons. They were able to find Lee County sheriff Campbell in Dixon and enlist him as an ally in the affair. Back at the Wassons, Reynolds and Wilson cleverly took on the disguise of Mormon elders, allowing them to approach the house without alarm. They caught the family at the dinner table and arrested Smith at gunpoint. Holding a revolver to his ribs, they muscled the prophet out to a tavern in Dixon, where they locked him up. But soon they were met by Sheriff Campbell, who counterarrested them on charges of false imprisonment. After some delay, Smith was able to visit with and retain three attorneys, including candidate Cyrus Walker, who was one of the most respected attorneys in northern Illinois. The attorneys, along with Sheriff Campbell, accompanied Smith, who was in the custody of Reynolds and Wilson, to Ottawa, where a habeas proceeding could be held. They rode some thirty miles to Paw Paw Grove, where in the morning the Missouri sheriff Reynolds was harassed by local citizens who accused him of kidnapping. Smith reported that the head of the local claim society appeared and took his side in the matter, stating: "You cannot kidnap men here, if you do in Missouri; and if you attempt it here, there's a committee in this Grove, that will sit on your case; and sir, it is the highest tribunal in the United States, as from its decision, there is no appeal. Reynolds, no doubt, aware that the person addressing him was at the head of a Committee who had prevented the Settlers on the public domain from being imposed upon by land speculators, sat down in silence."[32]

Upon arriving in Ottawa on the next day, the party found that the presiding judge was absent, so they returned to Dixon. A new writ of habeas corpus was made out to be served at Quincy, and the group proceeded there in a stagecoach. Then "in the afternoon after the second day after leaving Dixon," they were met on the road by a steady trickle of Mormon rescuers.[33] It was unclear who they were at first. As historian Richard Bushman narrates: "When two Mormons finally intercepted the convoy, Joseph greeted his friends 'with tears [in] his eyes.' Then he turned to his captors: 'I am not going [to] Missouri this time these [are] my boys.'"[34] Smith was apparently worried that a posse from Missouri was intercepting the stagecoach, since, as he wrote, "the whole country was swarming with men anxious to carry me there," but when the Mormons arrived, they escorted the convoy back to Nauvoo.[35]

After the event, Ford was concerned about rumors that "the citizens of Nauvoo have turned out in Military force to prevent the arrest of Smith." If the Nauvoo Legion had been used in this illegal way, the action was likely to "so excite the already combustible state of public feeling in Missouri as to lead to collision of hostile forces." To ascertain the truth, Ford sent his trusted friend and respected attorney Brayman as a "special agent" to Nauvoo on July 3 to investigate. Ford had Brayman's report in hand on July 26 when he wrote to Governor Reynolds informing him of his refusal to send out the militia to enforce the arrest warrant. He later wrote a letter to Reynolds on August 13 to provide more detail. He explained that the Mormon posse intercepting the convoy was made up of "parties of the citizens of Nauvoo; some, or most, of whom are said to have been members of the Nauvoo Legion, though there is no evidence that they appeared in a Military capacity."[36] The governor rested his decision not to call out the militia on the narrow claim that the

Mormon band had not acted officially as a rogue body and so had not broken an Illinois law. This legalistic claim was backed up by Thomas Gregg's summary of the events in the *Warsaw Message:* "No threat or intimidation was used by any person whatever to induce Mr. Campbell, the sheriff of Lee County, to go to Nauvoo with [Sheriff] Reynolds. . . . No attempt was made either at Dixon or after the company started, by the friends of Smith, to rescue him from the custody of the officers having him in charge."[37]

Without a militia to intercede for them and with a de facto militia against them, the Missouri sheriff Reynolds and Hancock deputy Wilson, together with Smith and the Lee County sheriff, went along with the Mormon posse to Nauvoo. The Missourian and the deputy surely went under protest. Ford later wrote to Governor Reynolds, "Smith immediately brought an action . . . for false imprisonment . . . and had [the Missouri sheriff] to bail in the sum of four hundred dollars." Being "in a strange country and unable to give bail," Sheriff Reynolds was "taken by the sheriff of Lee County and held prisoner; whilst [he] held Smith as his prisoner."[38] The sheriff's case was never adjudicated, and Reynolds and Wilson "stormed off to Carthage, demanding that the government dispatch the militia to arrest the Prophet."[39] Seven days later the prophet attended the Nauvoo Municipal Court, where a habeas proceeding was heard. By then he had retained the Whig candidate Cyrus Walker, from McDonough County, to present his case. Ford reported that Walker "made a wonderful exertion in a speech three hours long, to prove to the municipal court, composed of Joe Smith's tools and particular friends, that they had the jurisdiction to issue and act on the writ under the ordinance of their city."[40] Smith was granted the writ, the case immediately reviewed under it, and he was again discharged. But Walker's retainer came with a steep fee and the promise of Smith's vote in the coming election.[41]

This third writ again implicated both political parties in a highly politicized way. On the Whig side, there was Walker's defense of the municipal power to hear habeas petitions and the promise he extorted from prophet. On the Democratic side, Ford did not call out the militia to make the arrest the Missouri governor had requested. Political in another way was the rumored use of the Nauvoo Legion. Some scholars claim that Ford secretly pledged to the Mormons that he would not call out the militia against Smith if they would vote for the Democrats; others think the Mormons committed to

Ford independently due to his earlier efforts on their behalf.[42] Ford denied in his *History* that he made any such pledge; he noted that "a managing democrat of Hancock County was sent as a messenger to Springfield to ascertain positively what the governor would do if the Mormons voted the democratic ticket."[43]

This Democrat was Jacob B. Backenstos, who would play a leading role throughout the remainder of the troubles. He was serving as Hancock circuit clerk at the time; the Mormons would soon elect him to be state representative in 1844 and sheriff in 1845.[44] A protégé of Stephen A. Douglas, Backenstos claimed he was given Ford's pledge and so communicated the fact to Smith. Ford later learned that "during my absence [in St. Louis] . . . a prominent democrat of Springfield . . . had given a positive pledge in my name to Backenstos."[45] This Springfield democrat was likely none other than Ford's ally and agent Mason Brayman. He had sent a letter to Smith on July 29, 1843, in which he conveyed "the Governor's views and feelings." Brayman carefully added, "I do not speak for him, having no authority to do so." One can imagine that Brayman, perhaps engaged in a careless and informal conversation with Backenstos, stepped over the line he had so carefully crafted in writing.[46]

As politicized as the events were, the Mormons made them more so, managing to leave both political parties thoroughly discredited among their adherents in Hancock County. The Mormon side of the story played out as follows. Smith had pledged himself to vote for Walker, but the rest of the Mormons were not so obligated. In fact, as scholar Marvin Hill first uncovered, a Mormon eye-witness, Oliver Olney, later testified that after the public addresses by Walker and Hoge before the Nauvoo masses in June, the Mormon leadership decided for "Political union in favor of the Democratic Party [and Hoge]."[47] The decision was communicated to the Mormon faithful in the following way: a few days before the election, Hyrum Smith publicly announced that a last-minute revelation had directed him and the Mormons to vote for Hoge. Walker lost by 534 votes overall and by 1,500 votes in Hancock; the vote was 818 to 98 in Hoge's favor in the Nauvoo and Commerce Precincts, while at the Carthage and Warsaw Precincts, it was 232 to 110 in Walker's favor.[48] After the election, the story of Hyrum's "vision" and Mormon duplicity roiled the Whig flagship paper, the *Sangamo Journal*.[49]

In Hancock County at large, the issue of the General Assembly's failed repeal of the Nauvoo city and Nauvoo Legion charters rankled. A public meeting of anti-Mormons at Carthage on September 7, 1843, published resolutions complaining that both charters were being illegally used by Smith. On the city charter, they wrote, "He has caused the writ of habeas corpus to be issued by the Municipal Court of the city of Nauvoo, in a case not provided for in the Charter of that city, and indeed contrary to the letter of that instrument."[50] Walker had argued the opposite, and jurist Dallin H. Oaks argues that he had a case. Oaks points out that since the mayor and the city council members already constituted the municipal court, no additional purpose could be served by the charter's habeas power reaching only to the ordinances passed by the city council.[51] Furthermore, as historian James L. Kimball Jr. has shown, the Nauvoo charter's powers were by no means unique. Alton's municipal court also had the power to issue writs of habeas corpus, though the city populace rescinded this right in a referendum in August of 1839.[52] Historian A. T. Andreas notes that the press of judicial business was so great in Chicago in 1837 that the Chicago Municipal Court was granted all the powers of the state circuit court and that by a special act of the legislature Judge Thomas Ford was made the first judge of this court.[53]

But is it possible that the legislature wanted to create charters that put the cities beyond the reach of state and federal laws—if still bound by their constitutions? In fact, evidence suggests the legislature was in the habit of exempting municipal powers from state and federal laws; Galena and Springfield had been so exempted, though not Galesburg, Macomb, Marion, Rock Island, and Tremont.[54] Indeed, the tendency to devolve power to the locality is precisely what could be predicted under the institutional bias of the Jacksonian regime; it was just this spirit, when applied to extralegal frontier conditions, that Whigs like Abraham Lincoln ridiculed as "squatter sovereignty."[55] Given that the "General Assembly of Illinois . . . deliberately attempted to create the impression that the city lawmakers were not to be limited by state or federal law," Oaks concludes, Walker's interpretation of the Nauvoo municipal powers—finding a squatter "Old Citizen" spirit behind the letter of the law now applied in a frontier urban setting—was not unreasonable.[56] But if this power could be reasonably ascribed to the old settlers, Illinoisans generally reacted in alarm when they realized it was in the hands of a newly arrived group who lived separately, as did the Mormons. Here the institutional biases of the regime conflicted with its societal culture: the Mormons had lost their status as independent producers. Governor Carlin, who lacked a legal cast of mind but who nicely represented the average man, confidently told Emma Smith that the Mormon claims to the habeas powers in a municipal court were "most absurd and ridiculous . . . a gross usurpation of power that cannot be tolerated."[57]

Of the Nauvoo Legion charter, the anti-Mormons at Carthage wrote: "He has caused large bodies of his ragamuffin soldiery to arm themselves, and turn out in pursuit of officers, legally authorized to arrest himself; he being charged with high crimes and misdemeanors committed in the State of Missouri, and placed in duress, that he might enable himself, to march triumphantly into Nauvoo, and bid defiance to the laws of the land."[58] Later that fall, the status of the legion was raised by state officials. When one of the legion's brigade majors requested reimbursement from the state for expenses incurred while training, William Lee D. Ewing, serving as state auditor, asked the state's attorneys general to examine the legal authority behind the legion's request. On November 30, 1843, they sent Ewing an answer in public letters: because the legion's charter made it an independent body created by the city of Nauvoo, the state was not responsible for its expenses.[59] Ford must have disagreed, because on January 1, 1844, Smith thanked Ford in a letter: "Your Excellencys opinion that the Nauvoo Legion are part of the Militia of the State of Illinois, seems so consistent with the spirit and genius of the charter and the common law of the land, as well as the intention of our constitutions . . . the Attorneys Generals opinions, to the contrary not withstanding."[60] Ford's view was in accord with the "advisory opinion" Judge Douglas had issued back in May of 1841. At that time, Thomas Sharp had organized the citizens of Warsaw to resist serving their militia duty under Smith and Bennett's command. Douglas's opinion, however, stated that service in the Nauvoo Legion was open to any citizen of Hancock County, as indeed the ordinance organizing the legion read; service there sufficed to fulfill the state's mandated militia duty and should be supported financially by the state.[61]

But by the fall of 1843, the Nauvoo Legion was no longer viewed as a creature of the Illinois state. Locally, party leaders from both sides had by then joined together against the Mormons. Whig Thomas Gregg's conversion to anti-Mormonism at this time was likely influenced by partisan reasons, notably the realization that

Hancock County and the surrounding area had become so thoroughly anti-Mormon that the popular Walker might have won if he had come out against the Mormons "and received the full and enthusiastic Whig vote."[62] An anti-Mormon militia with men of both parties began drilling at Green Plains under leader Levi Williams in mid-September 1843.[63] A local decision point had been reached; the state of parties would be discarded. Hancock's united gentlemen of property and standing would resist the house of power in order to enforce their foundational belief in local independent-producer authority against the Mormons.

Although Ford warned Smith repeatedly about staying within the law, the prophet increasingly politicized the Nauvoo Legion by using it as a tool to protect himself and his people. This had begun early on. In December of 1841 the city council called out the legion to destroy a grogshop declared a nuisance on the temple hill.[64] From this kind of use, it was but a short step, from Smith's perspective, to use the legion to protect his city against Missourians; at a July 4, 1842, parade, he praised the legion for its capacity to "yield obedience to the institutions of our country, *and protect the Saints from mobs.*"[65] Governors Carlin and Ford repeatedly forbade Smith to call out the militia for routine protective services. In May of 1843, Smith felt pushed to the point of open civil disobedience. In a speech before a legion parade, he lamented, "When we have petitioned those in power for assistance, they have always told us they have no power to help us, *damn such traitors.*"[66] In a June 30, 1843, speech before a large gathering at Nauvoo, the prophet told his people, "The time has come when forbearance is no longer a virtue." He increasingly defended Nauvoo's powers as "chartered privileges," vested rights he would never give up regardless of repeal. Perhaps to underscore the fact, the legion marched for two successive weeks in September following the anti-Mormon meeting and drill at Carthage.[67] The Mormons were using martial arts to register their presence in the Hancock status order. If war was "a continuation of policy by other means" as Prussian general Carl von Clausewitz argued, the Mormons were performing citizenship by other means.[68]

In December 1843 two Mormons, Daniel Avery and his son, were kidnapped by an armed group of Missouri and Hancock County residents. They were abducted and taken across the Mississippi River for interrogation on an informal charge of thievery. Smith again asked Ford to call out the militia for protection; this was something Brayman in his earlier letter to Smith had suggested Ford would do "should the state be threatened with invasion . . . for the purpose of . . . carrying off one of its citizens."[69] But in his December 12 letter to Smith, Ford denied the request; he now defined cases of emergency more narrowly.[70] He used his lawyerly precision to avoid such calls in the future from either side. Indeed, a month later Ford rejected a similar request made by a group of anti-Mormons from Carthage on the same grounds. The conflict was resolved when the two Mormon prisoners were released on Christmas Day, but not before Levi Williams, charged with kidnapping by the city council, gathered his own posse at Warsaw to avoid arrest.[71] Williams insisted that the Averys, accused horse thieves, had been pursued by victimized Missourians.

Soon thereafter, Gregg noted in the *Warsaw Message* that "the neighborhood has been the scene of considerable excitement" due to the arrest of a Warsaw citizen on kidnapping charges by Deputy Sheriff King Follett from Nauvoo.[72] The citizen, John C. Elliott, was being tried at Nauvoo when word came of the Williams's posse. Smith decided to back down when he heard "some dozen or twenty citizens of Green Plains, excited by the circumstances of the arrest, had armed themselves and followed on as far as Warsaw." "Joe turned his tune very considerably," Gregg wrote. Vehement anti-Mormons like Walter Bagby and Levi Williams learned the dangerous lesson that "General Joe" retreated when threatened with organized force.[73] In November of 1843, the Hancock tax collector Bagby, who lived in Carthage, wrote to his brother in Kentucky that he would not visit or leave Illinois until he saw "the arrogances of that abomination in human shape [Joseph Smith] humbled low in the dust."[74]

Even when the two opposing sides aimed to appease and back away from violence, distrust on the other side conspired against peace. As in the classic security dilemma between "competing political groups independent of a central government," new defensive preparations only looked like aggressive acts to the other side and thereby exacerbated the conflict.[75] In December the Nauvoo City Council passed an ordinance "to select and have in readiness" forty police officers for the city.[76] Thomas Sharp replied that it looked like the prophet was preparing his forces for battle. Later, when "the Twelve" ordered twenty-four pieces of "heavy ordnance" from a foundry in Ohio, the same inference was drawn.[77] The charter also created misunderstanding. Similar as it was to the Galena and Springfield charters, the Nauvoo charter's section 17 did grant the mayor and the council at least one unique power: the mayor had "exclusive jurisdiction of all cases arising under the ordinances" of the city; and the mayor and the aldermen had the power to review appeals to their rulings at the municipal court.[78] Two days after the Avery kidnapping, the city council added to the mayor's power, passing an ordinance making it illegal to arrest Joseph Smith. When things cooled off, Smith had the council rescind the ordinance, which had been called "an extra ordinance for the extra case of Joseph Smith," but the appearance of liberal neutrality had been shattered and the taboo against open particularist bias flaunted.[79]

On the anti-Mormon side, a public meeting after the first of the year resolved to petition the governor to seek the state's assistance for the old citizens of Hancock County. In his reply, dated January 29, 1844, Ford carefully explained the limits of his powers and the need to treat all parties fairly. In the course of the letter, he also fell to scolding the anti-Mormons for their suggestion that the two parties were already at war and that they would act accordingly in an emergency if the governor refused assistance. Ford's position failed to acknowledge the lack of midrange police options left to peacekeepers because of the regime's too-narrow (due process via habeas corpus) or too-blunt (the militia) law enforcement capacity. Perhaps more damagingly, it failed to convey an understanding of the fears of the loss of local control motivating the anti-Mormon request.[80] Ford's position was legally accurate because the old citizens' desire to retain control rested arguably on an extraconstitutional regime bias. Still, he could be accused of falling prey to "seeing like a state," to viewing the problem from the perspective of the tools at hand. As the old adage runs, when all you have is a hammer, every problem looks like a nail, and to Ford every problem looked like a common-law puzzle in need of solving.[81] In his defense, the common-law state was an unwieldy tool, too narrow for some purposes and too blunt for others, but he left the little Jacksons with little recourse; they decided to take the responsibility for their own self-government. Ford's pretty liberal cloak of neutrality was viewed as an ugly abandonment by the one party and a feminine weakness by the other.

Soon the little Jacksons broke out everywhere. The prophet, in the spring of 1844, pushed his power beyond its legal limits to mete out justice to Mormon apostates. Smith had earlier used his unique mayoral power to call on the Nauvoo Legion to enforce city ordinances.[82] Then on June 7 a prominent group of apostates led by R. D. Foster and Wilson Law published in Nauvoo the first (and only) edition of a dissenting Mormon newspaper, the *Nauvoo Expositor.* Smith used the legion in a way that would demonstrate his need to use force to make the law authoritative among his own people. The dissenters announced their belief in the basic Mormon creed—"the pure doctrines of Jesus Christ . . . set forth in the Bible, the Book of Mormon, or the Book of Covenants"—but savagely attacked the prophet's recent moves to make plural marriage a doctrine and to raise his national political profile. The paper mixed a tone of high purpose with vindictive prose. The editors began "with the greatest solicitude for the salvation of the Human Family, and for our own souls" but at the same time determined "to explode the vicious principles of Joseph Smith and . . . [his] abominations and whoredoms." They were especially alarmed the prophet was redoubling efforts at religious control and asserting primacy in the political sphere. They demurred in both cases: "We do not believe that God has ever raised up a Prophet to Christianize a World by political schemes . . . [and we] abhor and protest any council or tribunal in this Church, which will not suffer the accused to stand in its midst and plead his own cause."[83]

Both Foster and Law also had personal grievances. They had competed with Smith to secure the scarce lumber needed for their private building projects and the Nauvoo House. The prophet publicly castigated them for being greedy by accusing the Law brothers of "grinding the poor" at their gristmill.[84] They in turn resented his effort to take their wives in celestial marriage.[85] In a rapid, escalating series of actions, they formed the Reformed Church of Jesus Christ of Latter-Day Saints in April, bought a printing press in May, and published their first edition in June.[86]

Feeling pressured from all sides, the prophet made a fateful decision: he browbeat city council members into declaring the *Expositor* a nuisance in need of immediate abatement.[87] The common-law state's reliance on foundational beliefs is apparent in cases in which the nuisance at issue is a public newspaper.[88] One council member voted against the motion, considering it "rather harsh." When he suggested "giving a few days limitation and assessing a fine, . . . the Mayor remarked he was sorry to have one dissenting voice in declaring the 'Expositor' a nuisance."[89] The proceeding violated the charter on its face, for it had granted the mayor and council jurisdiction over "all cases arising from the ordinances . . . provided that the parties litigant shall have a right to trial by a Jury of twelve men, in all cases before the Municipal Court."[90] Throwing all caution to the wind, the council issued a summary judgment and called out the Nauvoo Legion to assist the city marshal that evening in destroying the printer and the newspaper office.[91] Smith's "Proclamation" on June 16 explaining the council's actions to the city made a point of noting that "after a full and impartial investigation, it was voted, without one dissenting vote, a public nuisance to be immediately destroyed."[92] In all, Governor Ford counted nine separate illegalities in the operation, which included the issuing of yet another writ of habeas corpus.[93]

This final habeas proceeding was considered irrefutable evidence by the anti-Mormons of the seemingly limitless reach of Mormon rule. On June 12, Smith was arrested in Nauvoo by Carthage deputy sheriff David Bettisworth on charges of riot for the destruction of the *Expositor;* the prophet refused to be taken to Carthage and was again granted a habeas review from the Nauvoo Municipal Court.[94] That same day Thomas Sharp reported on the *Expositor*'s destruction and declared war in the *Warsaw Signal:* "We have only to state that this is sufficient! War and extermination is inevitable! Citizens arise ONE AND ALL!!! . . . We have no time for comment, every man will make his own. Let it be made with POWDER AND BALL!!!"[95] Sharp was by no means alone in this reaction. Governor Ford was visited by an anti-Mormon committee from Carthage on June 17 requesting that he call out the militia to assist in the arrest of the mayor and council.[96] As Ford later informed Smith in his letter of June 23, 1844, "Your conduct in destroying the press, was a very gross outrage upon the laws and liberties of the people. . . . There are many newspapers in this State which have been wrongfully abusing me for more than a year; and yet such is my regard for the liberties of the press, and the rights of a free people, in republican government, that I would shed the last drop of my blood to protect those presses from any illegal violence."[97] On June 16, Smith wrote Ford that a Carthage mob had been gathering, adding, "The Nauvoo Legion is at your service to quell all insurrections and support the dignity of the common wealth."[98]

Smith had declared martial law in the city, and the legion marched nearly every day until June 23, when the governor arrived.

Ford immediately assumed command of the anti-Mormon posse comitatus and several militia companies that had been called to Carthage. The next day, the governor requested that "the officers of the Nauvoo Legion . . . surrender the State arms in their possession." These amounted to "three pieces of cannon and two hundred and twenty . . . small arms." That same day, Smith, his brother Hyrum, and the entire city council came to Carthage and were arrested on charges of riot for the destruction of the press. They were all discharged by the justice of the peace on their own recognizance except the Smith brothers, who were rearrested on a charge of treason and detained.[99] The prophet predicted that he would not survive arrest and jailing in Carthage. His gift of prophecy did not fail him. Four days after their detention, the brothers were dead.

FOR FORMS OF LAW LET FOOLS CONTEST

Reconstructing how the Carthage mob justified its defiance of Governor Ford and the law requires that we look carefully at Illinois's structural dependence on local gentlemen of property and standing for the enforcement of the law. This dependence was well known, and party leaders supported it, but in "official" communications they frequently acknowledged the old Federalist regime's commitment to the rule of law. For example, after an antiabolitionist mob precipitated two murders during the attack on Elijah Lovejoy and his printing press on a cold night in Alton, the Democrat's *State Register* issued an editorial on November 24, 1837, with the obligatory statement "In the supremacy of the law ALONE is security." Given that the paper and the Illinois party had been all but proslavery and antiabolitionist from their inception, the sentiment rang hollow. Respect for the law would have to bow to respect for certain gentlemen. In fact, the rallying cry of law and order was being subtly undermined among the Whigs as they were adjusting to regime norms. The northern third of the state was beset with counterfeiters and horse thieves, and many respectable citizens, such as influential settler Charles Ballance, were organizing to enforce the peace by any means necessary, which included regulators and vigilance committees. Most Whig leaders still asked the people to respect sheriffs and the law, but as new converts to the Illinois way, they, too, realized that the law needed the support of local societal culture in order to be authoritative.

The question was not whether the law needed to be upheld, but by whom and how. National Whigs still took an altogether different perspective on the law—not a ground-level but a bird's-eye view of the law as a body of substantive social rules. Not unlike Governor Ford, they focused on due process. The view was a hegemonic fighting faith for those who learned it at the bar and in the law offices. If the "ruling class" described by Karl Marx had the mentality of "seeing like a state," Marx needed to look no further than the class of conservative lawyers to find it. However, their class rule was contested. Alexis de Tocqueville saw the lawyers' social weakness but hoped they could function as a pseudoaristocratic "temper" on the "tyranny of the majority" in a social order he viewed as all sail and no ballast.[100] But when due process failed to deliver order and protection, the Illinois way was to jettison the ruling class and impose rough justice.

The debate over law and order in Illinois revealed a rising tension within settler public opinion that boiled over in Hancock County. From one perspective the writ of habeas corpus was a way for the judiciary to check the arbitrary powers of the executive, like the sheriff. But the rules determining the writ's application evolved as they were applied. Ford and the Whigs accepted that the details of application would be shaped by judge-made case law. The rules were thus somewhat open-ended, and the standards, while broadly reflective of community sentiment, only applied in the context of an individual case. Opposed to this nuanced understanding of the law, many had little patience for precedent. The anti-Mormons viewed the Mormons' habeas appeals as actions outside the proper bounds of law and justice. In Thomas Sharp's view, Joseph Smith may have been within the letter of the law, but the spirit of justice was violated every time he was released. What was worse, each release encouraged him and his followers in the belief that the prophet was above the law. Smith was accused of treason or attempted murder, yet these accusations were never heard in court; legal procedure was enforced but the public peace denied. Furthermore, when the legislature granted the city of Nauvoo habeas powers and Smith used them to release "persons in custody by state officers," it was proof positive that the state's law had lost all power of enforcement.[101] The Mormon dissenters writing in the *Nauvoo Expositor* similarly focused on enforcement powers when they doubted the reach of the Nauvoo Municipal Court's writs of habeas corpus given that it had "powers . . . no more than coordinate . . . with a common justice of the peace."[102]

Of course, an experienced and well-trained legal mind like that of Cyrus Walker could and did use the letter of the charter to suggest otherwise. And while a court ruling on the matter might set precedent, the new rules reflected the facts of the case at hand and so were often not useful as general guides to action. Many scholars argue that judge-made law is either too narrowly focused or too general to be useful as a tool of public policy. It amounts to what historian Robert G. McCloskey describes as "playing baseball with a billiard cue."[103] It is some matter for debate whether the standards contained in the interstices of the antebellum American common law amounted to a coherent public policy. But in the end, it was not the rule of the judges but the rule of the militias and posses that drew respect during the troubles. And it was not the courtrooms which framed what was respected but leaders retailing a view shaped under pressure and guided by political culture. The state in Hancock County trifurcated under the pressure of the different kinds of legal enforcement urged by Smith, Sharp, and Ford under the terms of their respective political cultures. In performing citizenship as the three parties variously understood it, the house of power was torn asunder.

The local desire to control the enforcement of the law signaled a larger pattern of how Americans viewed the law during the heady days of their emerging democracy. Stressing such popular attitudes toward the law, legal scholars have transformed our understanding of the antebellum American state, which was radically decentralized not only politically but legally. A functional division of labor within the three levels of government developed. Those operating on the national level, such as senators, representatives, and justices, used the federal government's jurisdictional prerogatives to organize relations with the Indian nations, regulate banking and the public lands, set international trade relations, and establish communication systems via mail routes, turnpikes, and canals. State actors, such as governors, party leaders, and state justices, zeroed in on property law. Illinois's common law of torts and contracts were remade in the state supreme court during the 1840–60 period mainly to accommodate the coming of the railroad.[104] Public law, such as equity, probate, and criminal law, was largely left up to local courts. Scholars of Illinois have a rich sample of cases brought before the local courts due to the thorough record created by the Lincoln Legal Papers project, which covers the sixteenth president's legal practice as an attorney in the state from 1836 to 1861. Taken as a whole, the cases indicate the determination of marginal groups like married women and minors to press enforcement of a multitude of laws to their advantage.[105]

Historian Laura Edwards, in surveying recent scholarship in the field of legal history, depicts a hitherto hidden world of actors using the law from the margins of antebellum American society. She concedes that the law, abstractly considered, was a complex field consisting of multiple layers of written records, jurisdictional subtleties, and elite functionaries. But she and a new generation of legal scholars have uncovered evidence that the "law's very complexity made it more accessible . . . to ordinary citizens" and that if we expand our purview of legal forms to include society as a whole, we find that antebellum law "structured broad-reaching economic and cultural dynamics" reaching to the lives of Irish washerwomen and African American servants.

Key to the law's accessibility was a society free to ask "broad questions about governance" while the courts faced weak enforcement capacity "in the period before the emergence of the modern, bureaucratic state."[106] Edwards's own work uses the concept of the "public peace" to illustrate how the antebellum South developed a legal culture "in which all problems could develop public significance" and the "journey from private to public" was short.[107] The "peace" was popularly understood to encompass "the entire range of interpersonal relationships in the community" about which the point was "to restore order, not to protect individual rights."[108] Frequently, notables in local communities felt authorized to use their power of legal access and influence to deliver a punitive version of the law which eschewed rights and due process but vindicated a local sense of justice.

The new scholarship has shown how the forms of the law interact with politics, and how the administration of the law reflects power and culture. The same pattern emerges in the story of the Mormon troubles. Different versions of the rule of law followed for different persuasions and power dynamics in the 1840s. The Illinois Whigs saw a hope of grabbing power at the national level; they rallied around Henry Clay and devoted their efforts to securing the presidency. The Illinois Democrats focused on their controlling hand over state-level power and devoted their energies to maintaining control. Below this level, the Jacksonian regime allowed and depended upon a leakage of power to the local level. It might be noted that the leakage could only go so far before county jurisdictions were called upon to contain local power and state parties moved to rein in local independence. But Hancock's habeas and militia episodes illustrate how an open legal system, combined with a felt local need to impose order, could create significant political tension and lead to a condition of local anarchy and chaos for years before state-level authority was restored.

In Hancock the first sign of movement toward the dissolution of state-level authority appeared with the reports issued by Thomas Sharp in the *Warsaw Signal* during the summer of 1841. He made absolutely clear that the established settlers were feeling a loss of control. It may be true that Sharp soured on the Mormons at first only because of their role in impeding a paper town speculators were developing in the suburbs of Warsaw at Warren, Illinois.[109] But the results of the August 1841 local elections and his visit to the temple groundbreaking indicated the coming power of the Mormons. The feeling of vulnerability was then exacerbated by the reports of thefts which were given a prominent place in Sharp's paper. Just as it was realized that the people were losing control over the law and just as the call went out that its protection would be more than ever needed, stories were accumulating of the law's ineffectualness.

At this point a subtle juncture arrived to which the two parties responded by looking inward. Smith issued warnings against theft to his people, but he simultaneously raised the stakes of group membership by revealing the baptism of the dead doctrine. The anti-Mormons began meeting, organizing networks, and forming deep-felt daily attachments. Both sides were moving from group identification to "group consciousness," a term scholars use to describe the distinct ways of understanding the role of a group in the world that are developed and shared by members living under social pressure.[110] The bias of group consciousness spurred each side to demand much from Illinois's law; once dissatisfied, both sides came to view the state as weak or prejudiced against their side. Both sides responded by reaching out and grabbing a piece of the state for themselves: the Mormons with the use of habeas corpus and their militia, the anti-Mormons immediately after the assassinations with the vigilance Committee on Safety. The sequence of demand and disappointment was repeated several times during the troubles, each with increasing intensity until the anti-Mormons hit upon the self-help strategy of attacking those Mormons in southwest Hancock below Warsaw, who, because they lived in rural settlements, were isolated from the protection of Nauvoo.

With the assumption of self-governing powers, another critical juncture was reached. Both sides began the process of framing the other to make a case before the bar of public opinion; the Mormons raised the charge of religious persecution, and the anti-Mormons depicted the saints as an antirepublican and depraved people unworthy of independent status. When the anti-Mormons determined that their calls for "lateral support" would be heard by members in surrounding counties, they decided on the course of expulsion, while the Mormons' calls for aid fell on deaf ears, even in their favored town of Quincy.[111] Only once the trend of public opinion was clear did the informal Illinois state organize to gain control and authority in the county. It was as if the Hancock County settlers turned Alexander Pope's quip on its head. Pope had written, "For forms of government let fools contest, whate'er is best administered is best"; as the anti-Mormons had it, the local form of government was precisely the one best administered because they could control it themselves.[112]

The overall form of the Illinois state was democratic and open; its laws created openings that a wide assortment of marginal people used to demand popular justice. A sampling of the laws passed in the Fifth General Assembly (1826–27) offers some support for the law's openness and sensitivity to the claims of the marginal. Aliens and their widows were granted the same rights of holding and transmitting property as citizens. Minors over age fourteen were granted the right to select their own guardians. And apprentices were granted the privilege of "a new bible and two new suits of clothes" and the right to be "taught to read and write and the ground rules of arithmetic," though masters of "a negro or mulatto child" were exempted from having to fulfill this last duty.[113] Since the state legislature held the ultimate power over rules of this sort, an additional element of flexibility came in the body's habit of repeatedly revising the existing legal framework. The legislature's decision to revamp the entire judicial branch in 1841 confirmed the pattern. Ford explained: "A session of the legislature was like a great fire in the boundless prairies of the State: it consumed everything. And again, it was like a genial breath of spring, making all things new."[114]

The law's openness was a point of pride among universalist egalitarians like Ford. He conceded but contested Plutarch's adage that "written laws . . . were just like spiders' webs; they would hold the weak and delicate who might be caught in their meshes, but would be torn in pieces by the rich and powerful."[115] But the fact that the state's law enforcement powers were decidedly decentralized was also a key structural determinant. Many Illinois regime rules enforced decentralized control. One prime example was the ancient common-law rule still in place in Illinois of "the right of electing . . . sheriffs . . . secured to the people of the county."[116] Similarly ancient was the "Great Fyrd," the obligation of every local man to bear arms for king and country, from which the state's militia laws descended.[117] In practice, the written law of Illinois was frequently bent or revised in favor of local enforcement. Smith took advantage of this bias in the system. The state gave him enormous powers of local self-government in the Nauvoo city and Nauvoo Legion charters. The repeated use of these powers appeared to the anti-Mormons as a simple evasion of the law. They were left feeling threatened and resentful of the lack of a punitive power to check and correct Mormon behavior. In a countermove only open to them by a system relying on local populations to provide regime services, they took advantage of their own access to the militia and openly appealed to the citizens in the surrounding counties on the grounds that the norms of their shared frontier societal culture had been violated. Under the terms of the Illinois regime, they knew they stood a good chance of finding support.

The sequence of events leading to the Smith brothers' assassination demonstrates the limits of the Illinois regime as a governance system. The breakdown in trust and order that followed the Carthage mob murders must be understood in terms of the civic narratives and foundational beliefs of the agents who experienced the breach. The process began when available institutions and the predominant political cultures failed to generate a stable statewide public opinion looking with favor on the rise of local Mormon rule. After a brief period of sympathy for the saints following the assassinations, the narrative describing the Mormons as an unworthy and dangerous group deepened. Solidarity in Illinois was extended instead to Hancock's old settlers, who told anyone who would listen that Nauvoo and increasingly all of Hancock was under Mormon control, the jurisdiction of the state at Springfield notwithstanding.

Democratic states face the dilemma of needing to be open and accountable to the people while at the same time having enough power to make the law authoritative. The state is consequently presenting two faces, one open and inviting and another punitive and controlling. Many have argued that law in developing democracies is altogether too open to demands for public justice, with the consequence that the state's punitive face, with its flinty front of enforcement, is neglected in the name of maintaining popularity. Democracy as a form of popular government is all well and good, but if the law remains unenforced, its luster is considerably diminished, thus Pope's famous quip. The view is articulated by Samuel P. Huntington, who opens an influential political-development tome by asserting that "the most important distinction among countries concerns not their form of government but their degree of government. . . . The United States, Britain, and the Soviet Union have different forms of government, but in all three the government governs."[118] Emphasizing the enforcement side at the expense of the justice side is a pattern typical of conservative individualists like Huntington. Protection of individual rights and due process is criticized as allowing bad actors too many opportunities to evade the law altogether. In the case of the Mormon troubles, this view was articulated most prominently by Thomas Sharp. He would lead the charge for punitive enforcement in the name of local right of self-government and popular justice. We turn next to see how egalitarian and individualist leaders justified their performance of extralegal civic duties.

THE CULTURAL CONSTRUCTION OF CIVIC WORTH

The story of the habeas denouement in Hancock County indicates that the classic liberal democratic prescription for avoiding mobocracy—to promote respect for the law—is inapposite where and when it is needed most. It begs the question most people caught up in failed governance want answered: Whose law are we to respect, "ours" or "theirs"? The regime's assumption that if the enforcement of the law could be controlled locally by the people, it might always be supported and obeyed was shown to be flawed when traditional settlement patterns were disrupted. Further, disobedience and political conflict between the Mormon people and the Illinois people was inevitable once each group viewed itself in precisely this way—as a separate people. Amid two highly polarized groups, each claiming the authority to control the law, the only point on which they could agree was that the Illinois state government had failed in Hancock County. Given the premises of the prevailing Jacksonian regime, both had recourse to a rough extralegal remedy: rule by vigilantes made up of gentlemen of property and standing ready to defend the inherent right of self-government. The anti-Mormon Warsaw Committee of Safety, the Grand Military Encampment and Wolf Hunt, the Central Committee and its random bands of arsonists—all were a logical consequence of the old settlers' felt loss of control over local self-government.

Many scholars note the rise of establishment vigilantism in contexts in which "institutional instability and social ambiguity is pervasive."[119] Others document a pattern identical to the one in Hancock County, in which organized groups and networks use their control over "rough justice" to maintain "the hierarchical prerogatives of the dominant residents of the locality."[120] Under the Jacksonian regime, control by the "dominant residents" was the norm; locals only infrequently needed to "circumvent the state's legal apparatus" to get their way.[121] When pressed, they used congenial cultural lenses to frame all issues of law and order to their advantage. Vigilantism became an extension of politics by other means.

Before open lawlessness broke out in Hancock County, there were repeated efforts at compromise and legal resolution, but tragically no solution to the governance problem short of forced mass expulsion could be implemented. An attempt to forge a "two-state" solution was mounted, but neither side could secure a legal remedy. Smith petitioned the United States government for territorial status for Nauvoo in December of 1843, but he never received a reply.[122] On the anti-Mormon side, dividing Hancock County was a legal option discussed by the slate nominated by the Anti-Mormon Convention of May 29, 1842; but the idea failed to garner any support because it was acknowledged that moving the county seat would be unpopular at Carthage and the Mormons already had a quarter of the population living in what would have become the newly created gentile county.[123]

The local Whigs ran a slate of candidates in the 1842 election and attempted to reconcile with the Mormons during the first eight months of 1843. Thomas Gregg and his new partner William Y. Patch ran the *Warsaw Message* like a typical Whig paper, debating the merits of the tariff, denouncing Locofocos for endorsing the repudiation of the state debt, and organizing their partisans behind candidates in the coming congressional and presidential elections. But the Whigs lost all but one congressional seat among the state's seven newly configured districts in the August 7, 1843, election, and, as noted, the popular Cyrus Walker lost to the Democrat supported by the Mormons, Joseph P. Hoge. In the 1843 local elections the Mormons again carried their Democratic slate, and the local Whigs became anti-Mormon almost to a man from that point on. In response the local Democrats supported the Mormons for a longer period but were drawn into the anti-Mormon camp when Democrat Thomas Sharp regained the helm of the *Signal* to lead the push for removal. At the state level, the Hancock County Whigs would not regain control over General Assembly offices until the August 1846 elections, after most of the Mormons had left the area.

Smith's run for the presidency had the unintended consequence of cutting the Mormons off from all ties with the established regime in Illinois. After the Smith murders, the Whig Party leadership washed their hands of all things Mormon, having decided they were a political liability firmly in the hands of the Democrats and Governor Ford. The Mormons formed an alliance with Douglas's Democrats via the party's proxies, the consecutively elected sheriffs Minor Deming and Jacob Backenstos. The Democrat's state party newspapers strategically distanced themselves from the troubles and increasingly from the governor himself as he fought headwinds on the canal issue and later on future militia calls. The distancing was so apparent that the anti-Mormons had to publicly remind the people of Illinois that they were not made up simply of Whigs.[124] In October of 1845, Douglas, who had split with Ford over the issue of calling out the militia to arrest the Smith brothers' assailants, staged a high-profile intervention which resulted in the saints agreeing to leave the state in the spring. The de facto regime led informally but effectively by Douglas acted to end the conflict. Ford was relegated to a sideline position. The de jure state he led was now little more than a legal shell in the county. The governor relied on a contingent of military men from among the Whigs—first General John J. Hardin and then Major William B. Warren—to lead state militias to hold vigil while the agreement brokered by the real authority elsewhere was being implemented.

Institutional failure is a necessary but not sufficient cause of political dissolution; people act on interests shaped by ideas, and political ideas take shape among leaders using shared cultural materials in group settings. During the troubles, Hancock County experienced a level of group polarization and distrust reached by few communities in a liberal democracy. Civil society entities that previously took their respective places inside the parties and state status order came to view themselves as self-governing groups. The critical juncture reached in the summer of 1844 marked a point of no return. As Sharp put it in August of 1844, "We do not believe there can be any compromise. Hatred, venomous and deadly hatred, activates both sides."[125] The change durably marked the Hancock County landscape for a generation.[126] The story of peoplehood and the construction of worth as outlined by Rogers M. Smith were now in the hands of the anti-Mormons and the Mormons themselves. The conditions of possibility which follow from Smith's theory can be fleshed out using Mary Douglas's two key cultural frames, egalitarianism and individualism.

In modern political systems, political leaders competitively vie for resources and advantageous position; political development or durable change occurs as a result of competition over power. One of the more subtle ways leaders use the state to exert power is in defining the nation and its members. It is a truism in political science that the modern nation is the child of the state, but influence in the relationship runs in both directions.[127] The group of national members lurks like a shadow and exerts its own influence on state legitimacy. The surprise is that local leaders and groups in Illinois could engage in a "national" power struggle that, in the end, prompted them to separate from the regime's parties and partially at least from the Illinois state. In each case, Mormon and anti-Mormon, once the extralegal course was taken, an additional need to construct and defend group worth surfaced.

Like Mary Douglas and David Greenstone, Rogers M. Smith offers a compelling matrix for applying his theory of membership to a variety of group-worth cases. He categorizes political group membership by the degree of allegiance it commands and the range of issues it addresses. Smith creates nine categories, with "strong, moderate, and weak" degrees of allegiance varying along a range of "wide, midrange, and narrow" issue dimensions.[128] While all groups exert less or more pull on members, Smith's analysis focuses attention on the jealous demands of the "strong and wide" category. This is the house of power where the state lives. Political membership asks for an allegiance reaching to right and wrong and life and death; it spans a full range of public duties that deeply encumber private sphere freedoms. Smith argues that the "stories of peoplehood" used by state-building groups are constitutive of a public identity with the potential to reshape the interests of their members.[129] Leaders use peoplehood stories to induce trust in followers. When trust in state institutions is weak or new, as in settler societies like Illinois or the many developing democracies of the twenty-first century, worth and the civic narratives justifying trust and authorizing public sphere duties become proportionally more important. These stories generate new conceptions of worth that followers endorse and enforce on each other.

SMITH'S PEOPLEHOOD GROUPS

	WIDE ISSUE RANGE	MIDRANGE	NARROW ISSUE RANGE
STRONG TIES	US, China	Quebec	Jehovah's Witnesses
MODERATE TIES	Belgium, Navajo Nation	Wales	AFL-CIO, Greenpeace
WEAK TIES	Puerto Rico	Brooklyn	Oxfam

Adapted from *Stories of Peoplehood*, 21

Smith's matrix lays bare the fact that all political groups claim some degree of self-government and all political groups encroach to some degree on the public sphere duties of their members. In groups organized around a narrow range of issues calling for wholly voluntary attachment, the social setting is necessarily fluid and the personal ties created are largely negotiable private sphere matters. For example, a refugee rights organization's attachment is weak and its range narrow; membership duties may involve only annual dues and periodic meetings, events, and actions; its reach is almost exclusively limited to voluntary private sphere activities. But it is still a public sphere group with its own orbit of political allegiance in that members may be asked to put their refugee rights commitments ahead of obeying the law of the state in protests or demonstrations. By contrast, a group advocating greater autonomy for the Navajo within the United States can be characterized as moderate in the attachment it expects and midrange in the scope of its public sphere activities. Although the range of issues it addresses is broader than an advocacy group because it crosses fully into the realm of minority-group representation or self-government, its demands on members are moderate in that its goals are policies and laws, but they are laws that stop short of calling for self-rule as a fully independent nation.

Illinois was a semiautonomous department of the American state in which the emphasis on worth was strong and wide. Institutions like the militia, the posse, and claim societies provided regime services in exchange for the worth tied to a share of sovereignty. The setting in Illinois was thus conducive to self-governing varieties of worth; republican stories build solidarity by marking the boundaries between those deemed worthy of self-government and those not. Worth stories before the Enlightenment's liberal era were crafted from ascriptive materials. Over time, these born-into kinds of group worth were rejected as illiberal and were replaced with republican models more inclusive and universal in theory if not in practice.[130] The emphasis on choice and voluntary membership in liberal social contract theory has obscured the fact that republican worth stories offer majorities cultural and institutional means to exclude. Such exclusions operate even in settings that do not reinforce the predominant hierarchical and ascriptive traits of race/ethnicity, class, and gender. The Illinois story of peoplehood was one such republican worth story, the civic narrative of the independent producer. As we have seen, Illinoisans of all stripes celebrated the land of adventure their story projected.

Smith uses his matrix to detail the two general "processes through which political peoples are created . . . : coercive force and persuasive stories."[131] He refines the continuum of political power outlined by Alexander Hamilton in the first *Federalist* paper about societies building governments of either "accident and force" or "reflection and choice."[132] Force, on one far end of the power continuum, is always an option for state-building groups. But in democratic societies, according to Smith, leaders retail "economic, political, and ethically constitutive" themes to make reflection and choice persuasive. Economic stories claim that a separate people under nationhood will enjoy economic benefits and prosperity; this theme is perhaps emphasized most commonly in new nationalist movements, such as those in Catalonia and Scotland today. Political stories promise a separate people governing benefits like equality and freedom, themes prominently featured in the American and French Revolutions. But it is the last kind of story which has been the most overlooked if the most troublesome: the claim that as a separate state a people will constitute an ethically worthy group. Smith rightfully emphasizes the role played by leaders in the shaping, framing, and retailing of worth stories; in politically competitive liberal democracies, worth stories stand behind and justify specific political regimes that authorize elites to dole out power.

The story of peoplehood in Illinois emerged in the context of a backward-looking distinction between the settlers and the Indigenous people, but it quickly took on a forward-looking life of its own as a story of adventure and freedom. Here emerged the political theme of Illinois peoplehood. Looking forward or backward, most Jacksonian Democrats experienced membership in the group of independent White male producers as the primary fact of political life. Here the private sphere goals of getting clear of the land office converged with the public sphere duties of taking responsibility. Political leaders debated which groups best embodied the ethically constitutive public sphere ideal of the independent producer. Illinois's competitive party dynamic created constant adjustment over how the independent-producer narrative would be interpreted within the state's majority societal culture. The example of the 1841 court challenge defining "the right of Aliens to vote" illustrates how each party felt authorized to police the boundaries of the polity. The Whigs attacked alien suffrage as a means the Democrats used to direct the vote of dependent and unworthy foreign workers in places like Galena and Joliet, while Jacksonian papers like the *State Register* rejected out of hand Justice T. W. Smith's opinion simply because it would allow "a negro or Indian" to vote.[133]

At the state level, the Democrats heralded "equal rights" as a guiding principle. In practice this meant, according to the *St. Clair Banner,* "that government is best which governs least," because government intervention in the economy via the granting of monopolies so often left conditions unequal in its wake.[134] For the Illinois Jacksonians, governing less meant defaulting to local civil society as the locus for controlling and determining independent-producer status. The Illinois Whigs critiqued this "democratic dogma," which as the *Quincy Whig* had it, "let the government take care of itself and the people [take care] of themselves."[135] But the Whigs largely joined and competed under the political and ethically constitutive themes of the regime, which were attractive and powerful enough that even Joseph Smith flattered them with imitation. The Mormons plausibly fit the category of independent producers, and the language of equality ran throughout their own writings on political matters. Perhaps most surprising from today's perspective is the fact that the Democrats and the Mormons, most of whom could broadly be described as egalitarian, could have evolved such different political positions.

For the Democrats the most prominent negative reference was the Bank of the United States, with its chartered privilege. Particularist egalitarians extended solidarity to the White male farmer as a specific positive reference group, while universalist egalitarians conjured a positive reference in the form of "the laboring classes of the United States," as writer William Leggett had it.[136] Egalitarians under Mary Douglas's model orient themselves symbolically in opposition to a negative reference group, one perceived as unfairly favored in the social pecking order. While individualists do not emphasize reference-group loyalty or vertical equality, their horizontal equality—equality among individuals at the same social level—expects symmetrical reciprocity from others, an expectation carried over from the competitive societal settings which give rise to the subculture. When applied in the arena of group equity, the expectation of symmetry hamstrings the state's ability to justify the necessarily asymmetrical legal exceptions granted to minority groups or specific locales. The individualist culture motivates liberals to favor a law of general rules, which ensures equality but not equity or fairness to all.

Underneath this frame controlled by regime leaders in Illinois was a local zone controlled by county-based followers, where unwritten rules of standing prevailed. In Hancock County local leaders broke away from the state's regime leadership. Marginal groups like the Mormons actively attempted to navigate the majority culture's unwritten rules. Similarly, the anti-Mormons, who felt neglected and mistreated by Springfield, decided to take matters into their own hands. They had recourse to the many informal, locally negotiated rules governing social relations. These politically authoritative rules were made with the requirements of group worth in mind, with worthiness debated and defined in the newspapers, groceries, and halls of local power. In Illinois's Mormon troubles, de facto state leadership was driven on the Mormon side by Joseph Smith and, after June of 1844, Brigham Young and Jacob Backenstos; the anti-Mormon side was led by Thomas Sharp, Thomas Gregg, and Levi Williams. Each of these agents decisively shaped the conflict by taking pivotal actions presented by the political system at critical junctures.

After the second habeas proceeding in Monmouth and the inability of several sheriffs to locate the prophet at Nauvoo during the fall of 1842, Sharp concluded, "Joe cannot be taken. Situated as he is, he can set the laws of the state at our defiance, and never fear being apprehended." The problem was worse since it made the whole community above the law: "Mormons can only be punished by consent of their Prophet. This is the pass we have come to; and yet there are white men to be found, who tell us there is no danger to be apprehended from the Mormons!"[137] Sharp here quickly shifted from a focus on individual rights to the community's societal prerogative. Shifting so easily, he demonstrated the compelling logic of the Illinois regime's commitment to local majority control.

When Ford received the proceedings of the anti-Mormon meeting of January 1844, brought to him by a group seeking relief from Mormon control over the county, he offered a response that focused on Mormon and anti-Mormon rights as individuals alone. He wrote, "I am bound by the laws and the constitution to regard you all as citizens of the state, possessed of equal rights and privileges; and to cherish the rights of one as dearly as the rights of another." The group had asked the governor to "raise a militia to arrest a supposed fugitive" who Ford noted could be arrest legally only in the case of a state of war between the two groups. He warned the petitioners that if they "let it come to this, [and] let a state of war ensue," he would be compelled to arrest "the first transgressor." Sharp drew the obvious implication: Ford was cautioning the anti-Mormons against initiating any violent action. Sharp's reply requires a full quotation:

> The Governor here tells us that he can at present do nothing legally, in relation to the present difficulties. We conceive that he is right: But has there not been a time recently when executive power could have been legally exercised, by bringing to justice one who had set at defiance the Laws of the State?

> When Smith was arrested by a warrant from the Governor, and rescued by an armed force, was it not in his power to see that the Laws were faithfully executed, and to maintain their supremacy over the powers of insurrectionary violence? . . . It is said however that if Smith was rescued, it was the duty of the officer from whose custody he was taken, to raise the *posse comitatus,* and enforce obedience to the Laws. We think otherwise. Of what avail would a *posse* have been, when a majority of the citizens of the county, organized as a regular military band, were arrayed on the side of the prisoner? . . . We do not impugn the motives of his Excellency, in refusing to enforce the law by Executive Power. We believe he acted from the honest dictates of his judgment . . . [but] if a state of war should absolutely occur, might not his Excellency find some difficulty on determining who were the aggressors? And if he should not, might not, in this democratic country, the multitude who he should send here to mediate between the belligerents take a different view of the matter?[138]

As events proved, Sharp showed himself to be something of a prophet in his concluding remarks.

More importantly, he demonstrated how the enforcement of individual rights clearly depended upon local majority support. Sharp perhaps inadvertently raised the issue of what scholars today would call the boundary problem in democracies. Majority rule can give clear guidance to authorities on an issue, but the majority of which unit? The anti-Mormons constituted a majority in Hancock outside Nauvoo; the Mormons controlled the majority in Hancock County as a whole, but the anti-Mormons could likely call upon a majority from nearby counties to enforce Illinois regime rules and to come to their aid in an emergency. As Ford would discover, a focus on horizontal equality implemented neutrally by the state—the ideal of the rule of law—was insufficient to solving the Mormon problem.

A new spike of fear among the anti-Mormons was raised in August of 1845. Letters and editorials appearing in the *Warsaw Signal* commented on the recent election of Mormons to the offices of sheriff and the county commissioner's court. "Hancock," from Pontoosuc, argued the election had deprived the "old citizens" of privileges which "the poorest and humblest man in any other part of the Union" still retained; they had lost their voice from the federal level all the way down to the indignity of "exercising no agency in their own county affairs . . . [and even] in their own neighborhoods and villages."[139] Meetings of the county court held at Carthage, the county seat and anti-Mormon stronghold, were particularly tense. Any action taken in support of the Mormons, as when Sheriff Backenstos presented a large number of Mormons to be awarded pauper rights, was contested by the anti-Mormons who lined the courtroom and surrounded the court building. Of this episode Sharp commented, "The Mormons although they are the most numerous in Hancock are by no means the largest taxpayers yet they make all appropriations of the funds of the county and squander [them] away, according to the commands of the church."[140]

Since the Mormons had insisted on their own courts and juries, they were the side which eschewed a level playing field and sought special privileges; Sharp argued that the Mormons, in seeking and gaining their own city and militia charters, had gained undeserved advantages. The sense of unfairness grew among the anti-Mormons until it reached a breaking point in September of 1845. Shots fired near an anti-Mormon meeting at Green Plains, southeast of Warsaw, on September 9 generated the first spark. The next night, as Sharp related, "The Antis proceeded to commence immediate proceedings and drive the Saints from the lower [Morley] settlement as they had long been threatening to do."[141] Over the course of the next week, the anti-Mormons "burned down with fire about 150 or 175 houses, cabins, and hovels" in Morley, Green Plains, and the Bear Creek area. Later, during another arson attack, they murdered the old Mormon farmer Edmund Durfee. Episodes of rough justice followed in rapid succession: Sheriff Backenstos formed a posse of Mormons who roamed the county "stealing and plundering whatever was convenient to carry or drive away."[142] They searched for the arsonists until they found and killed one of the burners, Samuel McBratney.

On September 16, Sheriff Backenstos was moving his family from Warsaw to Nauvoo for protection when he was intercepted by a group of anti-Mormons led by Franklin A. Worrell, who would be killed in the chase. Worrell was not involved in the arson but was an officer of the Carthage Greys, "who commanded the guard at the jail at the time the Smiths were assassinated."[143] The details of Worrell's death were thus narrated by Oaks and Hill based largely on the official transcript:

> Franklin Worrell . . . was one of the four men who, in an attempt to intercept Backenstos, separated from the main body after a two-mile chase. As these pursuers closed to within 150 yards, Backenstos reached the railroad shanties north of Warsaw, where some members of the Mormon militia were escorting to Nauvoo some Mormon families who had been burned out of their homes. Backenstos shouted to the Mormons for help and got an instant response from Orrin Porter Rockwell, close friend and former bodyguard of the dead prophet. Rockwell reassured Backenstos that his men had fifty rounds of ammunition and two fifteen-shot rifles. Backenstos immediately commanded his pursuers to stop, but they kept riding toward him. At Backenstos's command Rockwell singled out Worrell, took careful aim, and shot him squarely in the belt buckle, knocking him out of his saddle. The other pursuers reined in, put Worrell in a wagon, and rode hard for Warsaw. Worrell died en route. He was buried in a ten-dollar coffin beneath a wooden headboard bearing the epitaph: "He who is without enemies is unworthy of friends."[144]

Sharp issued an editorial mourning "Poor Frank" and proclaimed, "To Arms! To Arms!"[145] Backenstos organized a Mormon march on Carthage. At this point Ford sent a militia under the command of General J. J. Hardin to restore order. Hardin found Backenstos "in control of [Carthage] and thirty men bivouacked in the courthouse. Hardin gave Backenstos twenty minutes to leave town."[146]

During and after these trying events, the anti-Mormons employed a two-pronged rhetorical strategy aiming to show that the anti-Mormons were as worthy as the Mormons were unworthy. Sharp advocated the local removal or sequestration of the Mormons on grounds that the saints were unfair to their neighbors. Sharp drew out the moral of every local news story, large and small, he printed. Mormon duplicity in trade was illustrated by the story of a Mormon woman who sold "a lump of beeswax to one of our [Warsaw] merchants which on examination, turned out to be nothing more than a large piece of limestone covered in beeswax."[147] After the Mormons suffered arson and murder southeast of Warsaw, the anti-Mormons addressed a public resolution to those outside Hancock County insisting they were not the aggressors; they preferred, "and the history of our difficulties will show that we have ever preferred, to suffer wrong rather than become wrong doers."[148]

At the time, however, Sharp issued a succession of extra editions in which he justified the aggression:

> It is unnecessary for us to recapitulate the causes which led to the recent disturbances in the south of our county. It was not one outrage alone, which roused our citizens, with the determination to rid the county of the outlawed villains that infest it; but for years, wrong upon wrong, insult upon insult, had been heaped upon us. We had been robbed of our property times without number; many of our citizens had been grossly abused and insulted; the lives of some of the most estimable men in our community have been threatened, for no crime other than opposition to tyranny; our political rights have been taken from us; we could get no justice in the courts of our own county; and, in short, every outrage, every wrong, every indignity, that the malice and cupidity of our enemies could suggest, had been inflicted on the old settlers of Hancock. They had borne it until to many it seemed that forbearance had ceased to be a virtue; and at last a small body of determined men, rendered desperate by the remembrance of long continued wrongs, commenced the work of ridding our neighborhood of the presence of the banditti that infested it. They did this on their own responsibility, but in the well-founded belief that the citizens of other counties would assist in driving from the State a community that any man at all acquainted with its character, admits to be entirely unfit to dwell in the midst of civilized society. Time and again have influential citizens of other counties, who were acquainted with our wrongs, averred that it was only necessary to set the ball in motion, and a force sufficient to keep it moving, would immediately flock to our standard. . . . Citizens of surrounding counties, you now have one of two things to determine. Will you have this banditti for your neighbors, or will you sustain the old settlers?[149]

In the extra editions, Sharp included proceedings of anti-Mormon meetings from other counties, including those in Adams, Henderson, McDonough, and Warren in Illinois and Clark in Missouri. The resolutions passed at these meetings provide ample evidence that Sharp had been successful in framing the issue as one of Mormon unfairness and asymmetry. At the Pittsfield meeting in Adams County, its attendees announced that the Mormons had "long enough trespassed upon the other citizens of Hancock." They added, "We shall not allow them those special privileges which they claim, and which they can only enjoy at our expense."[150]

Sharp was keenly aware that he needed the support of Illinois public opinion for the anti-Mormon cause to succeed. For months, his target audience was the citizens of Adams, Brown, Cass, Fulton, Pike, Marquette, McDonough, Morgan, Schuyler, and Scott Counties, whose militias held the balance of power in the region.[151] He organized a petition signed by 370 Democrats from Hancock County, reiterating the nonpartisan basis of the group. Most state politicians had washed their hands of the Mormons, and the Warsaw editor worked to protect the anti-Mormons from sharing the same fate. When the Democrats' *State Register* in 1845 presented the Whig Party with a bill of sale for ownership of the Mormon vote, the Whigs were said to have declined the bargain.[152] The lack of interest in the Mormons might have portended a lack of interest in Hancock County's seemingly endless troubles. The anti-Mormons feared being left to fight the Mormons alone. Indeed, without a countywide majority and the officers it elected, the anti-Mormons were even more vulnerable than the Mormons. When writing to the general public, as the anti-Mormons frequently did in open letters and resolutions, their leaders emphasized that the Mormons were a civic danger to all of Illinois, not just to their closest neighbors.

A sign that public opinion in the state concurred was the General Assembly's act of January 29, 1845, which repealed the Nauvoo city and Nauvoo Legion charters by an overwhelming vote and over the objections of the governor.[153] The *Sangamo Journal* censured the Mormons for a number of innovations "against the spirit and genius of our government" contained in their "extraordinary charter." A further complaint was that the "privileged Mormons" only had to work on the roads three days a week on the streets of Nauvoo while the standard was five days for all other Illinoisans.[154] Sharp emphasized that the Mormons relied on double standards: they asked for the protection of the law but asymmetrically would not enforce it against their own. Sharp made much of the fact that in theft cases Mormon witnesses were "sworn *to order* . . . [and] every Mormon culprit is to be shielded."[155] But public opinion could also backtrack on the anti-Mormons, as was intimated in the open letter sent to them on October 4, 1845, in which they were told the following in no uncertain terms: "Remember—whatever may be the aggression against you, the sympathy of the people may be forfeited. It cannot be denied that the burning of the houses of the Mormons in Hancock County, by which a large number of women and children have been rendered homeless, and houseless, in the beginning of winter, was an act criminal in itself and disgraceful to the perpetrators."[156]

Because of the stigma of such anti-Mormon crimes, Sharp purposely increased his rhetoric to justify such actions. He now sought to persuade all in Illinois that "a more dangerous, corrupt, and infatuated set of scoundrels, than are the Mormons, does not exist on the face of the earth." He detailed the statements made by Elder Heber C. Kimball in February of 1845 that "the Saints here in the city of Nauvoo and the region round about, have . . . confidence in the Twelve as a body." Sharp argued this confidence undermined Mormon claims to inclusion on grounds of an "anti-Republican" lack of independence; one set of Mormon rulers had been replaced by another with alacrity, yet the followers believed "the leaders should be obeyed *in all things*." Sharp concluded by quoting W. W. Phelps, who said: "As far as concerns myself, ye People of Illinois, I say goodbye to your justice, good bye to your legislative rights. . . . We have waited for [your] deliberations by minding our own business, but we have waited in vain, and consequently we have framed our own Constitution and adopted our own laws, and have agreed to a habeas corpus for ourselves, independent of Warsaw or the great state of Carthage." Here was reasoning and a public declaration of allegiance calculated to strike egalitarians and individualists alike as perverse.[157]

Given variability in degree and range, political groups are strongly reliant on leaders. Since leaders employ multiple cultural tropes, there is considerable room for maneuver in the shaping of any group's story of peoplehood. Leaders frequently take advantage of cultural variation to press definitions and frames that further their own interests. This was certainly the case in Illinois, where leaders Thomas Sharp and Joseph Smith dominated the responses of their "people." We can track Smith's presentation of Mormon worth and Sharp's direction of the anti-Mormon response in the many habeas corpus episodes occurring between 1840 and 1844. Each of the episodes resulted in Smith gaining his freedom, a fact which his opponents viewed as making a mockery of justice through an evasion of the law. In three of the episodes, the Nauvoo Legion was implicated in a way that played into the hands of Sharp's framing of that institution. The anti-Mormons plausibly argued that the Mormons were violating the common understanding of equal rights and the state's implicit rules of worthy peoplehood.

Sharp indicated that the anti-Mormons of Warsaw and Carthage were the real authority to be followed. When Murray McConnell, Governor Ford's special prosecutor, showed up at the offices of the *Signal* in September of 1844 with a writ of arrest for Sharp for the murder of the Smith brothers, the editor walked outside into the Warsaw town square saying, "We would abide by the decision of our friends." Upon "consultation [they] unanimously advised us not to go to Nauvoo, where the writ was properly returnable."[158] He thus acted out the civic script that in an anti-Mormon regime, the old citizens would rule.

In the two years from October 1844 to October 1846, both sides in the troubles erected makeshift vigilante organizations to enforce their own law. The Mormons met in "secret council" with a "body of Indians" and marched the Nauvoo Legion within four miles of Carthage while the circuit court was sitting. Brigham Young resorted to using an armed guard and requested another writ of habeas corpus to protect a witness during the trial of the Smith brothers' murderers.[159] Because the Nauvoo charter had been revoked, the Mormons resorted to an informal posse to keep order; the stable of Joseph Smith's old Nauvoo Mansion was converted into a makeshift prison.[160] The anti-Mormons also took law enforcement into their own hands. Levi Williams called out the Warsaw militia on his own authority multiple times during that pivotal September of 1845.[161] The group calling themselves the "Central Committee" organized the effort to insist on a Mormon exodus. Indeed, of the two groups, Sheriff Deming believed "the exterminators [the anti-Mormons] . . . [were] more fanatical than the Mormons and less regardful of the law."[162]

Sharp nevertheless stoutly refuted every charge of lawlessness. To the Whig editor of the *Alton Telegraph* he wrote: "Men may talk as much as they please about the sanctity of law, they never can and never will, prevent freemen from taking the law into their own hands when they feel they are aggrieved and that they have no legal remedy. If the law had provided or could have provided a remedy for the evils under which the people of Hancock were laboring, we should have been the last to justify illegal violence."[163] Governor Ford's only answer was that there was no legal remedy for prejudice. His letter in late July 1844 exhorted the anti-Mormons of Warsaw to reconsider their "infatuated resolutions."[164] When he sent his report to the legislature on the storming of Carthage Jail, he felt obligated to reassert the charge against the anti-Mormons of religious persecution. The Central Committee responded with a "Memorial" asking the General Assembly to investigate the "reported thefts and larceny" which the governor had dismissed as "without foundation."[165] The Mormons, for their part, supported Sheriff Backenstos, who defended his actions against the anti-Mormons as acts of self-defense against "lawless banditti" and "mobbers."[166] Backenstos issued several proclamations empowering the posse comitatus to restore the peace. Sharp duly published these—in all their militaristic language—which further incited resistance. When the sheriff marched into an abandoned Carthage with his Mormon posse to purge it of insurgents, the only peace to be restored was among the ghosts in the town graveyard.

6

Religious Toleration and Political Ideology in the Illinois Regime

The habeas and militia episodes detailed in the last chapter demonstrate that well before Carthage Jail was stormed and the Smith brothers were murdered, the Mormons and the Illinoisans in Hancock County experienced a series of altercations tearing the body politic apart. What from the Mormon perspective looked like Joseph Smith's effective use of the writ, prudent deployment of the militia, and adroit manipulation of the two parties looked to the Hancock settlers like a mockery of the law and a travesty of justice. The old settlers concluded they had lost control over their government and with it their self-determination.

Although the broken polity experienced few episodes of personal injury and only sporadic cases of the loss of property before June of 1844, simple operation of the legal system served to erode trust, and mutual respect evaporated. The anti-Mormons came to believe a larger conflict was inevitable. The power and unanimity of this belief suggests that our understanding is incomplete if we focus on the facts of physical harm and threat to property alone.

When governance breaks down, subtle differences in foundational beliefs nestled in political subcultures come to the fore. The recognition of difference creates openings which leaders use to highlight disagreement and reinforce group consciousness.

Anti-Mormon leaders framed the Mormon troubles as a crisis of local control, a theme the Illinois regime recognized and honored. But a more obvious explanation of the troubles has also been urged: religious persecution. Were not the Mormon troubles at root motivated by a religious conflict? Could it be that the anti-Mormons' concerns about self-government were a cover for a politically incorrect religious intolerance? John E. Hallwas and Roger D. Launius, in their comprehensive documentary history of Illinois's "Mormon War," argue that religion was at the root of the conflict. They use the term *myth* to explain the role of differing beliefs: the Illinoisans had a republican myth and the Mormons a Christian myth; these different interpretative frameworks drove the disagreement. Hallwas and Launius allow that the two frameworks overlap somewhat, but in their account repeated and salient mythic differences led to widespread disagreement, contention, and eventually violence.[1]

Literary scholar Terryl Givens also describes the Mormon-American relationship as one controlled by myth and religion, but he adds the dimension of hegemony. The "American investment in the ideal of religious tolerance has been a part of our self-presentation, our shared American mythology," so much so that, like a hegemonic belief system, it was not easily questioned. In Givens's account the challenge the Mormons posed to mainstream Americans needed to be worked out fictively over time. "America's ongoing process of self-definition," Givens argues, "has been facilitated by the appropriation of images of a handy, ready-made Other. The Mormon Villain, it turns out, is integrally related to the evolving American self-definition." Since the anti-Mormons in Illinois did not have the luxury of time, they may have sublimated religious hatred welling up during a compressed period into political grievances. In the literary canon he studies, Givens further establishes that since the constitutional norm of religious toleration was openly violated by many anti-Mormons, a "rhetorical strategy" disassociating "Mormonism from religion" was needed. The strategy was difficult to execute, doubly so, according to Givens, because the rejection of Mormonism was itself hard to place within a "Jacksonian America" committed to a broader social "tolerance of non-conformity."[2]

Givens documents the creation of a Mormon ethnicity in American literature and politics in the years following their expulsion from Illinois. Religious toleration was foundational and endorsed in a way that made it hegemonic—that is, an ideological force disguised as common sense in Antonio Gramsci's original understanding of the term.[3] Givens argues that the Mormons were "an example of radical otherness that did not blatantly manifest otherness." In sum, Mormonism was both familiar and threatening: "the viper on the hearth."[4] Besides the reality of religious prejudice, the Mormons also had to struggle against a commitment against religious prejudice which was assumed to be the common sense of American life and thus more powerful in precisely the way Gramsci observed. Could it be that anti-Mormons felt the force of hegemonic belief and denied their true motives?

THE LIMITS OF HEGEMONY

It is true that the ideal of religious toleration was hegemonic in the Illinois polity. It hovered in the background as an assumed commitment, an ideological product of the first American regime institutionalized under the United States Constitution. By the 1820s, specific American liberties like the freedom of religion came to the fore in contexts of comparison with European regime alternatives such as monarchy or aristocracy. Religious toleration was touted as a comparative advantage of the New over the Old World, a gift of an independent peoplehood inherited by the third generation of Americans after the Revolution. Arguments for religious toleration had won the day, and it had achieved a seldom-questioned legitimacy as a foundational belief. Separation of church and state was hegemonic in the sense that people of all classes and walks of life treated it as the most justifiable way to accommodate different religious practices in one polity. It was a legitimated status quo, a condition attained by other political freedoms like speech, press, and assembly.

But institutions like a free press can take more than one form, and different forms carry different ideological nuances. Working out the tensions between an old regime and a new one is what makes for the politics of regime consolidation; "articulating" new policies requires negotiating power while the tectonic plates of a political order shift.[5] Regime transitions keep a "polity suspended in a perpetual state of development, rendering it always to some degree imminent, unsettled, in the making."[6] In the case of the tension between the ideals of local self-government and freedom of religion, the conflict was not one of replacing old commitments altogether but finding a balance between two foundational commitments. The Supreme Court was not yet recognized as the final arbiter of the meaning of constitutional phrases, and much of the debate of the era, while not questioning the basic premise, focused on the specific form the constitutional inheritance should take.

The issue of postage reform serves as an example of the tension between two foundational beliefs hidden in what appears as a small change in institutional form and organizational policy. In a gambit at regime modification that failed, the Democrats proposed removing the franking privilege granted government officers and replacing it with universal free postage on newspapers. The idea was to make information less costly and allow the political news to reach every grocery. Free postage, it was argued, had been adopted with success in England and with modifications by "the Autocrat of Russia. . . . And shall republican America linger behind the monarchies of Europe? Must our government, the freest and most popular on earth . . . not risk a cent to promote the general circulation of knowledge, good will, and public virtue . . . ?"[7] Here the Democrats urged what modern scholars call a "deliberative" approach to First Amendment interpretation, one that allows government regulation of the speech market if the result is more information entering the public sphere, providing more opportunities for deliberation.[8] This approach carries nuances in favor of a local deliberative democracy, just as keeping government out of the speech market altogether biases the system in favor of libertarian democracy. Yet both approaches assume institutional support of a free press is a fundamental value. A similar nuance and diversity of approach lay just beneath the commitment to freedom of religion.

The hegemonic premises of religious toleration were tested by the Mormons in Illinois as early as 1836. Despite the efforts by mainstream Christian preachers to exclude the Mormons, religious independence in Illinois was defined broadly under the 1818 constitution, and in practice the law worked to include them. Evidence of this comes from a Whig lawyer's argument before a jury in an assault case carrying religious overtones. In 1836 attorney

Isaac Hendershot was representing plaintiff Harvey Green against Miles Van Miekle and others at the February session of the St. Clair County Circuit Court. Hendershot's speech to the jury was published in the *Alton Telegraph* along with the decision; not very remarkable newspaper material but for the fact that Green was a Mormon and the assailants charged with assault and battery were Methodists.[9] At the time, the Mormons were a tiny minority in the state and the Methodists were likely the largest religious sect.

The case was unique, the attorney argued, because of the assailants' motive. Why did they attack Green? During oral argument Hendershot asked and answered his own question:

> What is the character of my unfortunate client? And what is the justification offered by the defendants in this action, for so barbarously attacking and so inhumanely beating an innocent and unoffending man? . . . A man of strictly moral and Christian deportment, a man who has never attempted in any way whatever to offer a menace, or insult to any man in this community. . . . A man, too, who was just recovering from a severe and prolonged case of fever and ague? . . . It appears that he is guilty of the awful and dreadfully appalling crime of being a Mormon minister, for this alone have the defendants whipped him.

Hendershot reminded the jury of the standards laid down in the Illinois Constitution of 1818. He quoted from article 8, which declared a set of "general, great, and essential principles of liberty," including that "all men have a natural and indefeasible right to worship Almighty God according to the dictates of their own consciences; that no man can of right be compelled to attend, erect or support any place of worship, or to maintain any ministry against his consent; that no human authority can in any case whatever control or interfere with the rights of conscience."[10] Green's claim to worship his religion secured, Hendershot next established parity between his client and the jurors. Place yourself "in the situation of Harvey Green," he requested. Several members on the jury, he mentioned, were practicing Methodists; he himself "had been rocked in the very cradle of Methodism." Was not "religious prejudice," he asked, the cause of the "bloody history" of Europe? Was not "this same prejudice . . . [exercised] in Great Britain against the [Methodist] disciples of John Wesley?"

Hendershot beseeched the jury to relinquish its prejudices against Green: "If, gentlemen of the jury, there exists within your bosoms a single spark of prejudice, it is your duty, it is your sworn duty, to wrestle it from you. . . . I doubt not that every man in that jury box is a true patriot and a friend to his happy country, but *I* know that prejudice against the Mormons is natural, and *I* know that it is strong."[11] He concluded:

> Tear Religious prejudice from your bosoms . . . let the Mahometan, the Pagan, the Jew, the Catholic, and the Mormon have the same impartial justice at your hands as the Presbyterian, the Baptist, and the Methodist, for such is the spirit, such is the genius of our political institutions. . . . I will only say to you in conclusion that you are Americans and when you return to this court with a verdict, it will be here recorded, and let that record tell to posterity, that in the year of our Lord eighteen hundred and thirty six, there lived in Saint Clair County TWELVE PATRIOTS.

Allegiance to America, he implied, should overrule any mere denominational membership. The *Telegraph* records that "the jury found the defendants guilty."

The Methodist attorney's speech identified the legal institutions undergirding social and political relations in Illinois, but it also exposed some of the norms and attitudes shaping group life. It suggests that prejudice against Mormons as a group already marked the Illinois landscape as early as 1836. While the first mob scenes and three deaths had already occurred in Jackson County, Missouri—which Illinoisans had certainly heard about—the St. Clair jury met before the Mormon bank failed in Kirtland, Ohio, and well before the major episodes of the Missouri War. Thus it is likely that majority religious opinion alone drove the anti-Mormon prejudice that Hendershot referenced. Remarkably, the jury perhaps sided with common sense over religious sense.

Toleration of religious difference was a value that shaped the initial reception of the Mormons in Illinois. The people of Quincy endorsed the status of the Mormons as worthy refugees who had been persecuted unjustly in Missouri. As early as April of 1839, the *Quincy Argus* was publishing appeals requesting that "Illinois citizens [make] benevolent exertions to relieve this distressed people, who are now wandering in our neighborhoods, without comfortable food, raiment, or shelter."[12] Emma Smith wrote to her husband that "the people in this state are very kind indeed, they are doing much more than we ever anticipated they would."[13] Later in that summer of 1839, an anti-Mormon mob in Shelby County was thoroughly denounced by several newspapers throughout Illinois and was editorialized against in the *Daily Chicago American*.[14] The Chicago editor explicitly used the liberal language of religious freedom, although mixed with an egalitarian focus on persecution: "In this free country it is an abomination to persecute men for opinion's sake. Americans who spring from a persecuted stock, should be the last to interfere with religious opinion."[15] Prejudice, the source of illiberal intolerance, is here denounced as an "abomination."

If the treatment of the Mormons in Illinois was solely about tolerating individuals, their reception should have ended as Hendershot argued. Clearly, more was involved and perceived to be at stake. Notice, however, that even on liberal individualist grounds alone there were problems with applying Hendershot's argument fully to the Mormon case, for the Illinois Constitution, one paragraph after the one quoted above, contained the following principle: "that no religious test shall ever be required as a qualification to any office or public trust under this state." The Mormons themselves could not accommodate this principle because it clearly envisions a separation of church and state, a separation they, in their own communities, did not honor. Here the rhetoric of parity exposes an asymmetry—a failure on the Mormon side to reciprocate—that could and did lead to liberal intolerance on the Illinoisans' side. The intolerance here was driven not by bigotry but conceptions of fairness: the problem blocking accommodation was either one of allegiance to a different primary group, which especially disturbed egalitarians as a slight to worth, or an asymmetry of rights, which individualists especially believed induces distrust.[16] Hendershot's arguments and the setting in which they were made thus prefigure how both parties, Whig and Democrat, and both political cultures, individualist and egalitarian, conspired to impede the Mormon pathway to full membership in the Illinois circle of worthies.

In short, the existence of hegemonic premises in directed liberal democratic settings does not mean all debate is squelched, opposition quiescent, or that framing biases will leave foundational beliefs unmodified. The battle for and against hegemonic common sense has to be fought and won or lost, as Gramsci argued, across multiple arenas of civil society. Nor is it accurate to suggest that the critical self-fashioning opposed to hegemony works itself out exclusively or even primarily in the vicarious domain of literature or the media. The political arena is an ideological site of first-hand confrontation with the status quo and attempted revisions.

Take as an example the role played by the Whigs as a political opposition. The party was only too happy to defend freedom of the press from those who believed "the American press . . . level[ed] to an undistinguishable mass the educated, the ignorant, and the base," an assumption readily believed by that "portion of the European people who think that the happiness of mankind depends on the maintenance of Monarchical and Aristocratical Political Institutions. They cannot bear the idea that practical Republicanism should be found sufficient for the prosperity, stability, or happiness of nations."[17] But the Whigs hastened to add that some practical republican papers (generally Whig) were of much higher quality than others (generally Democratic). "Modern democracy," they argued, wrongly focused on quantity, an agrarian leveling aiming at a misguided "social equality"; the Whigs by contrast were keepers of republican quality.[18] The Whigs repeatedly made this argument in civil society by attacking the regime's common sense veneer of social equality using precisely the antihegemonic approach Gramsci prescribed. The hegemony of common sense existed, but in a relatively open (if still regime-directed) setting its power was contested and thus limited.

There are also reasons to resist a too-quick assumption that the disavowal of religious bigotry by opponents was a strategic ploy. In the Illinois case the anti-Mormons were not above casting aspersions on the Mormons and mocking their unconventional social practices. The bigoted approach is taken when one condemns all the members of a group for negative traits ascribed to and fixed on the group by nonmembers. Bigots illiberally prejudge individuals on the basis of a putative, indelible group trait. Ironically, some of the strongest bigotry during the troubles in Illinois was expressed by Mormon apostates like John C. Bennett or sophisticated critics like Jonathan Baldwin Turner. But bigots often do not need to hide their bigotry. They rely on traits conventionally ascribed to vulnerable groups by the societal pecking order—that other source of common sense.

Those in Illinois who rejected the Mormons on grounds of their religion being unacceptable frequently came out and said so, such as Democrat F. A. Snyder, editor of *The Politician* at Belleville, who ridiculed Smith for his "spiritual zeal" and all his followers as "fools."[19] In Bloomington, during the 1840 election season, a Mormon came to town to give a speech defending the Whigs and "was asked to leave town by the Democrats" simply because he was a Mormon.[20] Baptist preacher John Mason Peck, who debated a Mormon contingent in St. Clair County in 1834 and fared poorly according to John D. Lee, got his revenge the next year by publicly ridiculing "that distinguished antiquarian Joseph Smith" in his popular *Gazeteer,* a bestseller among prospective settlers.[21]

Bigotry was a real anti-Mormon motive, but it was far from the most powerful motive driving the local movement. The Hancock County tax collector Walter Bagby was famous for his anti-Mormon vitriol. He called the Mormons "vipers that wormed in our bosoms to turn and sting us."[22] Many opponents, however, even among the Mormon dissenters, claimed that the problem was not religious doctrine but the sect's political doctrine and its leader's capacity to exert power. The problem, Thomas Sharp argued, was the "anti-republican clannishness that gives them undue weight as a political body."[23] The real issue for these anti-Mormons was not anger at Mormon theology, which then had to be hidden because such anger expressed religious intolerance; the issue was how the Mormons organized and implemented their religion. The problem was not this or that Mormon belief, such as their rejection of the separation of church and state; the problem was in local actions like bloc voting that followed from the belief. Almost all Americans mixed church and state at some level given a societal culture descended from Puritanism. Whigs like Thomas Gregg, for example, attempted to use the influence of Christianity to reinforce "Law and Social Order."[24] Efforts of this kind constituted politics in towns like Springfield, Peoria, Quincy, Jacksonville, and Bloomington—all towns with strong Whig leadership. But that the Mormons could mix church and state without oppressing others and co-opting the usual outlets for political agency was not at all clear to their neighbors.

When the Mormon journal *Times and Seasons* editorialized on the topic of "Religion and Politics" in the spring of 1844, its position showed a family resemblance to the Whig view. Given the abuses of the "union of church and state . . . [in] our old European nations," the editor did not find it surprising that Americans had defended separation. But "the division [was] extending too far" such that they had "thrust out God from all [their] political movements." The editorial went on to apply precisely the kind of either-or thinking which it just denounced: "Either God has something to do in our national affairs, or he has not."[25] Since the latter view was untenable, the first option was logically entailed, which created an opening for some kind of official sponsorship. Nationally, while the parties agreed that religion was a sturdy prop of any free society, the Democrats viewed the role of religion as purely "voluntarist" and limited to civil society efforts, while the Whigs flirted with the view, articulated by Supreme Court justice Joseph Story in his *Commentaries,* that "Christianity ought to receive encouragement from the state."[26] The *Times and Seasons* editorial was taking the Whig view, but with the characteristic turn of insisting that the Mormon version of Christianity be preferred by the state. The paper went on to endorse Joseph Smith for president.

The local meaning of hegemonic beliefs like the separation of church and state and freedom of the press would be determined by how leaders like Joseph Smith and Thomas Sharp framed them. Among the anti-Mormons, competitive and conservative individualist leaders alike agreed the problem was not Mormon religion but Mormon politics. We will focus on the framing moves of Sharp, who left behind the most detailed account of the anti-Mormon position. How was the constitutional hegemony of republican freedom and independence deployed by Hancock's old settlers, and how was it resisted by the Mormons? The analysis first documents how both Mormon and anti-Mormon leaders became alienated from the Illinois law and state. We next consider Sharp's public claims that the Mormons failed the independent-producer test. Finally, we explore how the anti-Mormons justified their vigilantism, a response which also faced the headwinds of a hegemonic support for the rule of law.

CHALLENGING AND ARTICULATING REGIMES

Joseph Smith had always felt free to criticize and reject those parts of American politics that had rejected him. Late in 1841 the prophet said, "We care not a fig for *Whig* or *Democrat*."[27] This signaled a disapproval of partisan politics and an intention to keep his distance from the prevailing regime. Although Smith could be cagey about the matter, the progression away from regime norms was apparent in the Mormon church's public pronouncements. In September of

1840, when the *Times and Seasons* urged the Illinois governor not to grant the first extradition request from Missouri, its reasoning was not radical; the ground was that an exception to a general rule could be just and was needed in cases of tyranny: "The law requiring the Governor of our State to deliver up fugitives from justice, is a salutary and wise one, and should not in ordinary circumstances be disregarded, but as there are occasions that authorize the citizens of a State to resent a tyrannical and oppressive government, so there are occasions when it is not only the privilege but the duty of a Governor to refuse to surrender the citizens of his State."[28] The Mormons were accepting the authority of the law here but asking for accommodation in an exceptional case.

But a subtle shift was soon apparent. At a December 7, 1843, "public meeting of the citizens of Nauvoo," a resolution urged the "City Council of the City of Nauvoo . . . to use its powers . . . for [Mormons'] benefit and convenience" so that "hereafter if any person or persons shall come with process, demand, or requisition founded upon the aforesaid Missouri difficulties, to arrest said Joseph Smith, he or they shall be subject to be arrested by any officer of the city, with or without process."[29] Here the law was no longer a check; it had been co-opted as a source of Mormon power, power that could potentially replace the law. Challenging the Illinois regime eventuated in the articulation of a Nauvoo regime. By the spring of 1844, during Smith's campaign for president, the prophet was speaking familiarly of Vermont's Green Mountain Boys and the American Revolution as a part of his family history. His campaign statement had him "born in the land of liberty" and citing "the respected and venerable Thomas Jefferson."[30] But in Smith's narrative, a crisis had been reached and venerable tradition turned corrupt; the country was in need of a savior. Here Smith followed the logic of egalitarian dissent to voice an open criticism of the laws, denouncing the "counterfeit principles . . . [the] vanity, [and the] wasting . . . of the virtue . . . of the boasted American republic." He boldly offered an alternative: "I go for a Theodemocracy, where God and the people hold the power to conduct affairs of men in righteousness."[31]

A parallel progression and separation from the Illinois regime occurred among the anti-Mormons. They, too, had to distance themselves from mainstream opinion. They had been called out for illiberal persecution of religion, took stands against party government, and in the end embraced "mobocracy" by name. The anti-Mormon leaders expressed an individualist political culture. They advocated a self-help approach and described their group as "law-loving citizens."[32] They endorsed violence as the only means of restoring local self-government. The attack on partisanship was initiated by Sharp. After a remarkable early success organizing a slate of anti-Mormons for a few local offices in August of 1841, Sharp struggled for the next two years, with little political result, to lead a nonpartisan anti-Mormon political movement. The two established parties had their revenge, and he did not forget it. The comeuppance he engineered was long in coming, but it did come.

In the spring of 1842, the *Warsaw Signal* noted that party newspapers around the state responded in a predictable manner to Smith's announced support for his friend Stephen A. Douglas. The *Sangamo Journal* now declared the prophet a "dangerous man" who combined roles as religious leader and lieutenant general of the Nauvoo Legion. The *Chicago Democrat* was, for obvious reasons, more solicitous. Sharp was dismissive of both accounts: "Although we profess to belong to the same party with the Chicago Democrat, and would rejoice at the triumph of the principles which it advocates, yet [if] those principles be carried by a resort . . . to secure the favor of this detestable combination of fanatics . . . we say let us suffer defeat." He considered it "a humiliating sight" to have "the two great parties kneeling and sycophantically adoring . . . a *Money-Digger* selecting our candidates."[33] When the new election season began in the summer, Sharp committed an unthinkable snub to both parties: he took a "vacation of two months" until July 9, and Hancock's mainstream politicians were left without a newspaper. He felt justified because the anti-Mormon movement was in the doldrums; its nonpartisan group of leaders "did not expect a good turnout at the polls in August." But once the Mormons unexpectedly announced a slate for local offices on May 17, "the town was up almost en masse."[34]

But Sharp was not yet back in business. The anti-Mormon candidates lost the August 1842 elections, and Sharp, needing funds, brought on Thomas Gregg as a partner. They published the paper sporadically until the early fall, when Sharp again closed up shop, even issuing an obituary for the *Signal*.[35] At this point the *Signal* became the *Warsaw Message*, under Gregg's control. Gregg ran the paper as a Whig organ for the better part of the year. But after the Mormons again nominated a slate of local officers and again swept the August elections in 1843, anti-Mormonism took root locally for good. Gregg abandoned the paper's party affiliation and in February of 1844 handed the paper back to Sharp. The final two resolutions issued by the anti-Mormons at their August 19, 1843, meeting showed how far opinion had moved: "Resolved, 9th. That if the Mormons carry out the threats they have made in regards to the lives of several of our citizens, we will, if failing to obtain speedy redress from the laws of the land, take summary and signal vengeance upon them as a people. Resolved, 10th. That when the government ceases to afford protection, the citizens of course fall back upon their original and inherent right of self-defense."[36] This was the anti-Mormon declaration of independence. The process of group polarization had reached the point that rule by accident and force needed to replace rule by reflection and choice.

Sharp framed the rhetoric of the anti-Mormon movement using the materials of an individualist political culture. The setting he operated in—the setting of the Illinois regime—was one with a strong egalitarian bias. A predominant egalitarian culture in the state had produced a holistic political ideology with distinct understandings of democracy, equality, toleration, and inclusion. The Democrats' ideology was closest to the one shared by Smith and the Mormons. But for reasons relating to Illinois's three-tier settlement pattern, it was the individualists of the central part of the state, most of whom were Whigs, who first called out the Mormons and attempted to express a principled, nonbigoted opposition to the sect.

Scholar Daniel Elazar's three-tier model of traditionalists in the south, individualists in the middle, and moralizers in the north can be further differentiated and Sharp's setting mapped in the terms of political ideology. The traditionalists in the south were mainly particularist egalitarians. The individualists of the center combined in equal parts the sentiments of the universalist egalitarian and the competitive individualist. The moralists in the north could be grouped along a continuum featuring a nonconforming individualist strain, a predominant competitive individualist strain, and a conservative individualist strain. In the Illinois regime overall, egalitarianism was the majority culture, but the controlling Democrats gyrated between Douglas's particularist and Ford's universalist subcultures.

Individualists of all stripes see democracy as a tool for erecting equal and uniform processes upon which they can fairly display their worth and merit. Democracy is valued because it creates and protects a free and fair social arena. In political scientist Rogers M. Smith's model, individualist leaders emphasize the importance of trust in building a legitimate political order. Egalitarians of all stripes by contrast see in democracy a kind of social movement which seeks justice for groups long disadvantaged in society's pecking order. In telling a story of peoplehood, egalitarians vindicate the worth of social underdogs. Individualists fear the process-disrupting consequences of social disorder and chaos; they emphasize social control and order. Egalitarians fear unjust and tyrannical treatment, especially any oppression directed at their favored reference group. In Mary Douglas's symbolic scheme, it is the experience of living in a particular setting, at the boundary between the pure group and the impure world, which motivates egalitarian sensitivity to the social pecking order and the group's lowly position in it.

From these differing orientations, the two parties structuring Jacksonian political debate built distinct political ideologies of equality and toleration. Political toleration can be defined as a commitment to fair treatment of those who hold beliefs you do not respect. Fair treatment in a liberal democracy means equal treatment even for those whom the majority merely tolerates, but what equal treatment requires is variously understood. Equality can be about process or "equality of opportunity," as individualists would have it, or about results or "equality of condition," as egalitarians stress.[37] Furthermore, the reach of equality is determined by a prior understanding of membership and worth. In early Illinois there were five different answers to what equal treatment required, one each for the five predominant political subcultures, two egalitarian kinds and three individualist kinds. Egalitarians, as we have noted, can be arrayed on a universalist/particularist continuum. Individualists are found on a conservative/competitive/nonconforming continuum. Both these continua have equal process and equal result endpoints. The story of peoplehood which took hold in the Illinois regime could have both process and result emphases. As told by the Democrats, the narrative of the independent producer came in these two distinct subgenres of understanding membership, and each vied for dominance. The first was attractive to those of the universalist moral persuasion, which emphasized equal process.

The universalist camp was well represented by William Leggett, Illinois poet, short story writer, and Jacksonian newspaper editor.

Leggett's writings in the New York *Evening Post* and *The Plaindealer* made him a national figure during the second half of the 1830s. He had a unique set of foundational beliefs which, as did Joseph Smith, he hoped to spread throughout America. His reference group was "the Democracy"—the name the Jacksonians gave to the mass of worthy citizens who had been voting for Jackson and his followers since 1828. Although Leggett's foundational beliefs were different from Smith's, he started from an equally abstract desideratum. Leggett proceeded as would a formal political theorist. Rousseau, for instance, had stated the problem he was trying to solve in formal terms: "Find the form of association which defends and protects with all common forces the person and goods of each associate, and by means of which each one, while uniting with all, nevertheless only obeys himself and remains free as before."[38] Smith's goal was to find a form of American Calvinism which could withstand the corrosive effects of pluralism. Leggett aimed for a form of the American state that would solve the problem of ridding the democracy of particularist—he called them "subsociety"—attachments.

Leggett's cosmopolitan life experiences—as the son of an American Revolutionary War soldier, as a student at Georgetown, as a member of a family which lost its freehold on the Illinois frontier, as a (he believed) mistreated and discharged sailor in the US Navy, and as a New York City newspaper editor—exposed him to multiple social settings. In them he found himself on the outside looking in, barred informally from equal membership in the club of the American republic. From these experiences, he crafted an egalitarian political ideology as universally inclusive as he could make. In his literary writings, he created stories of victims of exclusion winning what consolations they could; in politics, his exclusion led him to support woman's suffrage and antislavery principles, wherein he presented women and Black people as wronged but worthy producers in exile, unfairly made socially dependent by fate.

Over time Leggett became, as historian Arthur Schlesinger Jr. calls him, the "spokesman for Jacksonian Democracy." He urged the party to dedicate itself to "the political maxim that the majority have the right to govern; but to the extent of the moral maxim, that it is the duty of the majority so to govern as to preserve inviolate the equal rights of all."[39] Here was a recipe for patterning the principles and policies of the Democratic Party after Leggett's universalist persuasion and for ensuring that whatever rules of recognition were developed, they would be inclusive. Under this formula, the value of fairness to outsiders could be achieved by prioritizing not ends but means—for example, equal process.

Leggett thought the best way to keep the focus on equal rights was to think in terms of society as whole. Pure republicans should refer to what James Madison called the public interest, not particular group or factional interest. Like a deductive mathematician, Leggett hoped to take advantage of the general form of rules; if the laws applied to all equally, and no special privileges or exemptions were allowed, a basic guarantee of fairness would be the axiomatic consequence of state action. While his main target was to limit the special benefits the wealthy garnered in the form of corporate or bank charters—his negative reference—his prohibition on organized "subsociety" advocacy extended to the reform-minded groups like the American Temperance Society and the American Anti-Slavery Society.

Leggett's attack on subsociety reformism came to a head in the summer of 1837, when he decided that "all or nearly all modern religious as well as merely charitable societies [were] radically objectionable."[40] He went on to explain: "Nothing can be more self-evident than the demoralizing influence of special legislation. It degrades politics into a mere scramble for rewards obtained by the violation of the equal rights of the people."[41] Although their reasoning was very different, both Leggett and Emma Smith agreed that groups like the Washingtonians were corrupting society, but Leggett feared the power of reform societies to distract the people from a broader set of republican purposes and processes, while Smith feared they would be distracted from an unworldly attachment to God's lost tribe of Israel in America.

Emma Smith's approach was typical of the more parochial Jacksonians in Illinois, who feared that if the Democratic Party followed a too-universalist course, it would be distracted from its primary purpose of lifting up the poor White settler. One leading Democrat who struck this particularist pose was William Kinney, state senator from St. Clair County, lieutenant governor in the 1820s, and a leading Jacksonian until the 1840 election. Kinney ran for Illinois governor in 1830 and 1834 as "the Farmer's candidate." Kinney was himself a notably successful farmer, having started out with no property and ending his life as a "big man," a pro-bank Democrat sitting on the Board of Public Works and overseeing the state's eight-million-dollar internal improvements plan.[42]

Kinney's assumption that his particular occupation—farming—could and should be taken as a proxy for all occupations, universalized, as it were, was a conceptual move typical of all particularists. It may also have been politically astute. For, as Whig Thomas Gregg conceded with some regret, "Farmers . . . control in all public matters throughout the West, except in a very few of the larger towns."[43] Farming was the majority occupation in settler Illinois, and the majority societal culture formed around the objects and desideratum of the settler's farm. Particularist Democrats, while committed in principle to an equal rights process, were eager first to secure the equal rights results of a particular group interest, which they took to represent the majority interest. They became the majoritarian or populist wing of the Democratic Party.

It is not surprising to find that Kinney's democracy was not as inclusive as Leggett's; his corollary notions of equality and worth intervened. Not all independent producers won his support. Kinney stood against any social force that stood in the way of the White male settler and stood for anything, slavery included, that might aid him. An antimission Baptist preacher and yeoman farmer who worked himself up to slaveholder status, Kinney justified slavery by arguing the institution was condoned in the Bible. He took a public leadership role in the movement to introduce "limited slavery" into Illinois and helped orchestrate the effort in 1823 and 1824 to call a constitutional convention for that purpose. Privately, he used the law to advance his property interests against his sister, his wife, and the eight enslaved persons he listed in the 1830 census. In 1838, Thomas Cook, enslaved by Kinney, complained in state court of Kinney's physical abuse, sued for his freedom, and won his case. In Kinney's thought, the shadow mark of group bias lurked behind his partially universalized rhetoric. The shadow obscured from Kinney the knowledge that his preference *was* particularist. Since, as he claimed, the "white folks," lowly in the world's eyes, were "the offspring of pure humanity," any regime enforcing their civic priority was implicitly pure and good and universal; those who argued otherwise were likely to be "foreigners," "aliens," or "men of color" and so without the "right" to make civic claims.[44]

Equal treatment for the universalist egalitarian required that government operate on general, society-wide rules with no special exceptions; for the particularist egalitarian, equal treatment required that government set policies which would result in equality of condition for White male farmers. The two views were able to converge by means of the independent-producer narrative. Since the overwhelming majority of heads of household in Jacksonian Illinois were White male farmers, society-wide rules favoring their interests satisfied both kinds of egalitarians within the Democratic Party. The Jacksonian newspapers framed policies from taxation to tariffs, internal improvements to corporate banking charters, and public lands distribution to Indian affairs, by reference to how they affected and benefited the poor White farmer.[45] Even when specific reform measures were under view, as when Gallatin County senator William Jefferson Gatewood proposed using public lands to erect county-based seminaries of learning to educate common school teachers, the focus was on the roll they would play in uplifting the poor. Gatewood emphasized the fact that Illinois's "republican government . . . [was] based on the broad principle of equal rights . . . [its] bold principle of *universal suffrage* . . . [giving] to every man, however humble his condition, the power of effecting a real influence upon its measures."[46]

Among the narrative materials provided by leaders like Leggett, Kinney, and Gatewood, the Mormon story found a home in 1839. Only five years earlier, another New Englander, Stephen A. Douglas, had found a similar home in Illinois and become a "western man," as he put it in 1834.[47] It is not surprising that Douglas and Smith became fast friends. The Mormon understanding of the dominant independent-producer narrative of worth shared many elements of the universal and particular varieties offered by people like Douglas. Another example of shared understanding between Mormons and Illinoisans was Thomas Ford, who, once elected governor in 1842, tried with legalistic precision to be an inclusive universalist. Ford would have posed the problem facing Illinois's universalists as follows: find a set of membership rules deracinated enough to include those of both egalitarian and individualist cultural biases. Ford fretted that when Illinoisans lived in separate group settings, no set of membership rules could overcome the biases which separation would cause. He settled on the idea of adventure as a unifying membership trope.

The Mormons had a lot of promise as adventurous independent producers. As summarized by scholar Bruce Flanders, they were recognized in Illinois as "Jacksonian Democrats . . . of westering New England stock, Puritan in religious background, and lower-middle class rather than peasant or proletarian in outlook . . . committed to group development to be sure, but they were also committed to upward socio-economic mobility for themselves as individuals."[48]

Economic productivity was certainly one indicator used to judge the Mormons as worthy of inclusion. The number of new businesses opening in the city and the general tone set by their secular paper, the *Nauvoo Neighbor,* strongly suggested they were a people driven by "the spirit of improvement and enterprise."[49] In a July 1843 letter, Democrat Mason Brayman sought to reassure Joseph Smith of Governor Ford's support in their fight with the Missourians. He confirmed that Ford viewed the Mormons as an "industrious and sober population" and that the governor was "anxious for the time to arrive when this vexatious persecution against you shall cease when your people like all other of citizens whatever religious sect will be left free to worship God in your own chosen way, and to vote as the predilections and opinions of Each man shall dictate—Each choosing for himself."[50]

But the Mormon vote in the August election of 1843 belied these premises; as Thomas Gregg argued in the pages of the *Warsaw Message,* not "each man" but "revelation now has the balance of power."[51] Brayman and Gregg were asserting the premises of individualism, a cultural view existing alongside and in competition with the generally egalitarian Illinois regime. Brayman was hoping to shape the Mormons into the mold of competitive individualists, just as Gregg hoped to shape them into conservative individualists. Gregg was disappointed the Mormons abandoned what he recognized as authentic Christian individualism, opting instead for prophecy and revelation directed by Smith. Beginning in the fall of 1843, Gregg's conservative vision took a back seat to Thomas Sharp's competitive vision.

No leader influenced the reception of the Mormons in Illinois more than Thomas Coke Sharp. It was his political ideology which framed how the Mormons were assessed as members in Hancock County. Like Smith, Sharp encountered in Illinois a script he had read before. For Sharp, it was the rise of the Masons and the Anti-Mason reaction he had watched play out back East. There he had succeeded as an Anti-Mason, and he would do his best to shape the anti-Mormon movement along similar lines. He had come to Illinois in 1840 from Carlisle, Pennsylvania, where he attended

FIG. 6.1. Thomas Sharp (from Gregg, *History of Hancock County*). Courtesy of Newberry Library

Dickinson College, took a law course, and supported himself by teaching high school math. His biography, written by Thomas Gregg in the *History of Hancock County, Illinois,* reports that he was raised a Jacksonian Democrat and "had been drawn to the Harrison ranks by the cry of retrenchment and reform" but soon "drifted back to his first love."[52] Sharp turned to newspaper editing after he struggled in the courtroom due to a hearing impairment.[53]

An unsigned letter in the *State Register* from Warsaw suggested Sharp came to the Whig Party via the influence of the Anti-Masonic

Party.[54] The Anti-Masons are best understood as a social movement born in the towns and counties of northern New York that formed a political party to counter the influence of the Masons in local politics. Masonry, a club-based organization that promoted sociability and various civic purposes, was viewed by the Anti-Masons as an antirepublican secret society. Scholars note that the Anti-Masons never mounted a very effective political organization, but the movement provides a fascinating window into two conflicted and debated features of American political development.[55] The first was the persistence of a nonpartisan and antipartisan tradition within a system that otherwise fully embraced partisanship. Historian Gerald Leonard emphasizes the persistence of this tradition in antebellum Illinois,[56] and Mark Voss-Hubbard stresses how this tradition persisted throughout the nineteenth century to reemerge and fight another day during the Progressive Era.[57] The tenacity of this tradition indicates that ideas can have a life of their own even when not successfully institutionalized or running counter to the bias of an organized regime.

The second tradition exemplified by the Anti-Masons pushes against the claim that disembodied ideas can have power; it points in the opposite direction by suggesting that regime structures can deeply influence how ideals are expressed. This argument begins with the fact that the Anti-Masons thrived in Vermont but never managed much of an organized presence in New Hampshire. As historian Michael F. Holt observes, the political cultures of Vermont and New Hampshire were virtually identical in the Jacksonian era. It is not that Anti-Masonic beliefs were lacking in New Hampshire but that the early development (1828) of the duopoly in that state crowded out the institutional space available for the latter (post-1828) Anti-Masonic movement. Because of the difference in timing, Anti-Masonic dissent was co-opted in New Hampshire by the Democrats, while in Vermont, the weakly developed two-party structure was unable to block and co-opt Anti-Masons, who proceeded to form their own party.[58] Structure displaced ideals and transferred agency. In Illinois, however, Sharp's anti-Mormonism agency found fertile ground for organization and action in Hancock County despite having to fight through an entrenched duopoly.

With the strange disappearance, murder, and badly managed trial of Mason apostate William Morgan in Genesee County, New York, the Anti-Masons had tangible evidence that Masons as judges and jury members had conspired to put protection of their brotherhood ahead of their allegiance to the truth and a proper "Christian republic."[59] A misplaced allegiance, Anti-Masons urged, undermined the legitimacy of republican institutions and needed to be stopped. When other Masons attempted to cover up the bad behavior of a few of their members, the Anti-Masons concluded that the rot of corruption was endemic to the breed. While the Anti-Masonic Party became a viable third party in many eastern states by 1832, it never had an organized existence in Illinois. It is plausible, however, to see the anti-Mormons of west-central Illinois as a frontier counterpart: Illinois never had Anti-Masons; it had anti-Mormons instead. Like the Anti-Masons, the anti-Mormons turned first to working within the political system in their effort to oppose the Mormons.

Sharp likely brought over from the Anti-Mason repertoire a very specific social category: the Mason sympathizer, those who took a noncommittal attitude toward Masonry or, more problematically, openly sympathized with the Masons. It was claimed that he served as an Anti-Mason editor in western New York, where "he invented the name Jack Mason."[60] He certainly was the first to use the term *Jack Mormon* in Illinois, which he applied to Mormon apostate John C. Bennett. The term was taken up by Sharp's Whig ally Thomas Gregg and soon became ubiquitous to describe those in Hancock County who sympathized with or actively allied with the Mormons.[61] The term, a framing tool for keeping compromise and accommodation between non-Mormons and Mormons at bay, was used most effectively after August of 1845 to describe newly reelected Hancock sheriff Jacob Backenstos, whom the *Warsaw Message* at first politely described as "in heart a Mormon."[62] Sharp's worldview fit the Anti-Mason profile in other ways too. Raised by a Methodist minister, he was a strong advocate for reforming civil society through the means of "voluntary benevolent societies."[63] His public praise of the beneficence and effectiveness of the Washingtonians in Lima, a town twenty miles south of Warsaw, in the early spring of 1842 perhaps influenced Emma Smith's strong reaction against them as a reform organization.[64]

Sharp's support for temperance, the library, and the lyceum made him a potential candidate for what historian Daniel Walker Howe denominates the "evangelical dimension of Whiggery."[65] This dimension is easy to caricature as driven by a "paranoid" need for social control.[66] The way Sharp moved so quickly in 1841 from the idea that the Mormons were not sufficiently independent to be included as Illinois members to the claim that they were dangerous to the American republic *was* arguably paranoid. But here we need a more precise cultural distinction than party membership can provide. Sharp was a Democrat, but one who, like many others of that party, such as William Kinney, strayed into Whiggery by voting for William Henry Harrison in 1840.

Competitive individualism is a more accurate description of Thomas Sharp's political ideology. Those expressing the competitive individualist subculture are preoccupied with fair process and order; for them social control ideally occurs not through coercion but through the discipline of voluntary market transactions. Believing open markets to be free and fair, competitive individualists prioritize equal processes and a level playing field. Only in times of conflict and crisis do embattled individualists move "up grid" in Mary Douglas's matrix to fall back upon the power of tradition and the ordering of hierarchy; at these times the institutional moorings of liberal democracy, which aim to keep processes fair and treatment equal, are threatened with dissolution. In these times, individualists of the competitive and conservative stripes tend to display Elazar's moralistic political culture.

The individualist premises of Sharp's view are everywhere expressed in his editorials. From the start, the Mormon threat for him was twofold. Latter-day Saints made democratic culture difficult if not impossible for the rest of the people in Hancock County because they did not act in the public sphere as individuals. Democracy required an open society in which interests and opinions freely circulated. Here was the commercial counterpart to the postal reform ideals of deliberative democracy. Sharp argued that because the Mormons congregated in one settlement at Nauvoo and because of their overwhelming numbers, only the Mormon interest was being furthered in Hancock County. This was a bad thing because it meant that the town of Warsaw, where he lived, and the rest of Hancock would not be able to compete in the struggle for trade in the Illinois race. "The point is settled," he wrote in December of 1841, "that *free* men and Mormons cannot live together in peace and harmony." "Who wishes," he asked rhetorically, "to make his homestead where there is a prospect of nothing but bickering and strife[?] . . . But what can we do, when every capitalist objects to invest his funds here, lest he may be compelled to abandon all by the absorbing influence of Mormonism." He concluded, "We feel that the Mormon Church is a perfect incubus resting upon us, preventing the proper kind of citizens from coming in, and destroying all enterprise."[67] In an irony of political development, it is the individualist's need and emphasis on trust that itself generates distrust; Sharp had created not a security dilemma but an escalating comparative development dilemma.

Sharp thought of competing towns as engines of prosperity, but generally he took the individual as the unit of analysis. We see this in his article on "Learning a Trade." Many parents, he observed, thought "meanly of him who wears an apron" and looked down on mechanics. Sharp added, "If a child have talents, they will not remain hid . . . no matter what his profession." But parents saved for a college education not appropriate for their child, and thus the world had "so many pettifoggers and vagabonds." Being a liberal arts graduate himself, Sharp thought "highly of [the country's] college institutions, and rejoice[d] to see them prosper; but [he was] more pleased to see an individual's mind turned in a right current." It was individuals and their minds that mattered for building community prosperity: "Our mechanics are, generally speaking, the most industrious part of our community. They are almost always busily employed, [whereas] professional men are frequently involved in unprofitable business."[68] Sharp here indicated his openness to producers of all varieties. Yet the Mormons failed to meet his test; he judged the Mormons to be unworthy of inclusion on both independent and producer grounds.

Sharp's equal openness to all producers raises the question of whether he should be considered an egalitarian. In fact, the word *equality* plays tricks on us. It is a big-tent term capable of holding many distinct conceptions of worth.[69] The fluid dimensions of equality as a concept construed by both individualists and egalitarians means that there can be wide latitude for disagreement within both cultures about who qualifies for inclusion under the big tent of civic membership. Defining the worthy for egalitarians begins conceptually with attachment to a particular unjustly treated reference group, such as the poor laborer. This specific solidarity is then expanded or universalized as the story of peoplehood is crafted. Civic narratives may reference all of humanity, as they did in Illinois, but a specific group is favored implicitly. The state may aspire to neutrality, but majoritarian interests and control over implementation biases all regimes. This is the pound of flesh democracy, as a form of government, requires all true believers in popular sovereignty to pay. Competitive individualists are loath to accept as fellow members those who rely on others to achieve worth and salvation; yet they are themselves far from consistent. Under pressure in times of crisis, individualists typically find themselves retreating to hierarchical and ascriptive norms entailed in the status quo.

Performing citizenship in civil society biases all regimes; exclusion is enforced in contexts in which multiple individualist and egalitarian subcultures compete. Even the most liberal universalist egalitarians apply exclusionary membership rules, as settlers did when colonial bias or racial prejudice led them to misrecognize Native American cultivation practices. The "shadow" side of group reference means that one or another group is disfavored under the regime order, a reality Democrats like Thomas Ford tried to deny in the case of Illinois's Black Codes. On the individualist side, equality is interpreted as the guarantee of the level playing field necessary for individuals to demonstrate worth according to their merit or salvation status. In other words, competitive individualists—who belong to the predominant strain of this subculture—valorize individual effort and self-help because they believe the efforts made to demonstrate worth mete out what individuals deserve. Self-interest is not seen as selfish but rather as a necessary consequence of any system capable of measuring individual merit. Of course, individualists also experience the pull of groups, but they strive to deny the impact of group life on individual freedom of choice.

In today's usage, *egalitarians* are thought to be fully inclusive and are seen as favoring the disadvantaged, but we should resist applying today's meaning to developing democracies. Early Illinois egalitarianism was promoted by a distinct social group, White male settlers, often to further their own interests, whereas, as political theorist Judith Shklar remarks, "one of the more notable aspects of contemporary egalitarianism is that it is usually promoted by the competent and relatively rich for the sake of the feeble and poor."[70] In Illinois, egalitarians authorized the unfair treatment of Black and female nonmembers; there could be no mistaking the public displays of the power of exclusion, but the bias often went unnoticed. As philosopher Peter Singer argues, it often requires a "liberation movement" to force "an expansion of our moral horizons and an extension or reinterpretation of the basic moral principle of equality." Speaking from the perspective of the privileged, Singer notes that these social movements, if successful, are able to unsettle "our most fundamental attitudes" about social equality under which "we may discover a pattern in our attitudes and practices that consistently operates so as to benefit one group—usually the one to which we ourselves belong—at the expense of another."[71] In the absence of a reformist social movement and because egalitarian and individualist political leaders frame the idea of equality to match the status quo, their bias for some groups over others is hidden.

Sharp also argued that the Mormons did not merit equal treatment and full membership, because they unfairly refused to extend such treatment symmetrically to non-Mormons. Indeed, the problem of Mormon unfairness went deeper: their beliefs and behavior, if unchecked, would threaten the rest of the community. This is why for people like Sharp the success of the anti-Mormon political movement was so important. The movement's success would set Hancock County on a new course by reaffirming its independence and self-determined direction.

In April of 1842, when a convention was announced for the "Great Mass Convention of the People of Hancock County," to take place on May 30, the key point for Sharp was that, contrary to Mormon dictation, it would "allow the *independent* citizens a voice in the nomination as well as the election of their officers."[72] This was a far cry from "Jo Smith's Proclamation" at the start of the year, which Sharp ridiculed as "a wonderful document . . . directing his followers how to vote."[73] It was precisely for these reasons that the early anti-Mormon leaders were so disappointed when, after their first electoral success in 1841, the movement showed so little energy. But support for the anti-Mormon cause suddenly reemerged in July of 1842, when the Mormons announced their slate for local offices: "Joe Smith can thank himself for the Anti-Mormon nominations."[74]

Sharp's reaction to the Hancock situation was not unlike how nonpartisan thinkers across the nation reacted to the partisan imperative: they viewed it as a threat to republican independence. As another newspaper editor and liberal arts graduate, Whig Jonathan Baldwin Turner, put it in one of his editorials, "Let every man be first a MAN, whether he is ever anything else or not, and not a *mere tool,* and then the republic is safe, all is safe." Like Sharp, Turner saw worth in those who thought for themselves and stood on their own intellectual grounds, not members of a "drilled and servile party."[75] In the same editorial, Turner explicitly argued that the maneuvers between Smith and the two parties in Illinois had been bad for all concerned.[76] Here Turner expressed a reformed liberal version of the independent-producer story: a liberal state dedicated to independence cannot deem dependent minds worthy of respect, nor can it accommodate as citizens mere subjected bodies. Nonconforming individualists like Turner believe the ideal form of life is the life of the freethinking, autonomous individual, the agent committed to self-scripted (as opposed to group-scripted) projects and ideas of the good.[77]

The attraction of autonomy as an ideal was strong among individualists. The defense of autonomy often took the form of defending rights. Especially in the early years of his leadership, Sharp made the case against the Mormons almost purely in terms of individual rights. It was the individual right to vote that the Mormons took away or the individual right to property which was harmed through theft. But it was not long before a public sphere, foundational belief in what scholar David Greenstone calls the "New England Way" appeared in Sharp's writing.[78] This was the idea that not only individuals but the community as a whole had an independent, self-governing moral character that could be threatened. Here were the roots of Elazar's moralistic political culture. This aspect of Sharp's thinking pushed him to organize and advocate for his beliefs in the community. When Sharp performed citizenship, he did so as a moralist, and here the tools of Illinois's settler regime came in handy.

Under the regime, the local majority of old settlers came to have a right to their own societal culture, a right the Mormons refused to respect. When the *Quincy Herald* questioned Sharp's anti-Mormon position, he could not help but assert the county's collective interest (the local status quo really) as a kind of sacred convention; he also referred to the need to protect anti-Mormon rights. The *Herald* asked in early 1844, What tangible harms have the Mormons committed? It replied to its own question: "none." Perhaps with the Missouri episode as a warning in mind, the editor went on to state that regardless of their religion, if Mormons owned property, their rights should be respected. Sharp's reply was telling:

> We object not to the [*Herald's*] sentiment, but we object to the impression intended to be conveyed, viz., that the hostility

> to Mormonism in this county, is on account of the religion of the sect. Now the editor of the Herald knows full well, that the old citizens care not a straw about the religion of the Mormons. They may worship as they please and whom they please—they may believe every tom-foolery that knavery ever invented, wherewith to dupe the ignorant for its own benefit. We have nothing to do with their mummeries or their gullibility. Let them act in temporal matters as other men, not unite to impose on others and screen themselves, not threaten our personal liberties when we are guilty of no crime, not obey the dictates of one man in political matters, which render him as complete a despot as though he had the tiara on his head, and they may live here as elsewhere unmolested.[79]

Sharp's exasperated exhortation "Let them act in temporal matters as other men" belied his individualist premises; certainly it showed a lack of sensitivity to the conventionality of the settler status quos. Other autonomy liberals, such as nonconforming individualists like philosopher J. S. Mill, attacked social conformity as much as governmental tyranny. Behind Sharp's comment was the picture of free and independent individuals as participants in an overlapping consensus who were able to shape their own societal culture, not have it hijacked locally by one individual with a controlling influence.

Sharp uncovered a whole host of additional assumptions about what the old settlers required before the Mormons would be recognized locally as worthy. When respect for the ways of the old settlers was the matter under discussion, it was not individual injury and harm but the tyranny and slavery of a "tiara" that were at issue. Joseph Smith, in setting up "a military church," threatened to "enslave" the citizens of Hancock. "Ask yourselves," Sharp queried, "what means this array of military force which is paraded under the direction of this church? Is an army necessary to propagate religion? . . . Are they so patriotic to have no other end than the safety of the state in view? Why all these weekly parades? Why all this strictness of discipline?"[80] The key issue was not any immediate harm but the future identity of the Hancock people and their societal culture. The threat was to their political identity as freemen.

The appeal of the image of the rational, deliberating individual is strong in liberal democracies. Thomas Ford even felt compelled to apologize for the way the party duopoly he endorsed trenched upon the free thought of the autonomous individual: "The privilege of changing principles and measures is only the privilege of the great [party] leaders, upon consultation and agreement with the lesser ones. . . . This gentle reader is government by moral means; and it seems, in the present state of civilization, that without this kind of government, imperfect and abhorrent to the freedom of thought as it may be, we are to have our choice between anarchy and a government of stern force."[81] But did Ford need to apologize? Did not even strong nonconforming individualists like the abolitionists end up finding succor in groups and a type of group conformity of their own kind? Scholar Lawrence J. Friedman documents the "familial warmth," the tight-knit "Boston clique," that abolitionists enjoyed as "gregarious saints" in their struggles with a world of conformists to proslavery beliefs.[82]

Individualists in Warsaw like Sharp and Gregg in fact sought out group affiliations as part of their anti-Mormon struggle. The Anti-Mormon Convention meetings, the gatherings of the Warsaw Legislature (the name given to the town's lyceum), the creation of the Warsaw Library Association—all became group vehicles for Sharp to perform citizenship and demonstrate his worth as an independent republican in the Hancock status order. After being indicted for the murder of the Smith brothers, Sharp went so far as to join the Warsaw Masons in the fall of 1844, a group founded by anti-Mormon Mark Aldrich. Sharp was inducted to the group, along with fellow defendants Jacob C. Davis and Levi Williams, perhaps with the motive of using Masonic influence on the jury soon to be empaneled to judge their case.[83] Sharp, it might be said, was forced to compromise his commitment to Anti-Masonry and his deeper commitment to individual autonomy. He used his opposition to the Mormons to build a group identity in order to protect the kind of republic that would be safe for individualism. The premier scholar of American violence notes that on the frontier the connection between "Freemasonry and vigilantism was frequently an intimate one."[84]

It should be recalled that Sharp was a bachelor who was a relative newcomer to Hancock County, having only arrived in September of 1840, a season after Joseph Smith himself.[85] He was thus susceptible to the need to seek not only group protection but the protection of a particular worthy group—the old settlers of Hancock County. It did not take Sharp long to follow the Illinois regime's local logic to an exclusionary conclusion when applied to the Mormons: the saints were apparently oblivious to the claims of the early settlers and did not appear to respect the authority of their ways. Tellingly, the Mormon apostates publishing the *Nauvoo Expositor* also used this alternative allegiance to demonstrate their distance from Smith and the Mormon norm: they valorized "the old citizens of the county who have born the heat and burden of the day; who have labored hard as the pioneers of the county; who have settled and organized the county; who have rights that should be respected by every principle of honor and good faith; and whose wishes should be consulted in the choice of officers, and not have men opposed upon them."[86]

Sharp did not hesitate to generalize from the idea that the Mormons posed a threat to local control to the claim that they threatened the republican order that stood behind it. When he reopened the *Signal* in February of 1844, the two concepts had merged to produce an urgency which the nation as a whole should notice: "Never since the formation of our Government did it ever behoove any class of people to stand more firmly together, for the protection of each other, and each other's rights, than the old citizens of this community are called upon to do in the present crisis. In our midst is a dangerous combination—bound together by the power of superstition—the strongest bond that ever united the minds of men—led on by one man, and that man a dangerous and aspiring knave."[87] Here Sharp ascribed the trait of superstition to a whole group, a move characteristic of bigotry.

The truth is that Sharp had reached a point of no return already by the summer of 1842 and perhaps before.[88] His rumormongering, name-calling, and character assassination as editor would soon serve to further isolate the prophet and his group. When a Lee County, Iowa, Whig convention allowed 150 Mormons to sway the outcome of a June 1842 proceeding, Sharp wrote, "A majority of the delegates possessed so little independence, and were so sycophantic, as to bow down to the dictation of these fanatics." Sharp was questioning the manliness and hence republican virtue of potential allies his movement dearly needed. Sharp would clash in this way with actual allies, such as his onetime publishing partner at the *Warsaw Signal*, Whig Thomas Gregg. He raised the same impurity charge against the Whigs which Smith had used against him: "Have we so little respect for the character of the American citizens—for the purity of our free institutions[?]"[89]

In an 1841 address to the "Anti-Mormon Convention," Joel Catlin (a Whig), Thomas Sharp (then independent), and William D. Roosevelt (a Democrat), writing together, demonstrated by their very union that "the old party landmarks . . . are now laid aside."[90] They proposed undoing half a decade of intense party organization in Hancock County and all the transactional dealings which had greased it—something easier said than done. Printing party lists cost money, and party workers needed to be rewarded with jobs, even modest jobs like justice of the peace, probate judge, recorder of deeds, deputy sheriff, postmaster, or road surveyor; access to such spoils required winning elections. Furthermore, old partisan allegiances persisted among the anti-Mormons. Whigs like Gregg persisted in the desire to promote their party's voice in the community; as we have seen, he bought out the *Warsaw Signal* and opened the *Warsaw Message* as a Whig organ in January 1843. It would take Sharp more than two years to get the anti-Mormons to pay up front for his newspaper.[91] The lines of interest, organization, and discourse within the Jacksonian regime had a structural reality that would not be easily set aside.[92]

Gregg's hopes for rapprochement with the Mormons came crashing down when the August 1843 elections were carried by Mormon candidates. There followed the "Great Meeting" of August 19, 1843, at which the anti-Mormons began articulating claims of an "inherent right" of self-defense. After this, only the names Mormon and anti-Mormon had meaning in the county. Indeed, those supporting the Mormons who were not of the religion had to be given an honorary Mormon name—that is, Jack Mormon—to emphasize the duality; there was no neutral or middle ground. Minor Deming had been elected sheriff of Hancock in August of 1844, and after Deming died unexpectedly, Jacob Backenstos followed him into the office; both nominally Democrats, they received Mormon support and were savagely attacked as Jack Mormons.

Beginning in the fall of 1841, rumors functioned as sparks to violence. Sharp's newspaper was a fertile breeding ground for "hoaxes" and "stories going the rounds." Sharp profoundly damaged Mormon reputation by falsely running a headline describing three Mormons as "murderers" of Colonel George Davenport of Iowa; in fact, they had only been arrested on suspicion and were later released.[93] One rumor that very nearly led to an outbreak of violence involved a conflict over stealing among land developers in

Warsaw and the Mormons who were living temporarily in Warren, the new development in the bottoms along the river below Warsaw.[94] The new stake in Warren was announced with great excitement in the *Times and Seasons* but created anxiety in Warsaw.[95] The sense of the anxiety this could create in the local population can be glimpsed in the no doubt exaggerated prose of B. F. Morris, an American Home Missionary Society minister writing to the home office from the upper town: "This deluded fanatical and ignorant sect is about to be poured upon us. . . . In view of this prospective state of things nearly all the old citizens are anxious to sell their property."[96]

When Sharp and Gregg comanaged the *Warsaw Signal* (July to September 1842), they debated in public about whether the Anti-Mormon Society of Hancock County was a "law-loving" group and what that meant. Gregg was a conservative individualist very much in the "Law and Social Order" camp.[97] He still held out hopes of converting his friend Sharp to the Whig Party, and Sharp had in fact voted for Harrison in 1840. But the success of the Mormon slate in August of 1843 was a turning point for Sharp, even as the Whigs were preparing to use the Warsaw printing press for one last partisan run. It pushed him to become a public advocate of violence as the most effective means of achieving Mormon removal. After Smith had evaded the law in an early scrimmage, Sharp wrote: "Our citizens were in hopes that the scamp would have been taken or else made open resistance. . . . If he had resisted, we should have had the sport of driving him and his worthy clan out of the state *en masse*."[98] But Gregg would not countenance the reference to any extralegal "taking the responsibility" and wrote so in the next edition. He noted that "the great body of anti-Mormons in this county" would disagree with Sharp's tack, as it was against "every principle of right and justice, or law and order." In another section of the paper, Sharp replied that Gregg was too sensitive. Not to be outdone, Gregg found a place to insert that law and order is something "about which we all *should* be 'sensitive.'"[99]

It was a rare occurrence for an editor and publisher to disagree in print.[100] Sharp responded predictably: he took the disagreement as a competitive challenge. He investigated all things Mormon to ferret out their antirepublican tendencies. He discovered the congressional report on the Mormon troubles in Missouri, published apostate William Harris's story, and, most damaging of all, highlighted Bennett's claim that Danite Porter Rockwell was in Nauvoo and then went missing one week before the Boggs assassination attempt. Bennett reported that Smith had issued a prophecy that Boggs would be dead within a year; when Bennett asked Smith where Rockwell was, he replied mysteriously, "Gone to fulfill prophecy!"[101] Sharp published the letter in the revived edition of the *Signal* on July 9, 1842. Under attack within his own movement for suggesting extralegal violence, Sharp must have felt vindicated in the debate he was having with the law-and-order Gregg. Still, the ideological tension between the two leaders reminds us there was no automatic unity within the individualist camp. A consensus on how to treat the Mormons and how to challenge regime norms had to be crafted, not discovered.

INDIVIDUALISTS AND EGALITARIANS UNDER PRESSURE

Individualists of the nonconforming variety in Hancock County likely resisted Sharp's effort to stigmatize the Mormons as a group. Examples of nonconforming individualists at the national level willing to tolerate the Mormons were Thomas Kane and John Greenleaf Whittier. These writers emphasized the long tradition of religious diversity in the Northeast reaching back to the antinomians. Nonconforming individualists had in fact defended pluralism on the ground that the autonomy sponsored by the New England Way was a societal culture needing group support like any other form of culture. In other words, individualism, too, had a membership dimension to its culture.[102] Thoughtful writers like Herman Melville probed the nature of individualism as a way of life and joined dissenting egalitarians like Joseph Smith and Daniel Parker in critiquing the "missionary position" needed to support the individualistic republic the Whigs envisioned. Melville explored the idea that a life structured around individual autonomy would itself be subject to hidden group biases.

That even the unconventional and the nonconforming share a culture was one of the themes of Melville's first novel, *Typee,* published in 1846. His protagonist, Tommo, is an American sailor who finds himself surrounded by "savages" on a South Pacific island. He is welcomed and adopted by a local tribe. Melville set Tommo's cultural openness against the backdrop of the tainted results of missionary attempts to convert the local people to Christianity. In one of the book's most compelling passages, Tommo studies a "very lady-like personage, a missionary spouse," being conveyed by "two of the islanders": "Not until I visited Honolulu was I aware of the fact that the small remnant of the natives had been civilized into draught horses, and evangelized into beasts of burden. . . . They have been literally broken in their traces, and are harnessed to the vehicles of their spiritual instructors like so many dumb brutes!"[103] When crusading individualism leads to brutalization, something is amiss. Melville invites his reader to ask, Who are the savages and who the brutes in Hawaii? As the book progresses, it seems to dawn on the author that his protagonist's individualism carries with it the seeds of Tommo's own Massachusetts societal culture and its conventions. Tommo attempts to urge woman's rights on Fayaway, one of the local women the tribe's chief is hoping he will marry. But before he can champion her rights, he needs to have his face tattooed as part of his initiation into the tribe. He realizes that the tattoo would permanently mark him and bar an easy reentry back into the West. Free spirit that Tommo is, he recognizes he is a member after all.

One of the greatest ironies of the Mormon troubles in Illinois was that the individualist fight against Mormon particularism turned many Hancock County anti-Mormons into particularists themselves. Articulating the regime's rules on self-government led them to put their duties to anti-Mormonism ahead of their duties as Illinois citizens. The most celebrated instance was the acquittal of the defendants in the Smith brothers' murder trial. The prosecution struggled to find witnesses to an event that dozens of people had witnessed. Those who did come forward were easily discredited. The presiding judge, Richard M. Young, who had previously served as a US senator, allowed the defense's motion to repanel the jury on the grounds that the first jury was prejudicial; they had been selected by a process overseen by Mormon-elected county commissioners and a Mormon-elected sheriff. Those witnesses who did agree to testify were either limited in their knowledge or cagey and elusive. When Sharp, Williams, Aldrich, and Davis stood as defendants in the Carthage courtroom to hear the jury foreman announce the verdict of "not guilty" after a nine-day trial, the jury had been out for only two and a half hours. It was not just jury nullification; it was community nullification.[104]

The anti-Mormons were willing to brave public calumny and hegemonic disapproval of their behavior. Once the majority of

Mormons were expelled, Sharp felt secure enough to justify the anti-Mormon violation of the taboo against participating in mobocracy. If there was contemporary opinion that faced hegemonic disdain across the nation, this was it. Mormons and Jack Mormons, Sharp recognized, relied on the people's "settled antipathy to mobs." He thus took it upon himself to explain cases of liberal intolerance in which it was "not only justifiable but proper" to have recourse to what was later called vigilantism or extralegal measures to enforce the law.[105] But in making his case for "mobocracy," he relied on so many exceptions and qualifying background assumptions that he no longer could claim universality. He also took on a particularist stance in defense of anti-Mormonism by becoming the self-appointed amplifier of seemingly every rumor and slander against the saints ever uttered in the vicinity. In the face of Sharp's rumormongering, the Mormons predictably and plausibly decried the specter of religious persecution.

In an open letter to the Hancock community in his brother William's paper *The Wasp,* Joseph Smith in the summer of 1842 appealed to "the old citizens of the county." He denounced the recent Anti-Mormon Convention and its candidates; they evinced "a spirit of intolerance and exclusion incompatible with the liberal doctrines of true republicanism." Smith reached out to the saints' "fellow citizens" who were "still desirous of equal participation with [them] in the selection of candidates for office."[106] Sharp replied: "Really this is great condescension. The prophet is ready to *yield* us the right to say who shall be candidates for office."[107] After the election, which almost all the Mormon candidates carried, both sides would retreat deeper and deeper into their respective civic narratives. Anti-Mormons began to question their own allegiance to the Illinois state. Sharp had valued the American story of peoplehood in a nonpartisan way precisely because, Leggett-like, he saw it as an elevated story focused on the common good. His primary allegiance was to the collective worth of the Illinois people as a group of individuals seeking to use majority rule to produce a society fair for all. The people were now threatened by a group whose subsociety biases made them place the particular over the universal. Distrust had displaced worth in Sharp's writing: the Mormons' allegiance simply could not be trusted.

All egalitarians sense a lack of independence in the failure to declare primary allegiance to the democratic regime. Egalitarians view society as composed of a vertical pecking order of groups. They claim that their own group, a positive reference, is disrespected by the hierarchy and under threat. They develop a group consciousness that grows in persuasive power to the degree that it is reinforced by the social setting. For Mormons the threatening negative reference group was the whole of the unconverted gentile world. The corrupt world had its ordering, and the Mormons had theirs; indeed, they had been selected by God to upset the world's order. This was the basic background assumption which, while it often motivated their actions, was only acknowledged in rare moments of joy or stress. Egalitarians living in a communal setting, as did the Mormons, are especially prone to making sense of the buzzing reality of social life through a positive reference group lens. For particularist egalitarians, the group of worthies overlaps mainly with those who share their daily setting and who thus value their particular mark of worth, those whom, for these reasons, they treat like family. In this way setting reinforces proximity and proximity becomes a proxy for ethical worth.

Dissenting egalitarian groups are commonplace in developing democracies, and they were common in frontier Illinois. Opposition to hierarchy within society was the starting point in Illinois for antimission Baptists and Jacksonian Democrats like William Kinney. While potentially a principled and universal group whose membership was determined by liberal recognition rules, those whom Kinney included among the worthy were frequently marked off from the world not by any principle or worldly accomplishment but by a status arbitrarily selected by God. When this side of Illinois's dissenting democracy was emphasized, as it was for political Baptists like Daniel Parker, the positive reference group was implicitly defined by a particular status: its members were worthy because, as "the dear children of the spiritual kingdom . . . [they were] beyond the reach of corruption . . . [and] secured in his book forever."[108] The Mormons viewed their own status in this way; baptism of the dead allowed whole families to be sealed for eternity. It was a view tantamount to creating a Calvinist purgatory and one more reason why "Mormons were hated and feared by otherwise rational and religious Americans."[109]

But if Mormon particularism was not unusual in Illinois, why would Sharp consider it a special threat to Jacksonian democracy? Here again the power of framing cannot be discounted. Sharp had already framed a similar story back East. The Masons were a group whose secret practices and group loyalty threatened the republic even though they had once been worthy members of it. In the Mormon case, their ideas of worth and salvation had developed an explicit and necessary communal component. This violated the basic premise of self-help, that the actions of individuals indicated their salvation (or lack of it). Sharp subtly felt the pull of Mormon communalism and the sanctification of proximity. He perceived the Mormon effort at friendship in the temple ceremony in April 1841 as an insulting effort "to bribe us to flattery."[110] Instead of taking advantage of the offer, he was repulsed by it. It is remarkable how rapidly he read the situation in Hancock County as one in which the Mormons had not only questioned his own independence and manhood but were working to undermine the very possibility of such independence in Hancock County, in Illinois, and in all of the United States. The problem for Sharp was not merely the quantity of Mormons in the county but their quality. They upset the civic logic of independent republicanism because they relied on the prophet for salvation in the next world and deferred to him politically in this one. "If not checked in another year," Sharp noted in the summer of 1841, "they will have a decided majority in this county . . . and men who have no minds of their own, but move, and act and think at the bidding of one man, are to be our rulers"[111]

Illinois's individualists had a gripe against the Mormons, and they framed their gripe in such a way to make it stick. In the scholarship on political culture, this finding has to be considered something of a surprise. In Elazar's model, individualists are presented as a culture which "emphasizes the centrality of private concerns . . . [and] limiting community intervention—whether governmental or nongovernmental."[112] In his model, it is the moralists and the traditionalists who view government as a tool to be used for reform or for reassertion of the status quo. In the end, it was the threat to an independent community life that brought the anti-Mormons together "en masse." Sharp's individualism of the market merged under the pressure of Mormonism with the moralism of the New England Way. It might be suggested that the merger makes cultural sense: individualists under pressure turn into moralists, their offended sense of competition driving efforts at exclusion. If the pattern is general, then the idea that individualists always move the political system in a more inclusive direction is false. Equality will be defined in particularist ways by some egalitarians; the regime will be biased by commitment to nonneutral reference groups by even universalist egalitarians. But competitive individualists will also define equality in such a way as to justify prescription in the societal culture. Contrary to expectation, governance dilemmas in pluralistic democratic societies will not be solved simply by embracing more perfectly the solution of solidarity favored by egalitarians or more forcibly the solution of denial of the realities of group life favored by individualists.

The cultural and ideological patterns generated by the governance failure in Hancock County prompt some general observations about managing diversity in developing democracies. All subcultures, when under extreme pressure, will fray. Whenever he met the determined opposition of physical force, Smith did what we would expect of an egalitarian under pressure: he retreated into the purity of his group's protection. Beginning in early 1841, while the prophet tried to present a congenial face to the public, privately he was facing pressures and laboring under anxiety. Under the threat of existential danger, even the most universalist of egalitarians react with particularistic biases, misrecognize the other, and use dualism to avoid confrontation with the repressed shadow side of the self all groups hide.

Stories of egalitarians behaving badly under pressure abound in the Mormon troubles. Historian Fawn Brodie observes that the "threat of extradition to Missouri" for Smith began in earnest in the "spring of 1841." Being "harassed," he "had said some bitter things."[113] Sharp's early attack on the conditions of the English Mormons had hit a sore point. As wave after wave of English converts immigrated in response to Orson Hyde's and Brigham Young's missionary work, many settled in Montrose, across the river from Nauvoo. The diary of William Clayton, an immigrant from Manchester who later became secretary to the prophet, indicates the struggles faced by the Mormon settlers in this weakly governed frontier region. Their land titles were in doubt, they squabbled daily, and they were repeatedly accused of stealing. Sharp documented and exposed to the world these problems. In October and November he published a series of letters from Iowa store owner David Kilbourne, who explained that Isaac Galland never held title to the "Half Breed Tract" lands he sold the Mormons. Kilbourne also listed as many as thirteen robberies that Iowans at Montrose had experienced in the last year.[114] Sharp reported, as public knowledge, that Smith had publicly chastised the Manchester Mormons: in a "sermon . . . on the subject of 'baptism for the dead,' he stated the facts nearly as we have stated them—adding that he did not want to hear any more of their 'whining' about him, that 'if they did not like things here, they might *go to the devil*.'"[115] In in his diary, Clayton noted that at Nauvoo "the saints had frequently told us the devil was over the river" in Iowa where the English lived.[116] In an April 1841 visit to Montrose, Clayton reported that Smith told them to "prepare for what [was] in store," adding that they had "Haun's Mill as a sample."[117] Bitter outbursts like these were a telling indication that Smith was already beginning to feel besieged by this early date. But after the fall of 1842 and going forward, such outbursts become more common and more intense.[118]

Feeling cornered, the prophet responded by manically adding layer upon layer of new ritual at Nauvoo, many of them secret. Joseph Smith early on created an Aaronic priesthood open to all males and a more exclusive Melchizedek priesthood.[119] He crucially embellished the Melchizedek priesthood in a January 1841 revelation. Then he ritualized baptism for the dead sealing ceremonies at the temple and added Masonic "degrees" to the practice of celestial marriage. On September 6, 1842, a revelation detailed an elaborate ritual of "recording" baptism for the dead ancestry; revelations in May and July of 1843 explained that "in the celestial glory there are three heavens or degrees . . . and in order to obtain the highest, a man must enter into [celestial marriage]."[120] Such attention to ritual worked to cement attachment to the group. This primary meaning should not obscure how the cover of secrecy created an inner circle, which added a special motive to stay loyal to the group. But it was precisely the magnetic attraction Smith's followers felt toward making the whole Mormon sect one big family in eternity that made his leadership so compelling in the first place.[121]

By the spring of 1843, Smith appeared to reach an impasse. He had managed up to this point to view his two primary allegiances—to the Mormon people and to the American people—as compatible. Historian Richard Bushman presents this moment as a shift away from premillennial thinking, in which outsiders worked to defeat American corruption from the outside. The run for president suggests Smith would now work for change on the inside. But he was running as an outsider who would overturn the inside; the change was that he no longer hid his egalitarian resentment of the established order. His adorable group, the saints, would now be held high—not only in heaven but here on earth. This was allegiance to the group over the whole.

The move to a more mainstream postmillennial theology pushed some within the special circles of Mormon group life to feel betrayed; many loyal followers began to make a disgruntled exit. The pattern was repeated in so many Mormon settings that it cannot be arbitrary; during this period, ritual complexity was added by members of the Danites, the Nauvoo Legion, the Council of Fifty, and the new Masonic lodge. On April 5, 1841, Joseph married Louisa Beaman in a secret ceremony.[122] Here began a bitter and permanent feud with his wife Emma and a series of actions which would lead directly to the expulsion of Bennett in June of 1842.

When Bennett publicly exposed the Mormons' practice of "plural marriage," code language was developed to allow members to make public statements denying the practice by distinguishing their "divine" version from Bennett's corrupted worldly version. Eliza Snow, one of Joseph Smith's wives, later explained she signed a statement denying the practice of plural marriage at Nauvoo using the following ruse: "We made no allusion to any other system of marriage than Bennett's. His was prostitution. . . . In those articles there is no reference to divine plural marriage. We aimed to put down its opposite."[123] For months, the prophet denied the rumors when Emma confronted his use of the same code. From this point on he lived, as scholar Lawrence Foster puts it, "between two worlds."[124] The *Nauvoo Expositor* apostates R. D. Foster and Wilson Law felt excluded from the innermost circle of celestial marriage. If it was a test of loyalty, they did not pass. In Emma Smith's case, when the true extent of "celestial marriage" was revealed to her by Hyrum Smith, she felt tested in her faith as she never had been.

The dualistic mental world Smith and the Mormons created had its counterpart in the egalitarian group setting in which they lived. So much about the Mormon view of the outside world contained an all-or-nothing quality; parts of the American republic were to be saved, but much, like all the rest of the world, was damned. There was no in between. Such dualism is apparent, for example, in Smith's letter to the *Times and Seasons* of May 6, 1841, in which he commended reasonable and supportive leaders of opposing parties, such as Douglas and Walker of Illinois, in contrast to the "poison of adders" which he had found among "the official characters in the state of Missouri."[125] As for loyal friends, Sharp could have been one, but he had turned away and was thus of the devil. Here was the asymmetrical stance toward favored pure friends and hated impure apostates that so bedevils isolated groups in a rapidly developing society. Individualists live by reciprocity, which requires the symmetrical recognition of rights and duties by all involved agents. Market settings reinforce more or less symmetrical exchange as their preferred mode of interaction. Particularists under stress, by contrast, surround themselves with loyal friends; they act asymmetrically to prepare for the battles of the future.

As an ethical stance, particularism can be accused of making a mistaken conflation: proximity is a factual relation, not an ethical category. Yet how often do we develop obligations based on setting—for example, to those we interact with daily, kin or not? Surely mere physical nearness is not always a sign of commitment or consent to the local group. But if an individual is nearby and has once consented and then turns his or her back, the revision of that person's original choice is construed by particularists as inauthentic. The individualist sees the simple case of a person choosing to exit the group, an exit the individualist believes should be simple and voluntary. Protestants, who generally follow a voluntarist ethical premise, agree in theory; they respect all apostates or those who consent to join but then change their minds. Universalists, who extend their solidarity more broadly—they may simply be reformed particularists who have experienced a diversity of settings—would agree. But as a practical matter, egalitarians of the particularist persuasion use shunning and other devices to disallow ex-members a costless, seamless exit option. The Mormons enforced costs on apostates as a matter of course.

Social pressure was also having its way on the anti-Mormon side. The progress of bad feeling toward the Mormons by December of 1843 meant that even Thomas Gregg and the local Whig establishment had reached a point of no return. At this time, established Whig papers like the *Alton Telegraph* were arguing that while the Mormon leaders were "unprincipled and unworthy," they were "nevertheless *Citizens of the State of Illinois*" and thus "entitled to the protection . . . [of] their person, property, and liberty . . . [as] the most worthy and favored in our midst."[126] But in advertising the *Message* for a second year, Gregg wrote:

> In local matters—especially on the all-absorbing question of Mormon Dictation and Tyranny—[the *Message*] will firmly maintain its old position—advocating, with all the zeal of which we are capable, the just rights and interests of the Old Citizens; and exposing "without fear, favor, or affection" the crimes, villainies, and dangers of that irresponsible and growing power at Nauvoo, which is daily fastening deeper and deeper its fangs upon the community. That a crisis is fast approaching in the affairs of this and the contiguous counties, is the opinion of most sober and reflecting citizens; and that it must be met—firmly—unyieldingly—and yet rightfully met—is also the opinion of every good citizen and friend to his country.[127]

The pressure of a Mormon "crisis" had welded "Old Citizens" and anti-Mormons, egalitarians and individualists, conservatives and competitors, together under a moralistic popular front. The door that had been open to a diverse array of citizens save those openly violating the harm principle now had closed to the viper on the hearth. Gregg and Sharp together would be busy articulating and legitimating a new justification for establishment vigilantism to be added to the civic repertoire of the Illinois way.

7

Thomas Ford and the Politics of Civic Worth

In February of 1844 two portentous developments occurred a week apart in Hancock County which, though they likely escaped the notice of the governor, loomed large in determining his future reputation and the course of the troubles. The two leading antagonists in the brewing conflict decided on subtle but crucial changes in their respective group operations. Thomas Sharp took over sole proprietorship of the only anti-Mormon paper in the county, and Joseph Smith told his followers of his decision to run for the United States presidency. On February 14, 1844, Sharp resumed the editorial duties at the *Warsaw Signal*. In announcing his purposes "to the reader," he noted that "probably in no portion of the Union [was] the public mind so violently and dangerously affected, as it [was] at the present time, in this vicinity."[1] Sharp was not exaggerating. While the Anti-Rent War in central New York was equally entrenched, it had entered a lull; and the tensions between nativists and Catholics in Philadelphia did not break into the open until May of 1844.[2] In Hancock County on February 8, the prophet had moved to raise the stakes. He explained to the faithful that the presidential run was his strategy to vindicate the "injured innocence" of the Mormon people.[3]

In Sharp's case the contents of the day's paper abundantly supported his assertion. The Saturday edition led with two items foretelling a future of violence in Hancock County: one, a letter from Governor Thomas Ford to the citizens of Hancock County; and the other, the proceedings of a public anti-Mormon meeting held in Warsaw four days earlier. In his January 29, 1844, letter Ford made clear his commitment to neutrality toward the polarized groups. As he interpreted state law, the citizens of Hancock were to order their own affairs; he would not intervene to disarm the Nauvoo Legion, raise a militia to arrest a fugitive, or repeal certain ordinances issued at Nauvoo. "I as Governor have no right to interfere in your difficulties," he wrote. "I am bound by the constitution and laws to regard you all as citizens of the state, possessed of equal rights and privileges." The only condition upon which he would intervene was if "a state of war" broke out, and he warned the anti-Mormons that were that to happen, his "interference [would] be against those who [were] the first transgressors."[4] Ford was raising state neutrality to a higher level of principle, a rule of order becoming an object of justice. His goal was to focus on the humanity all parties had in common. The Mormons had not heeded his advice to refrain from group voting or group settlement, but they were still "human beings . . . citizens of the State," as he later told the legislature.[5]

The *Signal*'s other lead item was a report of the contentious anti-Mormon meeting held on February 10 "at the church" in Warsaw.[6] Democratic senator Jacob C. Davis apparently made one last attempt to reassert party control over the county on the ground of his own personal authority. He and others packed the church with supporters of a putative "anti-excitement" platform. This faction among the anti-Mormons did not want to "pass inflammatory resolutions for the express purpose of creating and keeping up the excitement in the minds of one against another class of our own citizens." They further complained about a too-open endorsement of "Mobocracy," and one among them said "it filled him with alarm, when in this town he saw a packed jury, who gave in a verdict evidently contrary to law, merely because one of the parties was a Mormon."

Sharp, who was in attendance, gained control over the meeting by accusing Davis of reverting to personal "political interests." The purpose of the meeting, he observed, was simply to elect representatives to attend the larger anti-Mormon gathering in Carthage on February 17. The obstructionism was especially surprising according to Sharp because Davis himself "had been one of the very first who started the *ball* of anti-Mormonism—acted with the anti-Mormons until he saw an opportunity of gaining the political influence of the Mormons."[7] The senator evidently was adept at this game; he won the Hancock senate seat in 1842 with Mormon support and was reelected to the same seat in 1846 after they had largely left the state. He eventually went on to serve in Congress.[8] Davis may very well have been distracted by political calculation. He objected to the resurrection of the anti-Mormon megaphone that was the *Signal,* adding that he would "rather see the Mormons driven out at once than this constant excitement about them." But Senator Davis also had a majoritarian point: political focus in a democracy should be on the majority and their story of peoplehood; it should not be distracted by the minority and their constant failures to attain civic worth.

At this point in the meeting "the Chairman rose and stated that the call was for an anti-Mormon meeting, that those who moved the resolution had no business there if they did not come to promote the objects for which the meeting was called." This chairman was none other than Thomas Gregg, who was hereby signaling his intention to throw the support of his "conservative" Whig faction behind Sharp and the "inflammatory" anti-Mormons.[9] Only a few weeks earlier, Gregg had rejected the goal of forced Mormon expulsion on the grounds that not "*all* who reside[d] at Nauvoo [were] deserving of punishment" and that anti-Mormons could not go "beyond . . . the LAW."[10] The anti-Mormons agreed to disagree on how far they would go in publicly endorsing illegal actions; they left moot whether the "right of self-defense" was part of the law. The countywide meeting at Carthage the following week cautiously passed the motion that a report be prepared on "the available means of defense . . . [and] the number of men who [could] be depended upon to act in cases of emergency."[11] But a significant barrier to anti-Mormon unity had been overcome; when pushed to act in a public forum, Gregg had sided with Sharp.

Senator Davis's fears about Sharp's anti-Mormon juggernaut soon proved prescient. Over the course of the next two years, Davis's political leadership would be eclipsed by the civic leadership of men like Sharp and Gregg. Regime officers like Davis and Ford found their state authority reduced considerably, if not rendered "nugatory."[12] The settler state in Illinois had little capacity to direct from its center the power to enforce the law at the local level. Its already meager directive powers failed spectacularly when local communities degenerated into polarized self-governing groups.

Where competing majorities lived in separate enclaves, as in Hancock County, the temptation to miscalculate the other side's civic worth was too great to resist. Rumors became self-fulfilling prophecies, at which point the reconciliation of differences was impossible because each side painted the opposition in colors that by definition made them unacceptable—the Mormons as deluded and dependent, the anti-Mormons as corrupt and culpable. In these circumstances, the threat of violence lingered. With the regime's informal rules in play, the Springfield state no longer monopolized the routine use of force. Opposing groups took on the tasks of self-government and relied on their members. Individuals acted to reinforce group allegiance. Small changes in individual attitude, such as Thomas Gregg's, led to large differences in group behavior. The Mormon youth formed a "whittling and whistling" club to keep Nauvoo strangers under surveillance; the anti-Mormons organized militaristic "wolf hunts" to display their power. The path to "civil war" was set.[13]

FORD'S NEUTRALITY AND THE RULE OF LAW

When he first came to Hancock County at the head of a militia in June of 1844, Governor Ford appears to have predetermined himself on the course of neutrality. He had decided to treat the Mormons as a religious sect, which they were, but not as what they had become, a self-governing community. Ford's decision to continue to recognize the Mormons as legitimate citizens of Illinois left the anti-Mormons feeling betrayed and abandoned. The governor rejected the claim that the Mormons posed a unique threat to property rights; he also ignored the charges that the Mormons had failed as members because they violated the norms of the old settlers. Though such norms might be informal, they mattered, as Whig George T. M. Davis knew. When Davis had arrived in Alton as a young lawyer in 1832, he learned immediately that "the refusal of the newcomer to participate" in the local ways "was looked upon with disfavor and distrust."[14]

Ford had wagered on Mormon belief: that the saints' beliefs should be recognized and credited as autonomous, validly grounded, and not some form of false consciousness, and that Joseph Smith's beliefs were a new, apparently good-natured version of American Protestantism. The point about Mormon beliefs was thrown into doubt, Sharp suggested, because they so quickly adopted a new leader, Brigham Young, and appeared to follow the Twelve without qualification.[15] Such a rapid and unanimous substitution indicated a degree of credulity and dependence inconsistent with republican independence. The presence of Mormon dissenters like the Law brothers made concluding this point debatable, but Ford would come to regret his extension of civic worth to the Mormon prophet. Smith's stream of revelations was dynamic and creative, but it had the consequence of consolidating his power and control; the action against the *Expositor* and the run for the presidency under the terms of "theodemocracy" confirmed the pattern. These shifts in Smith's public posture made the charges of antirepublicanism all but impossible to deny.

Ford's January 1844 letter ignored all this and retreated to a defense of the harm principle and equal rights. In his *History* he observed, "In framing our governments it seemed to be the great object of our ancestors to secure the public liberty by depriving government of power."[16] He was reminding readers that liberal governments were limited governments, and that his powers as governor were limited to carrying out a preexisting property and criminal law. If executive discretion was called for, he would be committed to evenhanded enforcement. Ford's stance of neutrality was hard to fault, but it did not address the case at hand. Despite his denial, the state Ford was leading was concerned with worth as much as harm. Neutrality in the matter of worth was not possible in the Illinois regime because it was precommitted to an independent-producer bias.

Hegemonic belief dies hard, and of all the victims of hegemony in Illinois, Ford was perhaps the most tragic. In this sense the Illinois governor exemplifies perfectly the state-formation trap Pierre Bourdieu predicts is inevitable: the blindness to state bias that state command imposes on its operators or, as Bourdieu puts it, the "endeavor to think the state is to take the risk of taking over (or being taken over by) a thought of the state."[17] Ford was wholly captured by the thought of the liberal state, by thoughts of equality, the rule of law, and the possibility of absolute neutrality. He seems not to have bargained that the anti-Mormons would rally their members around public sphere duties. They quickly and effectively recruited supporters from among the settlers and citizen-soldiers in nearby counties. Once they did, Ford had little choice but to treat the matter as one of "war," a decision making real a final critical juncture he had attempted to avoid.

Ford's stance had the paradoxical effect of energizing the old settlers, who redoubled their efforts to invoke the informal rules of the Illinois regime while publishing to the world that the state's ordinary police powers had failed. The informal state, with all its biases, was triumphant while the formal state retreated, forced to act on emergency powers alone. The governor was left with a single extraordinary and unwieldy tool, the militia. He would use it repeatedly over the coming two years to impose peace in the short term, but a durable, locally endorsed peace did not return until almost all the Mormons were forced to leave. Ford's January 1844 decision bequeathed the Mormon War to the state. The war label was used in earnest by those outside Hancock, used in derision by those inside the county, and used everywhere to brand Ford's administration a failure.

The long tail of this point of no return was passed a half year later, on a fateful day in June. It was early in the afternoon of June 27, 1844, a few hours before the storming of Carthage Jail, when Sharp used his platform as a civic leader to address a rump contingent of the anti-Mormon militia, comprising "the Warsaw, Green Plains, and Rocky Run Troops, five companies in all," in an open field outside of Carthage.[18] From atop a "big bay horse," he spoke to the remnant of already disbanded and discharged soldiers: "My Fellow Citizens! . . . Now is the time to put a period to the career of the Prophet—sustained as he is by a band of fanatical military saints! We have borne his usurpations until it would be cowardice to bear them longer."[19] In perhaps the single most significant act of citizenship in the long Mormon troubles, Sharp exhorted the anti-Mormons to "take the responsibility" now or never. The editor may only have been urging the militia, as Gregg later claimed, to grab Joseph Smith and escort him out of the county and into the hands of a sheriff in Missouri, but the result of storming the jail was a shootout and the murder of the Smith brothers.[20]

After arresting the two brothers for destroying the *Expositor,* the governor had considered the Smiths safe in the Carthage Jail and sent most of his militia home. Once the men were assassinated, Ford quickly called out a second militia to stymie retaliation. This militia was also quickly disbanded when it was clear the Mormons did not intend to act in vengeance. Then, in the fall of 1844, Ford returned with a third militia. His request for federal troops was denied and he believed a force was needed to keep the peace in Hancock over the winter. The third militia also sought to implement the law, but this time it was the anti-Mormons who were under indictment, specifically for the murder of the Smiths. Temporarily leaderless, the Mormons were persuaded at the last moment by a Democratic Party operative to vote en masse in the local elections. They succeeded in electing a sheriff and three county commissioners, officers empowered to empanel a grand jury to hear indictments for the Smith murders during the meeting of the circuit court. Again prompted by a loss of local control, the anti-Mormon Committee of Public Safety organized several wolf hunts in the vicinity of Nauvoo.

The governor feared the anti-Mormons would use their military might to disrupt the legal process unfolding at the Carthage courthouse. He called out the militia preemptively to squelch any violence which might intimidate the court and derail the law. Since the perpetrators were not yet arrested, it was speculated that he was also using the militia to carry out arrests of the leading figures. This surreptitious goal turned the anti-Mormons permanently against him. Sharp, who had been his defender, now became a constant critic. He ridiculed Ford for attempting to raise a militia of 2,500 men and howled with vindication when the governor could muster only 450 volunteers (almost all Whigs) to monitor the "Grand Military Encampment" (a.k.a. wolf hunt) the anti-Mormons had planned. Stephen A. Douglas did not endorse Ford's move. The Democratic Party's lack of support for Ford's militia call was not lost on astute political observers in Hancock. It enabled the anti-Mormons to act secure in the knowledge that the state's societal culture was on their side. This emboldened them throughout Joseph Smith's murder trial, which ended in acquittal in June of 1845. In the fall of 1844, however, the anti-Mormons played it safe. Before Ford arrived, they called off their encampment and military display; Sharp explained that "the Governor was the real hunter, and . . . some arrests were planned."[21]

All evidence indicates Ford did indeed intend to use the third militia to arrest the accused. As the governor wrote in a report to the General Assembly, he expected the prosecution of the perpetrators of the Carthage conspiracy to vindicate "the honor of the State and the supremacy of the laws."[22] Levi Williams and Thomas Sharp were sought on writs of murder issued by Ford's special prosecutor, Murray McConnell.[23] But when Ford arrived on September 27, he learned the accused had slipped across the river at Warsaw and into Missouri. Ford intended to pursue them there and organized a contingent of reluctant militia volunteers. But with the Whig press full of accusations of a "corrupt bargain" between Ford and the Mormons over the August election, Illinois militia volunteers were reluctant to extend regime services to a mission perceived as unpopular and politically motivated. The governor was forced to accept a plea deal under which the two men avoided jail and were granted their freedom.

The anti-Mormons now viewed Ford and the state's prosecutors as outside interlopers. The Whig papers made the most of his "foolish" efforts; one quipped, "If ever there was a man who deserved a straight-jacket, I think it is Governor Ford."[24] Ford's own party had already informally turned off the militia spigot and now distanced itself from him altogether as it became clear the Mormon War would be the lame-duck governor's bane.[25] Democratic rival Douglas was now publicly mocking him: "Gentlemen this matter has passed beyond ridicule; it is time for sympathy."[26]

A SOLVER OF PROBLEMS AND A PROBLEMATIC SOLUTION

Given the fateful impact of Ford's decisions on the course of the Mormon troubles, we should make an effort to see the conflict from his perspective. Scholars Dallin H. Oaks and Marvin S. Hill, who look closely at the Carthage trial, conclude that Ford "had done as well as he could in upholding the appearance of law in Hancock County."[27] But after the passage of time and especially after the acquittal of all the accused in the trial on Joseph Smith's murder, Ford's attention to the matter drifted.[28] Without the federal support he had sought, he acted mainly to keep the conflict contained within Illinois. In September of 1845 he issued a proclamation to the anti-Mormons organizing in Iowa and Missouri warning them to stay out of the conflict.[29] The following summer and fall, the anti-Mormons again threatened war, this time on some "new citizens" who had moved to Nauvoo, but Ford hesitated to call another militia. The *Alton Telegraph and Democratic Review* could state as common knowledge that "Gov. Ford has been greatly censured by the public press, both in and out of the State, for an alleged neglect of official duties in failing to prevent or suppress the late riots in the county of Hancock."[30] He is accused by scholars of all stripes of exacerbating the conflict through careless and inept decisions.[31] What can be said on his side of the matter? Who was Thomas Ford?

As a frontier judge, Ford had familiarity with the powers and limitations of the settler state. Where the state had the power to act, he showed himself to be an adroit manager, as he demonstrated in his effective maneuvers to address the state's financial woes and its stalled canal project. Although the Mormon issue was more intractable, from the start Ford proposed an array of proactive measures: get the Mormons to withdraw from politics; end the threat of Joseph Smith's removal to Missouri; reform the charters; divide the county. These last two required time and cooperation from the legislature. Some of his measures were unfolding when the unexpected happened: Smith had the Nauvoo City Council declare the *Nauvoo Expositor* a nuisance. Smith and the Nauvoo City Council went further; they acted summarily and used force immediately and directly on abatement. Ford had no option but to call out the militia. Multiple militia calls followed, but they were increasingly ineffective because west-central Illinois societal culture deemed them illegitimate. And therein lay the rub, as he later claimed: "The people cannot be used to put down the people."[32]

The real power of popular justice the frontier judge knew firsthand. In fact, perhaps no official in the state was more prepared by temperament and by training to address the conflict in Hancock than Ford was. His extensive experience with extralegal justice in the northern third of the state was especially pertinent. If Thomas Ford could not find a way to avoid bringing the stain of mobocracy and religious persecution down on his "goodly" land, it was likely that no one could. The Illinois state did not have an effective structure going for it, but it did have Ford's will and agency. Even so, the politics of civic worth remained intractable, a source of frustration for the governor, who considered solving problems his special skill.

Ford shared many traits with his Democratic colleagues. Like William Kinney he was born in Pennsylvania in a frontier area near Pittsburgh in 1804, and like Kinney he grew up in New Design, one of Illinois Territory's first American settlements.[33] His father

FIG. 7.1. Thomas Ford (from Gregg, *History of Hancock County*). Courtesy of Newberry Library

died under mysterious circumstances, and his widowed mother abruptly moved to Illinois, though "the family was very poor, and the children necessarily engaged at work on the farm." Like William Leggett, Ford was a protégé of Ninian Edwards, Illinois's only territorial governor and first US senator. As early as 1818, he was working in the law office of Daniel P. Cook, the state's sole US representative and, in 1826, the talented chairman of the powerful House Ways and Means Committee. "But finding his preparatory education insufficient," Ford's stepbrother sent him to Transylvania University in Lexington, Kentucky. The Panic of 1819 brought his higher education to an abrupt end less than a year later. Making his way back home without any funds, Ford found himself in rural Indiana forced "to stop on the roadside . . . in the neighborhood of a new settlement." But he made the most of his misfortune. He persuaded the local people to hire him as a teacher and to build a schoolhouse, which "he assisted with his own labor." He was "more proud," he later wrote of this action, "than anything he ever did in after life." He came upon a problem and answered at one go his own and the community's pressing need.

Returning home, he got a newspaper position just across the border in St. Louis, studied law, and eventually opened a legal practice in Edwardsville. When his stepbrother was appointed secretary of state by Edwards in 1829, Ford moved to Galena to write for the *Miners' Journal* to support the Edwards-Reynolds faction among the Democrats. While Ford came out for Reynolds in the governor's race, he adroitly remained friendly with the opposing Kane-Kinney faction. Since the latter was proslavery in politics and particularist in other ways, Ford was indicating his allegiance to the universalist side of the party, which at this same time fellow Illinoisan William Leggett was beginning to make popular among the Locofocos in New York City. Ford was made state's attorney in Galena for his efforts and later served many years as a circuit judge for an area that covered the entire northern third of the state.

In May of 1842, Adam Snyder, the Democratic Party's nominee for governor in the upcoming August election, suddenly died. Under Douglas's leadership, the party swiftly called several emergency meetings culminating in Ford's nomination. Given that the state was at the time greatly divided over the canal and internal improvements—which some in the southern counties believed would only benefit Chicago and the counties adjacent to the canal—Ford's appointment was a shrewd move. While he had "homely features," a "naturally diffident, modest and reserved disposition," and lacked charisma, he was a loyal and capable party organizer who had grown up in the southern tier of the state but who had spent the last decade in the northern tier.[34] Ford's circuit riding gave him name recognition in the central tier of the state, and his reputation as a "bright, conscientious, and just man" there made him popular in many Whig strongholds, as it did at Quincy, where in 1833 he earned acclaim by ministering to the sick during the cholera epidemic.[35]

Perhaps most salient was the fact that he had recently published in the Rockford paper a learned defense of keeping the state's northern boundary in place, echoing congressional representative Nathaniel Pope's 1818 argument that Illinois needed a northern tier to perform its destined role as unifier of the nation. The northern boundary had been recently contested by Wisconsin Territory, whose proposal was almost unanimously supported by referenda held in Illinois's Stephenson, Boone, and Winnebago Counties.[36] Ford's defense of the state's national role resonated, and he was elected by an overwhelming majority in all three sections despite a rather feeble effort at stumping. The public, for the first time in its history, had a governor who was both a man of the people and effective. These were valuable assets if the people could overlook his "squeaking voice," which Ford could not make heard in the large General Assembly hall when reading his inaugural address.[37]

In print, the December 8, 1842, inaugural speech turned out to be a rhetorical masterpiece and a problem solver's tour de force. The new governor eschewed party dogma and assumed the average citizen would be able to follow his detailed financial analysis. In setting priorities, his stance was one of working with the banks—not blaming them—and firmly rejecting any further work on any internal improvement projects, however popular they may be. He said he would place all his focus on completing the canal project. As he put it, the work on the canal "has progressed nearly five-eighths toward completion"; this made it the closest to completion of all the state's projects.[38] Ford laid out a plan to responsibly retire the state bank and carefully manage the state's bonds and other debt. He pledged to liquidate the assets to be salvaged from all unfinished internal improvements projects, use the proceeds to pay creditors, and leverage the value in the yet-to-be-completed canal to secure the funding needed to finish the project.

Nearing his peroration, Ford appended a note urging reform of the Mormon charters, which he found "objectionable on many accounts, particularly on account of the powers granted." He continued, "The people of the state have become aroused on the subject and anxiously desire that those charters should be modified as to give the inhabitants of Nauvoo no greater privileges than those enjoyed by others of our fellow citizens." The short speech, about one-third as long as Governor Carlin's farewell address given the day before, caused consternation in the Democratic press—the *State Register* editor did not even print it, while Carlin's blame-the-banks partisan effort was printed as a separate pamphlet. By contrast, the Whig flagship paper, the *Sangamo Journal,* gave Ford's address a front-page spread. The Whigs appreciated that Ford had avoided Locofoco (antibank) fundamentalism. The "Springfield clique" running the Democratic Party no doubt found the Mormon policy consternating and arrogantly ungrateful given that Douglas had just succeeded in recruiting the Mormons to their side. It was a maneuver which had paid off in the Mormon vote for Democratic candidates in 1842, Ford himself being a primary beneficiary.

Ford would later clash with Douglas over the US Senate position and with Lyman Trumbull, the secretary of state held over from the previous administration, over the bank issue, but his overwhelming election victory gave him a cushion of authority he was determined to use. The state was deep in debt; Ford's estimate came to over fifteen million dollars. The people had been "rendered unhappy and looked with alarm at the prospect before them." His purpose was not to cast aspersions; had he been at the helm, he would likely have succumbed to the same "delusion . . . the same phrenzy which . . . surrendered . . . judgments to the dictates of a wild imagination." The General Assembly that raised and passed the extravagant internal improvements plan had included Stephen A. Douglas and Abraham Lincoln, two of the state's leading lights, both of whom had supported it.

It would be hard to get up enough in tax money to pay the interest on one year of the debt, let alone more. But there was another way, and he systematically laid out a solution. Working with the banks instead of castigating them offered a quick and easy means of retiring $2,650,000 in bonded debt. These and other maneuvers enabled the state to change completely its relationship with bondholders in New York and England. As Ford put it, "Instead of reproaching us and getting up a moral crusade against us, as against a confederated band of unprincipled swindlers, with the view to coerce us to our duty, [the banks] will be directly interested in doing us all the good in their power."

The plan had several moving parts. The General Assembly would have to move to improve the currency—that is, the bank notes in circulation—by "compelling" the state bank to resume specie payment and to burn its script as it was redeemed. The canal's engineers would have to backtrack on their favored "deep cut" canal plan; the ambitious six-feet-deep, sixty-feet-across dimension would have to be scaled back to the original measurements of four feet deep and forty feet across. The shallower cut removed less granite and was less expensive, though without the Lake Michigan water utilized by the deep cut, a feeder from the Little Calumet River needed to be added. Nonetheless, this change reduced the canal expense by $1.4 million.[39] All in all, the *Sangamo Journal* commended the address and Ford for his "determination to do what he believes to be best to subserve the interests of the people."[40]

In the meantime, Ford determined to use what powers he had as governor to put an end to Missouri's efforts to extradite the prophet. He used the tools at hand—his powers to issue warrants, to apprehend and arrest, and put out writs of habeas corpus—but he would use them on his terms. As we have seen, the arranged case before federal judge Pope at Springfield did not end the Missouri harassment. Just as Ford was poised, as he believed, to resolve the Mormon problem, he was "thwarted in ridding the State of the Mormons . . . by the insane frenzy of the anti-Mormons."

The governor was roundly criticized during his term and after for the problematic way he handled the troubles. He was attacked as biased by both the Mormons and the anti-Mormons. After the Carthage shootout, he repeatedly blamed the anti-Mormons for purposely endangering his own life. He argued they must have believed he would be killed at Nauvoo (where he was heading) when the news of the Smiths' mobbing reached the city. Gregg argued that the idea the anti-Mormons were plotting to kill either the governor or the Smiths with their jail rush was simply wrong, a product of the governor's "too excitable and suspicious nature." Had they lived, Ford's ultimate plan for the Smith brothers was not too different from the anti-Mormon plan Gregg disclosed.[41] Ford was considering a plan for an "escape" by "the leaders of Mormons," who would then take their people with them into the West; he claimed that he "had never breathed [the plan] to a living soul."[42]

But there is some evidence to suggest that in fact he did. Scholars see a kind of collusion with the anti-Mormons in the fact that, the day before the murders, he disbanded all the militias he had called to Carthage except three companies, two from the Carthage Greys, which he left to guard the Smiths in jail, and one company of

Augusta Dragoons, which he took with him to Nauvoo. But if Ford did share his plan, it is likely that he did so in an inadvertent way. Thomas Geddes, a commander of the Greys at Carthage, later told Gregg the following story:

> While the Smiths were in jail, I went to the jail in company with Gov. Ford, and there conversed with them for some time, the burden of Smith's talk being that they were only acting in self-defense, and only wanting to be left alone. After leaving the jail, and while returning from it, the Governor and I had still further conversation about the subject matter. After some time the Governor exclaimed, "O, it's all nonsense; you will have to drive these Mormons out yet!" I then said, "If we undertake that Governor, when the proper time comes, will you interfere?" "No, I will not," said he; then, after a pause, adding, "until you are through."[43]

While this conversation or something like it may have happened, there is some reason to suspect the anti-Mormons of seeking the cover of official authority for their act. They did not seem to seek it at the time. Certainly, Thomas Sharp never denied that "it was common talk and in the camp [among the Carthage Greys] and the opinion greatly prevailed, that Joe ought to be killed while the opportunity presented itself."[44]

Beside the general anti-Mormon animus directed at Ford, which was to last until the end of the troubles, three specific charges were leveled against him in Illinois at large: that he used the Mormons for political advantage during the August 1844 election, a charge made by Whig opponent George T. M. Davis; that he should have protected the Smiths better at the Carthage Jail, a charge made by the *Sangamo Journal* and the Mormons themselves; and that he did not do enough to enforce the supremacy of the law throughout the crisis, a charge prevalent in Whig public opinion.

The first charge is perhaps the easiest to answer. Ford repeatedly denied he had authorized the Democratic operative who arranged the Mormon vote. In truth his own party and the Mormons themselves were acting against his wishes. Despite Davis's plausible case—the Democrats stood to gain; Ford was actually on good terms with Minor Deming, the man elected sheriff; and the Mormons were told the governor was behind Deming's sheriff run—Ford's adamant denial of complicity is believable because he had consistently urged the Mormons to refrain from voting altogether. He repeatedly proclaimed his belief that Mormon group voting only threatened and antagonized the anti-Mormon opposition.[45]

On the second charge, the most plausible defense of Ford's approach was offered by Sharp:

> Some have attempted to make political capital out of the conduct of Governor Ford. The Sangamo Journal says that the leaving of only seven guards at the jail was a blunder. We do not know that he would have bettered the matter, had he left a thousand; only as they could have prevented an escape. The troops the Governor had ordered from a distance [i.e., the units he disbanded] were daily imbibing the animosity of the citizens—they were disaffected, and were anxious to return home, where their crops needed their attention.[46]

Under these circumstances, Ford's perceived neutrality actually undermined his capacity to sense what was happening on the ground. Precisely because all knew he was committed to a fair application of the law, "unusual pains were taken to conceal . . . the secret measures resolved upon." Still, the excuse of secrecy is hard to credit. One eye-witness claimed that William D. Roosevelt had proclaimed in Carthage, "We have willing minds, and God almighty has given us strength, and we will wield the saber and make our own laws." Further, it was common knowledge that Levi Williams had made a public speech calling for volunteers to murder the Smiths. Thus, it is hard to credit Ford's claim that the machinations were secret, though he added, "Whether such a speech [by Williams] was really made or not is yet unknown to me."[47]

Sharp described the group that stormed the jail as "a company of about one hundred armed men." The anti-Mormons were following the Illinois regime's informal rules of order, Ogle County Regulator style: no legal charge of murder could stand against one hundred people. It is doubtful that anyone could have stopped a united civic effort by the gentlemen of property and standing. This was a point Sharp emphasized: "The impression has gone out that the deed was done by the militia under military command. It is false. The men concerned had been discharged, and acted in this affair as citizens and not as soldiers." They acted from civic purpose and felt justified given the slow-moving, ineffectual law: "It is a well-known fact that Joe Smith had eluded every effort which had been made for the last four years to bring him to justice. . . . Our citizens have regretted and still regret the necessity that existed for taking the law in this particular instance, into our own hands; but that it sooner or later would have to be done, no one acquainted with the facts of the case, could deny."[48]

When hard-pressed and sent into hiding in the fall of 1844, Sharp still found time to produce a piece satirizing the "farcical" governor and his Mormon War. It is worth noting that he only used the term *war* when referring to the governor's actions against the anti-Mormons.[49] Anti-Mormon actions were by contrast described by Sharp as civic duties performed on a volunteer basis to further the public interest. If anti-Mormon citizen action had taken a decided military turn, this simply followed from the Illinois regime's citizen-soldier model. Immediately after the Smith murders, several anti-Mormon militias began daily parades, including the Warsaw Dragoons, the Warsaw Cadets, the Warsaw Rifle Company, the Green Plains Guard, and the Rocky Run Minute Men. "A military spirit seems to pervade all classes of our citizens," Sharp noted. He further framed, "This is right—Freemen, by the blood and toil of our fathers, by our vigilance let us hand down to our children the same precious legacy."[50] It was a time, George Davis remembered, when "the clans of the old settlers were gathering for combat."[51]

The third charge, about Ford's failure to enforce the rule of law, is more powerful and takes us to the very core of the dilemmas posed by the politics of civic worth. Many in Illinois held that Smith acted a tyrant and disdained the law only when he had the power; the prophet acted demurely, it was observed, when he was trapped and the power was against him. This view fit precisely the Illinois regime's recipe for dealing with outlaws: they could be controlled only by overwhelming power. The law would have to awe them; if it failed, the punitive, rough justice of the community would serve as a last-ditch backstop. Sharp claimed that when Ford called out the troops to enforce the law in the *Expositor* case, "the Prophet, seeing this determined position of the Governor, suddenly began to feel that he was not unlimited, in authority, and that there was power to assert the majesty of the insulted law. Immediately the haughty, proud, vain, and self-sufficient despot duffed his imperial robes, and mantling himself in hypocritical humility, he bowed seemingly to the dictates of the law. But could the law reach him? No! Its arm was palsied and to him it was nothing more than a spider's web."[52]

Here the Warsaw editor was implicitly rebuking Ford for not executing the law forcefully enough. This was a position commonly adopted during and after the troubles by anti-Mormon opinion and by the Whigs in the northern tier of the state whenever they justified the use of regulators.

Advocating for the use of an overawing law was far different from what Lincoln had in mind in his 1838 Springfield Lyceum address. It is true Lincoln pleaded with his fellow citizens to embrace the rule of law as a matter of "civil religion," but the awe of religion, as Lincoln had it, was far different from the awe of the rod. The regulators intended to use the correcting rod to cudgel the disobedient into submission. Charles Ballance of Peoria, for example, argued that the governor could have maintained control in Hancock, if he was "*man* enough to rule Illinois."[53]

In short, had Ford acted with an overwhelming show of force earlier in the conflict, he could have gotten Smith, the Mormons, and any recalcitrant anti-Mormons to submit to the supremacy of the law. This line of thinking simply ignores the real constraints on the governor—the harvest the militia members needed to get back to, the lack of support for the Mormons in the surrounding counties, and the bankrupt state's inability to pay the costs of a lengthy militia occupation. Behind this third charge was a simple frustration with the state's lack of enforcement capacity, which was manifest in the feeling that Ford was somehow failing in his "manly" republican duties. Historian Rodney O. Davis notes in his introduction to Ford's *History* that "one is struck by the frequent references his contemporaries made to . . . Ford's small stature and unprepossessing physical presence."[54] The anti-Mormon women tried to publicly shame Ford in the fall of 1846 when they greeted him and his fifth militia with two "trophies," one black and one red, made from the petticoats of "the ladies of Nauvoo."[55] The symbolism is unclear, but there are at least two intended meanings: that Ford was partial to Mormon red-bloomer ladies of ill repute; or perhaps that his military prowess was akin to a eunuch in a harem.

The attack on Ford for what the anti-Mormons supposed was a lack of manliness might also be understood as an attack on his refusal to recognize, authorize, or in any way credit the informal particularist side of the Illinois regime. His judicial cast of mind gloried in the law's due process while resisting the majority's need for the punitive enforcement of popular justice. Ford's universalist framing of the Jacksonian regime meant that he insisted on an allegiance to state neutrality. It was an allegiance he learned in the school of the law office, a hegemonic cultural institution if there ever was one. Here the "thought of the state" considering itself as a body committed to equal justice under the law was taught; it became a foundational belief, one typically mixing fact and value, description and prescription. Sharp's reference to the law as a mere spider's web is reminiscent of the egalitarian dismissal of law as the plaything of the wealthy. By accusing Ford of violating equal rights, of allowing the law to be ineffectual against the powerful Joseph Smith, Sharp was attacking the formal ideal of the law that Ford held dear. In his *History* Ford paraphrased but disputed the Athenian aphorism that the law is like a spider's web, which catches the weak and poor while the powerful and rich break through.[56]

Ford dedicated his hardscrabble life to contesting this cynical if arguably accurate truth about Illinois's democracy. He believed the Illinois regime contested it as well. He related a humorous episode about when "a hurricane of popular indignation" was raised after "the legislature passed a law for the improvement of the breed of cattle by which small bulls were prohibited. . . . The law was denounced as being aristocratic and intended to favor the rich, who, by their money, had become possessed of large bulls."[57] His evenhanded approach to the Mormon troubles was the sacrifice to his popularity he was willing to make upon the altar of egalitarianism. But he insisted on resisting particularism at the local level by asserting universalism at the state level. He counted the Mormons among the weak who needed the protection of the law, whereas the old settlers counted them among the powerful who were evading it.

Ford, of course, never denied that the community was the ultimate authority behind the law. As he put it in 1846, "The Governor of the state can do nothing unless he is supported by the people of the state and public opinion."[58] Lincoln had made the same concession in his temperance address when he observed that "universal public opinion . . . is an argument, or at least an *influence,* not easily overcome" in a democracy.[59] But while actually administering the law, Ford resisted as much as possible the influence of public opinion and the informal rules of the Illinois regime. It was an act of denial which he shared with Whig moralists. Those Democrats who dismissed Ford's administration as a "lamentable and pitiable failure" were really complaining about Ford's high-minded resistance to the authority of local majority opinion, a force the Democrats as a party were committed to representing.[60] As with his treatment of the Black Codes, Ford knew the law at base reflected independent-producer biases, but he resisted the power of local rules of recognition and he sought to enforce the law upon the grounds of a higher, public-interested majority, one above the fray and substantively and procedurally neutral.

But a universalist public interest was something the polarized groups in Hancock County and the party duopoly would not allow. It is not clear that self-interest, rightly understood, ever rises to the level of the public interest, which as an empirical matter the neutrality claim requires. Achieving the rule of law through democratic governance will not come through denying the fact of the bias inherent in the societal culture and particularist conceptions of the good of the majority. The only path to combining both fairness and accountability is to fully acknowledge the power of societal culture and its majoritarian biases and take measures to correct for them to allow for a minority voice where justified. It requires a level of self-awareness and honest reflection on group status which members of the Illinois regime appeared incapable of reaching. Ford, for all his introspection, seemed incapable of reaching it, and indeed, it is a level of reflection we will be incapable of reaching today unless we learn to recognize and own our public sphere commitments.

FROM GROUP POLARIZATION TO GROUPTHINK

In times of group polarization, the background assumptions contained in discursive structures, what we have called foundational beliefs, become salient and more important to members than the hegemonic principles espoused by the political regime. At these times, hegemonic principles like religious disestablishment and the rule of law can fail to command obedience. This reality indicates the limits of the incompletely theorized agreement strategy, which has been otherwise quite successful in liberal constitution making. The case of religious toleration again illustrates the problems involved. Limiting the power of Congress to establish a religion is a principle that can be supported from any number of foundational beliefs: the Democratic Party's support for voluntarism, the Whig Party's support for state-level—as opposed to federal-level—establishment, and the support of freethinkers, who wanted religion out of the public sphere altogether. The effort to downplay differences in foundational beliefs and to compromise on ambiguous principles where possible is a key strategy employed by compromise-seeking individualists in order to produce agreement on religious toleration. But when subsociety groups are pushed to take the law into their own hands and act on their own principles and beliefs, the lack of fundamental agreement is shockingly exposed; the consensual state has no clothes.

When social conflict and polarization exposed the diversity of opinion in the settler state, groups like the Mormons, who acted in public on their own beliefs, were seen as not playing the democratic game fairly. They could credibly claim to be continuing in the modern era the early Christian experience with revelation and the miraculous, but for Sharp this was a kind of preying upon the people's weakness for "mania . . . [or the] undue appreciation for the new and wonderful," or what George Davis called "the *prevailing epidemic* of the human mind to grasp at the marvelous and seize hold of every new absurdity upon the subject of religion."[61] Once converted, Mormons manipulated the rules of fair competition when they acted in mindless consort. "If the Mormons consent to act as other citizens," Mormon apostate William Harris wrote in *Mormonism Portrayed,* published in Warsaw, Illinois, in 1841, "they will not be molested on account of their religion, but freemen will not submit to be trampled on by an organized body of men, no matter what the name they are called, or whose standard they follow."[62] The theme echoes throughout anti-Mormon writing: the Mormons were "organized" around their own goals first; they put allegiance to the secular state second. In response, the anti-Mormons organized to resist what they saw as an antirepublican preference for a minority group over the majority interest. When in October of 1845 they assembled a convention to create a "committee on Military Organization," they requested the Hancock County Court be suspended because Mormon influence had spread so far through the criminal justice system that no fair trial could be conducted.[63]

In attempting to explain how individuals are motivated to act in the public sphere on behalf of group interests, scholars distinguish identity, consciousness, and action. Individuals can move progressively from awareness of the group's interests (identity) to endorsement of the group's worldview (consciousness) to public initiatives on behalf of the group (action). This triad must be understood in the context of the collective action problem all organized groups face. Members face incentives to free ride on the benefits provided to all members of the group as a result of the efforts of a few members. Why, then, do some members, especially of marginalized groups, go to the trouble and cost to act on behalf of group goals? Scholars Dennis Chong and Raoul Rogers see a "psychological dynamic" at play among members of socially stigmatized groups: "Attributing responsibility to the system for unequal group outcomes produces stronger feelings of personal efficacy. Efficacy and trust are thus inversely related to each other. High trust and high efficacy lead to allegiant participation [i.e., in support of the larger regime] while low trust and high efficacy produce protest activity."[64]

Hancock County during the Mormon troubles was an arena of low trust and high efficacy. It became that way because the egalitarian Mormons were retreating inward in distrust due to the Missouri conflict; for their own reasons they were adding layers of doubt and barriers to good faith between themselves and the impure world. The move increased group consciousness, inducing multiple and repeated actions in defense of the saints. The individualist anti-Mormons experienced the group bias of the newcomers as an affront to settler norms; they had reason to blame the system for outcomes they viewed as harmful—for example, thievery and failed economic development. In Hancock County the link between group consciousness and political efficacy may have been exacerbated by anti-Mormon individualism: the consciousness of anti-Mormon disadvantage shared by activists like Sharp, Gregg, and Williams improved their sense of self-worth, thus incentivizing political behavior.[65] Over time the anti-Mormons also increasingly became group conscious to the point of renouncing the Illinois state and advocating for a suspension of its laws.

The Mormons underwent a similar process of incentivizing protest activity. In 1841 the sect was already greedy of members' time, talents, and tithes. But increasingly thereafter, Smith retreated further and further into the protection of purity his people provided. Throughout 1842 he built additional layers of allegiance in the Masonic-like rituals and institutional rules of the Melchizedek priesthood, plural marriage, and the Nauvoo Legion. At this time, Richard Bushman observes, a new focus emerged on "priesthood sealing," the power to make marriages eternal, for "the powers of this world ended at death; only the power of God could ordain eternal marriages."[66] That the new focus was motivated at least in part by a concern with the purity of Mormon women and the masculinity of Mormon men was suggested by an 1842 publication at Nauvoo of a *Treatise on Religion and Jurisprudence,* by Udney Hay Jacob.

Jacob's tract endorsed plural marriage in the context of a crisis in the "lost . . . original dignity . . . of the masculine mind . . . [which had] become effeminate." This crisis was caused by the power of modern women, Jacob argued, for "nothing is further from the minds of our wives in general, than the idea of submitting to their husbands in all things." "Adam was enslaved by the woman, and so are we," he added; it was a circumstance "altogether unlawful and ruinous to the families of the nation."[67] These doctrines coalesced into a new rite under which the prophet gathered actors incentivized by a newly granted high status. In a "ceremony first called 'the holy order' and later referred to as the 'endowment,'" "a select group of men" dressed in "white clothing that was not part of their daily apparel."[68] Historian Michael A. Homer emphasizes how Brigham Young used the secrecy of the endowment process and temple veils to cement women to men and overall attachment to the group just before the saints began their exodus to Utah. As he notes, "Between December 10, 1845, and February of the following year, 5,634 members received their endowments including more than three thousand women."[69] Perhaps most telling of the power of the turn inward and the lure of membership during this period is the fact that Joseph's wife Emma Smith, who so adamantly opposed the new rite that the prophet was forced to admonish her by name in a revelation published in the Doctrine and Covenants, partially endorsed the practice so that she, too, could be "sealed to Joseph" for eternity.[70]

In addition, after the prophet was gone, leaders within the Twelve continued the process of separate state action. Away on a mission trip in Boston during the assassinations, Brigham Young returned to Nauvoo on August 6 of 1844.[71] Soon thereafter he had the Mormons acting again as a separate self-governing entity. Smith had prepared the way for this outcome by establishing so many parallel state institutions. But the Mormon followers' recognition of their separate status was confounded in the spring of 1844 by the prophet's reassertion of his constitutional rights and his recommitment to the American republic. The focus shifted from vindicating the lost cause against Missouri to reaffirming the place of the Mormons in the national story of American peoplehood. This countermovement spurred its own reaction: the more the Mormons worked to see themselves in the American state, the less the older settlers of Hancock County saw themselves in it.

These parallel sequences in the two opposed Hancock County groups support the claim that institutional breakdown and concomitant group polarization, not religious intolerance, caused the Mormon troubles in Illinois. When local agents emphasized the problem was Mormon "fanaticism," this was their way of referring to Mormon particularism and group polarization. Given that this is precisely how Illinoisans referred to abolitionists, the somewhat different treatment of the two movements creates a telling comparative test. Fanatics of all stripes took the minority part for the whole. It could be argued that similarly prescriptive and judgmental beliefs in favor of a minority on the part of both the abolitionists and the Mormons taunted the old settlers to lawless behavior.

When abolitionists acted repeatedly and publicly to defy local authority, as Elijah Lovejoy did in St. Louis and Alton and as the Peoria abolitionists did, violence erupted.[72] George Davis reports how nonplussed the Alton antiabolitionist mob leaders were to find Lovejoy repeatedly and perversely siding "with the niggers of the South" over their respectable local group, led by a "physician" and two other prominent men.[73] But other abolitionists in Illinois, such as Hooper Warren and Owen Lovejoy, who lived in the northern tier, were allowed to act in public unmolested. In the northern tier the societal culture was dominated by competitive individualists who tilted toward the moralism of the evangelical Whigs. Abolitionists there, while still actively discouraged by duopolistic competition, were left free to create the Liberty Party. "Fanatical" beliefs alone, then, did not prompt violence; unconventional belief, when organized and pointedly opposed to the authority of local majorities, as historian Leonard Richards argues, did meet violent response.[74] Not ideas alone but the way the ideas were institutionalized and how they were interpreted by civil society made the difference in the case of the Mormon troubles.

The importance of the institutionalization was confirmed openly. During the winter of 1841–42, when Smith announced his support for Adam Snyder, who had just been nominated by the Democrats for governor, the *Sangamo Journal* had a long spread on the issue of freedom of religion. The editor noted that even Catholics were to be admitted into free exercise of religion—but only because, having been assimilated into the United States, they made no attempt to create an established church. The key to toleration was that no attempt was made to unify church and state; that would be the one religious belief that individuals could not act on, because it would threaten public safety—the reason Locke disqualified Catholics from toleration in his *Letter Concerning Toleration*. The editor proceeded to argue that Joseph Smith, "when he enters into the civil office of the state, and as a lieutenant general, speaks to his friends, whom he knows as a Prophet *he can command*, and uses the religious influence he possesses, under the Military garb he has acquired . . . becomes a dangerous man, and must look to the consequences."[75] Here the Whig paper explained how the Illinois regime's discursive strategy ordered its background assumptions of majority control over local societal culture and limited the free exercise of religion.

Particularist defenses of local ways were part of the regime, and they could come from both sides of the party divide. One kind of particularism came from an unexpected direction, from Jonathan Baldwin Turner, a Presbyterian at Illinois College. Turner is an interesting case because he shows that even elite groups manifesting an individualist culture could feel threatened by Mormonism. Turner was a self-described Congregationalist, one of the "Yale Band" who came to Illinois in 1831 to found Illinois College at Jacksonville in Morgan County. A professor of rhetoric, Turner also edited the *Illinois Statesman*, wrote several books, advocated at the federal level for the creation of land-grant colleges, and pioneered the use of the Osage orange tree as an economical solution to the problem of fencing farmland on the treeless Illinois prairie.

Turner published *Mormonism in All Ages: Or the Rise, Progress, and Causes of Mormonism* early in 1842. The book argued that the Mormons were "the most dangerous and virulent enemies to our political and religious purity, and our social and civic peace, that now exist in the Union."[76] This was so not because of their direct acts but indirectly because of the impact of their arguments on non-Mormons. Mormons argued that their prophet's visitations by angels and revelations were no more miraculous than those of Jesus: "If the Book of Mormon in whole or in part is ridiculous, the Bible is too." "No church," Turner contended, "pretends to these gifts . . . of miracle, healing, prophecy, etc . . . except their own." He continued: "They claim to possess these gifts, and bring forward witnesses from among the initiated who testify that they have seen them exercised. Thousands are convinced by this argument that the Bible is false, and tens that Mormonism is true." The Mormons had thus established a pact with the devil by aligning themselves with atheists and those who secretly reasoned that "by tolerating the dreamy visions of Joe Smith, they . . . [could] with more ease . . . dispense with Jesus Christ and his doctrines."[77]

Here, we may surmise, is the voice of sophisticated anti-Mormonism in the early days of the Mormon arrival. The Illinois College professor explicitly disavowed violence and denounced the "mobocrats" in Missouri. He wrote:

> In this quarrel the Mormons were much in the wrong, and their leaders, Smith and Rigdon especially, deserved a much sorer punishment at the hands of the Missourians than they will ever get. But were the women and children at fault? Did they deserve banishment or death? Were those dissenters who did all they could for the state, worthy of death? Who began the quarrel? Was it the Mormons? Is it not notorious, on the contrary, that they were hunted, like wild beasts, from county to county, before they made any desperate resistance? Did they ever, as a body, refuse obedience to the laws, when called upon to do so, until driven to desperation by repeated threats and assaults on the part of the mob? Did the state ever make one decent effort to defend them, as fellow-citizens, in their rights, or to redress their wrongs?[78]

Turner's opposition to the Mormons, then, was not rooted in simple intolerance; it was rooted in a nuanced sense of the impact on public morals (however conventionally defined) as a result of competition among religious groups. It was ultimately rooted in a fear of the effects of pluralism—a value that individualists and their logic of reciprocity ordinarily support.

Turner's position is an ominous reminder that even nonconforming individualists can quietly maintain a submerged stance of solidarity with particularist group narratives. In Turner's case, his allegiance to mainstream Protestantism was strong enough to overrule any support for the individualist commitment to open competition and equality of opportunity. His objection to the Mormons was their threat to the American Protestant master narrative. What many have noted as the liberal individualist's need for control is often the result of the fear of "a cosmos crumbling," of losing a larger justification as a result of shifting background assumptions—namely that God gave North America to Protestants to signal their salvation.[79] Despite his master narrative, Turner's critique highlights the individualist concern with the fairness of group competition.

The nuances of Turner's position are echoed in the political theory of toleration. As John Rawls considers the case of the "toleration of the intolerant" in *A Theory of Justice,* he concludes that an "intolerant sect" might be restricted in its freedom "only when the tolerant sincerely and with reason believe that their own security and that the institutions of liberty are in danger."[80] Philosopher Barbara Herman also emphasizes the issue of security. While she presses the harm principle into service as adjudicator of when a threat to security or danger is involved, she cautions the following: "Whether a practice or a set of values is harmful has to be to some extent an open question in circumstances of pluralism. An action might be benign in one social context and not in another; the harmfulness of an action may arise from its contingent and local support of objectionable values."[81]

Thomas Sharp, for his part, made his case against the Mormons on the harm principle basis from the start. At times, he would emphasize a tangible harm like widespread thievery, but when he let his guard down, he could retreat to a simple defense of the status quo—the Mormons did not act as others did and did not respect the way society was organized in Illinois. Sharp's second approach was often as dispositive for the United States Supreme Court as for Illinois locals. In *Reynolds v. United States* (1879), the court upheld an antibigamy law as enforced in Utah on the grounds that polygamy threatened "social duties" and was "subversive of good order."[82] Here the court was explicitly following Thomas Jefferson, who said the magistrate could intervene after religious belief turned to action if the action threatened "peace and good order." In Illinois the local community was empowered to make judgments about future harm and definitions of good order.

If civil society is pluralistic and contains distinctions among groups, as is common in modern democracies, there will be competition; and social ranking typically relies on ascriptive traits that are easy for leaders to manipulate. With the addition of state power, ascription can be used to include and exclude, reward and punish. From mere disagreement it is but a small leap to a broader intolerance, and from there to a sense that the other is evil and bent on domination and tyranny. The leap is so common in the politics of developing democracies as to be almost unremarkable and unremarked upon. Yet it is a crucial product of groupthink that social psychologists have detected in settings as brief and casual as a few boys on a week-long summer camp.[83] It is not surprising the anti-Mormons spent the winter of 1844–45 sending in putative instances of Mormon theft to fill the pages of the *Warsaw Signal*. These were evidences of tangible harm, and they had time to make converts gradually. But even a small number of converts can make a difference, as scholar Thomas Schelling has shown; small changes in antagonism toward a group at the individual level can lead to larger shifts at the collective level.[84]

Modern scholarship also confirms the importance of local context, which figured so prominently in the Illinois regime. V. O. Key's masterwork, *Southern Politics*, uncovered a recurring pattern: counties with majority Black populations in the South of the 1950s had the strongest, most-organized White supremacists. The pattern was confirmed by later studies over three decades.[85] This suggests that the logic of the antebellum regime of local control lived on in the nation; it certainly continued to exert political power in the post-Reconstruction South. Contemporary scholars confirm the importance of the universalism/particularism continuum which shapes the societal culture in the United States today.[86]

Group difference has always been difficult for liberal democracies to manage. Race and ethnicity are key examples of groups that are hard for the bargaining pluralist system to digest. But from a regime perspective, the problem is one of who at the local level is going to enforce the larger regime allegiance. When the local representatives of the existing regime are weak or absent, then the situation can move from minority toleration to minority control or threat of minority control. The Illinois regime enforced order using not the law but the coercion exercised by the parties on each other and their own members, a very weak tool when trained against a majority of local constituents. As we have seen, the regime set the basic order, but when it came to interpreting specific principles or managing discrete tasks, the political parties were notoriously weak. The state in these instances followed what Theodore J. Lowi calls a "distributive" logic: it only distributed goods to all equally; it lacked the authority to discriminate, to deny anyone.[87] Illinois's Internal Improvements

Act, passed in 1837, is a key example. The parties could find no discrete decision rule whereby to order the projects, so the General Assembly authorized work on all of them *simultaneously.*

The attempt to manage the political leanings of the Mormons exhibited a similar fecklessness. When the Nauvoo city and militia charters were up for revision, both parties ducked and parried. The goal became creating plausible claims of support and hiding any opposition. Governor Ford openly pushed for the revision of the charters, but the Democrats in the legislature, fearing the political consequences, hemmed and hawed and tried to hide their opposition. Illinois historian Charles Thompson recognizes, "With the fluctuation of opinion as expressed in the various notes recorded in the Journals, one can see back of the scenes a skilled manipulator in the Democratic ranks." Thompson believes the manipulator to have been Stephen A. Douglas, who likely was trying to achieve repeal and reform but on consensual, nonpartisan terms so as to avoid any cost to his party.[88] In democracies, legislatures frequently lack the authority to discipline majorities; here the issue is not capacity but will.

Weakness of the will and lack of state capacity to enforce the law in the lightly settled areas only invited vigilantism. In fact, vigilantism was quite common in Illinois and was even a topic of lyceum debate. A Peoria group queried: "Is it right, in any case, to resort to force and violence, without the authority of law, for the purpose of restraining the utterance of opinions and doctrines, the expression or publication of which is not prohibited by the laws of the land?"[89] In all three tiers of the state, groups called "regulators" were endorsed once it was seen that the state would not enforce order. The problems in the north involved horse thieves; in the south, counterfeiters; the troubles with the Mormons in the central section found their counterparts there. But everywhere in the country the problem was one of the slow movement and incapacity of the legal process. As one Wyoming lyncher rhymed in a public "NOTICE" pinned to his victim: "Process of law a trifle slow, So this is the way we have to go, Murderers and thieves beware! PEOPLE'S VERDICT."[90]

It is the nature of political agency that individuals will often act in unexpected ways. Surely Joseph Smith in his last days at Nauvoo continued to reinforce group cohesiveness in ways that in hindsight appear tragically mistaken. In Greek tragedy, empowered individuals respond predictably with a hubris driven by overconfidence. How far did confidence drive Smith and the Mormons to go in their own strong and wide group particularism? Believing that the Illinois state had granted him free rein with the Nauvoo charter and Nauvoo Legion, Smith had created his own state. But it is unclear how ready he was to use it as a state per se; he appears to have viewed it as a purely defensive mechanism. Historian Klaus Hansen argues that by the spring of 1844 the move to create a separate kingdom under the tutelage of the newly created Council of Fifty was leading Smith to use the Nauvoo Legion in provocative ways.[91] Bennett, Black, and Cannon argue there is little evidence for Hansen's claim of a "revolutionary Mormonism" or of Smith using the Nauvoo Legion as an extension of Zion's Camp. They see Hansen's claim as "rather radical" and dismiss the connection between the legion and the council as "purely speculative." Far from seeing the legion as a tool for acting outside the law, they suggest a case can be made for its "worth as a deterrent to wanton persecution" by the anti-Mormons against the saints.[92]

THE SETTLER STATE'S CIVIL SOCIETY BACKSTOP

And just what kind of thing was the antebellum American settler state, which Illinois regulator and Mormon alike were disrespecting? How would an accurate assessment characterize it? Going back to Aristotle, we see that debate has raged over how to describe the state. Aristotle opened his *Politics* with the claim that "every state is a community of some kind." He later defined the state as the kind of community which controlled a collection of offices. Those who controlled the offices, ruled the city, they were "the regime"—that is, the state. Control over offices was indeed precisely what the second party system was organized to produce. Martin Van Buren was willing to break the first American regime's taboo against openly expressing and organizing partisanship because he believed that slavery posed an existential threat to the Constitution and the Union. The only way to avoid that conflict was to overlay it with—and thus divert attention to—another cross-cutting conflict. The overlaid conflict, if principled and thus debatable in a managed way, could be contained, unlike the conflict over slavery.

To fashion a cross-cutting cleavage, Van Buren selected the old Federalist and Anti-Federalist conflict between the powers of the federal government and the states. The Whigs took the national government's side (Federalist), and the Democrats took the states' side (Anti-Federalist). Van Buren correctly predicted that mobilizing bias around this conflict would allow the Democrats to win the lion's share of votes and offices. With these, they would be able to shape public policy to suit their principles and interests. Democracy became party government. But it also became government by civil society. The state was not simply government offices but all the informal offices and positions held in the local status order. This order, and the voluntary associations and, later, interest groups it spurred, vied for influence on par with and ahead of government officers, whose capacity to enforce the law was limited. In sum, in describing the early American state, we cannot proceed as if it developed in a societal vacuum. It shared its authority with counterparts in successive sectors of civil society: the courtroom had its law office, the post office had its lyceum, and the militia had its vigilance committee. At each decentralized layer, the state's formal offices were paired with informal groups that served as an authoritative backstop ready to direct order when formal efforts failed.

Whig leaders like Abraham Lincoln had meditated deeply on the problem of mobocracy in the early American state. He saw that when a societal dispute involving vested interests or foundational beliefs developed over slavery or religion, powerful emotions and ambitions would be unleashed. It is telling that when he cast about for a solution to the problem of injustice in the antebellum state, he looked to civil society, not to the institutions of government. In his Young Men's Lyceum address in 1838, Lincoln, at the time only twenty-eight years old, put his solution this way: "Let every American, every lover of liberty, every well-wisher to his posterity, swear by the blood of the Revolution, never to violate in the least particular, the laws of the country; and to never tolerate their violation by others. . . . Let reverence for the laws . . . become the *political religion* of the nation."[93] Lincoln recognized the crucial role of public opinion within civil society, and he realized that republicanism would need a degree of attachment that transcended the secular, one that drew membership into a spiritual realm.

His greatest fear was not that the people themselves would turn against republicanism but that ambitious leaders would usurp the system the founders put in place. Serving the public interest through the institutions set up at the founding brought fame, but would it be enough to satisfy the ambitions of "an Alexander, a Caesar, a Napoleon"? He continued: "Is it unreasonable then to expect that some man possessed of loftiest genius, coupled with ambition sufficient to push it to its utmost stretch, will at some time spring among us? And when such a one does, it will require the people to be united with each other, attached to the government and laws, and generally intelligent, to successfully frustrate his designs."[94] Lincoln may have been thinking about Aaron Burr as the archetypal ambitious genius. A thorough partisan himself, Lincoln certainly was not thinking of Van Buren, who did introduce a new set of institutions, including the party duopoly, which durably replaced the founders' nonpartisan system. In fact, Lincoln likely had in mind someone more along the lines of Joseph Smith, perhaps not in birth and education, but one whose genius and ambition was now driving him to run for president on a belief that the American republic had fallen into a morass of pluralism and needed to establish a higher, more authoritative "theodemocracy" at the federal level.

Lincoln's solution of civil society reverence for the laws was unlikely to work in a frontier setting. As Alexander Hamilton believed, it is effective enforcement of the laws, not attitudinal support, which creates respect for government, and enforcement was not a strong suit of the settler state.[95] It was not hard to get both sides in the Mormon conflict to agree upon the sacred duty to obey the law. Smith and the Mormons showed their agreement by appealing again and again to their own allegiance to the law in an effort to contrast themselves with the many mobs they faced that ignored or overrode the law. They continued to press for damages from the federal government and relief from the courts despite repeated rebuffs. Anti-Mormons like Sharp also watched for and diligently documented every legal violation the Mormons committed. At the Convention of Anti-Mormon Delegates, held on February 18, 1844, at Carthage, it was moved "to maintain peaceable and orderly action in all their difficulties with the Mormons, and to make it a paramount object to sustain the Laws." But the motion was not passed as written, and a great debate ensued over adding a clause about also sustaining "our reserved rights of self-defense." Sharp, in his commentary on the meeting, admitted: "There is a difference of opinion among the Anti-Mormons. . . . One portion believing the Mormons are so obnoxious, that sooner or later they must be driven out. . . . Another portion are conservative. They say that however obnoxious the Mormons may be . . . if at last we are driven to arms, let it be the result of an inevitable necessity."[96]

Sharp recognized the difference of opinion was not very great. He was willing to affirm, "We are ever prepared to assert the supremacy of the law over brute violence," but quickly asked a follow-up question: When the laws "are cheated of their efficacy by the cunning knavery of designing men . . . [must we] submit without a murmur or be branded disturbers of the peace?"[97] Sharp was appealing to the tradition of critical citizenship, the capacity of members of civil society to engage in acts of disobedience with the aim to expand the scope of justice by contesting the law. The strong wells of this tradition, reaching back to Socrates in ancient Athens, forward to Henry David Thoreau in the nation, and contemporaneously to the Underground Railroad in Illinois, were powerful enough to meet and even swamp the grounds of Lincoln's plea. On the side of disobedience, scholars and activists in our time show how hegemony and an ill-formed societal status quo can introduce biases in the enforcement of the law, deprive protestors of the resources they need to change it in lawful ways, and encourage disrespect for the law itself.[98] From this position, critical citizens conclude that civil disobedience is the more moral route, one following the course of the higher law of conscience.

Indeed, some have argued that the Mormon troubles were contested on the altar of the "higher law" tradition. On the anti-Mormon side, the higher authorities were popular sovereignty and the right of self-defense. On the Mormon side, Joseph and Hyrum Smith swore an allegiance to God above the laws. Given these different ultimate loyalties, a clash was as inevitable as the one between Creon and Antigone.[99] While the higher-law frame can be made to fit the Illinois troubles, it ignores the real conflicts on the ground and leads us to the wrong lessons. As a newly minted attorney, Lincoln already knew that the law was not one but many things; it could be interpreted many ways. Was it against the 1818 constitution's "invaluable right" of the "free communication of thoughts and opinions" to shut down a libelous newspaper, or was it the proper application of a city charter that allowed nuisances, whether libel or ball games, to be regulated? Does a writ of habeas corpus run from a municipal court to cover crimes alleged against state law? Does the US Constitution's rule requiring extradition of treasonous individuals fleeing from one state to another apply to charges of murder when the defendant, after the alleged murder, had not fled the state? Such questions can be given firm answers under the party bias mobilized by a regime setting, but as abstract matters they are open to multiple interpretations.[100] It is not higher law which creates the ambiguity but weakly developed regime institutions which allow civil society groups too many inroads, offer too many opportunities for misrecognition on the part of informal local leaders, and promote too much fatalism and desperation on the part of minorities.

Further conflicts can arise over who is to settle the dispute over interpretation—a first-order interpretation problem spawns a second-order authority problem.[101] The Jacksonian regime's answer to the authority question—the majority of the local civil society—was a familiar rule recognized by all gentlemen of property and standing. This was the failsafe backstop Democrats had relied on in Illinois counties or towns whenever a lone individual or a minority took actions that the majority deemed harmful to the person or property of one of its own but which the law itself left unspecified or could not prevent. The backstop method was applied to claims jumpers, desperados, and abolitionists. No matter that this meant that the rights of minority persons and/or property would be violated in the exercise of majority authority. Since the local majority was divided in Hancock County, applying the rule did not settle and indeed only exacerbated the conflict. In order to avoid having a conflict over beliefs become a violent contest for majority power, statewide, not local, institutions would be needed. Yet in frontier Illinois, the only statewide institutions available in Hancock County between 1840 and 1846 were all the usual suspects of the decentralized settler state—local party-organized elections, local volunteer militias, and local court-enforced rules.

At one level, members of the Illinois regime had an easy answer to the question of what the state was. As Thomas Ford knew, the people were the state; their authority was the ultimate one in the land. But, if so, then Ford was still stuck, for he needed rules of recognition to determine who the people were in the first place. This issue, which scholars call "the boundary problem," is one all democratic communities face. A second issue was finding a common rule to follow when "the people" disagreed among themselves. In both these areas civil society came to the aid of the state and became an indispensable adjunct to state power. The civil society solution would not have been surprising to Hegel, the nineteenth century's premier theorist of state development. He recognized, as John Keane observes, that civil society was a "*historically* produced sphere of ethical life" and that it was, for better or worse, "*wreckable*."[102] The same could be said for the Illinois regime: it was a historical product which used the independent-producer civic narrative to answer the boundary problem and the option of voluntary regime services, which allowed self-help to answer the disagreement problem. Both solutions put enormous pressure on Illinois civil society. In times of state incapacity and group polarization, it too was wreckable.

The group interest civil society authorized could be narrowly concerned with security and control, as it was so often in frontier Illinois, or it could be broad, "properly understood," and public spirited, as Alexis de Tocqueville thought it should be so that there could be "freedom, public peace, and social stability."[103] In the former case, popular justice was often constrained by a scarcity of public order; when order was secured, the more public-spirited varieties of popular justice emerged. Thus, popular justice in settler states ran on a continuum: it could issue in vigilante societies and it could create prison-reform movements. The one replaced and wrecked state authority; the other reformed and strengthened it, albeit under a directing ethic of moralism. Following the one or the other side of the continuum, the Illinoisans were forced back to the medieval definition of "state," the condition or quality of the officeholder. Since the twelfth century, the Latin *status*, or "condition of the ruler," had been the focus of political disquisitions. Over time these evolved into the study of the "state," the condition of the institutions the ruler created.[104] In Hancock County, Illinoisans—Mormon and anti-Mormon alike—decided the state authority they had inherited was insufficient in quality; they appealed time and again to civil society to supply the last word.

The conditions of possibility in developing Illinois wrecked civil society. The repeated use of the writ of habeas corpus by the Mormons began to look like an effort to evade the law altogether. Only when the administration of the law was stably controlled locally were the conditions of reciprocity possible, and only under these conditions was toleration made fair or palatable to majorities. Here, then, is one oft-repeated pattern: when rights get associated in the popular mind with special protections for minorities, the possibilities that the majority will act illiberally increase. This is the majoritarian logic recognized by Senator Jacob C. Davis and before which Thomas Sharp repeatedly had to genuflect when apologizing for "yet another story about the Mormons." Resentment among the old settlers, the recognized independent producers, grew as they felt their interests were being neglected in lieu of the "special" Mormons.

A second durable pattern is that since local institutions like the militia are by definition geographically based, they are difficult for a centralized authority to control. Even when some control is obtained, there will be leakage of authority since those undertaking voluntary service are always tempted to redeem in influence a payment for the regime services they render. Both the writ and the militia, institutions devised to enforce the law in extraordinary circumstances, leak power and undermine the ability of the state to enforce the law in ordinary times.

As the old settlers stopped seeing themselves in the law, the county became more and more ungovernable. In early July of 1844 the Warsaw Committee of Safety made an appeal to Governor Ford for protection; the plea was another true opportunity for negotiation. Tragically, Ford's anger at anti-Mormon duplicity, both in killing the Smiths and placing his own life in danger, led him to misread and ignore the plea. Elections had become Mormon weapons, and Ford's own party provided ammunition. George Davis accused Ford of drumming up the Mormon vote with a "Warsaw handbill . . . the production of a political maneuver . . . just days before the August 1844 election."[105] But in truth the Illinois regime was stronger than either Ford or the anti-Mormons. "The war of party," Ford explained in the run-up to the election of 1844 between Polk and Clay, "was never more fierce and terrible than during the pendency of these elections." He said he was "anxious that the Mormons should not vote at this election, and [he] strongly advised them against doing so." But partisan strife was too strong to be contained: a Democratic Party operative "went to their city a few days before the election and the Mormons, ever disposed to follow the worst advice they could get, were induced by him and others to vote for all the democratic candidates."[106] The settler state split in two as the county offices and officers became de facto tools of the Mormons while the anti-Mormons created counterparts in the informal world of civil society.

Immediately after the prophet's assassination, amid a furious search for a new leader, the Mormons entered what Annette P.

Hampshire denotes a period of "partial quiescence."[107] Their attention was turned to Minor R. Deming, the newly elected sheriff, through whom they decided to give the gentile justice system a chance to find, indict, and convict the perpetrators of the crime. The anti-Mormons responded to Mormon passivity with aggression. In the fall of 1844 they organized a tristate "great wolf hunt," as Ford called it, to intimidate those Mormons living in rural areas in the county.[108] The wolf hunt idea seems to have been percolating within anti-Mormon plans since the spring, as its notice by Thomas Sharp suggests.[109] Foiled by Ford's militia in the fall, the anti-Mormons returned to the strategy of rural intimidation in the fall of 1845, when they burnt barns and houses in several isolated Mormon settlements. In this way, the anti-Mormons used their own military services to implement a rural pogrom strategy their leaders had devised.

The endgame of the troubles for the Mormons came in the period between the fall of 1845 and the fall of 1846. Certainly, the number of murders rose dramatically in 1845; Gregg, in his *History of Hancock County*, stated, "If the year 1844 was one of blood, that of 1845 was more bloody still."[110] After the anti-Mormons attacked unprotected Mormon settlements in rural Hancock, the Mormons responded by marching into Carthage with their own sheriff and militia. Governor Ford sent in a fourth state militia led by Major William B. Warren to restore order in October of 1845. Warren remained over the winter and into the next spring. When Ford made his third and final visit to the county in the fall of 1846, at the head of a fifth militia, he was astonished by the ferocity of anti-Mormon opinion against him: "So far had the mob scenes which they had passed through beclouded their judgments and so far had they imitated the Mormons in their modes of thinking that they really believed that the people of Hancock had some kind of government and sovereignty of their own, and to interfere with this was to invade their sacred rights."[111] Both the Mormons and Hancock's old settlers believed themselves to be separate peoples guiding separate states.

By 1845 the Mormons throughout Hancock County had been implicitly charged and found guilty of the crime of holding an allegiance higher than the club of independent producers. They were again outsiders and again other than republican. This status may explain an additional mystery associated with the rise of anti-Mormonism more generally: the symbolic behavior reported in the use of "red flags," "tar and feathers," and face painting.[112] The sense that the Mormons were treated by the "old citizens" as a group apart and indeed, like the abolitionists, as a class of traitors to the cause of their "race" of free republicans, is suggested in the painting of faces that occurred with the anti-Mormon mobs in Missouri. It may simply have been a way for mob members to hide their identity and protect themselves from prosecution. But when anti-Mormon groups painted their faces, Parley Pratt felt that a deeper slight was intended. He described a Missouri mob he faced as "a murderous gang," which attacked "painted like Indian warriors." Pratt complained that while these men, "when openly committing murder, robbery, house burning, and every crime known to the laws, were denominated citizens, whites, etc., in most journals in the State," his people "were denominated 'Mormons,' in contradistinction to the appellation of 'citizens,' 'whites,' etc., as if we had been some savage tribe, or some colored race of foreigners."[113]

Further evidence of a deeper division comes from Susan Rugh's detailed study of the Mormon troubles as they played out in Fountain Green Township in the far southeastern corner of the county. Rugh argues that, in the spring of 1845, when the anti-Mormons decided they needed to publicly proclaim the nonpartisan basis of their group, their statement was significant not simply because it was signed by Democrats; she finds that it was mainly signed by men who originated from southern states. Before this, opposition to the Mormons was led by Whigs and men who had emigrated from the northern states. Now even rural outposts like Fountain Green were closing ranks. Non-Mormon southerners would rather extend recognition to Yankees and Whigs than to their old Mormon neighbors.

On September 10 and 11, 1845, anti-Mormon arsonists from Green Plains precinct led by Levi Williams blackened their faces and rampaged through the isolated Mormon villages of Morley Settlement, burning down every house they encountered.[114] Macedonia, another rural Mormon settlement, was by the spring of 1846 a "Deserted Village," in large part, as the anti-Mormon *Nauvoo Eagle* had it, because of "that trait in the Mormon character, which enables them to concentrate their energies and form communities of their own. In a locality of this kind, they mingle but little with the world."[115] But as Rugh documents, this separateness was a recent development, because several strong kin and trading ties had previously existed between the Mormons and the old settlers in rural Mormon settlements like Fountain Green. Being different and living alone did not mean that you would be attacked; these were necessary but not sufficient factors. Repeated state incapacity and the moves to group consciousness and groupthink were needed to complete the tragedy of misrecognition. Groupthink certainly had taken over by the spring of 1844 in Green Plains precinct, where anti-Mormon doggerel sent to Sharp referred to "some Green Mountain boys in Green Plains" who would "be firm and not flinch one iota until [their] bayonets are wore to the hilt and the butt ends broke off before [yielding] to such an infamous wreck as Joe or any of his merauders."[116]

The story of the rise of anti-Mormonism in Illinois illustrates the power of state capacity and group polarization as explanatory variables. Even in an increasingly individualist society like settler Illinois, groups matter. When state authority is tenuous and a majoritarian story of peoplehood is under construction, groups matter greatly. It was a fact Ford denied to the end, his problematic ideal of blind justice blinding him to the politics of civic worth. The second party system he had worked to erect in Illinois rested on a tacit consensus that civic narratives of worth needed to be separately determined and applied in every locality. On the frontier, where both enforcement capacity and trust were weakly developed, the politics of civic worth took on even more importance. Inclusion within the group of worthy republicans was granted only to independent producers by local gentlemen of property and standing who served as judge, jury, and executioner.

Conclusion

The Perils of Democratic Storytelling

The story of the Mormon troubles in Illinois has been little noted. Outside Illinois and the Mormon community, many only know of it through a brief reference in J. S. Mill's essay *On Liberty.* Mill highlighted how "antipathy" to "Mormonite doctrine" led to the sect's "prophet and founder" being "put to death by a mob . . . for his teaching." Mormon polygamy, he added, had induced many in Britain to "openly declare that it would be right (only that it is not convenient) to send an expedition against them, and compel them by force to conform to the opinions of other people."[1] Mill, who worked on his magisterial essay between 1854 and 1859, pointed to the Mormon troubles in Illinois to defend the freedom to dissent from conventional opinion. His story offers a lesson democracies need to learn even if his version of the events is not accurate.

We should question the very nature of the stories we tell ourselves in democratic society. Stories often refer to events that never happened, yet they get told and remembered because they express truths that people cannot live without. In this way, even false stories can indeed tell the truth. Democratic stories are also subject to selective memory. Groups in power have a way of editing out the participation and roles of minorities and nonmembers who participate in the margins or who seek membership. In this way, stories of peoplehood convey collective identities in which, scholar Richard Sennett suggests, "community [is] cemented as an act of will rather than by acts of experience."[2] In the decentralized power structure created under the first American regime, the prevailing civic narrative was enforced by the will of the locality as much as by the principles of the national parties. The capacity of the national elite to enforce its hegemonic principles paled in comparison to the majority on the ground. In the Illinois case, Thomas Ford noted, the Mormon troubles became infected with the prejudices of local civil society and exacerbated by "the everlasting intrigues of politicians."[3] In the tough story Illinoisans lived and told, truth and falsity became hostage to political necessity.

When they are considered necessary, factually false beliefs can take on a life of their own. As an illustration, consider the story of when Massachusetts senator John Davis visited Governor Ford in 1844. The story was told to James Armstrong and retold many times in his prominent northern Illinois Whig family. "As a small boy I was puzzled as to why my father thought it so important and told the story many times. . . . The State was bankrupt at that time and had not even the money to pay the interest on money borrowed in Boston to say nothing of the bonds that should have been redeemed. The holders of these bonds sent Senator Davis to see what could be done." The big question was if the state would repudiate its debt. Davis arrived in Springfield unannounced and inquired "where he might find the Governor's mansion." He was directed to a "small half story cottage" and "was met by a woman in a calico dress and a checkered apron. He was surprised beyond measure when she told him that this was the Governor's house." The governor himself was in "the backyard where he was sawing wood." After, Ford took him to the statehouse to show him the state's financial books: "Here the Governor who kept his own books personally went over the figures showing the amount of taxable property in detail." Ford's meticulous attention to detail and his simple lifestyle won over the visitor.[4]

As Armstrong's brother Perry remembered the story, Ford, "in his Kentucky blue jeans suit," also offered figures on "the number of horses, cattle, sheep, hogs, and their value, as returned by the assessors," which, together with other assets minutely detailed, showed "a sufficient sum to pay all the interest and create quite a sinking fund to apply towards paying the principal indebtedness of the state." The moral of the story was that when Senator Davis returned home, he reported that "any state whose people have the good sense to elect such a man as Governor Thomas Ford—a man whose character is an example of simplicity and economy of living—who resides in a small frame house, devoid of all the luxuries of life, and saws his own wood, will pay their debts in full with interest, and this you can depend upon."[5]

Now as it happens, we know this story is not true, or in any case could not have happened as related. It is true that Ford's clothes "were not strictly after the latest style," that during his time as governor "he totally neglected his own financial interests," and that he firmly denounced repudiation of the state's debt.[6] But we know from the journal John Davis compiled at the time that while he and Ford met several times during late 1843 and early 1844, they only met at Lockport and Chicago.[7] But stories are told for many purposes. The Whigs had reason to project an identity of frugal and hardworking individualism onto Ford; it helped in their struggle to discredit and limit the egalitarian image of citizenship valued by their Jacksonian opponents, and it covered with sacrifice and virtue the extension of state capacity they sought.

Northern Illinois Whigs were fighting a culture war, asserting an individualist culture against the prevailing egalitarian culture. The Whigs had a different model for how the state should render its regime services. They wanted governance to come through building state capacity; it was effective enforcement of the law by state officers, not the self-help of citizens, which would secure the rule of law. As Whigs turned Republicans, the Armstrongs told the story to cement a new societal culture in the state. They worked to solve the governance problem in the long term by increasing state capacity at the national level, even if they were willing to employ the vigilante cry of "prompt and sure punishment" in the short term. They could justify expanding federal power only on grounds of republican sacrifice and hard work; they appropriated Thomas Ford to their need to tell a trust-building, moralist story.

Ford may have been frugal, but the story told of his frugality was not sufficient to carry the weight of the state. Other stories needed to be told. One democratic story is the importance of getting the facts right. Whether others' actions are harmful or not is at some level a matter of fact. If the majority of voters in a democracy become deluded to the point of rejecting all reality of empirical fact, no state institutions can save them from infatuation or corruption. Exposing falsehoods and getting at the truth is how the marginalized and the powerless contest entrenched injustice; it is an inherent part of any developing democracy's focus on popular justice. Developed democracies, too, need to continually learn and relearn the lesson of the importance of adhering to evidence and the truth; presumably, they rarely fall into complete denial of arguments based on fact, or if so, the society dissolves or the state turns authoritarian and the call for order replaces popular justice as the orientation of the regime.

But hard as that lesson is, it is not the hardest one to learn. Ford pointed to a more challenging lesson for democracies: "The most difficult argument to answer is one founded partially on fact, but mostly upon guess work and conjecture."[8] There are always guesses to be made in reckoning the facts bearing on a society's political future; guessing the probability of future harm from a concentrated minority of citizens was the problem Ford faced with the Mormons. Settled at Nauvoo, Joseph Smith was involved in an ever-deepening series of revelations and prophecies. The prophet incrementally expanded his power in ways which made Ford's guesswork precarious. Smith's revelations included a call for all Mormons to gather at Nauvoo, a concentration that soon led to their outnumbering Hancock County's old settlers. The estimation of danger and risk was made more treacherous still when Smith came out as a candidate for the US presidency in early 1844 on a platform joining church and state.

At the time, there was not much received wisdom to direct Ford on how to manage tensions created by the revelations of new religions. John Adams and Thomas Jefferson had canvassed the political dangers of prophecy in American politics in some of the first letters they exchanged in old age after they rekindled their relationship in 1812. Their thoughts can stand as indicative of the considered opinion of the day. Adams deemed prophecies "not only unphilosophical and inconsistent with the political Safety of States and Nations; but that the most sincere and sober Christians in the World ought upon their own Principles to hold them impious, for nothing is clearer from their Scriptures than that Their Prophecies were not intended to make us Prophets."[9] Jefferson agreed. Prophets were often susceptible to "hypochondriac affections and the gloomy forebodings they inspire." They so frequently importuned the presidency that Jefferson assumed Adams would not have forgotten "the correspondences of that crazy class, of whose complaints, and terrors, and mysticisms, the several presidents have been the regular depositories."[10] This President Martin Van Buren could confirm—he was beseeched by Joseph Smith and a Mormon contingent in the summer of 1839.

But why was Adams so sure "sincere and sober" Christians would reject the idea that biblical revelation sanctioned the idea of prophecy continuing into the present? It may have been the transformation in biblical exegesis that was sweeping Europe and the divinity schools of America at this time. Adams was likely apprised of new hermeneutic principles which read the Old Testament prophets and their revelations in context as referring to specific events in the near future that would happen unless the Israelites changed their ways. It wasn't until later, the new learning further argued, that the early Christians, beset by Roman oppressors, developed the idea that their Son of God was the fulfillment of the Jewish law and its prophecies.[11] The new learning thus supported the idea that modern-day revelation was an unauthorized innovation. That it was dangerous to republican government was a claim the founders applied broadly to secular (French Revolution) and Native American prophecies.[12] In Illinois their view was endorsed by Jonathan Baldwin Turner, who dismissed the Mormon prophet on behalf of the state's Protestant establishment.[13]

After the founders, Lincoln worried about ambitious men who would subvert the Constitution because they sought fame and untrammeled power in "regions hitherto unexplored."[14] Ford faced the dilemma of how to assess the public consequences of the unexplored regions of Smith's prophecies. He struggled to know what to believe about Smith's beliefs. To his detriment, he focused less on the common courtesies of sharing public norms and the civic duties of reciprocity, instead offering a legal assessment of the prophecies' potential for harm or absolute power. Would the beliefs inspire actions spilling into the public sphere? Would they exert harm on others in a way that would force the state to act to protect individual safety and "the public peace"? Ford gambled that they would not and decided to follow his party's equal rights playbook by enforcing the law neutrally, at least until he could arrange a safe removal. The anti-Mormons of Hancock County thought it a poor wager.

Ford twice called out the militia to protect the Mormons from the harm of those who would force them to leave the state immediately. Politically, it was a miscalculation because statewide public opinion and the overwhelming majority in the surrounding counties (including in Iowa and Missouri) had shifted in support of the anti-Mormons. But such calculations are always a matter of wager and are not to be determined conclusively by simple reference to the falsity of the beliefs involved. Here is a political reality with which developing democracies must contend. A clear verdict on the truth or falsity of many beliefs often takes too long to formulate to be useful in real political time. Stories—true, false, and fabled—are the lifeblood of democratic politics. Civic narratives are used and exert power. When performed by citizens in society, they can shape the course of events. Without the ordering power of the majority, denial or belief by a few universalist egalitarians like Ford or conservative individualists like his Whig critic Charles Ballance has little scope to alter civic norms at the local level.

Ford's story ended tragically. An accidental governor, he did not choose the Mormon accident waiting to happen. The one problem he did choose—saving the state of Illinois from bankruptcy—he resolved successfully, and he lived long enough to see the canal open. His strategy was to redeem the state's honor in order to build its authority. Compared with his fellow Democrats, he sought to build state authority more on trust than on worth. He aimed to build trust through what the *Sangamo Journal* called his "manly and frank" communication style.[15] Much as the Whigs tried to recruit him to their needs, and much as he was temperamentally different from the Democrats who controlled the rump state at Springfield, Ford was unable to play the game of politics in the ways prescribed by the conservative Whig playbook. He would not impose a manly moral order on the community in the implicit belief that he was right—a luxury in a pluralistic society that even Whigs like Abraham Lincoln disavowed. Ford did not endorse and could not access, as Adams and Jefferson had, the cultural supremacy of establishment Protestantism. He was personally areligious, and his wife, Fannie, was a Catholic.[16]

The little governor preferred a broader, more universal version of the Democratic Party's political culture. His ideal of reason operated on a rarified plane independent of the empirical world. A legal formalist, his juridical view of democracy did not allow the state to secure order by cracking heads, Mormon or anti-Mormon, without due process. Because of his philosophical idealism, many of Ford's fellow Democrats dismissed him as politically useless or worse, calling him "vain of his intellectual endowments" yet "totally ignorant of the arts and methods of electioneering" and "totally wanting in [the] penetration and tact" needed to direct the Democratic majority.[17] Ford's idealist approach meant he would take the high road, as he saw it, a road the institutionally independent governor's office in Illinois allowed. He disdained the particularist civic narrative on which the regime relied. The party regulars in Springfield did not appreciate his high-minded independence and clipped his wings by taking as many offices away from him as they could.[18] A contrast to the three previous governors, who were physically large, Kentucky-born military men, Ford was neither party's image of a leader.[19] Trust would have to be cultivated using legal tact and practical judgment, not physical prowess.

Ford's view of the state rejected its informal shadow side, its civil society counterpart. But there was no rejecting the fact that settler state institutions, out on the frontier, were often overextended in multiple arenas. To be authoritative, they needed the support of civil society, that part of society which "involves citizens acting collectively in the public sphere."[20] In the Jacksonian regime, political leaders generated this support by authorizing worth-based civic narratives telling who deserved membership. By this means they extended to locally constituted majorities the power of granting civic recognition, the power of inclusion and exclusion. It is a pregnant power in democracies in which the two conflated devotions of the state—one to justice and the other to order—meet and conflict. Ford only recognized the state's power to seek justice by enforcing the rights of individuals. He denied the state's role as arbiter in the societal culture's status order; he sought fairness to the Mormons by using the individual right of habeas corpus. The route to group fairness based on confronting and adjusting the regime's status order eluded him.

The state's role in managing the societal culture's status order eludes us still. Most democratic states today contain more than one people and more than one potential societal culture. They are multicultural in this sense and face the task of managing deep pluralism. Many employ consociational schemes—institutions for sharing power and limiting the ways the majority can impose winner-take-all policies on minority groups—to give minority cultures some leverage against the dominant societal culture.[21] James Madison's confederated republic functioned in similar ways, and schemes like John C. Calhoun's "concurrent majority" aimed to extend the regime's consociational capacity.[22] However they approach power sharing, most democratic regimes ask that minorities, Indigenous and otherwise, conform to majoritarian norms and rules of reciprocity. Shared citizenship "presupposes a level of sociability that makes for reciprocal engagement, rule-learning behavior, and socialization."[23] The Mormons in Illinois can be seen as positing a worst-case scenario for multicultural socialization: a minority asks for and receives special legal exemptions and protections, develops separatist tendencies, and is expelled. Neither justice nor order is served.

That the Mormons were later forced back into the nation at the end of the nineteenth century and today have ceased to be a separate people is little comfort to those who argue that multiculturalism leads inevitably to civic disintegration. The story of the Mormon troubles from this perspective teaches the clear lesson that multiculturalism is bad for republics. While the degree to which they were pushed by others or pulled by their own reasons will be forever contested, the fact remains that, between 1830 and 1846, the saints executed a remarkable evolution from religious sect to seceding people. Illinois could not make its rule of law general and universal enough to hold them. In republican terms, they committed the political sin of secession from the national community.

The perspectives of multiculturalism, universalism, and republicanism remain relevant to developed and developing democracies today. The Illinois case has special relevance for the United States. The Mormon testing of the political system, straining a state government's capacities, reaching and exceeding its limits, if repeated in the early twenty-first century, would undoubtedly be resolved by the intervention of the federal government. Such has, in fact, transpired in Antelope, Oregon, with the Rajneeshee settlement in the 1980s.[24] But if the American state now has more capacity and more institutional fixes available, many of the civic and cultural patterns leading to breakdown are arguably still in place. The majority societal culture expects assimilation and deference to majority civic norms in most localities, and control over the police power at the local level is still contested and leads to violence and protest, as it did notably in Ferguson in 2014 and Minneapolis in 2020. Overall, the hegemonic belief in state neutrality still prevails, societal cultures are ignored, and the framing role of political culture is not well understood. Believing the story of state neutrality leaves American democracy vulnerable to dissolution and injustice.

~

The Mormon troubles in Illinois exposed persistent political development patterns that are worth cataloging and discussing separately. First off, it is remarkable that in the Mormon case the Illinois regime was pressured to the breaking point by a religion of purely indigenous materials similar to mainstream Protestantism.[25] Others in Illinois had group practices that differed from the norm enough to require special exceptions to general rules (e.g., the French in the American Bottom), others lived separately (the English at Albion), others voted as a group overwhelmingly for the same candidates (the Methodists for antislavery candidates), and others yet mistook their favored group interest for the public interest (particularist factions within the Jacksonian Democrats and the Whigs). In their tendency toward egalitarianism, the Mormons could even be described as mainstream, itself strong evidence for taking the Mormon case seriously. As a group, they were in many ways not exceptional but typical of the kind of societal minority with fair claims to accommodation in any American regime.[26] The case suggests that the need for accommodation may be more common than otherwise appears, though the need for accommodation says nothing about the degree or extent of accommodation appropriate and its likelihood of success. When minority groups become separatist and nationalist in orientation, a common allegiance to the larger society is abandoned. Toleration under these conditions often requires a degree of accommodation and autonomy which majorities rightly resist.

The tension here points to a second pattern in multicultural democracies: the need to find a balance between the fair demands for accommodation that minorities make and the fair claims to direct policy and set priorities majorities make. The balance is a matter of political judgment and should be considered on a case-by-case basis. Many argue in the twenty-first-century United States, for instance, that claims of majority bias against African Americans facing arrest and mass incarceration are rational and pressing. Accommodating these claims can and should be addressed as a matter of justice.[27] At the same time, there are public-interested, if nonuniversal, civic policies relating to democratic societal cultures that majorities can and should as a matter of justice require that minorities meet.[28] The

Amish, for example, live in separate enclaves in the United States today, but they forgo local voting or efforts to control county government. This is a position which has evolved over many years of internal dialogue, external socialization, and engagement with the larger civic community.[29] Many groups in the United States today vote nearly unanimously for one party, but none recognizes a single political leader or lives purposely in a concentrated setting. In the Mormon case, the combination of living separately, voting in unison, and advocating for a merger of church and state under one political prophet exceeded the limits of the toleration to be expected of the preexisting local majority. Each case presents its own challenges and should be considered separately, but a societal balance, an informal social contract crafted from multiple cultural perspectives, is needed to approach fairness.

A third pattern the Illinois case elucidates is the pivotal role played by civic narrative in democracies. Americans still adhere to and apply the independent-producer narrative. It is worth considering whether it remains a useful story of peoplehood. Usefulness is an appropriate measure since truth or falsity is moot with foundational beliefs. Independence is an aspiration which admits of many degrees. On the high end of the continuum, independent people pursue life projects of their own devising. In the terms of political theorists, they follow "individually scripted ideas of the good." Such a high degree of individualism, while inspiring to many as an ideal, can be exclusionary as a norm. Leslie Pickering Francis and Anita Silvers acknowledge that the focus on individual ideas of the good allows a liberal society to respect and tolerate a wide array of "identities and personal characteristics," but they argue that "this very feature introduced to ensure inclusiveness might instead defeat it in the case of people with intellectual disabilities" as well as, for different reasons, the Amish and conservative traditionalists of all varieties.[30]

The lack of universal reach develops along the producer continuum as well. Producerism arguably excludes the unemployed and most retired people.[31] For those who are included, the role of producer is hard work and tends to foment punitive resentment against those considered loafers. Rogers M. Smith suggests the alternative image of "a pioneering people," a trope in the genre of "political adventure stories" that is identical to Thomas Ford's embrace of an adventuring people.[32] The shift to agency broadly conceived is more inclusive and can be made to fit nontraditional kinds of production. But even at its broadest, the pioneer ideal indicates the origin of all settler-worth approaches in the exclusion of Indigenous people.

Such limits on universal inclusion will never be overcome and should serve as a reminder that politics is a domain of the contingent. The limits suggest that the goal in setting political ground rules, as the American founders recognized, should be to doubt and limit power by setting up procedures to check and control inevitable bias. Since all democratic societal cultures contain particularist biases, the goal should be to recognize and control for biases where reasonable.[33] The paradox is that cultural biases are so ingrained they appear natural and go unrecognized. The Mormon story reminds us that consociational accommodation and efforts in the name of due process, while necessary to fairness and ultimately the legitimacy of democratic governance, will be unpopular, especially in times of great distrust leading to unrest. Among the majority, those with an individualist cultural lens will focus on groups made unworthy by lack of reciprocity, and egalitarians will seek out groups made unworthy by a misplaced allegiance.

The politics of misrecognition is an inherent part of all worth stories. The Mormon troubles indicate how tentative the recognition of membership can be in a developing democracy. The party duopoly in Illinois drove competition for Mormon votes; the sect's increasing social power in the local arena goaded their neighbors to distrust and then misrecognize them. Organized as anti-Mormons, Hancock County citizens used their agency to define membership in the Illinois regime in ways that excluded the Mormons. The Mormons were at first recognized as producers under the informal rules of the Illinois regime, but accusations of thievery brought their reputation into question. While charges of property theft persisted, it was their communal settlement, political deference to their leaders, and surging electoral power which led their neighbors to label them publicly as a threat and reject them as fellow independent republicans. They may have been producers, but having been judged dependent, they failed the local test administered in Hancock County.

For a period of at least two years, the political elite of the state resisted their exclusion; they and the people outside Hancock County sought ways to make the Mormons fit the story line under which Illinoisans welcomed all to their state universally. They really meant that they welcomed producers who were dependent only on the

American state. Enslaved people had their masters and women their husbands and fathers; these groups, while they were producers as a matter of fact, were designated not truly independent as citizens. The Mormons were found to fall into the same unworthy category as enslaved people and women because of their dependency and attachment to the Mormon church and its leadership. From the Illinois perspective, the Mormons had perversely placed themselves in the dependent category; they were dependent not by ascription but by their own choice. By belief and action, they were found to have put their attachment to a particular "strong and wide" group, as the Mormons are classified under Rogers M. Smith's formulation, above their attachment to the civic nation.

The anti-Mormon exclusion of the Mormons on grounds of excessive dependency was not wholly unfounded. Separate egalitarian groups like the Mormons often find allegiance to the state less compelling than allegiance to their favored cause. Strong and wide groups require a state-like commitment and allegiance from their members. Seeing like a state, Joseph Smith did not want to share his members with any other organization.[34] The Mormons believed the gentiles were misguided and going to hell; Mormon inclusiveness was aimed at other outsider groups, such as the Native Americans or the poor English immigrants. In their view, other dissenting Protestant groups might through grace happen upon the truth, but the correspondence was accidental and temporary.

The anti-Mormon concern about Mormon dependency leading to tyranny was thus not unjustified. When Mormon ends diverged from those of other groups, as they did inevitably, the Mormons' ferocity in their critiques was shocking. Mormon anger and rage was on display in Smith's 1844 letters to national figures Henry Clay and John C. Calhoun. In the letters he permanently wrote off both parties because he hated "the imbecility of American Statesmen" and longed "for a day of righteousness."[35] Smith seemed more and more determined to act on his belief that secular pluralism in America had produced too much compromise and too much corruption.

The emphasis on their own worth and purity that preoccupies excluded groups is a fourth pattern the Illinois case highlights. Minority groups who ask to be fairly accommodated will be judged unfair themselves by the majority when they act illiberally toward their own members.[36] This pattern was seen in the Mormons' lack of reciprocity in practicing toleration internally, most notably in the case of the *Nauvoo Expositor.* In 1843 Smith claimed to be "willing to die in defending the rights of a Presbyterian, a Baptist, or a good man of any other denomination for the same principle which would trample upon the rights of the Latter-day Saints."[37] But in practice, in Nauvoo's majoritarian Mormon setting, such reciprocity was a mere abstraction. The Nauvoo City Council ordinance "in relation to religious societies" was more telling. The *Nauvoo Neighbor* promoted it as exhibit A in the case for Mormon toleration. While it did open "free toleration and equal privileges" in the city to "Catholics, Presbyterians, Methodists, Baptists, Latter-Day Saints, Quakers, Episcopalians, Universalists, Unitarians, Mohammedans, and all other religious sects and denominations," it still allowed the Nauvoo mayor or the municipal court the power to fine up to five hundred dollars or imprison for six months any person "guilty of ridiculing, abusing, or otherwise deprecating another in consequence of his religion."[38] Offensive speech was thus criminalized in a way at odds with the norms of the frontier Illinois speech market.

The abatement of the *Expositor* as a common nuisance relied on seeing an analogy between the reputations of individuals and groups. Libel was a civil tort; private individuals might sue to recover damages to their reputations. It did not obviously extend to the reputations of municipalities and groups. Further, the rough-and-ready style of journalism conventional on the frontier could and frequently did lead to physical threats and duels; attacks on character, name-calling, and false claims were the norm, not the exception. The Mormons were running up against a different societal culture that contained a different set of foundational beliefs. If a group libel tort had existed, Thomas Sharp was guilty of violating it when he falsely reported in the fall of 1845 that several Mormons were charged in the murder of old-settler George Davenport; no single news story was more damaging to the group's reputation.[39] Stories like this emboldened opposition to the saints in Hancock.

The anti-Mormons, while a local minority, felt sure they would be backed by overwhelming majorities in nearby counties and indeed by settler state public opinion as a whole. Not only were the Mormons ignoring Illinois's widespread practice of rough journalism but they were repeat offenders by ignoring implicit premises like deferring to the old settlers. One or two such differences might be elided in the common-law method of authorizing the evolution of local custom, but the Mormons were risking misrecognition by insisting that so many value choices go their way. Given the importance of extralegal norms in clarifying the meaning of the law, the need to include civil society actors in the definition of the state becomes imperative. The realities of state formation require that William Novak's concept of the "well-ordered" common-law state be widened to include direction from the majority's societal culture. The move opens the exercise of the police power to include both the "punitive" antebellum tradition Gary Gerstle emphasizes and the "popular" legal tradition Laura Edwards documents.[40]

The presence of background assumptions within societal culture underscores a final repeating pattern in the troubles, one about group competition in democratic regimes. Conflicts between minorities and majorities often develop simply from the fact that the lines dividing members' allegiance to their group and to the larger society are unclear. Navigating these unwritten codes can be especially treacherous for minority outsider groups but particularly for religious groups, which typically have their own set of unwritten public commitments. As religious scholars note, the "discursive structure" of religious creeds, the set of cosmological background assumptions, very frequently does not allow for a clear delineation between the religious domain and other spheres of life. "In the discursive structure of the worldview of elective monotheisms," Robert Erlewine writes, "the boundary between the individual and community as well as between the public and the private is quite blurry."[41] It was certainly blurry in Mormonism, and made more so when Joseph Smith's King Follett sermon put its monotheism in doubt. On the one hand, Mormons, as individuals, were born members of the American republic who considered themselves members of a group pledged to redeem it; on the other, their group believed redemption would come in an eventual apocalypse, after which families would share separate worlds. Their ultimate salvation would be through temple rites, not state rights.

While the diaries of Mormons living at Nauvoo indicate life as group and family members eclipsed all other interests, as individuals and citizens they were still property owners and producers liable to pay taxes and obey state laws. These Illinois obligations could easily be reframed and redirected by the standards of group life. In December of 1841, Sharp pointedly observed that Smith's unique status as both a religious and political leader placed on him special civic obligations. Smith was far from unique as a tax scofflaw, as was apparent in the city's published delinquent tax rolls, but he had a special duty to pay on time, Sharp argued, because otherwise "of course his followers will feel themselves justified in doing likewise."[42] By pointing to the Mormons' tentative reciprocity in a matter of ultimate allegiance to the state, Sharp crafted civic reasoning which appealed to both individualists and egalitarians in Illinois societal culture. Leaders like Sharp were able to exploit cultural biases to frame the inevitable group competition in ways that favored his side.

These five patterns converged during the Mormon troubles to create a perfect storm of mistrust and violence. While both sides in the conflict were culpable, a question about the merits of toleration remains. Clearly, there are illiberal behaviors that simply should not be tolerated. Did the Mormons cross a line of tolerability? The anti-Mormons believed their strong separatism made the reciprocal support for other people's rights problematic and supplied evidence of a lack of allegiance to the republic. The case has been made here that Mormon separatism, their recurring emphasis on a separate final destiny for their members, did make them distinct. Still, it may well be asked, Did not other denominations exude distinct and shared public identities? Did not other religious denominations in Illinois also demand much time and money of their members? Indeed, did not other groups deemed independent producers by the Illinois settlers in fact vote as a group?

As a factual matter, the answer to all these questions is yes. There is an ambiguity in the nature of "independence" that people like Sharp often overlook. He simply assumed that independent thinkers would as a unit end up voting in a normal or bell curve distribution. Smith could have replied that the distribution of a group's votes is a statistical artifact, not a sign of common intent. He might have pressed further: if members all share a common experience of oppression and liberation, is it necessarily a sign of direction and dependence on groupthink? What of African Americans who voted nearly unanimously for the Republican Party in Mississippi during Reconstruction or for the Democratic Party after the civil rights movement? Smith answered the perceived problem of Mormons voting as a group with a Methodist analogy: "With regard to elections, some say all the latter-day Saints vote together and vote as I say. But I never tell any man how to vote, or who to vote for. . . . Should there be a Methodist society here and two candidates running for office, one says: 'If you will vote for me and put me in governor I will exterminate the Methodists, take away their charters, etc.' The other candidate says 'If I am governor, I will give all an equal privilege.' Which would the Methodists vote for?"[43] It is a telling example in a state where it was notorious that the Methodists had been a nearly monolithic antislavery force in the 1824 convention vote.[44]

But there was this difference: the Methodists did not live in one neighborhood, whereas the Mormons and other misrecognized groups did. Some groups, such as the Methodists, were assimilated, while others, such as the abolitionists or Black settlers, were not. This fact highlights how group geography challenges toleration in part because the local setting is an electoral setting, and elections matter in democracies. As we have seen, the Illinois regime's discursive structure included deference to the first settlers of a county. When abolitionists were newcomers to a middle-tier Illinois community, as in Alton or Peoria, they were mobbed; when they were able to found their own communities in the state's northern tier, as in Putnam County, they were not. The timing of settlement and its geographic location carried political weight in Illinois. Sundiata Keita Cha-Jua argues that establishing an early status as a "majority-Black town" made it possible for the African Americans in Brooklyn, Illinois, to keep control over their town in a way that eluded Free Frank McWorter's biracial town of New Philadelphia in Pike County.[45] Control over offices explains the difference. In Hancock County it was repeatedly noted by the anti-Mormons that the offices of "the County Commissioner's Court, which selects the panel of grand and petit jurors, the Sheriff, the jailor, a majority of all the Justices of the Peace and Constables, the clerks of the County Commissioner's as well as the Circuit Court, the Assessor and Collector" were all in the hands of the newcomer Mormons.[46] The newcomers proceeded to gain the majority and use control over offices to prioritize their own ways.

The anti-Mormons were claiming in essence that the Mormons were violating republican norms by putting their group interest above the public interest. Their allegiance to the American state was called into question. It should be noted that the same could be said about the Illinois regime. In Illinois the local majority interest was christened the public interest by the settlers.[47] The part swallowed the whole in precisely the way the holist Whigs resisted. By endorsing the settler logic, the Democrats appeared to eliminate the problem of the tension between mere local interest and the national interest. This was a decisive move against the logic of the first national regime. James Madison believed that voters in a republic needed to be committed to the public interest. But he stressed that the check on majority tyranny would come primarily through the institutional nudge of large voting districts. His reliance on institutional means as opposed to moralistic exhortations obscured the importance of the public interest to his theory of republicanism. Under Madison's regime, allegiance to the national good and the authority of the United States superseded any other membership. Andrew Jackson seemed to agree with him by his insistence on the priority of federal authority over US bank authority and state nullification.

As the 1830s wore on, the first regime's norms began to slip away. Alexis de Tocqueville confirmed that the Americans he met had begun to experience the public interest "rightly understood" as a commitment arising spontaneously from membership in multiple civic associations.[48] The national regime's authority was curiously hidden, and the public interest was enforced at the state government level or in settler states like Illinois at the local level. In such places and under the new regime, the Madisonian assumption that the larger sphere would be a public-spirited check on the majority was easily ignored or abandoned. As so often happens in democracies today, Jacksonian democracy was lived as majoritarian democracy. In our day, appeals to check majority power using deep pluralism are rejected as giving in to a "minority formula" or succumbing to group identity politics.[49] Clearly, there are limits to accommodation, but the limits follow from the logic of republicanism itself and apply equally to majorities and minorities.

Both the Illinois settlers and the Mormon saints often placed their group allegiance ahead of their allegiance to the state. The 1830s context of civil society multiplicity and pluralism encouraged group engagement. New religions, agricultural societies, the Masons, the Washingtonian Temperance Society, lyceums, the American Colonization Society—voluntary associations of all kinds were pioneered and flourished. The Jacksonian ideal was multiplicity of identities at the civil society level but unified identity and membership at the level of popular sovereignty. It was an elusive ideal amid so many "subsociety" ties, as William Leggett recognized; many opposed to Leggett and the Democrats sought a solution not in partisanship but in its antipartisan opposite. They judged the political party to be like any particular group attachment, a violation of the first regime's foundational republican beliefs, since intense adherence to the party's interest could and often did overcloud allegiance to and recognition of higher allegiances.

Partisans like Martin Van Buren argued that it was precisely the commitment to the republic that required the partial combination of Leggett's "laboring class of America" to defeat the ever-present forces of hierarchy and privilege from hijacking the state. In a similar way, it was Mormon dedication to the higher purpose of establishing the Christian millennium in America that drove the Mormons to a separate group adherence. While many religious denominations thought of America as a millennial nation, the Mormons exploited anew the timeworn tradition of emphasizing their uniqueness in the eyes of the creator. They so adamantly rejected the norm of civil society pluralism that they became as a practical matter intolerant of most other religions. The anti-Mormons followed a similar course to an opposite conclusion. They reacted against a deep pluralism that allowed the Mormons to become so independent that they became their own people, seemingly with the permission to build their own state. In anti-Mormons' eyes the Mormons had become so separate that they had become ungovernable and intolerable.

~

How to navigate the problem of toleration has by no means been solved formally, let alone practically. We think of toleration as one idea, but it is many ideas with many separate rationales, each leading to many discrete dilemmas, and the interface of these dilemmas with the problem of governance is still contested. They remain issues of concern for those living in emerging democracies around the world. Indeed, they remain contested for contemporary Americans approaching democracy. Toleration is a wicked problem because it combines multiple domains. As experienced by majority communities in settler Illinois, it included four discrete issues: the dilemma of tolerating unconventional beliefs, the dilemma of knowing where a belief ends and a harmful action begins, the dilemma of asymmetry in tolerating those who are intolerant or who perversely appear to thrive on persecution, and finally the dilemma of the incomplete universality of state neutrality—of recognizing that regime authority rests, even under civic nationalism, on religiously and ethically charged narratives of worth.[50]

The case for toleration based on "respect for persons" illustrates the difficulties created by the first dilemma. This rationale for toleration is that we should tolerate unconventional beliefs, even those one views as morally wrong, because we should respect all persons as moral agents responsible for their own choices and entitled to choose their own conception of the good. In this vein, Mill argued that polygamy "was as much voluntary on the part of the women concerned . . . as is the case with any other form of the marriage institution."[51] His reasoning runs into a problem in the Illinois case because there Mormonism was considered "an imposition"—that is, a cultish fraud. Respect for persons in conditions of fraud might arguably lead more properly to intolerance since fraudulent manipulation subverts the autonomy of moral agents.

For those who did argue for toleration of the Mormons in Illinois, their lived experience included many moments of exasperation. Critical junctures made the demands of toleration appear foolish and the whole project of accommodation futile or wrongheaded. One critical moment was in 1844 when Governor Thomas Ford had the Smith brothers imprisoned in Carthage Jail. Joseph Smith had previously evaded imprisonment through the use of a writ of habeas corpus.[52] Ford sent the wrong message to Hancock County civil society when he suggested that, even after a trial and possible conviction in the *Expositor* nuisance case, the people of Hancock would need to figure out a long-term solution to the Mormon problem. The officials took this as a free pass to confront the Smiths in jail, which led immediately to their assassination.

Fairly managing majority-minority relations is the state's most important role in establishing toleration in democracies. It is a role with both structural and attitudinal aspects. Lincoln's "civil religion," an attitudinal solution he urged at the age of twenty-nine, is insufficient. Toleration fights against other moral goals—such as protecting individuals from harm or realizing republican self-government. The anti-Mormons refused to succumb without a fight to what they considered tyranny. We can recognize Lincoln's brilliance as a leader in attempting to synthesize, however unsuccessfully, the egalitarian attitude of solidarity toward the marginalized and the individualist bias toward horizontal equality. The synthesis replicated, David Greenstone argues, Lincoln's version of "the New England Way," a pairing he would later urge in his second inaugural speech to heal a broken nation.[53] Unfortunately, settler Illinois was not ready for reform; it was not ready for a new public sphere commitment.

Much of what passes for toleration is really indifference; trust in government authority enables indifference toward the perceived transgressions of others to grow and survive. But such trust is a function of regime legitimacy and stability, which coevolve: majorities are more likely to ignore minority difference if there is trust that the government will enforce reciprocity and control accommodation. Governor Ford tried but was unable by himself to build and project this appearance of control. His failure to project virtue, defined as manly control, was graphically illustrated by the anti-Mormon women publicly presenting him Mormon petticoats in 1845.

There is much to be said for toleration; it may be ethically fair, good for pluralism, and necessary for democratic regime stability. But it is not clearly a virtue. Susan Mendus reminds us that we tolerate what we think is wrong.[54] Since it is not an unmixed good to countenance what we believe to be evil, we need to have strong reasons to tolerate. The state-formation perspective focuses on how failed governance weighs on participants and produces climates of popular justice dismissive of due process. The narratives of worth that legitimate regimes form a crucial lens through which democratic toleration is viewed by the agents involved. In developing democracies where state capacity to enforce the law is weak, one condition above all seems to be needed to justify toleration: clear allegiance. For democratic toleration to work in practice, allegiance to regime authority and its good must be seen as prevailing over allegiance to individual or group conceptions of the good. Without it, what a tolerating democratic state asks of the majority in the name of a minority is frequently demeaned as complicity with evil, mere "politics," or at best "compromise."

As influential as cultural frames were in constructing Illinois's civic narrative, the predominance of one political subculture or another did not cause or prevent the failure of governance in Hancock County. As we have seen, the egalitarian Mormons were preoccupied with American worth, which ended up bringing on misrecognition of their own worth. At the same time, the competitive individualist Thomas Sharp, characteristic of his culture, was quick to mistrust, which ended up bringing on the cascade of distrust that engulfed the troubles. It was the dynamic these cultures and their agents produced together which drove the Mormon troubles in Hancock County: the anti-Mormons' competitive individualist distrust jarred against the Mormon group, threatened it, and spurred its egalitarian need to express worth. Given the regime services west-central Illinois volunteers were providing in the form of the militia, the Illinois state could not carry the governance load the dynamic created.

Young Lincoln thought Americans might solve the tolerance problem by conjuring a sacred commitment which combined an individualist commitment to rights and the law with an egalitarian stance of allegiance to a special republic. Lincoln's solution failed because the two cultures in Illinois were under the pressure of distrust and incapacity; they were more often arrayed against each other than brought into cooperation and combination. Jefferson's compelling idea of toleration as a passive virtue, one only requiring indifference or that people not act, also failed. Governor Ford placed blame precisely on the passive "moderate party," who, while they eschewed violence, took no action to support due process in times of crisis. Surreptitiously addressing his Whig counterpart George T. M. Davis, he wrote bitterly: "These moderate men, if force is necessary to put down force, are always the last whose services can be obtained; and yet they are always the readiest to find fault with the government which they have failed to assist."[55] Many on the other side, dubbed by Ford "the men of property," were active on behalf of protecting and enforcing values they held dearer than toleration, such as property rights or self-government or, as they insisted, self-defense, which they believed an intolerable group had violated.[56] Unlike the moderates, Ford's "old citizens" were active; they were motivated, as they stated in a public apology after the Carthage murders, "by a high sense of duty to themselves, and to their County."[57]

The right to a writ of habeas corpus is a perfect embodiment of the lack of capacity which hamstrung the solicitous settler state. It embodied all its strengths and weaknesses. Its strength as a right was its blunt power to limit state action; its weakness was its narrow and usually constrained scope. The Illinois legislature, when it created the habeas power for Nauvoo, did not limit its scope. The lack of constraint created a strong common-law tool, one greatly favoring individual liberty and due process. The Mormons made full use of their broad and blunt tool and could be forgiven if they believed Illinois was the land of refuge it appeared to be upon their arrival. What the story of the Mormon troubles allows us to see, as Gary Gerstle and Laura Edwards point out, is that behind the state's solicitation hid a shadow police power. What Ford did not see was that while the Illinois state could provide for popular justice, it had a hard time enforcing it because it was accountable to various civil society groups seeking a return on their regime services by using the state to mark the excluded with punitive disapproval.

Illinois's settler state was neither balanced nor neutral, despite its rhetoric or any appearance of "statelessness" emanating from its common-law form. William Novak rightly denounces as a "myth" the idea that, in the nineteenth-century, Americans had an exceptionally weak state.[58] The regime the Jacksonians created only appeared so because at the state level it relied on the executive branch to administer the details of public policy. At the local level, this meant relying on sheriffs and constables, county commissioners courts (county boards) and state's attorneys, and mayors and city councils. In practice, filling in the details of rule at the local level meant deferring to the majority in civil society to empower action. Local citizens in settler Illinois were granted a platform on which to perform citizenship; they used it variously to both include and exclude.

Governance and toleration in developing democracies confront many challenges. None are so great that the project of liberal fairness should be abandoned, as many on the political-spectrum right and left routinely suggest. If the democratic state is to live up to the ideals of true believers like Thomas Ford, we will need to learn to accept a realistic assessment of its powers. We must recognize that democratic state majorities are a loaded weapon. Such majorities are not inherently illegitimate; in fact, they can be the only body capable of authorizing needed changes in political order or directing broad shifts in policy.[59] But majorities must own their biases and the ordering power of those biases. Denial, the option Ford chose, will not reduce or resolve these biases; it is the surest path to entrenching them. Instead, the state should take steps to make transparent all the majoritarian biases of its societal culture. Majorities committed to public sphere duties should make them clear and obvious to all. If a sudden change in majority group control threatens individuals, geographical districting policies should be developed to break up at-large voting or exclusive control over local offices. On the minority side, a duty to assimilate to a minimum of public-interested behaviors should be recognized and practiced. A fair democratic society requires republican sacrifice from both majorities and minorities. Perilous and unheeded as it is, the republican story is one Americans need to keep telling themselves.

Advocating for a majority-minority dialogue is not the same as forfeiting the ideal of fair government in liberal democracies. Fairness remains the ideal, but the imperfections of neutrality need to be acknowledged. Some believe the lure and thrall of neutrality is so great that its hegemonic siren song will be impossible to recognize, acknowledge, and contest. The story told here suggests that this is not necessarily the case. The state is a powerful weapon, but its power is not so subtle that its biases are seamless and go unrecognized, at least not in open societal settings in which citizens have access to and exercise the freedoms of speech and press. The Mormon resistance to the American state demonstrates that hegemonic power can be recognized and contested by the relatively powerless in the course of expressing civic agency. The story of the Mormon troubles in Illinois in this way contains one last surprise. In resisting the combined power of state and society in America, the saints, like other outsider and marginal groups, showed that they could write themselves into the story of American democracy by nudging its believers to become fairer and more self-aware.

Notes

PREFACE

1. This series of laws began in 1802 in the Old Northwest and was revised multiple times. See Eugene H. Berwanger, *The Frontier against Slavery: Western Anti-Negro Prejudice and the Slavery Extension Controversy* (1967; repr., Urbana: University of Illinois Press, 2002), 22. The quotation is from the title of the first of many Black laws the state of Illinois passed beginning in 1819. For a compendium of these laws, see Stephen Middleton, *The Black Laws in the Old Northwest: A Documentary History* (Westport, CT: Greenwood Press, 1993), 271–339.
2. Thomas Ford, *A History of Illinois: From Its Commencement as a State in 1818 to 1847*, ed. Rodney O. Davis (1854; repr., Urbana: University of Illinois Press, 1995), 18.

INTRODUCTION: SETTLER ILLINOIS AS A DEVELOPING DEMOCRACY

1. Clinton Rossiter, ed., *The Federalist Papers* (New York: Penguin, 1961), 33.
2. Laurence Whitehead, "Three International Dimensions of Democratization," in *The International Dimensions of Democratization: Europe and the Americas*, ed. Lawrence Whitehead (Oxford: Oxford University Press, 1996), 4–5.
3. See Robert A. Dahl and Bruce Stinebrickner, *Modern Political Analysis*, 6th ed. (Upper Saddle River, NJ: Prentice Hall, 2003), 79–80. Charles Tilly, the foremost scholar of democratic development, summarizes Dahl's list in five elements: "effective participation; voting equality; enlightened understanding; control of the agenda, and inclusion of adults." *Democracy* (Cambridge: Cambridge University Press, 2007), 9.
4. See Michael J. Pfeifer, *Rough Justice: Lynching and American Society, 1874–1947* (Urbana: University of Illinois Press, 2004).
5. "Equal rights" was made the rallying cry of the Democrats by William Leggett. For Leggett, the whole point of "equal rights"

was its limitations on the power of the majority. As he wrote in the first edition of *The Plaindealer* on December 3, 1836, "It is the duty of the majority so to govern as to preserve inviolate the equal rights of all." See Laurence H. White, ed., *Democratic Editorials: Essays in Jacksonian Political Economy* (New York: Liberty Press, 1984).

6. See Marie Gottschalk, *The Prison and the Gallows: The Politics of Mass Incarceration in America* (Cambridge: Cambridge University Press, 2006), 94.
7. "Stories of peoplehood" is a phrase pioneered by Rogers M. Smith, in *Stories of Peoplehood: The Politics and Morals of Political Membership* (Cambridge: Cambridge University Press, 2003).
8. Joel Feinberg, *Social Philosophy* (Englewood Cliffs, NJ: Prentice Hall, 1973), 25.
9. See Elmer Baldwin, *History of LaSalle County, Illinois* (Chicago: Rand McNally, 1877), 195.
10. Amin Maalouf, *In the Name of Identity*, trans. Barbara Bray (1996; repr., New York: Penguin Books, 2000), 96.
11. Tilly defines state capacity as "the extent to which interventions by state agents into non-state resources, activities, and interpersonal connections alter existing distributions of those resources, activities, and interpersonal connections as well as relations among those distributions." *Democracy*, 16.
12. Larry Diamond, *Developing Democracy: Toward Consolidation* (Baltimore: Johns Hopkins University Press, 1999), 16.
13. Charles Tilly, *Big Structures, Large Processes, Huge Comparisons* (New York: Russell Sage Foundation, 1984), 11.
14. See Havel's remarks in Cong. Rec. S2153–55, quote at 2155 (February 21, 1990).
15. Two prominent political scientists who study ethnic conflict in India emphasize these two additional factors, with each focusing on a favored variable. Paul Brass stresses the impact of elite manipulation of ethnicity and religion to gain advantage in the electoral process, while Ashutosh Varshney looks to the role of bridging and bonding groups in civil society. See Brass, *The Production of Hindu-Muslim Violence in Contemporary India* (Seattle: University of Washington Press, 2003), and Varshney, *Ethnic Conflict and Civic Life: Hindus and Muslims in India* (New Haven: Yale University Press, 2002).
16. The state-formation literature that undergirds the approach taken here includes Peter B. Evans, Dietrich Rueshemeyer, and Theda Skocpol, eds., *Bringing the State Back In* (Cambridge:

Cambridge University Press, 1985); Sven Steinmo, Kathleen Thelen, and Frank Longstreth, *Structuring Politics: Historical Institutionalism in Comparative Analysis* (Cambridge: Cambridge University Press, 1992); George Steinmetz, ed., *State/Culture: State Formation after the Cultural Turn* (Ithaca: Cornell University Press, 1999); Karen Orren and Stephen Skowronek, *The Search for American Political Development* (Cambridge: Cambridge University Press, 2010); and Richard M. Valelly, Susanne Mettler, and Robert C. Lieberman, eds., *The Oxford Handbook of American Political Development* (New York: Oxford University Press, 2016).

17. For the debate over the nature and power of the antebellum state, see Stephen Skowronek, *Building a New American State: The Expansion of National Administrative Capacities, 1877–1920* (Cambridge: Cambridge University Press, 1982); William J. Novak, *The People's Welfare: Law and Regulation in Nineteenth-Century America* (Chapel Hill: University of North Carolina Press, 1996); Richard R. John, *Spreading the News: The American Postal System from Franklin to Morse* (Cambridge, MA: Harvard University Press, 1995); Gottschalk, *The Prison and the Gallows;* Richard L. McCormick, *The Party Period and Public Policy: American Politics from the Age of Jackson to the Progressive Era* (New York: Oxford University Press, 1986); Howard Schweber, *The Creation of American Common Law, 1850–1880: Technology, Politics, and the Construction of Citizenship* (Cambridge: Cambridge University Press, 2004); J. M. Opal, *Avenging the People: Andrew Jackson, the Rule of Law, and the American Nation* (New York: Oxford University Press, 2017); and Gary Gerstle, *Liberty and Coercion: The Paradox of American Government from the Founding to the Present* (Princeton, NJ: Princeton University Press, 2015).

18. For the hidden side of the federal government in this era, see Brian Balogh, *A Government out of Sight: The Mystery of National Authority in Nineteenth-Century America* (Cambridge: Cambridge University Press, 2009); for the popularity of the state level's coercive capacities, see Gary Gerstle, "The Resilient Power of the States across the Long Nineteenth Century: An Inquiry into a Pattern of American Governance," in *The Unsustainable American State,* ed. Lawrence Jacobs and Desmond King (New York: Oxford University Press, 2009).

19. Daniel Brinks and Sandra Botero, "Inequality and the Rule of Law: Ineffective Rights in Latin American Democracies," in *Reflections on Uneven Democracies: The Legacy of Guillermo O'Donnell,* ed. Daniel Brinks, Marcelo Leiras, and Scott Mainwaring

(Baltimore: Johns Hopkins University Press, 2014), 214–39, quote at 221.

20. For the concept of "status quo neutrality" and its role in constitutional law, see Cass R. Sunstein, *The Partial Constitution* (Cambridge, MA: Harvard University Press, 1993), 3–7, 68–92.
21. Alexis de Tocqueville, *Democracy in America,* ed. J. P. Mayer, trans. George Lawrence (1836–39; repr., Garden City, NY: Doubleday, 1969), 525.
22. Tocqueville, *Democracy in America,* 526.
23. Thomas Ford, *A History of Illinois: From Its Commencement as a State in 1818 to 1847,* ed. Rodney O. Davis (1854; repr., Urbana: University of Illinois Press, 1995), 3–4.
24. Feinberg, *Social Philosophy,* 24–25.
25. Amy Gutmann uses the concept of "conscious social reproduction" to make the same point in *Democratic Education,* 2nd ed. (Princeton, NJ: Princeton University Press, 1999), 39.
26. Will Kymlicka, *Contemporary Political Philosophy: An Introduction* (Oxford: Oxford University Press, 1990), 4. Kymlicka argues that all modern liberal philosophers share this "egalitarian theory," first expressed by Ronald Dworkin in *Taking Rights Seriously* (Cambridge, MA: Harvard University Press, 1977).

CHAPTER 1: ILLINOIS IN 1839

1. See Susan Easton Black and Richard E. Bennett, eds., *A City of Refuge: Quincy, Illinois* (Salt Lake City: Millennial Press, 2000).
2. See the "Proclamation" by Joseph Smith, Sidney Rigdon, and Hyrum Smith in *Times and Seasons,* January 15, 1841.
3. *Daily Chicago American,* April 12, 1839.
4. See Fawn M. Brodie, *No Man Knows My History: The Life of Joseph Smith,* 2nd ed. (New York: Vintage Books, 1995), 256; Thomas O'Dea, *The Mormons* (Chicago: University of Chicago Press, 1957), 54, relates that the Mormon Elders in 1833 employed Joshua Seixas for a seven-week course in Hebrew. In a revelation on April 26, 1838, Joseph Smith changed the church's name to The Church of Jesus Christ of Latter-day Saints. See Doctrine and Covenants 115:4. The original name in 1830 was the Church of Christ; this was changed to the Church of the Latter Day Saints in 1834; it was changed to The Church of Christ of Latter Day Saints in 1836. See Klaus J. Hansen, *Mormonism and the American Experience* (Chicago: University of Chicago Press, 1981), 38.
5. Thomas Ford, *A History of Illinois: From Its Commencement as a State in 1818 to 1847,* ed. Rodney O. Davis (1854; repr., Urbana: University of Illinois Press, 1995), 117, 315.

6. *Black* and *White* are capitalized to underscore the constructed nature of these terms.
7. See the address published in the *Belleville Advocate,* July 21, 1842.
8. Ford, *History of Illinois,* 43 argues that the term *sucker* was originally tied to the lead miners of Galena, who were like the fish on the Mississippi River because they would ride a steamboat up to Jo Daviess County for a summer of mining, only to float back down south when the winter came. This view is confirmed in "Meaning of the Term Sucker," *Illinois State Register,* October 27, 1837.
9. See Douglas K. Meyer, *Making the Heartland Quilt: A Geographical History of Settlement and Migration in Early-Nineteenth Century Illinois* (Carbondale: Southern Illinois University Press, 2000), 141, 173.
10. Willene Hendrick and George Hendrick, eds., *On the Illinois Frontier: Dr. Hiram Rutherford* (Carbondale: Southern Illinois University Press, 1982), 45. Vernacular spelling will be retained in quotations throughout the book and will not be accompanied the intrusive *sic.*
11. For a typical ad, see the *Illinois Advocate,* February 23, 1831.
12. Scholars estimate the Native American population at about thirty-three thousand in 1660 and six thousand by 1700. See Paul A. Shackel, *New Philadelphia: An Archaeology of Race in the Heartland* (Berkeley: University of California Press, 2011), 3.
13. For the Shawnee story, see Colin G. Calloway, *The Shawnees and the War for America* (New York: Penguin Books, 2007).
14. For the "Sloopers" in Norway, Illinois (LaSalle County), see *Starved Rock Country* (Fall 2014): 50–51. For Brooklyn and New Philadelphia, see Sundiata Keita Cha-Jua, *America's First Black Town: Brooklyn, Illinois 1830–1915* (Urbana: University of Illinois Press, 2000), and Juliet E. K. Walker, *Free Frank: A Black Pioneer on the Antebellum Frontier* (Lexington: University Press of Kentucky, 1983).
15. Robert Bruce Flanders cites 1,135 British immigrants in 1841 and 1,614 in 1842. See *Nauvoo: Kingdom on the Mississippi* (Urbana: University of Illinois Press, 1965), 58n1. Contemporary evidence for these numbers is found in an article from the *Liverpool Chronicle* reported in the *Illinois Democrat,* December 19, 1840, which states that "upwards of 2,000 . . . passengers belonging to a sect called 'Latter Day Saints' . . . are entreaty to embark early next spring . . . bound for Quincy in the State of Illinois."
16. For the use of the term *Easterner* as a synonym for *Northerner,* see, for example, Caroline Palmer Clarke's letter of November 1, 1835, to her sister. She notes that in Chicago, "there are so many

Eastern people getting in now that their customs prevail over those of the South." For "Down Easters," see *Peoria Register and North-Western Gazette,* July 7, 1838.

17. Population estimates for Nauvoo vary. The *Warsaw Signal* reported 22,599 in 1846. See Richard E. Bennett, Susan Easton Black, and Donald Q. Cannon, *The Nauvoo Legion in Illinois: A History of the Mormon Militia, 1841–1846* (Norman, OK: Arthur H. Clark, 2010), 127n1. Thomas Ford, who was not given to exaggeration, estimated that there were 16,000 Mormons in Hancock County by the beginning of 1843. See *A History of Illinois,* 219. The best estimate for Nauvoo is found in Susan Easton Black, "How Large Was the Population of Nauvoo?," *Brigham Young University Studies* 35, no. 2 (1995): 91–94. She concludes that the population of Nauvoo "rose to about 12,000 in 1844, and stood at around 11,000 in 1845" (93). The census of 1845 listed Nauvoo's population at 11,036 inhabitants. It listed Cook County's population at 21,581 and Hancock County's at 22,559—making Hancock the most populous county in the state. Chicago's population was reported by census to be 100 in 1830 and estimated by Jessup W. Scott to be 5,000 in 1838. "Internal Trade No. 3," *Hesparian* 2, no. 5 (March 1839): 351. The *Sangamo Journal,* September 7, 1843, lists Chicago's population as 7,583. The next year the state fixed its debt issues and the canal project resumed funding; very quickly, Chicago's population outpaced Nauvoo's. Kenneth N. Owens gives Galena's population as 2,225 in 1841 and 6,000 in 1850, both by the city census. *Galena, Grant, and the Fortunes of War* (DeKalb: Northern Illinois University Press, 1964), 7.
18. See the 1838 report of chief engineer William Gooding in *Report of the Canal Commissioners of Illinois to Governor John R. Tanner, December 1, 1900* (Springfield, IL: Phillip Bros., 1901), 158.
19. See Gooding's 1836 report in *Report of the Canal Commissioners of Illinois,* 35.
20. Owens, *Galena, Grant, and the Fortunes of War,* 4.
21. See the secretary's report in S. Doc. No. 41, 20th Cong., 2d Sess, *US Serial Set,* vol. 181 (1829). For the political uses of the freeholder numbers, see James Simeone, "The 1830 Contest for Governor and the Politics of Resentment," *Journal of the Illinois State Historical Society* 102, no. 3/4 (Fall–Winter 2009): 282–306.
22. Kenneth J. Winkle, *The Politics of Community: Migration and Politics in Antebellum Ohio* (Cambridge: Cambridge University Press, 1988), 16.

23. This point is argued explicitly in Kenneth J. Winkle, "The Voters of Lincoln's Springfield: Migration and Participation in an Antebellum City," *Journal of Social History* 25 (March): 595–611 at 605.
24. See William Leggett, *Tales and Sketches by a Country Schoolmaster* (New York: Harper, 1829), 146.
25. See the reminiscences of a "Mr. Lee" who had visited the Mackinaw River area in 1805 and 1812. A. V. Pierson, letter, November 2, 1910, McLean County Historical Society, Bloomington, IL.
26. See Hendrick and Hendrick, *On the Illinois Frontier,* 20.
27. See John B. Newhall, *Sketches of Iowa, or the Emigrant's Guide* (New York: J. H. Colton, 1841), 139–40.
28. Newhall, *Sketches of Iowa,* 140.
29. Stephen Middleton, *The Black Laws in the Old Northwest: A Documentary History* (Westport, CT: Greenwood Press, 1993), 273.
30. See the *Compendium of the Enumeration of the Inhabitants and Statistics of the United States* (Washington, DC: Thomas Allen, 1841), 86. For Richardson's master, see Darrel Dexter, *Bondage in Egypt: Slavery in Southern Illinois* (Cape Girardeau: Southeast Missouri State University, 2011), 331–35.
31. For the census data, Richardson's indenture, and her legal counsel, see Carol Pirtle, *Escape Betwixt Two Suns: A True Tale of the Underground Railroad in Illinois* (Carbondale: Southern Illinois University Press, 2000), 62.
32. For the distinction between slave societies and societies with slaves, see Ira Berlin, *Many Thousands Gone: The First Two Centuries of Slavery in North America* (Cambridge, MA: Harvard University Press, 2000).
33. *Shawneetown Republican,* October 8, 1842.
34. See *Autobiography of George Washington Bean, a Utah Pioneer of 1847, and His Family Records,* comp. Flora Diana Bean Horne (Salt Lake City: Utah Printing, 1945), 16.
35. Alexis de Tocqueville, *Democracy in America,* ed. J. P. Mayer, trans. George Lawrence (1832–36; repr., Garden City, NY: Doubleday, 1969), 343–48.
36. Juliet E. K. Walker, *Free Frank: A Black Pioneer on the Antebellum Frontier* (Lexington: University Press of Kentucky, 1983), 77, 93–100. Shackel notes that McWorter was able to avoid the one-thousand-dollar requirement, perhaps because the 1829 law allowed "the solvency of said security" to be determined by the county clerk. *New Philadelphia,* 5.
37. See Cha-Jua, *America's First Black Town.*

38. Anna-Lisa Cox, *The Bone and Sinew of the Land: America's Forgotten Black Pioneers and the Struggle for Equality* (New York: Public Affairs, 2018), xiv–xv.
39. Quoted in Peter Way, *Common Labour: Workers and the Digging of North American Canals: 1780–1860* (Cambridge: Cambridge University Press, 1993), 255; see also 173, 290.
40. Craig Buettinger, "Economic Inequality in Early Chicago, 1849–1850," *Journal of Social History* 11 (1978): 413–18, as cited in Andrew R. L. Cayton and Peter S. Onuf, *The Midwest and the Nation: Rethinking the History of an American Region* (Bloomington: Indiana University Press, 1990), 138.
41. The forty-acre increment was passed as part of the preemption act signed into law in 1832. See Malcolm J. Rohrbough, *The Land Office Business: The Settlement and Administration of American Public Lands, 1789–1837* (London: Oxford University Press, 1968), 213–14.
42. "Claim clubs" are described in Robert P. Swierenga, *Pioneers and Profits: Land Speculation on the Iowa Frontier* (Ames: Iowa State University Press, 1968), 11–17; Elmer Baldwin, *History of LaSalle County, Illinois* (Chicago: Rand McNally, 1877), 119. For a typical settler society claims meeting, see the *Peoria Register and North-Western Gazetteer,* October 14, 1837.
43. See Bronson v. Kinzie, 1 How. 311 (1843). For a report of the protests, see the *Sangamo Journal,* March 16, 1843.
44. *Western World,* May 27, 1840.
45. Steven Stoll, *Larding the Lean Earth: Soil and Society in Nineteenth-Century America* (New York: Hill and Wang, 2002), 35.
46. See the letters of Bryant to his mother dated April 25, 1833, and August 23, 1832, in *The Letters of William Cullen Bryant,* ed. William Cullen Bryant II and Thomas G. Voss, vol. 1, *1809–1836* (New York: Fordham University Press, 1975), 371, 356.
47. See the *Peoria Register and Northwestern Gazetteer,* May 13, 1837.
48. See Seeley v. Peters, 10 Ill. 130–69, 5 Gilm. 130 (1848). The attorney for the plaintiff (Seeley) was Thomas Ford, and the attorney for the defendant (Peters) was William Herndon.
49. Alma Stevens to Miss Lucia Birdley, February 7, 1836, Edward Warren Papers, Chicago Historical Society.
50. Baldwin, *History of LaSalle County, Illinois,* 140.
51. See *The History of Livingston County, Illinois* (Chicago: Wm. Le Baron Jr., 1878), 130, and Erma D. Stuckey, *Darnall, Spence, Steers, Spangler, Stuckey, Sill* (Henry, IL: M&D Printing, 1983), 276.
52. Stuckey, *Darnall,* 276.

53. *The History of Livingston County,* 10.
54. *The History of Livingston County,* 10, 130–31.
55. Millie Troll, *Historical Account of the Origin, Growth, and Development of the Village of Tremont, Illinois* (Morton, IL: Johnson Printing, 1925).
56. *The History of Livingston County,* 12.
57. Stuckey, *Darnall,* 281.
58. See Jacqueline Peterson, "'Wild' Chicago: The Formation and Destruction of a Multiracial Community on the Midwestern Frontier, 1816–1837," in *The Ethnic Frontier: Essays in the History of Group Survival in Chicago and the Midwest,* ed. Melvin G. Holli and Peter d'A. Jones (Grand Rapids, MI: Eerdmans, 1977). For the Indian divers, see Henry S. Beebe, *History of Peru* (Peru, IL: J. F. Linton, 1858), 295.
59. John Francis Snyder, "General Ford and His Family," *Journal of the Illinois State Historical Society* 3, no. 2 (July 1910): 45.
60. Ford, *History of Illinois,* 63, 170.
61. Henry Clyde Hubbart, *The Older Middle West 1840–1880* (New York: D. Appleton-Century, 1936), 33.
62. John Mack Faragher, "'More Motley Than Mackinaw': From Ethnic Mixing to Ethnic Cleansing on the Frontier of the Lower Missouri, 1783–1833," in *Contact Points: American Frontiers from the Mohawk Valley to the Mississippi, 1750–1830,* ed. Andrew R. L. Cayton and Fredrika J. Teute (Chapel Hill: University of North Carolina Press, 1998), 325–26.
63. Baldwin, *History of LaSalle County, Illinois,* 109–10. Baldwin's memory was confirmed contemporaneously. The *Peoria Register and North-Western Gazetteer,* on August 5, 1837, noted: "The swarm of consumers in the shape of speculators and immigrants, have raised produce higher than it will be again for many years."
64. *A History of Livingston County,* 16–19.
65. *Warsaw Signal,* September 24, 1842.
66. Helen M. Cavanagh, *Funk of Funk's Grove: Farmer, Legislator, and Cattle King of the Old Northwest 1797–1865* (Bloomington, IL: Pantagraph Publishing, 1952), 69.
67. See Christopher Clark, "The Consequences of the Market Revolution in the American North," in *The Market Revolution in America: Social, Political, and Religious Expressions, 1800–1880,* ed. Melvyn Stokes and Stephen Conway (Charlottesville: University Press of Virginia, 1996), 23–42, quotes at 26 and 27.
68. Eliza W. Farnham, *Life in Prairie Land* (1846; repr., Urbana: University of Illinois Press, 1988), 54–56.

69. Stacy M. Robinson, *Hearts Beating for Liberty: Women Abolitionists in the Old Northwest* (Chapel Hill: University of North Carolina Press, 2010), 72–75.
70. Linda King Newell and Valeen Tippetts Avery, *Mormon Enigma: Emma Hale Smith: Prophet's Wife, "Elect Lady," Polygamy's Foe, 1804–1879* (Garden City, NY: Doubleday, 1984), 106–7.
71. For Mary Davis and the "Liberty women" in Illinois, see Robinson, *Hearts Beating for Liberty*, 37–66.
72. Cheryl Janifer LaRoche, *The Geography of Resistance: Free Black Communities and the Underground Railroad* (Urbana: University of Illinois Press, 2014), 23–37.
73. The history of the Underground Railroad in Illinois is still being written. One example is the work of Jeanne Schultz Angel on Sheldon Peck of Lombard, which she presented at the Illinois History Workshop on October 25, 2014.
74. See the notices for the Peoria meeting in the *Peoria Register and North-Western Gazetteer*, January 6, 1841, and for the Galena meeting in the *Northwestern Gazetteer and Galena Advertiser*, January 3, 1836.
75. See the account of attorney George Forquer's last-minute religious conversion in the *Sangamo Journal*, June 21, 1839.
76. For German Methodists, see Charles Ballance, *The History of Peoria, Illinois* (Peoria, NC: Nason, 1870), 103.
77. On the role of the Methodists in the convention controversy of 1823–24, see James Simeone, *Democracy and Slavery in Frontier Illinois: The Bottomland Republic* (DeKalb: Northern Illinois University Press, 2000), 166–88.
78. Quoted in the introduction of Juanita Brooks, ed., *On the Mormon Frontier: The Diary of Hosea Stout 1844–1861* (Salt Lake City: University of Utah Press, 1964), xiv.
79. See his letter dated June 19, 1832, at Jacksonville, in *Letters of William Cullen Bryant*, 348.
80. *Illinois Advocate and State Register*, May 31, 1834.
81. See the *Representative and Belleville News*, June 23, 1838.
82. *Juliet Courier*, March 26, 1842.
83. See the committee report summarized in Frank George Franklin, *The Legislative History of the Naturalization Laws in the United States* (1906; repr., New York: Arno Press, 1968), 199.
84. Caroline Palmer Clarke, letter, November 1, 1835, Clarke Papers, Chicago Historical Society.
85. See the act approved January 19, 1829, in *The Revised Code of Laws of Illinois* (Shawneetown, IL: Alexander Grant & Co., 1829), 138–39.

86. *Illinois Advocate,* July 15, 1831.
87. See the *Northwestern Gazetteer and Galena Advertiser,* July 11, 1835.
88. Beecher's *Six Sermons on Intemperance* (1843), quoted in Anne Norton, *Alternative Americas: A Reading of Antebellum Political Culture* (Chicago: University of Chicago Press, 1986), 72.
89. See Lois W. Banner, "Religious Benevolence as Social Control: A Critique of an Interpretation," *Journal of American History* 60, no. 1 (June 1973): 23–41, and Lawrence Frederick Kohl, "The Concept of Social Control and the History of Jacksonian America," *Journal of the Early Republic* 5, no. 1 (Spring 1985): 21–34. Banner and Kohl were mainly concerned with correcting the earlier view that held reformers were motivated solely by self-interest in an effort to reassert their upper-class status.
90. Banner, "Religious Benevolence," 23.
91. Newell and Avery, *Mormon Enigma,* 107.
92. The story of this split must be gleaned from histories favoring one side or the other. See Achilles Coffey, *History of the Regular Baptists of Southern Illinois* (Paducah, KY: Martin & Co., 1877), 35–99, and E. P. Brand, *Illinois Baptists: A History* (Bloomington, IL: Pantagraph Printing, 1930), 68–77.
93. See the meeting minutes for the "Presbyterian Synod" in *Peoria Register and North-Western Gazetteer,* October 6, 1838, and November 3, 1838.
94. The New York paper was the *Lockport Banner.* For the names given to the Mormon church, see Doctrine and Covenants 20:1; 115:4.
95. Harris is quoted in Brodie, *No Man Knows My History,* 38.
96. John D. Lee, *Mormonism Unveiled: Life and Confession of John D. Lee and the Complete Life of Brigham Young* (1877; repr., Albuquerque: University of New Mexico Press, 2001), 53.
97. See Alexander L. Baugh, "A Call to Arms: The 1838 Mormon Defense of Northern Missouri" (PhD diss., Brigham Young University, 2000).
98. Emil Joseph Verlie, ed., *Illinois Constitutions* (Springfield: Illinois State Historical Library, 1919), 435.
99. For an examination of constitutional principles as "incompletely theorized agreements," see Cass R. Sunstein, *The Partial Constitution* (Cambridge, MA: Harvard University Press, 1993).
100. Will Kymlicka, *Multicultural Citizenship: A Liberal Theory of Minority Rights* (Oxford: Oxford University Press, 1995), 76.
101. The "comity" rule between states is an example of one such constitutional norm. David F. Ericson explores a number of such

norms in Stephen A. Douglas's theory of democracy, including rapid mobility and "interpersonal comity." See *The Shaping of American Liberalism: The Debates of Ratification, Nullification, and Slavery* (Chicago: University of Chicago Press, 1993), 118–19.

102. For the characterization of the era as one of "personal freedom" and "individualism," see Roger D. Launius and John E. Hallwas, ed., *Kingdom on the Mississippi Revisited* (Urbana: University of Illinois Press, 1996), 4.

103. Charles Sellars argues that the era featured a central "clash of cosmologies" between an "antinomian farming majority" committed to "rural egalitarianism" and an "Arminian moralism [that] sanctioned competitive individualism and the market's rewards of wealth and status." *The Market Revolution: Jacksonian America, 1815–1846* (New York: Oxford University Press, 1991), 30, 31, 33. For the connection between reform groups and religion, see Lawrence J. Friedman, *Gregarious Saints: Self and Community in American Abolitionism 1830–1870* (Cambridge: Cambridge University Press, 1982); Paul Goodman, *Toward a Christian Republic: Antimasonry and the Great Transition in New England, 1826–1836* (New York: Oxford University Press, 1988), 34–53; John F. C. Harrison, *Quest for a New Moral World: Robert Owen and the Owenites in Britain and America* (New York: Charles Scribners' Sons, 1969), 100; and Carl J. Guarneri, *The Utopian Alternative: Fourierism in Nineteenth-Century America* (Ithaca, NY: Cornell University Press, 1991), 278–83, where Guarneri documents the intriguingly sectarian Socialist Church that developed among the otherwise secular Fourierists.

104. See Robert E. Shalhope, "Toward a Republican Synthesis: The Emergence of an Understanding of Republicanism in American Historiography" *William & Mary Quarterly* 29, no. 1 (Jan. 1970): 49–80, and Steven J. Ross, "The Transformation of Republican Ideology," *Journal of the New Republic* 10, no. 3 (Autumn 1990): 323–30.

105. See Kenneth H. Winn, *Exiles in a Land of Liberty: Mormons in American, 1830–1846* (Chapel Hill: University of North Carolina Press, 1989), and Marvin S. Hill, *Quest for Refuge: The Mormon Flight from American Pluralism* (Salt Lake City: Signature Books, 1989).

106. See Lawrence Frederick Kohl, *The Politics of Individualism: Parties and the American Character in the Jacksonian Era* (New York: Oxford University Press, 1989), and Sellars, *The Market Revolution.*

Kohl argues that the Jacksonians aimed in politics "to thwart the rapid change, the new institutions, and the new type of human relations which modernity had brought" (22).

107. For a critique of the putative appeal of Mormonism to the "socially disinherited," see Steven C. Harper, "'Dictated by Christ': Joseph Smith and the Politics of Revelation," *Journal of the Early Republic* 26, no. 2 (Summer 2016): 275–304, quote at 279.
108. Ira Katznelson, "Working Class Formation and American Exceptionalism, Yet Again," in *American Exceptionalism? US Working-Class Formation in an International Context,* ed. Rick Halpern and Jonathan Morris (London: Macmillan Press, 1997), 51.
109. For the "higher law" interpretation, see Dallin H. Oaks and Marvin S. Hill, *Carthage Conspiracy: The Trial of the Accused Assassins of Joseph Smith* (Urbana: University of Illinois Press, 1975).
110. See Robert Baron and Nicholas R. Spitzer, eds., *Public Folklore* (Washington, DC: Smithsonian Institution Press, 1992).
111. Robert C. Toll, *Blacking Up: The Minstrel Show in Nineteenth-Century America* (New York: Oxford University Press, 1974), 5.
112. Daniel J. Elazar, *Cities of the Prairie: The Metropolitan Frontier and American Politics* (New York: Basic Books, 1970).
113. Daniel J. Elazar, with Rozann Rothman, Stephen Schechter, Maren Allan Stein, and Joseph Zikmund II, *Cities of the Prairie Revisited: The Closing of the Metropolitan Frontier* (Lincoln: University of Nebraska Press, 1986), 56.
114. See Robert E. Erikson, Gerald C. Wright, and John P. McIver, *Statehouse Democracy: Public Opinion and Policy in the American States* (Cambridge: Cambridge University Press, 1993), 150–76.
115. Elazar, *Cities of the Prairie,* 257.
116. Elazar, 259. For a succinct explanation of Elazar's theory, a review of its reception in the political science literature, and a test of its validity, see Todd Zoellick, "Daniel Elazar, Bogus or Brilliant? A Study of Political Culture across the American States," *Res Publica: Journal of Undergraduate Research* 5 (2000): 1–11.
117. Ford, *History of Illinois,* 58.
118. Eliza R. Steele, *A Summer Journey in the West* (1841; repr., New York: Arno Press, 1975), 151.
119. Steele, *A Summer Journey,* 152–53.
120. Steele, 178, 181.
121. See Perry Miller, *Errand into the Wilderness* (Cambridge, MA: Harvard University Press, 1956), and Sacvan Bercovitch, *The Puritan Origins of the American Self* (New Haven, CT: Yale University Press, 1975).

122. For the secularizing trend, see Richard L. Bushman, *From Puritan to Yankee: Character and the Social Order in Connecticut, 1690–1765* (Cambridge, MA: Harvard University Press, 1967).
123. Herman Melville, *White-Jacket* (1850; repr., New York: Quality Paperback Book Club, 1996), 189.
124. J. David Greenstone, *The Lincoln Persuasion: Remaking American Liberalism* (Princeton, NJ: Princeton University Press, 1993), 267–68, 254.
125. Doctrine and Covenants 28:14, 9.
126. Enos 1:20 (Book of Mormon). The online versions of the Mormons' sacred texts are the easiest to access, and thus are used here. While this runs the risk of anachronism, the changes made to the texts by succeeding generations of Mormons appear to be efforts at clarification and not expurgation.
127. Richard L. Bushman, *Joseph Smith and the Beginnings of Mormonism* (Urbana: University of Illinois Press, 1984), 116.
128. 2 Nephi 1:9 (Book of Mormon).
129. Baugh, "A Call to Arms," 7.
130. John Reynolds, *"The Balm of Gilead": An Inquiry into the Right of American Slavery* (Belleville, IL: printed by the author, 1860), 11.
131. Reynolds, *"The Balm of Gilead,"* 12–13.
132. Reynolds, 6.
133. Reynolds, 15.
134. Reynolds, 15.
135. Reynolds, 7.
136. For the origins of the term *white folks* in Illinois and its use in context, see Simeone, *Democracy and Slavery*, 6.
137. See George E. Marcus, Sandra L. Wood, and Elizabeth Theiss-Morse, "Linking Neuroscience to Political Intolerance and Political Judgment," *Politics and Life Sciences* 17, no. 1 (September 1998): 165–78.
138. For the impact of the post office as an institutional force, see Richard R. John, *Spreading the News: The American Postal System from Franklin to Morse* (Cambridge, MA: Harvard University Press, 1995).
139. For the debate over the early American state, see Richard R. John, "The State *Is* Back In: Now What?," *Journal of the Early Republic* 38, no. 1 (Spring 2018): 105–18.
140. Ariel Ron and Gautham Rao, "Introduction: Taking Stock of the State in Nineteenth-Century America," *Journal of the Early Republic* 38, no. 1 (Spring 2018): 61–66, at 61.
141. Stephen Skowronek, "Present at the Creation: The State in Early American Political History," *Journal of the Early Republic* 38, no. 1

(Spring 2018): 100. One set of institutions in the state-building debate that has come under increasing scrutiny for the punitive "kind and location" of its power is state law. See, for example, Marie Gottschalk, *The Prison and the Gallows: The Politics of Mass Incarceration in America* (Cambridge: Cambridge University Press, 2006). Gottschalk focuses on the rise of state prosecutors during the Early Republic. See also Laura F. Edwards, *The People and Their Peace: Legal Culture and the Transformation of Inequality in the Post-revolutionary South* (Chapel Hill: University of North Carolina Press, 2009). Edwards looks at the role of state legislatures in consolidating legal power over slavery in the South after the 1820s. Gary Gerstle argues the American founders committed the nation to liberal principles of limiting governmental power but left the states free to administer the "police power" under a republican popular sovereignty confined only by representative structures. Gary Gerstle, *Liberty and Coercion: The Paradox of American Government from the Founding to the Present* (Princeton, NJ: Princeton University Press, 2015). The national parties and the federal state in large part ignored the Mormons, a luxury unavailable to governing outposts in Ohio, Missouri, and Illinois.

142. David Waldsteicher, *Slavery's Constitution: From Revolution to Ratification* (New York: Hill & Wang, 2010).
143. Michael Witgen, "Seeing Red: Race, Citizenship, and Indigeneity in the Old Northwest," *Journal of the Early Republic* 38, no. 4 (Winter 2018): 582, 583.
144. Max Weber, *Economy and Society: An Outline of Interpretive Sociology*, ed. Guenther Roth and Claus Wittich (New York: Bedminster Press, 1968), 2:938.

CHAPTER 2: JOSEPH SMITH AND THE NEW POLITICS OF BELIEF

1. R. F. Atkinson, *Knowledge and Explanation in History* (Ithaca, NY: Cornell University Press, 1978), 26.
2. Joseph Smith History, vol. A-1, pp. 1–2, The Joseph Smith Papers, https://www.josephsmithpapers.org/paper-summary/history-1838-1856-volume-a-1-23-december-1805-30-august-1834/1.
3. See Marvin S. Hill, *Quest for Refuge: The Mormon Flight from American Pluralism* (Salt Lake City: Signature Books, 1989).
4. Smith's 1826 deposition given before a justice of the peace on the charge of being a "disorderly person and imposter" in Chenango County, New York, is quoted in Fawn Brodie, *No Man Knows*

My History: The Life of Joseph Smith, 2nd ed. (New York: Vintage Books, 1971), 427.

5. Emily M. Austin, *Mormonism; Or, Life among the Mormons* (1882; repr., New York: Arno Press, 1971), 30.
6. Quoted in Brodie, *No Man Knows My History,* 35.
7. See the letter printed in the *Times and Seasons,* March 1, 1842; for Emma Smith's comments, see the story as related in Linda King Newell and Valeen Tippetts Avery, *Mormon Enigma: Emma Hale Smith: Prophet's Wife, "Elect Lady," Polygamy's Foe, 1804–1879* (Garden City, NY: Doubleday, 1984), 21.
8. As quoted from her "Last Testimony," in Newell and Avery, 26.
9. 1 Nephi 1:1–2, 13 (Book of Mormon).
10. Enos 1:20–21 (Book of Mormon).
11. 3 Nephi 11:8 (Book of Mormon). It perhaps should be noted that in the account Christ's visitation does create peace and unity for a couple hundred years.
12. Richard L. Bushman, *Joseph Smith: Rough Stone Rolling* (New York: Vintage Books, 2005), 130.
13. Doctrine and Covenants 27:5; 33:8.
14. Doctrine and Covenants 33:3; 31:7; 33:2.
15. *Times and Seasons,* March 1, 1842, 707–8.
16. This idea was not unprecedented because, as Brodie and others have pointed out, there were many contemporary theories that speculated about the Indian burial mounds and placed them among ancient civilizations, including biblical ones. See Brodie, *No Man Knows My History,* 71.
17. *Times and Seasons,* March 5, 1840, 68.
18. Bushman, *Rough Stone Rolling,* 58.
19. Brodie, *No Man Knows My History,* 54, 80.
20. Eudocia Baldwin March, Douglas L. Wilson, and Rodney O. Davis, "Mormons in Hancock County: A Reminiscence," *Journal of the Illinois State Historical Society* 64 (Spring 1971): 22–65, quote at 38; emphasis in original. For the opening of Smith's house as the "Nauvoo Mansion," see Robert Bruce Flanders, *Nauvoo: Kingdom on the Mississippi* (Urbana: University of Illinois Press, 1965), 190.
21. *Warsaw Messenger,* November 15, 1843.
22. Henry Caswell, *The City of the Mormons; or Three Days at Nauvoo* (London: J. G. F. and J. Rivington, 1842), 36 and preface.
23. Caswell, *The City of the Mormons,* 44.
24. *Times and Seasons,* October 15, 1843.

25. For the idea of essential contested concepts, see W. B. Gallie, "Essentially Contested Concepts," *Proceedings of the Aristotelian Society* 56 (1955–56): 167–98.
26. See "Notes on the State of Virginia," in *The Portable Thomas Jefferson,* ed. Merrill D. Peterson (New York: Penguin Books, 1975), 210.
27. John Stuart Mill, *On Liberty and Other Essays,* ed. John Gray (Oxford: Oxford University Press, 1991), 14.
28. Mill, *On Liberty and Other Essays,* 62–63; Brian Barry, *Political Argument: A Reissue with a New Introduction* (Berkeley: University of California Press, 1990), 88, suggests "privately-oriented" and "publicly-oriented" interests for this distinction.
29. Thomas Hobbes, *Leviathan with Selected Variants from the Latin Edition of 1668,* ed. and intro. Edwin Curley (Indianapolis: Hackett Publishing, 1994), 113.
30. John Locke, *The Second Treatise on Government and A Letter Concerning Toleration* (Mineola, NY: Dover Publications, 2002), 115–19, quote at 115.
31. The respect for belief continues in our own day. For example, Adam Laats and Harvey Siegel use the distinction between belief and knowledge to structure their case for balancing evolution and creationism. They argue that "the goal of evolution education should be to get students to *know* and *understand* it, leaving belief to fall where it may." *Teaching Evolution in a Creation Nation* (Chicago: University of Chicago Press, 2016), 73.
32. Kant thus pioneered today's "liberal," or a left-leaning person, as opposed to the conservative or classical liberal—that is, a right-leaning person.
33. Immanuel Kant, "What Is Enlightenment?," in *The Philosophy of Kant* (New York: The Modern Library, 1949), 132, 138.
34. William James, *The Varieties of Religious Experience* (New York: Collier Books, 1902), 378.
35. For more on incompletely theorized agreements, see Cass R. Sunstein, "Incompletely Theorized Agreements in Constitutional Law" (working paper, University of Chicago Public Law and Theory, number 147, 2007).
36. See Stephen Holmes, "Gag Rules or the Politics of Omission," in *Constitutionalism and Democracy,* ed. Jon Elster and Rune Slagstad (Cambridge: Cambridge University Press, 1988), 23–24.
37. *The Collected Works of Abraham Lincoln,* ed. Roy P. Basler (New Brunswick, NJ: Rutgers University Press, 1953), 1:272, 274, 275.

38. For the wings of the Whig Party, see Daniel Walker Howe, *The Political Culture of the American Whigs* (Chicago: University of Chicago Press, 1979); *The Collected Works of Abraham Lincoln,* 1:275, 277.
39. *The Collected Works of Abraham Lincoln,* 1:278.
40. See Holmes's dissent in the *Schenck* case (1919).
41. Jean-Jacques Rousseau, *Of the Social Contract,* trans. Donald A. Cress, intro. Peter Gay (Indianapolis: Hackett Publishing, 1988), 30.
42. Benjamin Franklin, quoted in Louis Hartz, *The Liberal Tradition in America* (New York: Harcourt, Brace & World, 1955), 44.
43. For Franklin's theory that the British Parliament was limited in its sovereign powers over those living in British territory, see Carl Van Doren, *Benjamin Franklin* (1938; repr., New York: Penguin Books, 1991), 377.
44. This shaped the politics of belief in that people not deemed members had little legal authority in the US, though laws like the Alien Tort Statute of 1789 did recognize the standing of international actors in making property claims before US courts.
45. G. W. F. Hegel, *Elements of the Philosophy of Right,* ed. Allen W. Wood, trans. H. B. Nisbit (1821; repr., Cambridge: Cambridge University Press, 1991), 80–81, 102–3.
46. "Second Inaugural Address," *The Portable Thomas Jefferson,* 318.
47. For the playing out of this general pattern, see Peter Onuf, *Statehood and Union: A History of the Northwest Ordinance* (Bloomington: Indiana University Press, 1987).
48. *Sangamo Journal,* November 11, 1842.
49. Scott Larson, "'Indescribable Being': Theological Performances of Genderlessness in the Society of the Publick Universal Friend, 1776–1819," *Early American Studies* 12, no. 3 (Fall 2014): 576–600, quote at 577.
50. Brodie, *No Man Knows My History,* 83.
51. Paul E. Johnson and Sean Wilentz, *The Kingdom of Matthias: A Story of Sex and Salvation in 19th-Century America* (New York: Oxford University Press, 1994), 6.
52. Johnson and Wilentz, *The Kingdom of Matthias,* 173.
53. Leonard J. Arrington and Davis Bitton, *The Mormon Experience: A History of the Latter-day Saints,* 2nd ed. (Urbana: University of Illinois Press, 1992), 73.
54. Bushman, *Rough Stone Rolling,* 518.
55. *A Narrative of the Adventures and Experience of Joseph H. Jackson in Nauvoo* (Warsaw, IL, 1844), 5–7.

56. Bushman, *Rough Stone Rolling,* 529; the details on the murder attempt are at 538–39.
57. Harold Bloom, *The American Religion: The Emergence of a Post-Christian Nation* (New York: Simon & Schuster, 1992).
58. Wallace Stegner, *Mormon Country,* intro. Richard W. Etulain (1942; repr., Lincoln: University of Nebraska Press, 2003), 131.
59. Craig Koslofsky pursues the idea of using cultural resonance tied to changes in everyday life to ground explanations of the appeal of the Protestant Reformation. "Explaining Change," in *The Oxford Handbook of the Protestant Reformations,* ed. Ulinka Rublack (Oxford: Oxford University Press, 2017), 585–600.
60. For the distinction between first- and second-order volitions, see Harry G. Frankfurt, "Freedom of the Will and the Concept of a Person," *Journal of Philosophy* 68, no. 1 (1971): 5–20.
61. Emily R. Gill, *Becoming Free: Autonomy and Diversity in the Liberal Polity* (Lawrence: University of Kansas Press, 2001), 23.
62. Thomas Ford, *A History of Illinois: From Its Commencement as a State in 1818 to 1847,* ed. Rodney O. Davis (1854; repr., Urbana: University of Illinois Press, 1995), 178.
63. Brodie, *No Man Knows My History,* 77.
64. Ford, *A History of Illinois,* 178.
65. Joseph Smith History, vol. D-1, p. 1432, The Joseph Smith Papers, https://www.josephsmithpapers.org/paper-summary/history-1838-1856-volume-d-1-1-august-1842-1-july-1843/75.
66. Quoted in William Muldur and A. Russell Mortensen, eds., *Among the Mormons: Historical Accounts by Contemporary Observers* (New York: Knopf, 1958), 10.
67. As Charles S. Peirce noted in the context of religious claims in general, even a one in twenty-five chance is confirmed about 2 percent of the time. On the evidence Ford compiled, he would have to concede that Smith's claims might have been true. In that case, following Peirce, we might have said "that he acted in accordance with reason, but that would only show that his reason was absolutely worthless." *Essays in the Philosophy of Science,* ed. Vincent Thomas (Indianapolis: Bobbs-Merrill, 1957), 64. Peirce's conclusion was that probabilistic truths must be acknowledged to be imbedded in a community of observers, and only within this larger set were they rational and fully "justified." See Hilary Putnam, *The Many Faces of Realism* (LaSalle, IL: Open Court, 1987), 53–56, for the role critical communal interpretation plays in justifying truth claims.
68. For the problems of indeterminacy when "rationality fails," see Jon Elster, *Solomonic Judgements: Studies in the Limitations of*

Rationality (Cambridge: Cambridge University Press, 1989), 1–35.

69. Arrington and Bitton, *The Mormon Experience*, 15.
70. Bushman, *Rough Stone Rolling*, 58.
71. Terryl L. Givens argues that "the Book of Mormon may usefully be compared to the Old Testament, insofar as both purport to be sacred narratives beginning as family history that expand into tribal and national history." *The Book of Mormon: A Very Short Introduction* (Oxford: Oxford University Press, 2009), 90.
72. Locke, *The Second Treatise*, 120.
73. See Rousseau, *Of the Social Contract*, 102.
74. Ernest Gellner, *Conditions of Liberty: Civil Society and Its Rivals* (New York: Penguin Press, 1994), 187–88.
75. Rousseau, *Of the Social Contract*, 41.
76. Brodie, *No Man Knows My History*, 404.
77. Thomas Ford, *Message from the Governor, in Relation to the Disturbances in Hancock County* (Springfield, IL: Walters & Weber, 1844).
78. Brodie, *No Man Knows My History*, 84–85.
79. Ford, *A History of Illinois*, 249.
80. For these failing prophecies, see Brodie, *No Man Knows My History*, 146, 199.
81. See R. G. Collingwood, *The Idea of History* (London: Oxford University Press, 1956), 213, where Collingwood claims that historians investigate "not mere events but . . . actions." He later draws out the implications of this idealist view as it applies to the historical study of religion: "If the reason it is hard for a man to cross the mountains is because he is frightened of the devils in them, it is folly for the historian, preaching at him from across a gulf of centuries, to say 'This is sheer superstition. There are no devils at all. Face facts, and realize that there are no dangers in the mountains except rocks and water and snow, wolves perhaps, and bad men perhaps, but no devils.' The historian says that these are the facts because that is the way in which he has been taught to think. But the devil-fearer says that the presence of the devils is a fact, because that is the way he has been taught to think. The historian thinks it is a wrong way; but wrong ways of thinking are just as much historical facts as right ones, and no less than they, determine the situations (always a thought-situation) in which the man who shares them is placed" (318). What Collingwood says about the historian as claim investigator applies with equal weight to Ford the governor as claim investigator.

82. Brigham Young, diary, quoted in Lawrence Foster, *Religion and Sexuality: The Shakers, the Mormons, and the Oneida Community* (1981; repr., Urbana: University of Illinois Press, 1984), 123.
83. Ford, *A History of Illinois*, 229.
84. Such, in effect, is the claim made by twentieth-century skeptics such as Michael Shermer. He explains the credulity of UFO believer Joe Firmage on the grounds that he was raised Mormon and is open to such beliefs since "Joseph Smith had a close encounter of a third kind." *Why People Believe Weird Things: Pseudoscience, Superstition, and Other Confusions of Our Time* (New York: Henry Holt, 1997), 308.
85. As quoted in R. Lawrence Moore, *Religious Outsiders and the Making of Americans* (New York: Oxford University Press, 1986), 25.
86. See the story "Burial of the Mormon Girl," *The Wasp*, April 16, 1842.
87. See *Times and Seasons*, January 1, 1842, 642–43.
88. For Ballance's story, see *The History of Peoria, Illinois* (Peoria, NC: Nason, 1870), 13–16. Ballance, as a settler on lands previously occupied by Native tribes, had an interest in denying any claim that Native Americans ever had "a great civilization." He thought the claim that Native peoples had built burial mounds "a delusion" shared by men addicted to "marvelousness." Such were not rational, as he was. He summed up these individuals as follows: "Men fond of the marvelous are averse to scanning evidence" (16).
89. See Campbell's quotation in *The Mormon Experience*, 31–32.
90. Givens, *The Book of Mormon: A Very Short Introduction*, 116.
91. Brodie, *No Man Knows My History*, 85, 25, 49.
92. See the affidavit Brotherton wrote upon arriving in St. Louis for John C. Bennett's exposé in *Cultures in Conflict: A Documentary History of the Mormon War in Illinois*, ed. John E. Hallwas and Roger D. Launius (Logan: Utah State University Press, 1995), 122–25.
93. Foster, *Religion and Sexuality*, 126.
94. *Belleville Advocate*, July 25, 1842.
95. *Times and Seasons*, January 1, 1842, 651; emphasis in original.
96. Brodie, *No Man Knows My History*, 272.
97. Simeon Francis, *Sangamo Journal*, June 3, 1842.
98. The Aaronic priesthood and other Old Testament parallels are explored by Jan Shipps, *Mormonism: The Story of a New Religious Tradition* (Urbana: University of Illinois Press, 1985).
99. The history of the Nauvoo Lodge is outlined in Mervin B. Hogan, *Mormonism and Freemasonry: The Illinois Episode* (Salt Lake City: Third Century Graphics, 1977).

100. For the state legislative history, beginning with the militia act of 1819 through the 1837 "Act Encouraging Volunteer Companies," see Richard E. Bennett, Susan Easton Black, and Donald Q. Cannon, *The Nauvoo Legion in Illinois: A History of the Mormon Militia, 1841–1846* (Norman, OK: Arthur H. Clark, 2010), 41–46.
101. Klaus J. Hansen, *Quest for Empire: The Political Kingdom of God and the Council of Fifty in Mormon History* (East Lansing: Michigan State University Press, 1967), 7.
102. For a typical harangue on the Mormon commitment to the freedoms of conscience and the press, and their violation by other Americans (in this case the Missourians), see William Smith's editorial in *The Wasp,* April 16, 1842.
103. See *Times and Seasons,* July 15, 1842, 855–57.
104. Hansen, *Quest for Empire,* 75.
105. Joseph Smith, *History of the Church of Jesus Christ of Latter-day Saints,* intro. and notes by B. H. Roberts, 2nd ed. (Salt Lake City: Deseret Book, 1969), 6:xxxiv.
106. Gordon B. Hinckley, *Truth Restored: A Short History of The Church of Jesus Christ of Latter-day Saints* (Salt Lake City: The Church of Jesus Christ of Latter-day Saints, 1979), 72.
107. Bushman, *Rough Stone Rolling,* 658n48.
108. Bushman, 519.
109. Bushman, 520.
110. It is clear that the wolf hunt was a preexisting tradition which in Hancock was being refitted as part of the anti-Mormon civic action repertoire. See the casual reference to a "Wolf Hunt on the Prairie" in the *Iowa Patriot* of June 25, 1839. Also, on August 1, 1839, in the same paper readers were reminded of the wolf hunt to which all were invited (including candidates for the upcoming elections) and which promised to be "first-rate entertainment."
111. For an argument that sketches a similar thesis in broad outline, see Klaus Hansen, "The Political Kingdom of God as a Cause for Mormon-Gentile Conflict," *Brigham Young University Studies* 2, no. 2 (1960): 241–60.
112. Will Kymlicka and Wayne Norman, "Return of the Citizen: A Survey of Recent Work on Citizenship Theory," in *Theorizing Citizenship,* ed. Ronald Beiner (Albany: State University of New York Press, 1995), 283–322, quote at 284.
113. Late in his career and during the 1860 race for the US presidency, Douglas made good on his promise to provide a history of this tradition of local control over practices like slavery. See "The Dividing Line between Federal and Local Authority: Popular

Sovereignty in the Territories," in *Harpers' New Monthly Magazine,* September 1860, 517–37.

CHAPTER 3: SAINTS AND SUCKERS IN THE SETTLER STATE

1. *Voice of the People,* July 27, 1838, Newberry Library, Chicago.
2. *Voice of the People,* July 27, 1838.
3. Theodore Calvin Pease, ed., *Illinois Election Returns, 1818–1848* (Springfield: Illinois State Historical Library, 1923), 111–13.
4. *Voice of the People,* July 27, 1838.
5. *Sangamo Journal,* April 2, 1841.
6. Thomas Ford, *A History of Illinois: From Its Commencement as a State in 1818 to 1847,* ed. Rodney O. Davis (1854; repr., Urbana: University of Illinois Press, 1995), 158.
7. Stephen Skowronek, *Building a New American State: The Expansion of National Administrative Capacities, 1877–1920* (Cambridge: Cambridge University Press, 1982), 3.
8. There is an enormous literature on this point. The approach taken here is that all states, even liberal states, must to some extent reflect societal conceptions of the good. My aim is to move the debate forward by gaining some empirical purchase on how regimes structure the way liberal settler states institutionalize societal conceptions of the good.
9. John Rawls, *A Theory of Justice* (Cambridge, MA: Harvard University Press, 1971).
10. Vernon Van Dyke, "The Individual, the State, and Ethnic Communities in Political Theory," *World Politics* 29, no. 3 (April 1977): 343–69, quote at 343; Rogers M. Smith, *Stories of Peoplehood: The Politics and Morals of Political Membership* (Cambridge: Cambridge University Press, 2003), 136. For a general critique, see Michael Sandel, *Liberalism and the Limits of Justice* (Cambridge: Cambridge University Press, 1982).
11. As Michael Walzer notes, "In a world of particular cultures, competing conceptions of the good, scarce resources, elusive and expansive needs, there isn't going to be a single formula, universally applicable." *Spheres of Justice: A Defense of Pluralism and Equality* (New York: Basic Books, 1983), 79.
12. See Rogers M. Smith, *Civic Ideals: Conflicting Visions of Citizenship in U.S. History* (New Haven, CT: Yale University Press, 1997); Smith, *Stories of Peoplehood;* Rogers M. Smith and Desmond King, "Racial Orders in American Political Development," *American Political Science Review* 99 (February 2005): 75–92; Desmond King and Rogers M. Smith, *Still a House Divided: Race*

and Politics in Obama's America (Princeton, NJ: Princeton University Press, 2011).

13. Will Kymlicka, *Multicultural Citizenship: A Liberal Theory of Minority Rights* (Oxford: Oxford University Press, 1995), 76.
14. Aristotle, *The Politics*, trans. Carnes Lord (Chicago: University of Chicago Press, 1984), book 3, chapters 6 and 7, pp. 94–96.
15. E. E. Schattschneider, *The Semi-Sovereign People: A Realist View of Democracy in America* (Fort Worth, TX: Holt, Reinhart, and Winston, 1975), 30.
16. For the concept of status quo neutrality, see Cass R. Sunstein, *The Partial Constitution* (Cambridge, MA: Harvard University Press, 1993), 3–7, 68–92.
17. For the concept of party duopoly and the "duopoly mechanism," see Wesley Hiers, "Party Matters: Racial Closure in the Nineteenth-Century United States," *Social Science History* 37, no. 2 (Summer 2013): 255–308, especially 261.
18. Gianfranco Poggi, *The Development of the Modern State: A Sociological Introduction* (Stanford, CA: Stanford University Press, 1978), 86–116.
19. Skowronek, *Building a New American State*, 3, cites H. G. Wells using the phrase "sense of the state" in Wells, *The Future in America: A Search after Realities* (1906; repr., New York: Arno Press, 1974). For the debate over the nature of American statelessness among American historians, see William J. Novak, "The Myth of the 'Weak' American State," *American Historical Review* 113, no. 3 (June 2008): 752–72, and the follow-on commentary in vol. 115, no. 3 (June 2010).
20. Poggi, *The Development of the Modern State*, 97.
21. For an assessment of this reception, see Susan Easton Black and Richard E. Bennett, eds., *A City of Refuge: Quincy, Illinois* (Salt Lake City: Millennial Press, 2000).
22. Desmond King, *In the Name of Liberalism: Illiberal Social Policy in the United States and Britain* (Oxford: Oxford University Press, 1999), 13.
23. Emil Joseph Verlie, ed., *Illinois Constitutions* (Springfield: Illinois State Historical Library, 1919), 440, 436.
24. For the 1812 militia numbers, see John K. Mahon, *The War of 1812* (New York: Da Capo, 1991), 100n. For the 1831 call, see Evarts Boutell Greene and Clarence Walworth Alvord, eds., *Governors' Letter-Books, 1818–1834* (Springfield: Illinois State Historical Library, 1909), 165–74; see also Frank E. Stevens, *The Black Hawk War* (Chicago: published by the author, 1903). Reynolds asked

for 700 men in 1831, but as Stevens notes: "Men left their plows, and, with little or no preparation, hastened to Beardstown, where twice the number of volunteers asked assembled. In bringing this expedition about, with as little hardship as possible, Governor Reynolds summoned none south of St. Clair or east of Sangamon counties." On April 16, 1832, Reynolds issued a call "To the Militia of the North-Western Section of the State," and 1,694 joined. See Cecil D. Eby, *"That Disgraceful Affair," the Black Hawk War* (New York: W. W. Norton, 1973), 97, 109.

25. Jill Norgren, *The Cherokee Cases: The Confrontation of Law and Politics* (New York: McGraw-Hill, 1996).
26. See Frank R. Grover, "Indian Treaties Affecting Lands in the Present State of Illinois," *Journal of the Illinois State Historical Society* 8 (October 1915): 379–419, and Theodore Calvin Pease, *The Frontier State 1818–1848* (1918; repr., Urbana: University of Illinois Press, 1987), 151–57.
27. See the address in the *Illinois Advocate,* June 11, 1831.
28. Nancy Fraser and Linda Gordon, "A Genealogy of 'Dependency': Tracing a Keyword of the US Welfare State," in *Fortunes of Feminism: From State-Managed Capitalism to Neoliberal Crisis,* ed. Nancy Fraser (London: Verso, 2013), 83–110, quote at 92–93.
29. See the speech of Melancton Smith of June 20, 1788, in David Wootton, ed., *The Essential Federalist and Anti-Federalist Papers* (Indianapolis: Hackett Publishing, 2003), 46.
30. The phrase *independent producer* was not commonly used at the time, but the meaning of the concept to simultaneously include and exclude is noted by Jan Lewis in her study of southern political ideology. She notes that John C. Calhoun insisted that "independent producers have easy access to the market" while otherwise making a strong republican case for slavery, making it "insulated from the language of liberalism." "The Problem of Slavery in Southern Political Discourse," in *Devising Liberty,* ed. David Thomas Konig (Stanford, CA: Stanford University Press, 1993), 265, 293, 297.
31. C. B. Macpherson, *Democratic Theory: Essays in Retrieval* (Oxford: Clarendon Press, 1973), vii, 163. He argues that this "preliberal democratic" egalitarianism is attractive to twentieth-century revolutionaries because "it upholds their one-party or dominant-party state, and validates their authority as leaders of it" (163).
32. See Michael Thompson, Richard Ellis, and Aaron Wildavsky, *Cultural Theory* (Boulder, CO: Westview Press, 1990). The theory was first developed by Mary Douglas. For an early rendition, see

Natural Symbols: Explorations in Cosmology (New York: Pantheon Books, 1970).

33. C. B. Macpherson, *The Real World of Democracy* (Oxford: Clarendon Press, 1966), 13.
34. George M. Fredrickson, *White Supremacy: A Comparative Study in American and South African History* (Oxford: Oxford University Press, 1981), 154–55.
35. On Jacksonian egalitarianism's vertical equality, see James Simeone, "Reassessing Jacksonian Political Culture: William Leggett's Egalitarianism," *American Political Thought* 4, no. 3 (Summer 2015): 364.
36. See James Simeone, *Democracy and Slavery in Frontier Illinois: The Bottomland Republic* (DeKalb: Northern Illinois University Press, 2000), 6, 16–38.
37. Leonard L. Richards, *"Gentlemen of Property and Standing": Anti-abolition Mobs in Jacksonian America* (London: Oxford University Press, 1970).
38. Verlie, *Illinois Constitutions,* 430, 440.
39. Skowronek, *Building a New American State,* 24–31.
40. Pease, *The Frontier State,* 36–37.
41. "Politics as a Vocation," *From Max Weber: Essays in Sociology,* ed. H. H. Gerth and C. Wright Mills (New York: Oxford University Press, 1946), 78.
42. Grant McConnell, *Private Power and American Democracy* (New York: Vintage, 1966), 51–90.
43. McConnell, 73. McConnell's original assessment of the agrarian local-control ideology appeared in *The Decline of Agrarian Democracy* (Berkeley: University of California Press, 1952).
44. Hannah Arendt, *On Revolution* (New York: Penguin Books, 1963), 251.
45. Ford, *A History of Illinois,* 302–3.
46. For the republican dancing, see Karl Marx, *The Eighteenth Brumaire of Louis Bonaparte* (1852; repr., New York: International Publishers, 1963), 45, 66. Marx notes in *The Communist Manifesto* that "the executive of the modern state is but a committee for managing the common affairs of the whole bourgeoisie." See Marx and Engels, "Manifesto of the Communist Party," in *The Marx-Engels Reader,* ed. Robert Tucker, 2nd ed. (New York: W. W. Norton, 1978), 469–500, quote at 475.
47. William A. Galston, *Liberal Purposes: Goods, Virtues, and Diversity in the Liberal State* (Cambridge: Cambridge University Press, 1991), 304.

48. The Illinois legislature passed a modest property tax in 1819 to fund its basic operations. But the lion's share of its revenue came from taxes on nonresident landowners, land sales, and the leased saline operations in Gallatin County. Its limited income set severe limits on the state's capacity to deliver services during the 1830s and 1840s. The best summary of the state's taxing power and its finances during this period is still Pease, *The Frontier State*, 52–69.
49. *Journal of the Senate of the Eight General Assembly of the State of Illinois* (Vandalia, IL: Greiner & Sherman, 1833), 41.
50. James Madison, *The Federalist Papers*, ed. Clinton Rossiter (1788; repr., New York: Penguin Books, 1961), 77–84.
51. Wootton, *The Essential Federalist and Anti-Federalist Papers*, 49, 47.
52. G. W. F. Hegel, *Elements of the Philosophy of Right*, ed. Allen W. Wood, trans. H. B. Nisbit (1821; repr., Cambridge: Cambridge University Press, 1991), 81.
53. See Wood's introduction to Hegel's *Elements*, xix. Misrecognition is emphasized in a contemporary context by Melissa V. Harris-Perry, see *Sister Citizen: Shame, Stereotypes, and Black Women in America* (New Haven, CT: Yale University Press, 2011).
54. For the details of Smith's life in New York, Ohio, and Missouri, see Fawn Brodie, *No Man Knows My History: The Life of Joseph Smith*, 2nd ed. (New York: Vintage Books, 1995).
55. As quoted in Bray Hammond, *Banks and Politics in America: From the Revolution to the Civil War* (Princeton, NJ: Princeton University Press, 1957), 430.
56. See Hammond, *Banks and Politics in America*, 438–45.
57. On this point, see Peter Temin, *The Jacksonian Economy* (New York: W. W. Norton, 1969), 64–78.
58. Temin, *The Jacksonian Economy*, 82. Temin uses species import and distribution data as evidence to support his claims.
59. *Chicago American*, November 18, 1836; emphasis in original.
60. Information on lot sales come from the *Report of the Board of Canal Commissioners of 1836*, as reported in James William Putnam, *The Illinois and Michigan Canal: A Study in Economic History* (Chicago: University of Chicago Press, 1918), 41.
61. For the attempt by Van Buren's Department of the Treasury to regulate the pet deposit banks in the interest of fiscal control, see John M. McFaul, *The Politics of Jacksonian Finance* (Ithaca, NY: Cornell University Press, 1972).
62. See Reginald Charles McGrane, *The Panic of 1837: Some Financial Problems of the Jacksonian Era* (1924; repr., Chicago: University

of Chicago Press, 1965), 209–36, for a summary of the bill's legislative history.

63. For the first option, see McGrane, *The Panic of 1837*, and Hammond, *Banks and Politics in America;* for the second option, see Temin, *The Jacksonian Economy.*
64. Washington Hitt to Daniel Hitt, May 7, 1840, Daniel Hitt Papers, Abraham Lincoln Presidential Library, Springfield, Illinois.
65. Daniel Webster, quoted in *Voice of the People,* July 27, 1838.
66. See the *Western World,* July 1, 1840. The Whigs did well in the 1838 elections, and in the run-up to the 1840 contest for president, they saw the opportunity to turn the tables on the Jacksonians with their own Indian-fighting general, William Henry Harrison. The flavor of the rhetoric from this "hard cider and log cabin" campaign is found in a report from Washington by a *Sangamo Journal* correspondent dated December 29, 1838. It complained that Van Buren was attempting "to carry on all the operations of government without the aid of Congress." The author hoped that Congress could fight back and "arrest the corrupt practices of the executive departments." If not, "the people . . . [would] be made to contribute to the grandeur and pomp and luxury of their sub-treasurer masters."
67. See Gerald Leonard, *The Invention of Party Politics: Federalism, Popular Sovereignty, and Constitutional Development in Jacksonian Illinois* (Chapel Hill: University of North Carolina Press, 2002).
68. Ford, *A History of Illinois,* 141.
69. Ford, 116.
70. Quoted in McGrane, *The Panic of 1837,* 233.
71. See the *Sangamo Journal* editorial cited in Leonard, *The Invention of Party Politics,* 109.
72. See Duncan's second address to the General Assembly at Vandalia on December 7, 1835, reported in the *Northwestern Gazetteer and Galena Advertiser,* December 26, 1835.
73. For Kane's role, see James Simeone, "The 1830 Contest for Governor and the Politics of Resentment," *Journal of the Illinois State Historical Society* 102, no. 3/4 (Fall-Winter 2009): 286.
74. See the poll books held at the Abraham Lincoln Presidential Library.
75. For "slaughter pen," see the *Sangamo Journal,* April 2, 1841. The phrase was picked up and used by many others; for example, see Duncan's 1834 letter in the *Illinois Statesman,* April 29, 1843.
76. *Illinois State Register,* February 21, 1840.
77. See Charles Manfred Thompson, "Attitude of the Western Whigs toward the Convention System," *Proceedings of the Mississippi*

Valley Historical Association 5 (1912): 167–89, quote at 174. For the committee report, see the *Alton Telegraph*, March 25, 1843.

78. See Leonard, *The Invention of Party Politics*, 246–49, 256–66. Richard P. McCormick states that "the Whigs in Illinois never succeeded in developing an effective organization." *The Second American Party System: Party Formation in the Jacksonian Era* (Chapel Hill: University of North Carolina Press, 1966), 285–86.
79. See Richard Jensen, *The Winning of the Midwest: Social and Political Conflict, 1888–1896* (Chicago: University of Chicago Press, 1971), 178–208.
80. *Quincy Argus*, April 27, 1839.
81. *Warsaw Signal*, May 19, 1841.
82. *Northwestern Gazetteer and Galena Advertiser*, August 8, 1835.
83. *Peoria Register and North-Western Gazetteer*, November 10, 1835.
84. See the Joseph Duncan letter of March 23, 1843, published in the *Illinois Statesman*, April 29, 1843.
85. Ford, *A History of Illinois*, 114.
86. After a struggle with T. W. Smith, the state bank became an almost exclusive Whig venture whose purpose was to divert the lead trade of Galena from St. Louis to Alton. See Ford, 118–21.
87. See Paul M. Angle, ed., *Herndon's Life of Lincoln: The History and Personal Recollections of Abraham Lincoln as Originally Written by William H. Herndon and Jesse W. Weik* (1888; repr., Greenwich, CT: Fawcett Publications, 1961), 163.
88. Lincoln's address to the Springfield Washington Temperance Society was published in the *Sangamo Journal*, March 25, 1842.
89. Ford, *A History of Illinois*, 169.
90. See Mancur Olson Jr., *The Logic of Collective Action: Public Goods and the Theory of Groups* (Cambridge, MA: Harvard University Press, 1965).
91. See the summary of this trial in Alice Louise Brumbaugh, "The Regulator Movement in Illinois" (master's thesis, University of Illinois, 1927), 23–24.
92. Quoted in Christopher Waldrep, "Word and Deed: The Language of Lynching, 1820–1953," in *Lethal Imagination: Violence and Brutality in American History*, ed. Michael A. Bellesiles (New York: New York University Press, 1999), 228–58, quote at 232.
93. The vote was 278 for Ford and 479 for Duncan, his opponent. See *Illinois Election Returns, 1818–1847*, 127. This was Ford's home county at the time. Ford's opposition from "the lynching faction" in northern Illinois is noted by John Wentworth, *Chicago Democrat*, August 10, 1842.

94. For Lincoln's definition, see Lincoln's speech at Columbus, Ohio, on September 16, 1859, in *The Collected Works of Abraham Lincoln,* ed. Roy P. Basler (New Brunswick, NJ: Rutgers University Press, 1959), 3:405. For Douglas's view, see "The Dividing Line between Federal and Local Authority: Popular Sovereignty in the Territories," *Harpers' New Monthly Magazine,* September 1860, 517–37.
95. See the reports cited in Catharine Tobin, "The Lowly Muscular Digger: Irish Canal Workers in Nineteenth Century America" (PhD diss., University of Notre Dame, 1987), 129. Tobin cites an eye-witness account published in the *Boston Pilot,* July 13, 1839. See also Peter Way, *Common Labour: Workers and Digging of North American Canals: 1780–1860* (Cambridge: Cambridge University Press, 1993), 154. The LaSalle Mission Cemetery, an Irish Catholic cemetery located near the Illinois and Michigan Canal, was the burial place of many Irish diggers in that section of the canal. It was first used in 1838 and closed in 1857. While the community of LaSalle only numbered 200 people in 1850, Catholic church records indicate that 1,257 individuals were buried in the cemetery, and an archeological report in 2010 found 1,506 shaft graves. Personal communication with Bill Johnson, LaSalle County board member.
96. *Northwestern Gazetteer and Galena Advertiser,* June 27, 1835.
97. *Chicago American,* July 23, 1836.
98. Ford, *A History of Illinois,* 188.
99. *Sangamo Journal,* June 10, 1842.
100. Alexis de Tocqueville, *Democracy in America,* ed. J. P. Mayer, trans. George Lawrence (1836–39; repr., Garden City, NY: Doubleday, 1969), 668.
101. *Alton Telegraph and Democratic Review,* September 20, 1845.
102. See W. E. B. DuBois, *Black Reconstruction in America 1860–1880* (1935; repr., New York: Atheneum, 1979), 700.
103. *Belleville Advocate,* April 1, 1840.
104. *Sangamo Journal,* July 3, 1840.
105. Newhall, *Sketches of Iowa,* writing in August of 1840 mentions that "hundreds of buildings have sprung up, as if by magic, within the last twelve months in the city of this devoted people," 135.
106. For these charges, see, for example, *Fifty Years in Iowa: Being a Personal Reminiscence of J.M.D. Burrows, 1838–1888* (Davenport, IA: Glass and Company, 1888), 159: "From 1840–1845 this section of the West [Montrose, Iowa,] was infected with a desperate

gang of robbers, horse thieves, counterfeiters, and murderers, who kept the county in a constant state of alarm. Their headquarters were said to be at Nauvoo, among the Mormons, whence, from time to time, they issued forth on their expeditions of robbery and murder."

107. Robert H. Bates et al., eds., *Analytic Narratives* (Princeton, NJ: Princeton University Press, 1998), 4.
108. See "The Autobiography of Martin Van Buren," in *Annual Report of the American Historical Association for the Year 1981,* ed. John C. Fitzpatrick (Washington, DC: Government Printing Office, 1920), 2:137–40.
109. Political scientist Barry Weingast calls it the "balance rule" and argues that this institutional innovation, not the "liberal consensus" Louis Hartz emphasizes, explains American stability. As he puts it, "Political culture—the behavior of mass publics and elites—cannot be treated as indelible characteristics of the underlying electorate." in Bates et al., *Analytic Narratives,* 176.
110. See William Plumer Jr.'s letter of February 20, 1820, in Everett Somerville Brown, ed., *The Missouri Compromise and Presidential Politics, 1820–1825* (St. Louis: Missouri Historical Society, 1926), 11.
111. Ford, *A History of Illinois,* 190n. Ford's formulation bears a striking resemblance to the one used by Rogers M. Smith in *Stories of Peoplehood.*
112. Smith, 56–71.
113. See Richard E. Bennett, Susan Easton Black, and Donald Q. Cannon, *The Nauvoo Legion in Illinois: A History of the Mormon Militia, 1841–1846* (Norman, OK: Arthur H. Clark, 2010), 42.
114. Pease, *The Frontier State,* 158, 160; see also Bennett, Black, and Cannon, *The Nauvoo Legion in Illinois,* 41–46.
115. See census of 1845 in the *Illinois State Register,* May 15, 1846.
116. For Snyder as a Pennsylvania Dutch speaker, see Thomas J. McCormick, ed., *Memoirs of Gustave Koerner, 1809–1896* (Cedar Rapids, IA: Torch Press, 1909), 329; for his ties to the Germans in St. Clair, see John Francis Snyder, *Adam J. Snyder and His Period in Illinois History, 1817–1842* (Virginia, IL: E. Needham, 1906); for the election returns, see *Illinois Election Returns, 1818–1848,* 101.
117. On Carlin's parents, see Snyder, *Adam J. Snyder,* 241.
118. For the 1838 election returns, see *Illinois Election Returns, 1818–1848,* 111–12 (the Will Precinct was included in Cook in 1834).
119. On the precedent from other states, Ford laid out the reasoning plainly: "Citizenship alone was never construed in any State to

confer the elective franchise: there being many citizens in every state, some more and in others less, who were not allowed to vote. And it seemed to be a legitimate and unanswerable argument that if citizenship alone did not confer the right of voting, the want of it alone could not take it away." *A History of Illinois,* 147.

120. See Ford, 150. Snyder refers to "two Whigs, at Galena [who], agreed to an arranged case." *Adam J. Snyder,* 310. Ford's claim that the aliens who voted were "about 10,000 strong" may have been accurate, but a statewide estimate is harder to gauge than the three-county measure used here. *A History of Illinois,* 147.

121. After the vote, the *Sangamo Journal* bitterly noted that there was not one Whig in a state office under control of the Democrats. In a less partisan moment, President Andrew Jackson had appointed Abraham Lincoln postmaster at New Salem on May 7, 1833. See Harry E. Pratt, *Lincoln 1809–1839* (Springfield, IL: Abraham Lincoln Association, 1941), 25; for the fate of the "tender-foots," see Ford, *A History of Illinois,* 150.

122. On Smith's entrance into Springfield, see Brodie, *No Man Knows My History,* 327–28; for the militia laws, see Bennett, Black, and Cannon, *The Nauvoo Legion in Illinois,* 92.

123. Niccolo Machiavelli, *The Discourses,* ed. Bernard Crick, trans. Leslie J. Walker (New York: Penguin Books, 1986), 178.

124. *Journal of the Senate of the Twelfth General Assembly of the State of Illinois* (Springfield, IL: 1841), 45.

125. For the last three, see Robert Bruce Flanders, *Nauvoo: Kingdom on the Mississippi* (Urbana: University of Illinois Press, 1965), 148–51.

126. Andrew F. Smith, *Saintly Scoundrel: The Life and Times of John Cook Bennett* (Urbana: University of Illinois Press, 1997), 32–47.

127. Bennett, Black, and Cannon, *The Nauvoo Legion in Illinois,* 82.

128. *Warsaw Signal,* May 19, 1841.

129. See Susan Sessions Rugh, "Saints and Old Settlers: The Conflict in Hancock County, Illinois, 1840–1846" (paper 91–3, Newberry Papers in Family and Community History, 1993), 34.

130. See Richards, *"Gentlemen of Property and Standing,"* 84.

131. H. Jon Rosenbaum and Peter C. Sederberg, eds., *Vigilante Politics* (Philadelphia: University of Pennsylvania Press, 1976), 4.

132. Richards, *"Gentlemen of Property and Standing,"* 26.

133. See Susan Sessions Rugh, *Our Common Country: Family Farming, Culture, and Community in the Nineteenth-Century Midwest* (Bloomington: Indiana University Press, 2001), 41; emphasis in original.

134. For the stealing charges, see Rugh, "Saints and Old Settlers," 28–30.
135. Brigham Young, quoted in Dallin H. Oaks and Marvin S. Hill, *Carthage Conspiracy: The Trial of the Accused Assassins of Joseph Smith* (Urbana: University of Illinois Press, 1975), 194.
136. Rugh, "Saints and Old Settlers," 31.
137. Rugh, *Our Common Country*, 49.
138. On the Mormon's "political kingdom," see Klaus J. Hansen, *Quest for Empire: The Political Kingdom of God and the Council of Fifty in Mormon History* (East Lansing: Michigan State University Press, 1967).
139. Nicholas R. Miller, "Pluralism and Social Choice," *American Political Science Review* 77, no. 3 (September 1983): 734–47, quote at 734.

CHAPTER 4: NAUVOO PROPHECIES IN THE HANCOCK STATUS ORDER

1. A *Cincinnati Chronicle* article, cited in the *Western World*, September 9, 1840, noted that the Mormons first crossing the river at Quincy had moved north: "There are about 2,800 at Nauvoo, Illinois and about 2,000 in Lee County, Iowa."
2. As self-described by Ebenezer Robinson and Don Carlos Smith, editors of the *Times and Seasons*, in their opening "Address," published at Commerce in November 1839. The phrase "shut up in my bones," from Jeremiah 20:9, is applied to feelings in this time period by John D. Lee, *The Mormon Menace: Being the Confession of John Doyle Lee, Danite*, ed. Alfred Henry Lewis (1877; repr., New York: Home Protection Publishing, 1905), 112. Lewis, in the preface, explains the publication of this book. He says that after 1877, when Lee was put to death for his role in the Mountain Meadows Massacre, he issued his "confessions, so to call them." They were suppressed by Brigham Young, but "two volumes" escaped and were given to Lewis. He states that "much that was shocking and atrocious has been eliminated in the editing" (viii). An unexpurgated edition is available through the University of New Mexico Press.
3. *Quincy Whig*, April 27, 1839.
4. Brigham Young, Heber C. Kimball, John E. Page, Wilford Woodruff, John Taylor, and George A. Smith, "To the Elders of the Church of Jesus Christ of Latter Day Saints, to the Churches Scattered Abroad, and to All the Saints," *Times and Seasons*, November 1839, 12.
5. As quoted in Grant Underwood, *The Millenarian World of Early Mormonism* (Urbana: University of Illinois Press, 1993), 72.

6. Joseph Smith, discourse, circa July 19, 1840, as reported by Martha Jane Knowlton Coray, p. [21], The Joseph Smith Papers, https://www.josephsmithpapers.org/paper-summary/discourse-circa-19-july-1840-as-reported-by-martha-jane-knowlton-coray-b/13.
7. *Times and Seasons,* November 1839, 15; December 1839, 31.
8. See Fawn Brodie, *No Man Knows My History: The Life of Joseph Smith,* 2nd ed. (New York: Vintage Books, 1995), 272.
9. Stanley B. Kimball, "The Mormons in Early Illinois: Introduction," *Dialogue: A Journal of Mormon Thought* 5, no.1 (Spring 1970): 13.
10. See the letter of Sidney Rigdon to Joseph Smith reporting Young's counsel and hinting about a recent purchase of land at Kirtland. Sidney Rigdon to Joseph Smith, April 3, 1840, p. [2], The Joseph Smith Papers, https://www.josephsmithpapers.org/paper-summary/letter-from-sidney-rigdon-3-april-1840/2. Young raised fifty dollars in New York for the Illinois Mormons, an effort endorsed by Illinois governor Thomas Carlin. See the report in the *Peoria Register,* November 1, 1839.
11. Richard Lyman Bushman, "The Inner Joseph Smith," *Journal of Mormon History* 32, no. 1 (Spring 2006): 65–81, quote at 71.
12. See Memorial to Nauvoo High Council, June 18, 1840, The Joseph Smith Papers, https://www.josephsmithpapers.org/paper-summary/memorial-to-nauvoo-high-council-18-june-1840/1.
13. Richard Lyman Bushman, *Joseph Smith: Rough Stone Rolling* (New York: Vintage Books, 2005), 132.
14. John L. Brooke emphasizes that Smith's brother Alvin appeared "in a vision that Smith received in January 1836 at the charismatic meetings before the dedication of the Kirtland Temple." See *The Refiner's Fire: The Making of Mormon Cosmology, 1644–1844* (Cambridge: Cambridge University Press, 1994), 243.
15. Joseph Smith, discourse, September 29, 1839, as reported by James Mulholland, p. [13], The Joseph Smith Papers, https://www.josephsmithpapers.org/paper-summary/discourse-29-september-1839-as-reported-by-james-mulholland/2.
16. Bushman, *Rough Stone Rolling,* 421–22.
17. Thomas O'Dea, *The Mormons* (Chicago: University of Chicago Press, 1957), 57.
18. See the September 1842 letter to "All the Saints in Nauvoo," in *Doctrines and Covenants* (Nauvoo, IL: John Taylor, 1844), 128:14.
19. Doctrine and Covenants 128:18, 24.
20. The term is from John D. Lee, *Mormonism Unveiled: The Life and Confession of John D. Lee and the Complete Life of Brigham Young*

(1877; repr., Albuquerque: University of New Mexico Press, 2008), 81. A reprint of the 1891 edition, the text was originally published in 1877.

21. John C. Bennett to Sidney Rigdon and Joseph Smith, July 27, 1840, p. 170, The Joseph Smith Papers, https://www.josephsmithpapers.org/paper-summary/letter-from-john-c-bennett-27-july-1840/1.
22. Thomas Ford, *A History of Illinois: From Its Commencement as a State in 1818 to 1847*, ed. Rodney O. Davis (1854; repr., Urbana: University of Illinois Press, 1995), 255.
23. Joseph Smith, discourse, circa July 19, 1840, as reported by Martha Jane Knowlton Coray, pp. [12–13], The Joseph Smith Papers, https://www.josephsmithpapers.org/paper-summary/discourse-circa-19-july-1840-as-reported-by-martha-jane-knowlton-coray-b/4.
24. Joseph Smith History, vol. C-1, 1092, The Joseph Smith Papers, https://www.josephsmithpapers.org/paper-summary/history-1838-1856-volume-c-1-2-november-1838-31-july-1842/264.
25. *Times and Seasons*, December 13, 1841; emphasis in original.
26. See, for example, R. Lawrence Moore, *Religious Outsiders and the Making of Americans* (New York: Oxford University Press, 1986), 34–35.
27. See, for example, Louis Hartz, *The Liberal Tradition in America* (New York: Harcourt, Brace & World, 1955), 62. Hartz used the comparison to Europe to highlight the relative strength of competitive individualism as a subculture in shaping American liberalism, resulting in a political ideology quite different from European liberalism. In particular, he argued that the absence of a feudal tradition in America explained the lack of the development of a strong labor party in the US. For the impact of the Hartzian thesis on American political development scholarship, see John G. Gunnell, "Louis Hartz and the Liberal Metaphor: A Half-Century Later," *Studies in American Political Development* 19, no. 2 (Fall 2005): 196–205. See also the articles in the "commemorative panel" on Hartz in the same volume.
28. To adopt Weber's terms, organizing political power in the "legal order" shapes outcomes in the market's "economic order" and civil society's "status order." For Weber's definition of the state, see *Economy and Society: An Outline of Interpretive Sociology*, ed. Guenther Roth and Claus Wittich, vol. 2 (New York: Bedminster Press, 1978), 56; the focus on "orders" is found at 901–40. A powerful application of Weber's ideas to Jacksonian-era state building is Amy Bridges, *A City in the Republic: Antebellum New*

York and the Origins of Machine Politics (Ithaca, NY: Cornell University Press, 1987).

29. For the importance, and ultimate failure, of the neutrality project in the liberal treatment of religion, see Stephen D. Smith, *Foreordained Failure: The Quest for a Constitutional Principle of Religious Freedom* (New York: Oxford University Press, 1995). Emily Gill argues that neutrality, while not possible as a "constitutive" value of the liberal state, should remain as "a secondary or derivative value." Nonetheless, she also concedes that in the context of "accommodation of the practices stemming from religious belief . . . [and] because the appearance of neutrality is a function of one's interpretation of the factual circumstances, there can be no policy that all parties perceive as neutral." *Becoming Free: Autonomy and Diversity in the Liberal Polity* (Lawrence: University of Kansas Press, 2001), 17, 145.
30. Christopher Baylor, *First to the Party: The Group Origins of Political Transformation* (Philadelphia: University of Pennsylvania Press, 2018).
31. Emil Joseph Verlie, ed., *Illinois Constitutions* (Springfield: Illinois State Historical Library, 1919), 436.
32. See the Illinois constitution cited in *Revised Law of the Nauvoo Legion* (Nauvoo, IL: John Taylor Printer, 1844), 3. These provisions were retained verbatim in the 1848 Illinois Constitution.
33. Mrs. John H. Kinzie, *Wau-Bun, the Early Day in the North-West* (New York: Derby & Jackson, 1856), 190. This apparently anomalous phrase was replicated years later in a Pike County history (1935–39) using a similar locution, if in a different idiom: "The first white man in Hadley Township was a colored man." see Paul A. Shackel, *New Philadelphia: An Archaeology of Race in the Heartland* (Berkeley: University of California Press, 2011), 2.
34. William H. Herndon and Jesse W. Weik, *Herndon's Life of Lincoln: The History and Personal Recollections of Abraham Lincoln as Originally Written by William H. Herndon and Jesse W. Weik*, ed. Paul M. Angle (1888; repr., Greenwich, CT: Fawcett Publications, 1961), 111.
35. Verlie, *Illinois Constitutions*, 435.
36. Lee, *Mormonism Unveiled*, 41.
37. Verlie, *Illinois Constitutions*, 435.
38. George Washington Bean, *Autobiography of George Washington Bean, a Utah Pioneer of 1847, and His Family Records*, comp. Flora Diana Bean Horne (Salt Lake City: Printing, 1945), 18.
39. Mary Douglas, *Purity and Danger: An Analysis of the Concepts of Pollution and Taboo* (London: Routledge, 1966), 4.

40. See Mary Douglas, *Natural Symbols: Explorations in Cosmology* (New York: Pantheon Books, 1970).
41. See Richard J. Ellis, *American Political Cultures* (New York: Oxford University Press, 1992), and James Simeone, "William Kinney's Agrarian Dilemma," *Journal of Illinois History* 13 (Spring 2010): 2–32.
42. The transition to modernity is moderated by the state, as Ernest Gellner argues, because "the modern industrial state can only function with a mobile, literate, culturally standardized, interchangeable population." *Nations and Nationalism* (Ithaca, NY: Cornell University Press, 1983), 46. The role the political culture of egalitarianism plays in this transition has yet to be fully explored.
43. Evidence for this claim is found in Terryl L. Givens, *The Viper on the Hearth: Mormons, Myths, and the Construction of Heresy* (New York: Oxford University Press, 1997), and W. Paul Reeve, *Religion of a Different Color: Race and the Mormon Struggle for Whiteness* (Oxford: Oxford University Press, 2015).
44. Stanley Tambiah, *Leveling Crowds: Ethnonationalist Conflicts and Collective Violence in South Asia* (Berkeley: University of California Press, 1996), 14.
45. Brian Barry articulates most clearly the standard criticism that political culture is useless as an explanatory variable because it does not vary. See *Sociologists, Economists, and Democracy* (Chicago: University of Chicago Press, 1970).
46. Bean, *Autobiography*, 19.
47. Bean, 7.
48. Bean, 16.
49. Bean, 16.
50. Bean, 19.
51. Bean, 18.
52. Bean, 18. Bean's "absolute faith" gives "the simple candor of his remarks an unquestioned veracity," or so argues Samuel W. Taylor, *Nightfall at Nauvoo* (New York: Avon Books, 1971), 402.
53. Bean, *Autobiography*, 18.
54. Bean, 17.
55. Bean, 16.
56. Bean, 19.
57. The "politics of recognition" and the practices associated with "misrecognition" in contemporary American society are helpfully framed by Melissa V. Harris-Perry, *Sister Citizen: Shame, Stereotypes, and Black Women in America* (New Haven, CT: Yale University Press, 2011), 35–50.

58. H. Richard Niebuhr, *The Social Sources of Denominationalism* (1929; repr., Cleveland: Meridian Books, 1957), 3.
59. Niebuhr, *The Social Sources of Denominationalism,* 160.
60. Perry Miller, *Errand into the Wilderness* (Cambridge, MA: Harvard University Press, 1956), 59.
61. Miller, *Errand into the Wilderness,* 78.
62. John Witte Jr., "Blest Be the Ties That Bind: Covenant and Community in Puritan Thought," *Emory Law Journal* 36 (Spring 1987): 579–602, quote at 592.
63. Richard L. Bushman, *From Puritan to Yankee: Character and the Social Order in Connecticut, 1690–1765* (Cambridge, MA: Harvard University Press, 1967), 172.
64. Nathan O. Hatch, *The Democratization of American Christianity* (New Haven, CT: Yale University Press, 1989), 9, 17.
65. Ernest Lee Tuveson, *Redeemer Nation: The Idea of America's Millennial Role* (Chicago: University of Chicago Press, 1980), 175–86, quotes at 177 and 186.
66. The emphasis on communitarian groups creating living models of their ideas is found in Arthur Bestor, *Backwoods Utopias: The Sectarian Origins and the Owenite Phase of Communitarian Socialism in America, 1663–1829,* 2nd ed. (Philadelphia: University of Pennsylvania Press, 1970). See especially the appendix, "Patent-Office Models of the Good Society: Some Relationships between Social Reform and Westward Expansion" (230–52).
67. O'Dea, *The Mormons,* 53.
68. For these hints, see the *Warsaw Signal,* June 9, 1841.
69. The "portability and ceaseless transmutations of Zion" in the Book of Mormon is emphasized by Terryl L. Givens. See for example, *The Book of Mormon: A Very Short Introduction* (Oxford: Oxford University Press, 2009), 34.
70. For the logic of the jeremiad, see Sacvan Bercovitch, *The American Jeremiad* (Madison: University of Wisconsin Press, 1978).
71. The four letters are noted by George T. M. Davis, *An Authentic Account of the Massacre of Joseph Smith, the Mormon Prophet, and Hyrum Smith, His Brother, Together with a Brief History of the Rise and Progress of Mormonism, and All the Circumstances Which Led to Their Death* (St. Louis: Chambers & Knapp, 1844), 7.
72. Klaus J. Hansen, *Quest for Empire: The Political Kingdom of God and the Council of Fifty in Mormon History* (East Lansing: Michigan State University Press, 1967), 52.
73. *Illinois Advocate,* June 11, 1831.

74. For a representative view, see Underwood, *The Millenarian World,* 80.
75. Daniel Dunklin, quoted in Brodie, *No Man Knows My History,* 191.
76. Steven C. Harper, "'Dictated by Christ': Joseph Smith and the Politics of Revelation," *Journal of the Early Republic* 26, no. 2 (Summer 2006): 275–304.
77. Universalizing the particular, which might be seen as a mistake made by all liberals, is especially endemic to those influenced by the "restoration impulse" since these religious groups believe "that they are an innocent and fundamentally natural people, who, in effect, have stepped out of history, thereby escaping the powerful influence of history, culture and tradition. These Americans therefore have often confused the historical particularities of their limited experience with universal norms that should be embraced, they have thought, by all people in all cultures and all times." Richard T. Hughes and C. Leonard Allen, *Illusions of Innocence: Protestant Primitivism in America, 1630–1875* (Chicago: University of Chicago Press, 1988), xiii–xv.
78. Contemporary scholars have been convinced of the same. The thesis that Mormon doctrine represented a true, if dissenting, republican vision is argued by Kenneth H. Winn, *Exiles in a Land of Liberty: Mormons in America, 1830–1846* (Chapel Hill: University of North Carolina Press, 1989).
79. Wight and Smith, quoted in Robert Bruce Flanders, *Nauvoo: Kingdom on the Mississippi* (Urbana: University of Illinois Press, 1965), 218.
80. O'Dea, *The Mormons,* 56.
81. It is worth noting that during this same period, Matthias's message was quite similar. In 1832 he claimed that he was the literal "Spirit of Truth." See Paul E. Johnson and Sean Wilentz, *The Kingdom of Matthias: A Story of Sex and Salvation in 19th-Century America* (New York: Oxford University Press, 1994), 94–95.
82. Doctrine and Covenants 132:19–20.
83. Bushman, *Rough Stone Rolling,* 421.
84. For Finney's doctrine, see William G. McLoughlin Jr., *Modern Revivalism: Charles Grandison Finney to Billy Graham* (New York: Ronald Press, 1959), 65–121.
85. Bushman, *Rough Stone Rolling,* 209–10.
86. For Leland's conversion theology, see Donald G. Mathews, *Religion in the Old South* (Chicago: University of Chicago Press, 1977), 60. For the "Mammoth Cheese" incident, see Isaac Kramnick and R.

Lawrence Moore, *The Godless Constitution: A Moral Defense of the Secular State* (New York: Norton, 2005).

87. The story is found in Joseph Smith, *Elders' Journal,* July 1838, 42, and is retold in Underwood, *The Millenarian World,* 42.
88. J. David Greenstone, *The Lincoln Persuasion: Remaking American Liberalism* (Princeton, NJ: Princeton University Press, 1993), 269.
89. Zechariah Chafee, quoted in Vincent Blasi and Seana V. Schiffrin, "The Story of *West Virginia State Board of Education v. Barnette:* The Pledge of Allegiance and the Freedom of Thought," *Constitutional Law Stories,* ed. Michael C. Dorf, 2nd ed. (New York: Foundation Press, 2009), 409–53, quote on 422.
90. See Richard Mentor Johnson, *Review of a Report of the Committee, to Whom Was Referred the Several Petitions on the Subject of Mails on the Sabbath, Presented to the Senate of the United States, January 16, 1829, by the Hon. Mr. Johnson, of Kentucky, Chairman of Said Committee* (N.p.: 1829).
91. See Hatch, *The Democratization of American Christianity.*
92. Elias Smith, quoted in Hatch, 69.
93. Robert H. Abzug, *Cosmos Crumbling: American Reform and the Religious Imagination* (New York: Oxford University Press, 1994), 5.
94. *Warsaw Signal,* May 19, 1841.
95. Hatch is one of the few scholars to explore this aspect of Mormonism's appeal. See *The Democratization of American Christianity,* 113–22.
96. Norman Cohn, *The Pursuit of the Millennium,* rev. and exp. ed. (New York: Oxford University Press, 1970), 19–20. References to the "fulness of the gospel" are rife in Mormon writings.
97. Scholar Grant Underwood conducted a systematic study of the early Mormon textual citations from the early period of the group's development. He found an emphasis on "the restoration of Israel" and its location in America. The frequently cited Ether 13:4–8, for example, specified that "the New Jerusalem shall be built on this land." See *The Millenarian World,* 78.
98. See Underwood, 124.
99. See Bercovitch, *The American Jeremiad.*
100. See Tuveson, *Redeemer Nation.*
101. See the oration by Father Samuel Mazzucelli in the *Galena Gazetteer and Advertiser,* August 8, 1835.
102. Finney, quoted in William G. McLoughlin, *Revivals, Awakenings, and Reform* (Chicago: University of Chicago Press, 1978), 128–29.
103. On the attractions of Parker and antimission Baptists' "fee-simple salvation," see Simeone, *Democracy and Slavery in Frontier Illinois,*

174. For the notion of time as a corruptor in the republic tradition, see J. G. A. Pocock, *The Machiavellian Moment: Florentine Political Thought and the Atlantic Republican Tradition* (Princeton, NJ: Princeton University Press, 1975).
104. *Autobiography of Parley Parker Pratt,* 8th ed. (Salt Lake City: Deseret Book, 1970), 42.
105. For the "twistifications" comment, see the story "Burial of the Mormon Girl," published in *The Wasp,* April 16, 1842.
106. *Autobiography of Parley Parker Pratt,* 32.
107. *Autobiography of Parley Parker Pratt,* 37.
108. See Givens, *The Book of Mormon,* 7–8.
109. Alexis de Tocqueville, *Democracy in America,* ed. J. P. Mayer, trans. George Lawrence (1836–39; repr., Garden City: NY: Doubleday, 1969), 508.
110. Thomas Hooker, quoted in Edmund S. Morgan, *The Puritan Family Religion and Domestic Relations in Seventeenth-Century New England* (New York: Harper & Row, 1966), 1.
111. Morgan, *The Puritan Family,* 2.
112. Doctrine and Covenants 76:86.
113. See the *Baptist Almanac and Baptist Register* (1847): 344.
114. See Bushman, *Rough Stone Rolling,* 415.
115. See, for example, Hansen, *Quest for Empire,* 13–14, and Underwood, *The Millenarian World,* 3–8; Tuveson argues that the Mormons "fit awkwardly . . . in the pattern of millennialism." *Redeemer Nation,* 175.
116. See Marvin S. Hill, *Quest for Refuge: The Mormon Flight from American Pluralism* (Salt Lake City: Signature Books, 1989).
117. Joseph Smith History, vol. C-1, 1229, The Joseph Smith Papers, https://www.josephsmithpapers.org/paper-summary/history-1838-1856-volume-c-1-2-november-1838-31-july-1842/401.
118. Udney Hay Jacob, *An Extract from a Manuscript Entitled The Peace Maker, or the Doctrines of the Millennium: Being a Treatise on Religion and Jurisprudence, or a New System of Religion and Politics* (Nauvoo, IL: J. Smith, 1842), 3.
119. See Richard J. Ellis, *The Dark Side of the American Left: Illiberal Egalitarianism in America* (Lawrence: University of Kansas Press, 1998).
120. Taylor, *Nightfall at Nauvoo,* 65.
121. *Western World,* July 29, 1840.
122. *Western World,* October 7, 1840.
123. John E. Hallwas and Roger D. Launius, *Cultures in Conflict: A Documentary History of the Mormon War in Illinois* (Logan: Utah State University Press, 1995), 52.

124. John E. Hallwas, *Western Illinois Heritage* (Macomb, IL: Illinois Heritage Press, 1983), 135–36.
125. Ford, *History of Illinois,* 286.
126. See the letter of "J. Lanborn" in the *Sangamo Journal,* July 16, 1841.
127. Thomas Gregg, *History of Hancock County, Illinois* (Chicago: Chas C. Chapman, 1880), 272.
128. *Western World,* July 29, 1840.
129. Hallwas and Launius, *Cultures in Conflict,* 54–55.
130. Hallwas and Launius, 72–73.
131. Lee, *Mormonism Unveiled,* 56.
132. Lee, 58.
133. Lee, 74.
134. Lee, 116.
135. Lee, 117.
136. Lee's dismay with Rigdon was shared by many Mormons, including Joseph Smith. See Lee, 79–82.
137. Lee, 59, 63, 71.
138. See the address printed in the *Sangamo Journal,* March 25, 1842.
139. *Warsaw Signal,* August 28, 1844.
140. See the editorial titled "Thieves," *Times and Seasons,* December 1, 1841, 615. No author specified. For Smith, see "Hyrum Smith's Affidavit," 615.
141. *Western World,* January 20, 1841.
142. *Warsaw Signal,* June 9, 1841.
143. James Hall, *Illinois Monthly Magazine* (Vandalia, IL: Robert Blackwell, 1831), 420; emphasis in the original.
144. Hall, *Illinois Monthly Magazine,* 420.
145. *Northwestern Gazetteer and Galena Advertiser,* February 28, 1835.
146. See the *Sangamo Journal,* January 21, 1841.
147. See the report of the Lee County, Iowa, convention in the *Warsaw Signal,* June 9, 1841.
148. For the distinction between immigrants and national minorities, see Will Kymlicka, *Multicultural Citizenship: A Liberal Theory of Minority Rights* (Oxford: Oxford University Press, 1995), 13–15.
149. The literature on the role of norms in supplementing the legal order is extensive. For one illuminating empirical study of the key role played by norms and local convention in the legal regime's regulation of property harm in a northern California ranching community, see Robert C. Ellikson, *Order without Law: How Neighbors Settle Disputes* (Cambridge, MA: Harvard University Press, 1991).

150. *Warsaw Signal,* May 19, 1841.
151. *Warsaw Signal,* June 2, 1841.
152. "Report of the First Presidency," *Times and Seasons,* April 15, 1841.
153. Douglas, *Purity and Danger,* 3.
154. *The Wasp,* April 22, 1842.
155. *The Wasp,* April 16, 1842.

CHAPTER 5: PERFORMING CITIZENSHIP IN THE HOUSE OF POWER

1. For the description of the state as a house of power, see Max Weber, "Class, Status, Party," in *From Max Weber: Essays in Sociology,* ed. H. H. Gerth and C. Wright Mills (Oxford: Oxford University Press, 1964), 194. "House of power" is translated as "sphere of power" in Max Weber, *Economy and Society: An Outline of Interpretive Sociology,* ed. Guenther Roth and Claus Wittich, vol. 2 (New York: Bedminster Press, 1978), 938.
2. This point is emphasized by Richard Lyman Bushman, *Joseph Smith: Rough Stone Rolling* (New York: Vintage Books, 2005), 504–20.
3. Fawn Brodie, *No Man Knows My History: The Life of Joseph Smith,* 2nd ed. (New York: Vintage Books, 1995), 272.
4. George F. Partridge, "'The Death of a Mormon Dictator': Letters of Massachusetts Mormons, 1843–1848," *The New England Quarterly* 9, no. 4 (December 1936): 583–617, quote at 591.
5. Requisition, September 1, 1840, [extradition of Joseph Smith et al. for treason and other crimes], The Joseph Smith Papers, https://www.josephsmithpapers.org/paper-summary/requisition-1-september-1840-extradition-of-js-et-al-for-treason-and-other-crimes/1.
6. *Times and Seasons,* September 1840, 170.
7. See for example the June 10, 1842, edition of the *Sangamo Journal:* "They gave him power and he is to give them votes." This claim was echoed throughout the Whig press and, while unsubstantiated, was far from implausible given Governor Carlin's overwhelmingly partisan approach to governing.
8. See the citation of a revision of the law in 1833 in Dallin H. Oaks, "The Suppression of the *Nauvoo Expositor,*" *Utah Law Review* 9 (Winter 1965): 862–903, quote at 883n126.
9. When Smith was arrested by a Carthage constable on the charge of riot, he was eventually released by the Nauvoo Municipal Court. When the riot charge resurfaced as it moved through the legal system, Smith "argued that a second trial would deprive him of his right not to be put in jeopardy twice for the same offense,"

which was not true since the habeas proceeding was not a trial on the merits of the riot charge. See Oaks, "The Suppression of the *Nauvoo Expositor,*" 865n17. Two of the eleven Mormons charged with riot were later tried and acquitted on grounds of a lack of positive identification by the police. See Dallin H. Oaks and Marvin S. Hill, *Carthage Conspiracy: The Trial of the Accused Assassins of Joseph Smith* (Urbana: University of Illinois Press, 1975), 201.

10. For a careful review of these episodes, see Andrew F. Smith, *Saintly Scoundrel: The Life and Times of John Cook Bennett* (Urbana: University of Illinois Press, 1997), 78–94; for the bodyguard, see Brodie, *No Man Knows My History,* 315, which claims the bodyguard was formed after the first Missouri sheriff came in 1840.
11. *Warsaw Signal,* August 9, 1842; reprinted in the *Sangamo Journal,* August 18, 1842.
12. *Sangamo Journal,* October 7, 1842.
13. The swamp comment is from the letter "Alpha" published in the *Sangamo Journal,* January 26, 1843.
14. On Ford's brief campaign over the summer of 1842, see the introduction to Evarts Boutell Greene and Charles Manfred Thompson, eds., *Governors' Letter-Books, 1840–1853* (Springfield: Illinois State Historical Library, 1911), xxxv.
15. Thomas Ford, *A History of Illinois: From Its Commencement as a State in 1818 to 1847,* ed. Rodney O. Davis (1854; repr., Urbana: University of Illinois Press, 1995), 173.
16. *Journal of the Senate of the Twelfth General Assembly of the State of Illinois* (Springfield, IL: 1841), 33.
17. Francis's editorial in the *Sangamo Journal,* January 19, 1843, reports the vote to table the repeal bill as 69 to 43. He added, "We are pleased to see that a large majority of Whigs voted to lay the bill on the table."
18. For details on the steamboat *Nauvoo,* see *The Joseph Smith Papers,* ed. Dean C. Jessee, Ronald K. Esplin, and Richard Lyman Bushman, *Journals,* vol. 2, *December 1841–April 1843,* ed. Andrew H. Hedges, Alex D. Smith, and Richard Lloyd Anderson (Salt Lake City: Church Historian's Press, 2011), 177–78 (hereafter cited as *JSP,* J2).
19. For the bankruptcy issue, the Butterfield meetings, and Douglas's intervention, see *JSP,* J2:174–78.
20. Thomas Ford to Joseph Smith, December 17, 1842, p. [1], The Joseph Smith Papers, https://www.josephsmithpapers.org/paper-summary/letter-from-thomas-ford-17-december-1842/1.

21. Ford, *History of Illinois,* 219.
22. Linda King Newell and Valeen Tippetts Avery, *Mormon Enigma: Emma Hale Smith: Prophet's Wife, "Elect Lady," Polygamy's Foe, 1804–1879* (Garden City, NY: Doubleday, 1984), 133.
23. 22 F. Cas. 373, Ill. Circuit Court (1843), 133.
24. *JSP,* J2:210.
25. Nathaniel Pope, quoted in Newell and Avery, *Mormon Enigma,* 133.
26. *The Nauvoo Poems of Eliza R. Snow* (Mason County, IL: The Church of Jesus Christ of Latter-day Saints, 1989), 25–26.
27. Ford, *History of Illinois,* 220. Ford thereby ensured that the arrest warrant would be returned to him if and when it was not exercised.
28. For Smith's suspicions of Rigdon, see Newell and Avery, *Mormon Enigma,* 162.
29. For this evidence, see Smith, *Saintly Scoundrel,* 136–37.
30. Brodie, *No Man Knows My History,* 348.
31. Bushman, *Rough Stone Rolling,* 506.
32. Joseph Smith History, vol. D-1, 1584, The Joseph Smith Papers, https://www.josephsmithpapers.org/paper-summary/history-1838-1856-volume-d-1-1-august-1842-1-july-1843/229.
33. *Warsaw Message,* July 15, 1843; Ford thought it likely as not that the Missourians were following "the voluntary act of the Sheriff of Lee County." See Greene and Thompson, *Governors' Letter-Books, 1840–1853,* 98. The *Warsaw Messenger,* July 15, 1843, reported that Campbell "determined to conduct them to Nauvoo."
34. See the details in Bushman, *Rough Stone Rolling,* 505–6.
35. Joseph Smith History, vol. D-1, 1586.
36. Greene and Thompson, *Governors' Letter-Books, 1840–1853,* 98.
37. Thomas Gregg, *Warsaw Message,* July 12, 1843.
38. Thomas Ford to Thomas Reynolds, *Governors' Letter-Books, 1840–1853,* 97.
39. Bushman, *Rough Stone Rolling,* 507.
40. Ford, *History of Illinois,* 220.
41. Brodie, *No Man Knows My History,* 349. I have not found the official record of this proceeding. Joseph Smith's journal includes over thirty pages of testimony on the Missouri troubles and only one short paragraph from Walker, which discreetly skirts the legal technicalities. See the entry for July 1, 1843, in Joseph Smith History, vol. D-1, pp. 1600–1636. For the argument that the Nauvoo Municipal Court could reasonably be claimed to have the power to hear a wide variety of habeas petitions under the Nauvoo charter, see Oaks, "The Suppression of the *Nauvoo Expositor,*" 879–82.

42. For the first charge, see Samuel W. Taylor, *Nightfall at Nauvoo* (New York: Avon Books, 1971), 194, 204. Taylor also makes the false claim that Ford needed the Mormon vote to win his election in 1842. The second view is laid out convincingly by Andrew H. Hedges, "Extradition, the Mormons, and the Election of 1843," *Journal of the Illinois State Historical Society* 109, no. 2 (Summer 2016): 127–47.
43. Ford, *History of Illinois*, 222.
44. Thomas Gregg, *History of Hancock County, Illinois* (Chicago: Chas C. Chapman, 1880), 336.
45. Ford, *History of Illinois*, 222.
46. Mason Brayman to Joseph Smith, July 29, 1843, p. 7, The Joseph Smith Papers, https://www.josephsmithpapers.org/paper-summary/letter-from-mason-brayman-29-july-1843/7. See also the reasoning of Rodney O. Davis, *History of Illinois*, 315, who suggests it is Brayman. This is likely, as Ford does not disclose the name, which he would have done in the case of a political enemy.
47. Marvin S. Hill, *Quest for Refuge: The Mormon Flight from American Pluralism* (Salt Lake City: Signature Books, 1989), 132.
48. See the election returns published in the *Nauvoo Neighbor*, August 16, 1843.
49. See, for example, the *Sangamo Journal*, September 7, 1843.
50. *Warsaw Message*, September 20, 1843.
51. Oaks, "The Suppression of the *Nauvoo Expositor*," 881.
52. James L. Kimball, "The Nauvoo Charter: A Reinterpretation," in *Kingdom on the Mississippi Revisited*, ed. Roger D. Launius and John E. Hallwas (Urbana: University of Illinois Press, 1966), 39–47, especially 43.
53. A. T. Andreas, *History of Chicago: From the Earliest Period to the Present Time* (Chicago: A. T. Andreas, 1884), 1:443.
54. See Oaks, "The Suppression of the *Nauvoo Expositor*," 862, and Kimball, "The Nauvoo Charter," 41. Quincy is a contested case.
55. See Robert W. Johannsen, ed., *The Lincoln-Douglas Debates of 1858* (New York: Oxford University Press, 1965), 15–16.
56. Oaks, "The Suppression of the *Nauvoo Expositor*," 882.
57. See the letter of Governor Carlin to Emma Smith of September 7, 1842, published in "History," 1396.
58. *Warsaw Message*, September 20, 1843.
59. See the letters by J. I. Lamborn and J. A. MacDougal published in the *Nauvoo Neighbor*, December 6, 1843.
60. See Joseph Smith to Thomas Ford, January 1, 1844, p. [4], The Joseph Smith Papers, https://www.josephsmithpapers.org/paper

-summary/letter-to-thomas-ford-1-january-1844/4. Ford's position is inferred from Smith's letter. His opinion is not in the public record.

61. See the notice in the *Times and Seasons,* May 15, 1841, 417. For the Nauvoo charter, which sets out the powers of the Nauvoo Legion in section 25, see the *Warsaw Message,* September 20, 1843; for the ordinance organizing the legion on February 3, 1841, see Richard E. Bennett, Susan Easton Black, and Donald Q. Cannon, *The Nauvoo Legion in Illinois: A History of the Mormon Militia, 1841–1846* (Norman, OK: Arthur H. Clark, 2010), 271–72.
62. See Gregg, *History of Hancock County,* 296.
63. See Hill, *Quest for Refuge,* 135.
64. *Warsaw Signal,* December 8, 1841.
65. Joseph Smith, quoted in Bennett, Black, and Cannon, *The Nauvoo Legion,* 323; emphasis in original.
66. Joseph Smith History, vol. D-1, 1547; emphasis in original.
67. For the parading dates, see Bennett, Black, and Cannon, *The Nauvoo Legion,* 329.
68. See *War, Politics and Power,* trans. and ed. Edward M. Collins (South Bend, IN: Regency, 1962), 83.
69. See Brayman to Smith, p. 5.
70. Thomas Ford to Joseph Smith, December 12, 1843, The Joseph Smith Papers, https://www.josephsmithpapers.org/paper-summary/letter-from-thomas-ford-12-december-1843/1.
71. Bushman, *Rough Stone Rolling,* 511.
72. Thomas Gregg, *Warsaw Message,* December 27, 1843.
73. *Warsaw Message,* January 4, 1844. See Walter Bagby's letter of January 11, 1844, to his brother Charles in Glasgow, Kentucky, in the Bagby Papers at the University of Kentucky. This episode is summarized ably in Annette P. Hampshire, *Mormonism in Conflict: The Nauvoo Years* (New York: Edwin Mellen Press, 1985), 183–85.
74. Walter Bagby to Charles D. Bagby, November 26, 1843, in the Bagby Papers.
75. Robert E. Osgood and Robert W. Tucker, *Force, Order, and Justice* (Baltimore: Johns Hopkins University Press, 1967), 11. Osgood and Tucker define the security dilemma as one in which "the very search for security in a system of politics without government compels reliance on military self-help, which, in turn, fosters conflict and competition for military power" (11).
76. *Nauvoo Neighbor,* December 8, 1843.
77. See the letter under "Mormon Preparations" in the *Warsaw Signal,* May 21, 1845.

78. Kimball, "The Nauvoo Charter," 42.
79. *Nauvoo Neighbor,* December 13, 1843.
80. *Warsaw Signal,* February 14, 1844.
81. For the tendency of the modern state to try to solve social problems by a reduction to the management tools at hand, see James C. Scott, *Seeing Like a State: How Certain Schemes to Improve the Human Condition Have Failed* (New Haven, CT: Yale University Press, 1998).
82. Bennett, Black, and Cannon, *The Nauvoo Legion,* 331.
83. All quotations from the *Nauvoo Expositor,* June 7, 1844.
84. Gregg, *History of Hancock County,* 317.
85. Brodie, *No Man Knows My History,* 368–72.
86. Bushman, *Rough Stone Rolling,* 531.
87. William J. Novak argues that taken as a system, the common-law tools municipalities employed often approximated an ideal of "the well-regulated society." See *The People's Welfare: Law and Regulation in Nineteenth-Century America* (Chapel Hill: University of North Carolina Press, 1996), 2. Yet, precisely because common-law standards are created by precedents over time, they are retrospective and not particularly useful as guidance in public policy debates the way shared standards are. Nuisance standards are a case in point. Those which evolved during the era followed the broad outlines of the harm principle: individuals were free to act as long as their freedom did not harm other individuals or abridge their like freedom. Nuisances like slaughter-house waste dumped into a city stream are examples of indiscriminate harms that often went unregulated. Novak's "well-regulated society" is supported with numerous examples in which the harm principle and shared conceptions of the public good provided guidance in antebellum municipal regulation of conventional nuisances like slaughter houses, powder houses, stables, mills, dairies, and breweries. See Novak, *The People's Welfare,* 62.
88. The *Nauvoo Expositor* episode indicates how reliant the common-law state was on shared societal and cultural standards, which were lacking in multicultural settings. The Nauvoo City Council felt duty bound to stamp out the impurity represented by the *Expositor* and to smash its press as it would abate an open sewer. The anti-Mormons needed only to refer to the hegemonic commitment of freedom of the press to indicate how far the Mormons had strayed from allegiance to the American regime. Their view was widely shared in the Illinois newspapers of the time. Typical are the views expressed by George T. M. Davis in the June 24,

1844, *Alton Telegraph,* in which he doubted the Mormons could justify their destruction of the press, and in the edition of July 6, 1844, in which he commended Ford for telling the Mormons in his speech on June 27 at Nauvoo that destroying the press "had incensed the people of the State against them almost beyond control." This view prevailed despite the fact that municipal charters and codes were developing broad regulator powers during the antebellum period. The conflict between settlers and saints in Hancock County also confirms several general points about group competition in decentralized common-law regimes.

89. The full transcript is given in the *Nauvoo Neighbor Extra,* June 17, 1844, and is reprinted in Gregg, *History of Hancock County,* 303–19.

90. See the Nauvoo charter in John E. Hallwas and Roger D. Launius, *Cultures in Conflict: A Documentary History of the Mormon War in Illinois* (Logan: Utah State University Press, 1995), 23.

91. Recourse to shared notions of the public good and traditional harm principles was all but useless for governance here because the nature of harm and its boundaries were precisely the issues at hand. Joseph Smith felt he had legal precedent for the Nauvoo City Council's summary "abatement" proceedings—which included sending two hundred men to sledgehammer the doors of the building and the press. Smith cited a case in Ohio in which a press had been considered a nuisance. Governor Ford disagreed; he thought the Nauvoo council at minimum needed to present its case for abatement before a court and argued that the application of nuisance law to a newspaper was unprecedented. See the details related by Oaks, "The Suppression of the *Nauvoo Expositor,*" 877n104, 885–86. On the latter point, it would be over one hundred years before the United States Supreme Court decided the case of Minneapolis abating the *Saturday Press* in *Near v. Minnesota.* The court overturned the Minnesota Supreme Court's upholding of the city's action abating the paper as a nuisance on the grounds that it violated the First Amendment to the US Constitution's freedom of the press clause. The paper could be held responsible for its written claims in a libel proceeding, but summary nuisance abatements were declared akin to a prior restraint, which common-law practices had put beyond the power of government. For the case history and summary, see Fred W. Friendly, *Minnesota Rag: The Dramatic Story of the Landmark Supreme Court Case That Gave New Meaning to the Freedom of the Press* (New York: Vintage Books, 1982).

92. Gregg, *History of Hancock County,* 318. Joseph Smith viewed Nauvoo's nuisance power as a broad one, and William Novak rightly points out that the broad powers municipalities exercised in regulating entities like taverns belie any attempt to transpose today's notions of a libertarian or minimal state back into the nineteenth century. Novak cites an 1872 New Jersey case which emphasized that "at the common law, it is always the right of a citizen, without official authority, to abate a public nuisance, and without waiting to have it judged such by a legal tribunal." Novak, *The People's Welfare,* 227. But this case dealt precisely with the nuisance of putrid meat; libel was a different order of stench, and even the logic of analogical thinking so celebrated by common-law theorists is too weak a reed to span the chasm between meat and press. On the common law's reasoning by analogy, see Edward H. Levi, *An Introduction to Legal Reasoning* (Chicago: University of Chicago Press, 1962). Debate over what made a society "well ordered" was too wide open to justify a summary power to declare a newspaper libelous and close it. Instances of mobs organizing to close antislavery papers, as they did in Alton and Peoria, could be appealed to as civil society counterparts to legal precedents. But such "violent proceedings" were roundly condemned as illegal, even if the blame was often laid at the door of the abolitionists, as the *Missouri Republican* did in blaming Illinois College president Edward Beecher for inciting Elijah Lovejoy to act. See the November 18, 1837, editorial quoted in John Randolph Willis, *God's Frontiersmen: The Yale Band in Illinois* (Washington, DC: University Press of America, 1979), 210.
93. Ford explained the details of the episode in his message to the legislature later that winter. See *Message of the Governor of the State of Illinois, in Relation to the Disturbances in Hancock County, December 21, 1844* (Springfield, IL: Walters and Weber, 1844), 4–5.
94. Oaks and Hill, *Carthage Conspiracy,* 16.
95. Thomas Sharp, *Warsaw Signal,* June 12, 1844.
96. Ford, *Message of the Governor,* 3.
97. Thomas Ford, quoted in George T. M. Davis, *An Authentic Account of the Massacre of Joseph Smith, the Mormon Prophet, and Hyrum Smith, His Brother, Together with a Brief History of the Rise and Progress of Mormonism, and All the Circumstances Which Led to Their Death* (St. Louis: Chambers & Knapp, 1844), 10.
98. Bennett, Black, and Cannon, *The Nauvoo Legion,* 334.
99. Thomas Ford, *Message from the Governor, in Relation to the Disturbances in Hancock County* (Springfield, IL: Walters & Weber, 1844), 10–11.

100. Alexis de Tocqueville, *Democracy in America,* ed. J. P. Mayer, trans. George Lawrence (1832–36; repr., Garden City, NY: Doubleday, 1969), 263–70.
101. *Warsaw Signal,* February 28, 1844.
102. *Nauvoo Expositor,* June 7, 1844.
103. Robert G. McCloskey, *The American Supreme Court* (Chicago: University of Chicago Press, 1960), 13.
104. See Howard Schweber, *The Creation of the American Common Law, 1850–1880: Technology, Politics, and the Construction of Citizenship* (Cambridge: Cambridge University Press, 2004).
105. For concrete examples, see the cases surveyed in Daniel Stowell, ed., *In Tender Consideration* (Urbana: University of Illinois Press, 2002).
106. Laura F. Edwards, "Sarah Allingham's Sheet and Other Lessons from Legal History," *Journal of the Early Republic* 38 (Spring 2018): 121–47, quotes at 122–23 and 127.
107. Laura F. Edwards, *The People and Their Peace: Legal Culture and the Transformation of Inequality in the Post-Revolutionary South* (Chapel Hill: University of North Carolina Press, 2009), 101.
108. Edwards, *The People and Their Peace,* 103.
109. Hill, *Quest for Refuge,* 105, 239, cites a letter in the *State Register* of November 8, 1844, which claimed that, at the time, Sharp "made himself the organ of a gang of town speculators . . . who [were] afraid that Nauvoo [was] about to kill off their town."
110. For the identification/consciousness distinction, see Dennis Chong and Reuel Rogers, "Reviving Group Consciousness," in *The Politics of Democratic Inclusion,* ed. Christina Wolbrecht and Rodney E. Hero (Philadelphia: Temple University Press, 2005), 45–74, especially 46.
111. On the importance of the presence or absence of "lateral support" in the enforcement of minority rights in developing democracies, see Daniel Brinks and Sandra Botero, "Inequality and the Rule of Law: Ineffective Rights in Latin American Democracies," in *Reflections on Uneven Democracies: The Legacies of Guillermo O'Donnell,* ed. Daniel Brinks, Marcelo Leiras, and Scott Mainwaring (Baltimore: Johns Hopkins University Press, 2014).
112. See Pope's "An Essay on Man: Epistle III," in *Poetry and Prose of Alexander Pope,* ed. Aubrey Williams (Boston: Houghton Mifflin, 1969), 146.
113. *The Revised Code of Laws of Illinois* (Vandalia: Robert Blackwell, 1827), 49, 301, 56.
114. Ford, *History of Illinois,* 16.

115. See Ford's allusion to this anecdote in *History of Illinois,* 172. The direct quotation is from the Fourth Book on Solon, *Plutarch's Lives,* trans. Bernadotte Perrin (Cambridge, MA: Harvard University Press, 1967), 415.
116. Quoted in the report made by Jessie B. Thomas Jr. on December 27, 1834, in the Illinois senate. See *Journal of the Senate of the Ninth General Assembly of the State of Illinois* (Vandalia, IL: J. Y. Sawyer, 1835), 139.
117. See the history of militia practices outlined in Alexander L. Baugh, "A Call to Arms: The 1838 Mormon Defense of Northern Missouri" (PhD diss., Brigham Young University, 2000), 19.
118. Samuel Huntington, *Political Order in Changing Societies* (New Haven, CT: Yale University Press, 1968), 1.
119. Jonathan Obert and Eleonara Mattiacci, "Keeping Vigil: The Emergence of Vigilance Committees in Pre–Civil War America," *Perspectives on Politics* 16, no. 3 (September 2018): 600–616, quote at 606.
120. Michael J. Pfeifer, *Rough Justice: Lynching and American Society, 1874–1947* (Urbana: University of Illinois Press, 2004), 3.
121. The habit of "circumventing" the law is a persistent pattern of the "contradictions of democracy" in postrevolution societies like South Africa and El Salvador. See Nicholas Rush Smith, *Contradictions of Democracy: Vigilantism and Rights in Post-apartheid South Africa* (Oxford: Oxford University Press, 2019), 20n7.
122. See *The Joseph Smith Papers,* ed. Ronald K. Esplin and Matthew J. Grow, *Journals,* vol. 3, *May 1843–June 1844,* ed. Andrew H. Hedges, Alex D. Smith, and Brent M. Rogers (Salt Lake City: Church Historian's Press, 2015), 142, 149; also Brent M. Rogers, "Armed Men Are Coming from the State of Missouri," *Journal of the Illinois State Historical Society* 109, no. 2 (Summer 2016): 148–79, especially 155.
123. A letter by "an Anti-Mormon" raised the issue in the *Warsaw Signal,* July 23, 1842; Sharp editorialized against splitting the county on November 24, 1842, *Warsaw Signal;* the antidivision view was later supported by the letter of "Hancock" to the *Warsaw Message,* January 28, 1843.
124. See the statement signed by 370 Democrats rejecting any partisan Whig motivation behind the anti-Mormon movement. *Warsaw Signal,* May 14, 1845.
125. Thomas Sharp, *Warsaw Signal,* August 28, 1844.
126. For the definition of political development as "a durable shift in governing authority," see Karen Orrin and Steven Skowronek,

The Search for American Political Development (Cambridge: Cambridge University Press, 2004), 123.

127. Ernest Gellner, *Nations and Nationalism* (Ithaca, NY: Cornell University Press, 1983).
128. Rogers M. Smith, *Stories of Peoplehood: The Politics and Morals of Political Membership* (Cambridge: Cambridge University Press, 2003), 20–21.
129. Smith's work thus crucially links the issues of culture and identity with the state-building literature in political science. For a survey of the political science literature devoted to "bringing the state back in," see Orrin and Skowronek, *The Search for American Political Development,* 19.
130. Some scholars doubt that republican models of the public sphere and "civic public" can be fully universalized even in theory because "its rational and universal status derives only from its opposition to affectivity, particularlity, and the body. Republican theorists insisted on the unity of the civic public: insofar as he is a citizen, every man leaves behind his particularity and difference, to adopt a universal standpoint identical for all citizens, the standpoint of the common good or general will." Iris Marion Young, *Justice and the Politics of Difference* (Princeton, NJ: Princeton University Press, 1990), 117.
131. Smith, *Stories of Peoplehood,* 43, 44.
132. Alexander Hamilton, *The Federalist Papers,* ed. Clinton Rossiter (1788; repr., New York: Penguin Books, 1961), 33.
133. *State Register,* January 29, 1841.
134. See the motto on the first edition of August 1, 1843.
135. *Quincy Whig,* November 10, 1838.
136. For Leggett's use of this phrase, see James Simeone, "Reassessing Jacksonian Political Culture: William Leggett's Egalitarianism," *American Political Thought* 4, no. 3 (Summer 2015): 363.
137. *Warsaw Signal,* September 17, 1842.
138. *Warsaw Signal,* February 14, 1844.
139. *Warsaw Signal,* September 3, 1845.
140. *Warsaw Signal,* September 17, 1845.
141. *Warsaw Signal,* September 17, 1845.
142. Thomas Ford, *Mormon Difficulties: Report of the Governor in Relation to the Difficulties in Hancock County* (Springfield, IL: William Walters, Public Printer, 1846), 1.
143. Details stated by Ford, *Mormon Difficulties,* 1, 2; see also Hill, *Quest for Refuge,* 178.
144. Oaks and Hill, *Carthage Conspiracy,* 195. See the *Warsaw Signal,* October 15, 1845, for Sheriff Backenstos's "Proclamation II," which contains his account of the Worrell episode.

145. *Warsaw Signal*, September 17, 1845.
146. Oaks and Hill, *Carthage Conspiracy*, 198.
147. *Warsaw Signal*, June 4, 1845.
148. *Warsaw Signal*, November 26, 1845.
149. *Warsaw Signal*, September 24, 1845.
150. *Warsaw Signal*, September 25, 1845.
151. These were the county militias Governor Ford called to service on June 29, 1844, two days after the murder of the Smith brothers. See a copy of the order in Davis, *An Authentic Account*, 31.
152. See the report in the *Warsaw Signal*, May 21, 1845.
153. Hallwas and Launius give the vote as 25–14 in the senate and 75–37 in the house. See *Cultures in Conflict*, 267.
154. See the story on this matter in the *Sangamo Journal*, June 10, 1842.
155. *Warsaw Signal*, November 24, 1841; emphasis in original.
156. See the undated sheet titled "To the Anti-Mormons Citizens of Hancock and the Surrounding Counties," *Warsaw Signal*, October 4, 1845. Even within the anti-Mormon camp, leaders like Thomas Gregg and Dr. Samuel Marshall condemned illegal actions against the Mormons. See Gregg, *History of Hancock County*, 339–40.
157. *Warsaw Signal*, May 14, 1845.
158. *Warsaw Signal*, October 9, 1844.
159. For the Indian council, see the *Alton Telegraph and Democratic Review*, February 22, 1845; and for Young's actions, see Oaks and Hill, *Carthage Conspiracy*, 68–69.
160. Hallwas and Launius, *Cultures in Conflict*, 267, 278.
161. Hill, *Quest for Refuge*, 174.
162. Deming's letter to his family is quoted in Hallwas and Launius, *Cultures in Conflict*, 271.
163. *Warsaw Signal*, September 18, 1844.
164. For the text of the letter, see the *Warsaw Signal*, July 31, 1844.
165. See the text of the memorial reproduced in Hallwas and Launius, *Cultures in Conflict*, 264–65.
166. *Warsaw Signal*, October 15, 1845.

CHAPTER 6: RELIGIOUS TOLERATION AND POLITICAL IDEOLOGY IN THE ILLINOIS REGIME

1. John E. Hallwas and Roger D. Launius, *Cultures in Conflict: A Documentary History of the Mormon War in Illinois* (Logan: Utah State University Press, 1995), 5–8.
2. Terryl L. Givens, *The Viper on the Hearth: Mormons, Myths, and the Construction of Heresy* (New York: Oxford University Press, 1997), 21.

3. This use of *hegemony* was originated by the Italian anti-Fascist and Marxist revolutionary Antonio Gramsci. See "The Study of Philosophy," in *Selections from the Prison Notebooks,* ed. and trans. Quintin Hoare and Geoffrey Nowell Smith (New York: International Publishers, 1971), 323–80, especially 333. Unlike traditional Marxists, and following an approach he traced back to Machiavelli, Gramsci focused on the important role played by ideas originating in civil society and the arts in the process of legitimating the power of the state. For an effort to apply Gramsci's concept of hegemony to cultural studies more broadly, see Stuart Hall, "Gramsci's Relevance for the Study of Race and Ethnicity," in *Stuart Hall: Critical Dialogues in Cultural Studies,* ed. David Morley and Kuan-Hsing Chen (London: Routledge, 1996), 411–40.
4. Givens, *The Viper on the Hearth,* 23.
5. For the "politics of articulation" at the national level, see Stephen Skowronek, *The Politics Presidents Make: Leadership from John Adams to Bill Clinton* (Cambridge, MA: Harvard University Press, 1997), 41.
6. Stephen Skowronek and Mathew Glassman, eds., *Formative Acts: American Politics in the Making* (Philadelphia: University of Pennsylvania Press, 2007), 1.
7. *St. Clair Banner,* March 13, 1844.
8. For the deliberative approach to First Amendment law, and freedom of the press in particular, see Cass R. Sunstein, *Democracy and the Problem of Free Speech* (New York: Free Press, 1995).
9. *Alton Telegraph,* April 20, 1836.
10. All quotations from the 1818 constitution are found in Emil Joseph Verlie, ed., *Illinois Constitutions* (Springfield: Illinois State Historical Library, 1919), 43.
11. *Alton Telegraph,* April 20, 1836; emphasis in original.
12. *Quincy Argus,* April 13, 1839.
13. Emma Smith to Joseph Smith, March 7, 1839, p. 37, The Joseph Smith Papers, https://www.josephsmithpapers.org/paper-summary/letter-from-emma-smith-7-march-1839/1.
14. *Daily Chicago American,* July 23, 1839. The other papers included the *Illinois Republican* and the *Sangamo Journal.*
15. See the *Daily Chicago American,* July 23, 1839. The editor adds: "The practice [of persecution for religious opinion] is not only pitiful and unjust, but it always counteracts its purpose. . . . Nothing is so difficult to quench as religious enthusiasm. Human nature sympathizes with the oppressed, and nothing is more true than the saying 'the blood of martyrs is the seed of the church.'"

16. The problem of asymmetry in toleration has long been seen by liberal theorists as a glaring instance of the vexing problem posed by illiberal minority groups more generally. See, for example, Karl Popper, "Toleration and Intellectual Responsibility," in which he focuses on the problem of "minorities . . . who are unwilling to reciprocate the tolerance offered to them by the majority . . . minorities who accept a principle of intolerance." In *On Toleration*, ed. Susan Mendus and David Edwards (Oxford: Clarendon Press, 1987), 18.
17. See the article on "American Institutions—The Press" from the *Cincinnati Chronicle* excerpted in the *Warsaw Message*, June 10, 1843.
18. See Gregg's critique of Orestes Brownson's views in the *Warsaw Message*, May 24, 1843; for the idea that Democrats conceived of political progress in terms of quantity, freedom, and space and the Whigs quality, direction, and time, see Major L. Wilson, *Space, Time, and Freedom: The Quest for Nationality and the Irrepressible Conflict 1815–1861* (Westport, CT: Greenwood Press, 1974).
19. F. A. Snyder, *The Politician*, June 8, 1844.
20. Edith Packard Kelly, "Northern Illinois in the Great Whig Convention of 1840," *Transactions of the Illinois State Historical Society* (Springfield: Illinois State Journal, 1915), 137.
21. John Mason Peck, *A Gazeteer of Illinois* (Jacksonville: Goudy, 1834), 53–54.
22. Walter Bagby to Nancy E. Rogers, August 4, 1844, Walter Bagby Papers, University of Kentucky.
23. *Warsaw Signal*, September 18, 1844.
24. *Warsaw Message*, May 17, 1843.
25. *Times and Seasons*, March 15, 1844, 470.
26. Joseph Story, quoted in Steven K. Green, *The Second Disestablishment: Church and State in Nineteenth-Century America* (New York: Oxford University Press, 2010), 5; for the "voluntarist" view, see Stephen D. Smith, *Foreordained Failure: The Quest for a Constitutional Principle of Religious Freedom* (New York: Oxford University Press, 1995), 20.
27. *Times and Seasons*, December 20, 1841; emphasis in original.
28. *Times and Seasons*, October 1840, 188.
29. *Nauvoo Neighbor*, December 13, 1843.
30. *General Smith's Views on the Powers and Policy of the Government of the United States* (Nauvoo, IL: John Taylor, 1844), 3, 5.
31. Joseph Smith to the editor of *The Globe* (Washington, DC), April 15, 1844, *Times and Seasons*, May 1, 1844, 508–10.

32. *Warsaw Signal,* August 28, 1844.
33. *Warsaw Signal,* February 2, 1842; emphasis in the original.
34. *Warsaw Signal,* July 9, 1843.
35. For the obituary, see *Warsaw Signal,* October 1, 1842; Sharp did not resume the helm again until February 14, 1844. By then group polarization was complete, and the *Signal* was resurrected under a new series published steadily until the hostilities ceased in the fall of 1846.
36. *Warsaw Message,* September 20, 1843.
37. Ricahrd J. Ellis traces these two different conceptions of equality through many eras of United States political history in *American Political Cultures* (New York: Oxford University Press, 1992), 43–62.
38. Jean-Jacques Rousseau, *Of the Social Contract,* trans. Donald A. Cress, intro. Peter Gay (Indianapolis: Hackett Publishing, 1988), 24.
39. The quotation is taken from the first page of Leggett's newspaper, *The Plaindealer,* first published in New York City on December 3, 1836.
40. *The Examiner,* July 29, 1937.
41. *The Plaindealer,* June 3, 1837.
42. For Kinney's story, see James Simeone, "William Kinney's Agrarian Dilemma," *Journal of Illinois History* 13 (Spring 2010): 2–32. While the internal improvement resolutions introduced in the General Assembly by Douglas in 1836 left blank the amount to be raised, and while the cost ballooned over the years such that the state owed seventeen million dollars by 1842, the bill passed in 1837 asked for a loan of eight million. See Theodore Calvin Pease, *The Frontier State 1818–1848* (Urbana: University of Illinois Press, 1987), 212, 213, 231.
43. *Warsaw Message,* May 24, 1843.
44. William Kinney, quoted in James Simeone, *Democracy and Slavery in Frontier Illinois: The Bottomland Republic* (DeKalb: Northern Illinois University Press, 2000), 32.
45. Typical of the Jacksonian tendency to see equal rights through an oppositional egalitarian lens is the opening editorial by Robert K. Fleming to the *Illinois Mercury* published in Belleville, Illinois, on May 11, 1839: "In politics, the Mercury will lend its aid to the promotion of democratic principles. It will oppose the creating of monopolies, granting of chartered rights and special privileges to particular individuals which are denied to the great body of the People, and will at all times advocate the doctrines of Equal Rights—the interests of the many against the privileges of the few."

46. See Gatewood's speech in *Journal of the Senate of the Ninth General Assembly of the State of Illinois* (Vandalia, IL: J. Y. Sawyer, 1835), 419; emphasis in original.
47. *The Letters of Stephen A. Douglas* (Urbana: University of Illinois Press, 1961), 3.
48. Robert Bruce Flanders, "The Kingdom of God in Illinois: Politics in Utopia," *Dialogue: A Journal of Mormon Thought* 5, no. 1 (Spring 1970): 27.
49. See, for example, the *Nauvoo Neighbor,* September 6, 1843. New businesses include rope, spinning wheel, cabinet, lime, and shoe manufacturers.
50. Mason Brayman to Joseph Smith, July 29, 1843, pp. 4, 6, The Joseph Smith Papers, https://www.josephsmithpapers.org/paper-summary/letter-from-mason-brayman-29-july-1843/6.
51. *Warsaw Message,* September 6, 1843.
52. Thomas Gregg, *History of Hancock County, Illinois* (Chicago: Chas C. Chapman, 1880), 749.
53. Roger D. Launius, "Anti-Mormonism in Illinois: Thomas C. Sharp's Unfinished History of the Mormon War, 1845," *Journal of Mormon History* 15 (1989): 28.
54. See the letter and Sharp's silhouette published in *State Register,* November 8, 1844; Sharp's biography in Gregg, *History of Hancock County,* 748–57, makes no mention of this episode; see also Annette P. Hampshire, "Thomas Sharp and Anti-Mormon Sentiment in Illinois, 1842–1846," *Journal of the Illinois State Historical Society* 72, no. 2 (May 1979): 82–100.
55. See, for example, Donald J. Ratcliffe, "Antimasonry and Partisanship in Greater New England, 1826–1836," *Journal of the Early Republic* 15, no. 2 (Summer 1995): 199–239.
56. Gerald Leonard, *The Invention of Party Politics: Federalism, Popular Sovereignty, and Constitutional Development in Jacksonian Illinois* (Chapel Hill: University of North Carolina Press, 2002).
57. Mark Voss-Hubbard, "The 'Third Party Tradition' Reconsidered: Third Parties and American Public Life, 1830–1900," *Journal of American History* 86, no. 1 (June 1999): 121–50.
58. Michael F. Holt, *Political Parties and American Political Development from the Age of Jackson to the Age of Lincoln* (Baton Rouge: Louisiana State University Press, 1992), 5–6.
59. See Paul Goodman, *Toward a Christian Republic: Antimasonry and the Great Transition in New England 1826–1836* (New York: Oxford university Press, 1988).

60. See the anonymous letter in the *State Register,* November 8, 1844.
61. The first reference in print to a "Jack Mormon" is in an editorial by Thomas Sharp in the *Warsaw Signal,* February 9, 1842; Thomas Gregg began using the term in a casual reference to "a Jack Mormon exemplified" in the *Warsaw Message,* September 22, 1843.
62. *Warsaw Message,* August 6, 1843.
63. For a detailed overview of the Anti-Masons, see Goodman, *Toward a Christian Republic.*
64. *Warsaw Signal,* February 2, 1842.
65. Daniel Walker Howe, *The Political Culture of the American Whigs* (Chicago: University of Chicago Press, 1979), 150.
66. See Robert Hofstadter, *The Paranoid Style in American Politics and Other Essays* (Chicago: University of Chicago Press, 1979), 3–40, and David Brion Davis, "Some Themes of Counter-Subversion: An Analysis of Anti-Masonic, Anti-Catholic, and Anti-Mormon Literature," *Mississippi Valley Historical Review* 47 (September 1960): 206–24.
67. *Warsaw Signal,* December 29, 1841; emphasis in original.
68. *Warsaw Signal,* May 12, 1841.
69. Richard J. Ellis offers an excellent review of the varieties of equality claims in the American setting. See "Rival Visions of Equality: Process versus Results," in *American Political Cultures* (New York: Oxford University Press, 1992), 43–62. Ellis pursues the idea of illiberal egalitarianism, termed *particularist egalitarianism* here, in late-nineteenth- and twentieth-century American thought in *The Dark Side of the American Left: Illiberal Egalitarianism in America* (Lawrence: University of Kansas Press, 1998).
70. The quotation is from Judith N. Shklar, "Jean-Jacques Rousseau and Equality," in *Rousseau's Political Writings,* ed. Alan Ritter and Julia Conway Bondanella (New York: W. W. Norton, 1988), 260–74, quote at 261.
71. Peter Singer, "All Animals Are Equal," *Philosophical Exchange* 1 (1974): 103–16, quote at 103.
72. *Warsaw Signal,* April 13, 1842; emphasis in original.
73. *Warsaw Signal,* January 26, 1842.
74. *Warsaw Signal,* July 9, 1842.
75. *Illinois Statesman,* April 29, 1843; emphasis in original.
76. Turner's candidate, Joseph Duncan, drew out the particularist ethnocultural implications of this view for the larger Whig Party, indicating his tendency toward nativism. Duncan regretted seeing "the cringing of ambitious office seekers of both parties at

the feet of the Mormon Prophet," then added: "Formidable as this Mormon Prophet is becoming, his is not the only power ambitious of political sway . . . that may take advantage of our divisions. All know that there is another large and powerful church in this country, whose faith in its head is also superior to their political opinions, and we see by repeated accounts of late from Europe, that extensive arrangements are now making to send millions of his subjects to this country." *Illinois Statesman,* April 29, 1843.

77. For the definition of autonomy as agency committed to individual projects, see Doug Johnson, *The Idea of a Liberal Theory* (Princeton, NJ: Princeton University Press, 1991), 22–24, 79–86; for the concept of "individually scripted" ideas of the good, see Leslie Pickering Francis and Anita Silvers, "Liberalism and Individually Scripted Ideas of the Good: Meeting the Challenge of Dependent Agency," *Social Theory and Practice* 33, no. 2 (April 2007): 311–34.
78. J. David Greenstone, *The Lincoln Persuasion: Remaking American Liberalism* (Princeton, NJ: Princeton University Press, 1993), 269.
79. *Warsaw Signal,* February 28, 1844.
80. *Warsaw Signal,* June 22 and June 9, 1841.
81. Ford, *History of Illinois,* 150.
82. Lawrence J. Friedman, *Gregarious Saints: Self and Community in American Abolitionism 1830–1870* (Cambridge: Cambridge University Press, 1982), 50.
83. Dallin H. Oaks and Marvin S. Hill, *Carthage Conspiracy: The Trial of the Accused Assassins of Joseph Smith* (Urbana: University of Illinois Press, 1975), 66.
84. Richard Maxwell Brown, *Strain of Violence: Historical Studies of American Violence and Vigilantism* (New York: Oxford University Press, 1975), 106.
85. Roger D. Launius, "Anti-Mormonism in Illinois: Thomas C. Sharp's Unfinished History of the Mormon War, 1845," *Journal of Mormon History* 15 (1989): 27–45.
86. *Nauvoo Expositor,* June 7, 1844.
87. *Warsaw Signal,* February 14, 1844.
88. Sharp called Smith an "unparalleled knave" and "infamous blasphemer" in June of 1841. Simple religious intolerance then progressed rapidly to accusations of fraud; the Mormons were not only "religious imposters but swindlers." See *Warsaw Signal,* June 9 and July 7, 1841.
89. *Warsaw Signal,* June 9, 1841.
90. *Warsaw Signal,* July 7, 1841.

91. It was not until the spring of 1844 that Sharp in his notices began to suggest that his subscribers were paying him regularly.
92. Oaks and Hill, *Carthage Conspiracy,* note that "examination of court records from 1844 through 1846 shows that grand juries continued to indict accused persons, and voluntary dismissals of the prosecuting attorney continued to account for far more people going free than acquittals by a jury" (201). This provides some evidence for the claim that the Illinois regime did not completely dissolve in Hancock County, even during the worst of the troubles.
93. *Warsaw Signal,* September 30, 1845. Sharp never issued a retraction but two weeks later cited a witness who claimed the actual murderers had stayed locally with the Mormons. *Warsaw Signal,* October 15, 1844. For details, see Marvin S. Hill, *Quest for Refuge: The Mormon Flight from American Pluralism* (Salt Lake City: Signature Books, 1989), 172.
94. For the hoaxes and rumors, see the *Warsaw Signal,* July 17, 1841; for the story about the Warren settlers, see the November 24, 1841, edition.
95. See *Times and Seasons,* November 15, 1841, 602.
96. See the letter dated August 22, 1841, in Roger D. Launius, "American Home Missionary Society Ministers and Mormon Nauvoo: Selected Letters," *Western Illinois Regional Studies* 8, no. 1 (Spring 1985): 21.
97. See Gregg's use of these terms in his condemnation of the approach to jury nullification in the case of a posse homicide in New Jersey taken by the Jacksonville *Illinoisan, Warsaw Message,* May 17, 1843.
98. *Warsaw Signal,* August 13, 1842.
99. *Warsaw Signal,* August 20, 1842.
100. *Warsaw Signal,* August 20, 1842.
101. See Bennett's letter in the *Sangamo Journal,* July 2, 1842.
102. This point is too often denied by individualists, who are inclined to believe that it is only "the more vulnerable ones who need a collective identity to cling to." See Ian Buruma, *Murder in Amsterdam: Liberal Europe, Islam, and the Limits of Tolerance* (New York: Penguin Books, 2006), 181.
103. Herman Melville, *Typee: A Peep at Polynesian Life* (1846; repr., New York: Penguin Books, 1996), 196.
104. Oaks and Hill, *Carthage Conspiracy,* 185; see the compelling analysis of jury nullification on pages 210–14.
105. *Warsaw Signal,* April 22, 1846.

106. *The Wasp,* July 2, 1842.
107. *Warsaw Signal,* July 8, 9, 1842; emphasis in original.
108. Daniel Parker, quoted in Simeone, *Democracy and Slavery,* 174.
109. Richard K. Fenn, *The Persistence of Purgatory* (Cambridge: Cambridge University Press, 1995), 113.
110. *Warsaw Signal,* June 9, 1841.
111. *Warsaw Signal,* June 9, 1841.
112. Daniel J. Elazar, *Cities of the Prairie: The Metropolitan Frontier and American Politics* (New York: Basic Books, 1970), 260.
113. Fawn Brodie, *No Man Knows My History: The Life of Joseph Smith,* 2nd ed. (New York: Vintage Books, 1995), 323.
114. See the letters published in the October 27 and November 22 editions of the *Warsaw Signal.*
115. *Warsaw Signal,* June 23, 1841; emphasis in original.
116. James B. Allen and Thomas G. Alexander, eds., *Manchester Mormons: The Journal of William Clayton, 1840–1842* (Santa Barbara, CA: Peregrine Smith, 1974), 201.
117. Allen and Alexander, *Manchester Mormons,* 209.
118. In another example, Smith blew up at a minister who had come to visit him. See the extract of the interview, which had been proceeding calmly until Smith's outburst, published in *Warsaw Signal,* December 15, 1841.
119. "The Mormon priesthood," historian Klaus J. Hansen explains, "evolved into a lay organization ideally including all male members that have reached the age of twelve. A boy is first ordained to the office of deacon in the Aaronic priesthood, and then advances to the offices of teacher and priest. At about the age of nineteen, a young man who has moved up through the ranks, and who is deemed worthy, is then ordained to the office of elder in the Melchizedek priesthood." *Mormonism and the American Experience* (Chicago: University of Chicago Press, 1981), 37.
120. Doctrine and Covenants 131:1–2 and 132.
121. Richard Bushman sees in this institution a bastion against isolation: "Husbands who are sealed to their wives will attain to unimaginable glory, while those who are not sealed will remain alone. Glory is juxtaposed against loneliness." See "The Inner Joseph Smith," *Journal of Mormon History* 32, no. 1 (Spring 2006): 76–77.
122. See Lawrence Foster, *Women, Family, and Utopia: Communal Experiments of the Shakers, the Oneida Community, and the Mormons* (Syracuse, NY: Syracuse University Press, 1991), 153.
123. Eliza Snow, quoted in Linda King Newell and Valeen Tippetts Avery, *Mormon Enigma: Emma Hale Smith: Prophet's Wife, "Elect*

Lady," Polygamy's Foe, 1804–1879 (Garden City, NY: Doubleday, 1984), 129.

124. Foster, *Women, Family, and Utopia,* 124.
125. *Times and Seasons,* May 15, 1841, 441.
126. *Alton Telegraph,* December 30, 1843; emphasis in original.
127. *Warsaw Message,* December 27, 1843.

CHAPTER 7: THOMAS FORD AND THE POLITICS OF CIVIC WORTH

1. *Warsaw Signal,* February 14, 1844.
2. For the Anti-Rent lull between the fall of 1842 and the spring of 1844, see Henry Christman, *Tin Horns and Calico: A Decisive Episode in the Emergence of Democracy* (New York: Henry Holt, 1945), 46–72. For the Kensington riots, which exploded in May of 1844, in Philadelphia, see Michael Feldberg, *The Turbulent Era: Riot and Disorder in Jacksonian America* (New York: Oxford University Press, 1980), 9–23.
3. Joseph Smith History, vol. E-1, 1886, The Joseph Smith Papers, https://www.josephsmithpapers.org/paper-summary/history-1838-1856-volume-e-1-1-july-1843-30-april-1844/258.
4. See Ford's letter of January 29, 1844, in the *Warsaw Signal,* February 14, 1844. The letter was prompted by an unnamed "citizen of Hancock County" who had forwarded to the governor for his comment the "proceedings and resolutions" of the anti-Mormon meeting held at Carthage on September 6, 1843.
5. Thomas Ford, *Message of the Governor of the State of Illinois, in Relation to the Disturbances in Hancock County* (Springfield, IL: Walters & Weber, 1844), 20.
6. See the report of the meeting in the *Warsaw Signal,* February 14, 1844.
7. *Warsaw Signal,* February 14, 1844; emphasis in original.
8. See Theodore Calvin Pease, ed., *Illinois Election Returns, 1818–1848* (Springfield: Illinois State Historical Library, 1923), 351, 409.
9. Sharp described Gregg's faction as "conservative" in an editorial, *Warsaw Signal,* February 21, 1844.
10. *Warsaw Message,* January 31, 1844; emphasis in original.
11. *Warsaw Signal,* February 21, 1844.
12. See "Proposals for Resuscitating the Warsaw Signal," *Warsaw Signal,* February 14, 1844.
13. *Warsaw Signal,* September 17, 1844.
14. *Autobiography of the Late Colonel George T. M. Davis* (New York: Jenkins and McCowan, 1891), 50.

15. Sharp duly noted the disaffections and defections of Sidney Rigdon, Lyman Wight, and Emma Smith, but none of these issued in the dissolution of the main body of saints as he had often predicted.
16. Thomas Ford, *A History of Illinois: From Its Commencement as a State in 1818 to 1847*, ed. Rodney O. Davis (1854; repr., Urbana: University of Illinois Press, 1995), 172.
17. Pierre Bourdieu, "Rethinking the State: Genesis and Structure in the Bureaucratic Field," trans. Loic J. D. Wacquant and Samar Farage, in *State/Culture: State-Formation after the Cultural Turn*, ed. George Steinmetz (Ithaca, NY: Cornell University Press, 1999), 53–75, quote at 53.
18. *Warsaw Signal*, July 10, 1844.
19. Sharp's speech is found in William M. Daniels, *A Correct Account of the Murder of Generals Joseph and Hyrum Smith, at Carthage, on the 27th Day of June, 1844* (Nauvoo, IL: John Taylor, 1845), 8. Daniels's account no doubt includes many exaggerations and coached phrases, but it also includes many confirmed details, such as Sharp's speech at the railroad shanty here referenced and the "single file" approach the troops took to ambush the Carthage Grey guards at the jail. Sharp's speech is reported as follows by George T. M. Davis: "The officers formally disbanded their troops, but requested them to remain a few moments. They were called to order, when a citizen, (not connected with the troops), who believed he would be murdered, if the Smiths were allowed to escape, addressed them for a short period." *An Authentic Account of the Massacre of Joseph Smith, the Mormon Prophet, and Hyrum Smith, His Brother, Together with a Brief History of the Rise and Progress of Mormonism, and All the Circumstances Which Led to Their Death* (St. Louis: Chambers & Knapp, 1844), 28.
20. Thomas Gregg stated: "This purpose, and only this we are convinced—to take the prisoners and run them to Missouri—was as far as any purpose went, until they reached the door of the jail. There they were met with resistance—with fight; a defense certainly to have been expected; and it ended in death." *History of Hancock County, Illinois* (Chicago: Chas C. Chapman, 1880), 325.
21. *Warsaw Signal*, October 9, 1844.
22. Ford, *Message of the Governor*, 19.
23. Dallin H. Oaks and Marvin S. Hill, *Carthage Conspiracy: The Trial of the Accused Assassins of Joseph Smith* (Urbana: University of Illinois Press, 1975), 38. The details of Ford's prosecution of the case are laid out in this carefully researched book.

24. The Whig paper is quoted in Oaks and Hill, *Carthage Conspiracy*, 41.
25. The terms of the constitution of 1818 make the governor eligible for a second term only after an eight-year lacuna.
26. For the Douglas quotation, see Oaks and Hill, *Carthage Conspiracy*, 42.
27. Oaks and Hill, 42.
28. The state had decided to prosecute the brothers' murders separately. After the Joseph Smith murder trial ended in acquittal, the state declined to pursue the second Hyrum Smith trial.
29. See the *Warsaw Signal*, September 30, 1845, for the resolutions of the "Public Meeting at Churchville" in Clark County, Missouri, which denounced Governor Ford's "proclamation to the citizens of Missouri and Iowa, warning [the anti-Mormons] to take no part in the quarrel now pending in Hancock County." The proclamation, dated September 26, 1845, was reprinted in the *Warsaw Signal*, October 15, 1845.
30. *Alton Telegraph*, October 16, 1846.
31. Leonard J. Arrington and Davis Bitton, in *The Mormon Experience: A History of the Latter-day Saints*, 2nd ed. (Urbana: University of Illinois Press, 1992), 81, emphasize that "Governor Ford broke his promise not to leave Carthage without taking the prisoners along." Annette P. Hampshire, in *Mormonism in Conflict: The Nauvoo Years* (New York: Edwin Mellen Press, 1985), 252, reviews Ford's decision not to call out a militia to stop the mounting tensions during the summer of 1846. She sums up Ford's actions: "Since 1844 Governor Ford had moved from being inept to becoming ineffectual."
32. Ford, *History of Illinois*, 172.
33. See the "Autobiography of Thomas Ford," published in the *Peoria Democratic Press*, December 18, 1850. All the following quotations from Ford are from this piece.
34. See J. F. Snyder, "Governor Ford and His Family," *Journal of the Illinois State Historical Society* 3, no. 2 (July 1910): 45–51, quote at 45.
35. See the comments of "Mr. Asbury" in Gregg, *History of Hancock County*, 414.
36. John F. Snyder claims that Ford's efforts "almost alone" to combat the northern-tier "succession movement" clinched his selection by the party leaders at Springfield. *Adam J. Snyder and His Period in Illinois History, 1817–1842* (Virginia, IL: E. Needham, 1906), 415–16. Ford rehearsed his argument for the unique status of Illinois as a national unifier to open his *History*.

37. Charles Ballance, *The History of Peoria, Illinois* (Peoria, IL: N. C. Nason, 1870), 250.
38. See the speech printed in full in the *Sangamo Journal,* December 16, 1842. All quotations are from this source.
39. For the canal figures, see James William Putnam, *The Illinois and Michigan Canal: A Study in Economic History* (Chicago: University of Chicago Press, 1918), 35, 56; John Henry Krenkel, *Illinois Internal Improvements* (Cedar Rapids, IA: Torch Press, 1958), 38; and John M. Lamb, *Historical Essays on the Illinois-Michigan Canal* (Romeoville, IL: Lewis University, 2009), 55.
40. *Sangamo Journal,* December 16, 1842.
41. Gregg, *History of Hancock County,* 325.
42. See Ford's comments in a footnote in *History of Illinois,* 238.
43. Gregg, *History of Hancock County,* 372.
44. *Warsaw Signal,* July 17, 1844.
45. For Ford's detailed rejection of Davis's charge, see *History of Illinois,* 255. For Davis's charge, see the series of editorials he wrote for the *Alton Telegraph,* beginning with "Governor Ford and the Mormons" on September 28, 1844. Davis became an ardent opponent of Ford despite having praised his even-handed approach in his *Authentic Account* (18–22).
46. *Warsaw Signal,* July 17, 1844.
47. Ford, *History of Illinois,* 242. For the eye-witness account of Roosevelt's speech, see William M. Daniels, *A Correct Account of the Murder of Generals Joseph and Hyrum Smith, at Carthage, on the 27th Day of June, 1844* (Nauvoo, IL: John Taylor, 1845), 5.
48. *Warsaw Signal,* June 29, 1844, and July 17, 1844.
49. *Warsaw Signal,* October 9, 1844.
50. *Warsaw Signal,* July 17, 1844.
51. This is George Davis's phrase from his *Autobiography* (79). This work, published posthumously, contains many factual errors; it must be used with caution when citing specific events.
52. *Warsaw Signal,* July 17, 1844.
53. Ballance, *History of Peoria,* 211; emphasis in original. A similar approach to the law was typical in northern-tier Whig views of vigilante societies. See Elmer Baldwin, *History of LaSalle County, Illinois* (Chicago: Rand McNally, 1877), 194–95.
54. Ford, *History of Illinois,* xxv.
55. *Warsaw Signal,* November 14, 1846.
56. Ford, *History of Illinois,* 172.
57. Ford, 70–72.
58. See Ford's letter to the committee of "New Citizens" of Hancock County dated October 2, 1846, in the *Warsaw Signal,* October 20, 1846.

59. *Sangamo Journal,* March 25, 1842; emphasis in original.
60. See Snyder, *Adam J. Snyder,* 412.
61. For Sharp's claim, see the *Warsaw Signal,* November 24, 1841; for Davis's, see *An Authentic Account,* 5.
62. William Harris, *Mormonism Portrayed: Its Errors and Absurdities Exposed. And the Spirit and Designs of Its Authors Made Manifest* (Warsaw, IL: Sharpe & Gamble Publishers, 1841), 35–36.
63. *Warsaw Signal,* October 22, 1845.
64. Dennis Chong and Raoul Rogers, "Reviving Group Consciousness," in *The Politics of Democratic Inclusion,* ed. Christina Wolbrecht and Rodney E. Hero (Philadelphia: Temple University Press, 2005), 45–74, quote at 47.
65. For the empirical links, see Chong and Rogers, "Reviving Group Consciousness," 47–48, 68–69.
66. Richard Lyman Bushman, *Joseph Smith: Rough Stone Rolling* (New York: Vintage Books, 2005), 443.
67. Udney Hay Jacob, *An Extract from a Manuscript Entitled The Peace Maker, or the Doctrines of the Millennium: Being a Treatise on Religion and Jurisprudence, or a New System of Religion and Politics* (Nauvoo, IL: J. Smith, 1842), 4, 3, 11.
68. Linda King Newell and Valeen Tippetts Avery, *Mormon Enigma: Emma Hale Smith: Prophet's Wife, "Elect Lady," Polygamy's Foe, 1804–1879* (Garden City, NY: Doubleday, 1984), 139.
69. Michael W. Homer, *Joseph's Temples: The Dynamic Relationship between Freemasonry and Mormonism* (Salt Lake City: University of Utah Press, 2014), 232.
70. Newell and Avery, *Mormon Enigma,* 143.
71. Marvin S. Hill, *Quest for Refuge: The Mormon Flight from American Pluralism* (Salt Lake City: Signature Books, 1989), 154.
72. On the Peoria case, see Dana E. Weiner, "Anti-abolition Violence and Freedom of Speech in Peoria, Illinois, 1843–1848," *Journal of Illinois History* 11 (Autumn 2008): 179–204.
73. Davis, *Autobiography,* 62.
74. Leonard L. Richards, *"Gentlemen of Property and Standing": Anti-abolition Mobs in Jacksonian America* (London: Oxford University Press, 1970), 61–67, 84, 107–8.
75. *Sangamo Journal,* January 21, 1841; emphasis in original.
76. See J. B. Turner, *Mormonism in All Ages: Or the Rise, Progress, and Causes of Mormonism; with the Biography of Its Author and Founder, Joseph Smith, Jr.* (New York: Platt & Peters, 1842), 3.
77. Turner, *Mormonism in All Ages,* 3–4.
78. Turner, 57.
79. For the impact of the loss of political control within a "literally cosmic setting of divine judgment" as a driving force in the

reform Protestantism of this era, see Robert H. Abzug, *Cosmos Crumbling: American Reform and the Religious Imagination* (New York: Oxford University Press, 1994), 8.

80. John Rawls, *A Theory of Justice* (Cambridge, MA: Harvard University Press, 1971), 220.
81. See Barbara Herman, "Pluralism and the Community of Moral Judgment," in *Toleration: An Elusive Virtue,* ed. David Heyd (Princeton, NJ: Princeton University Press, 1996), 62.
82. Reynolds v. United States, 98 US 145 (1879), quote at 164.
83. See the pioneering study of Muzafur Sherif, "Experiments in Group Conflict," *Scientific American* 195 (1956): 54–58.
84. See Thomas Schelling, "Sorting and Mixing: Race and Sex," in *Micromotives and Macrobehavior* (New York: W. W. Norton, 1978), 137–66.
85. See V. O. Key, *Southern Politics in State and Nation* (New York: Vintage Book, 1949), 319–44. For a later study showing that before the Voting Rights Act, Black registration denials were greatest in counties where Black citizens threatened to have a majority, see Donald R. Mathews and James W. Prothro, "Social and Economic Factors and Negro Voter Registration in the South," *American Political Science Review* 57 (March 1963): 24–44.
86. See Paul M. Sniderman and Edward G. Carmines, *Reaching Beyond Race* (Cambridge, MA: Harvard University Press, 1997).
87. See Theodore J. Lowi, "Four Systems of Politics, Policy, and Choice," *Public Administration Review* 32, no. 4 (July/August 1972): 298–310, quote at 300.
88. Charles Manfred Thompson, *The Illinois Whigs before 1846* (Urbana: University of Illinois, 1915), 100.
89. This debate topic was on the agenda of the Peoria Lyceum a few weeks after the Lovejoy murder. See the *Peoria Register and North-Western Gazetteer,* December 16, 1837.
90. Michael J. Pfeifer, *Rough Justice: Lynching and American Society, 1874–1947* (Urbana: University of Illinois Press, 2004), 108. When the judge in *The Ox-Bow Incident,* a fictional account of a Nevada lynch mob, threatens to arrest one of the mob "for impeding the course of justice," she replies, as no doubt many frontier Illinoisans from every tier believed: "Judge, you can't impede what don't move anyway." See Walter Van Tilburg Clark, *The Ox-Bow Incident* (New York: American Library, 1940), 81–82. For a perceptive assessment of the novel from the perspective of social psychology, see Casey Plach, "Group Membership and Its Adverse Psychological Effects in *The Ox-Bow Incident*"

(unpublished manuscript, October 11, 2011), https://www.iwu.edu/political-science/casey-plach-essay-pdf.

91. Klaus J. Hansen, *Quest for Empire: The Political Kingdom of God and the Council of Fifty in Mormon History* (East Lansing: Michigan State University Press, 1967), 77–81.
92. Richard E. Bennett, Susan Easton Black, and Donald Q. Cannon, *The Nauvoo Legion in Illinois: A History of the Mormon Militia, 1841–1846* (Norman, OK: Arthur H. Clark, 2010), 229, 258, 269.
93. The Lyceum took place on January 27, 1838. See the copy of the speech published in the *Sangamo Journal*, February 3, 1838; emphasis in original.
94. *Sangamo Journal*, February 3, 1838.
95. See Alexander Hamilton, *The Federalist Papers*, ed. Clinton Rossiter (1788; repr., New York: New American Library, 1961), 120.
96. *Warsaw Signal*, February 28, 1844.
97. *Warsaw Signal*, February 28, 1844.
98. Howard Zinn, *Disobedience and Democracy: Nine Fallacies on Law and Order* (Cambridge, MA: South End Press, 2002), 12–38.
99. This is the tack Oaks and Hill take in *Carthage Conspiracy*. See the introduction (xi–xiv).
100. Put another way, this suggests that political questions can never be resolved by judicial opinions. Thomas Ford explained: "It may . . . be said of the ablest and best judges, those most celebrated for dispensing equity in common cases between individuals, that when any great political question on which parties are arrayed comes up for decision, the utmost that can be expected of them is an able and learned argument in favor of their own party, whose views they must naturally favor for the very reason that they prefer one party over the other. Such a decision, therefore, can never be satisfactory to the opposite party, which well knows that if the judges had been of a different political complexion the decision would have been otherwise." *History of Illinois*, 148.
101. For first- and second-order authority problems, see H. L. A. Hart, *The Concept of Law* (Oxford: Oxford University Press, 1961).
102. John Keane, *Civil Society: Old Ideals, New Visions* (Stanford, CA: Stanford University Press, 1998), 50; emphasis in original.
103. Alexis de Tocqueville, *Democracy in America*, ed. J. P. Mayer, trans. George Lawrence (1832–36; repr., Garden City, NY: Doubleday, 1969), 528. The full quotation runs as follows: "I do not think that the doctrine of self-interest as preached in America is in all respects self-evident. But it does contain many truths so clear that for men to see them it is enough to educate them. Hence it

is all-important for them to be educated, the age of blind sacrifice and instinctive virtues is already long past, and I see a time approaching in which freedom, public peace, and social stability will not be able to last without education."

104. Quintin Skinner, *Foundations of Modern Political Thought,* vol. 1 (Cambridge: Cambridge University Press, 1978), 353.
105. *Alton Telegraph,* October 29, 1844.
106. Ford, *History of Illinois,* 255.
107. Hampshire, *Mormonism in Conflict,* 228.
108. Ford, *History of Illinois,* 255.
109. See Sharp's comments in the *Warsaw Signal,* March 6, 1844. Information on the wolf hunt strategy is sketchy. Ford, who by the fall had "secret agents" deployed within both camps, claimed that for the fall 1844 hunt, "anti-Mormon leaders sent printed invitations to all the militia captains in Hancock and to the captains of militia in all the neighboring counties of Illinois, Iowa, and Missouri to be present with their companies." *History of Illinois,* 255. Regardless of its origins, there is evidence the wolf hunt specter succeeded in intimidating the Mormons, as is evidenced in the testimony of Wandle Mace, a mechanical engineer at Nauvoo. See John E. Hallwas and Roger D. Launius, *Cultures in Conflict: A Documentary History of the Mormon War in Illinois* (Logan: Utah State University Press, 1995), 317–19.
110. Gregg, *History of Hancock County,* 336, 347.
111. Ford, *History of Illinois,* 304.
112. For the reference to "red flags" and "tar and feathers," see "A History, of the Persecution, of the Church of Jesus Christ, of Latter Day Saints in Missouri," *Times and Seasons,* December 1839, 18.
113. See *Autobiography of Parley Parker Pratt,* 8th ed. (Salt Lake City: Deseret Book, 1970), 174–75.
114. See Thomas Sharp's history of the troubles for the Green Plains attribution. Roger D. Launius, "Anti-Mormonism in Illinois: Thomas C. Sharp's Unfinished History of the Mormon War, 1845," *Journal of Mormon History* 15 (1989): 31. For Williams's role, see Hill, *Quest for Refuge,* 173–75.
115. See Susan Sessions Rugh, "Saints and Old Settlers: The Conflict in Hancock County, Illinois, 1840–1846," paper 91–3, Newberry Papers in Family and Community History, 1993 (Chicago: Newberry Library, 1991), 34.
116. Thomas Sharp Papers, February 15, 1844.

CONCLUSION: THE PERILS OF DEMOCRATIC STORYTELLING

1. John Stuart Mill, *On Liberty and Other Essays,* ed. John Gray (Oxford: Oxford University Press, 1991), 100–101.
2. Richard Sennett, *The Uses of Disorder: Personal Identity and City Life* (New York: Vintage Books, 1970), 33.
3. Thomas Ford, *A History of Illinois: From Its Commencement as a State in 1818 to 1847,* ed. Rodney O. Davis (1854; repr., Urbana: University of Illinois Press, 1995), 4.
4. James E. Armstrong, *Life of a Pioneer Woman, as Illustrated in the Life of Elsie Strawn Armstrong, 1789–1887* (Chicago: John F. Higgins, 1931), 59.
5. Perry A. Armstrong, *The Sauks and the Black Hawk War with Biographical Sketches, Etc.* (Springfield, IL: W. H. Rokker, 1887), 133.
6. For Ford's personal dress and finances, see the recollections of a family friend in Jeriah Bonham, *Fifty Years Recollections with Observations and Reflections on Historical Events: Giving Sketches of Eminent Citizens Their Lives and Public Services* (Peoria, IL: J. W. Franks & Sons, 1883), 61, 65.
7. John Davis, "A Diary of the Illinois-Michigan Canal, 1843–1844," in *Papers in Illinois History and Transactions for the Year of 1941,* ed. Gus A. Lee (Springfield: Illinois State Historical Society, 1943), 59–71.
8. Ford, *History of Illinois,* 26.
9. Lester J. Cappon, ed., *The Adams-Jefferson Letters* (Chapel Hill: University of North Carolina Press, 1987), 298.
10. Cappon, *The Adams-Jefferson Letters,* 298–99.
11. Peter Stuhlmacher, *Historical Criticism and Theological Interpretation of Scripture* (Philadelphia: Fortress Press, 1977), 36–41. See also George M. Mardsen, "Everyone One's Own Interpreter? The Bible, Science, and Authority in Mid-Nineteenth-Century America," in *The Bible in America: Essays in Cultural History,* ed. Nathan O. Hatch and Mark A. Noll (New York: Oxford University Press, 1982), 79–100, and Robert E. Brown, *Jonathan Edwards and the Bible* (Bloomington: Indiana University Press, 2002).
12. While Adams noted that "the continual refutation of all their prognostications by time and experience [had] no effect in extinguishing or damping their ardor," he did not think that the ardor of the French millennialists was of a different order than that of their religious brethren. He added that even an Enlightenment thinker as respected as "Dr. Priestly . . . fully believed upon the authority of prophecy that the French nation would establish a free government." Jefferson, too, in his review of the

contemporary prophets, including a local Christian preacher in Virginia, treated the "Richmond and Wabash [Shawnee] prophets" as equivalent. See Cappon, *The Adams-Jefferson Letters,* 297–98.

13. See Turner's brief tutorial in the nature of the miraculous and biblical interpretation in *Mormonism in All Ages: Or the Rise, Progress, and Causes of Mormonism; with the Biography of Its Author and Founder, Joseph Smith Junior* (New York: Platt & Peters, 1842), 119–48.
14. *Abraham Lincoln's Great Speeches* (New York: Dover, 1991), 7.
15. *Sangamo Journal,* January 26, 1843. Rodney O. Davis speculates that Ford's formative years as a frontier judge may explain his "Whiggish concern for social order." See "Judge Ford and the Regulators, 1841–1842," in *Selected Papers in Illinois History 1981,* ed. Bruce D. Cody (Springfield: Illinois State Historical Society, 1982), 26.
16. The story of Thomas Ford's life after his term as governor is a sad one. He moved to Peoria to work as a lawyer after finishing his *History.* But on October 12, 1850, his wife, Fannie, died of cancer at the age of thirty-eight, and less than a month later Ford himself succumbed to consumption at age forty-nine. Their orphaned children were thrown upon the community. Two of their daughters died young, and their two sons died violent deaths on the Kansas frontier west of Wichita in the 1870s. See J. F. Snyder, "Governor Ford and His Family," *Journal of the Illinois State Historical Society* 3, no. 2 (July 1910): 45–51.
17. See the typical comments in this regard in John Francis Snyder, *Adam J. Snyder and His Period in Illinois History, 1817–1842* (Virginia, IL: E. Needham, 1906), 402–3.
18. See Emil Joseph Verlie, ed., *Illinois Constitutions* (Springfield: Illinois State Historical Library, 1919), 439. As Ford explained in his *History of Illinois,* this was something the constitution of 1818 permitted, for while it formally granted the governor in its third article control over several key offices, it later added a "Schedule," which granted that the public auditor, attorney general, and "other officers of the state as may be necessary may be appointed by the general assembly." *History of Illinois,* 12.
19. Bonham, *Fifty Years Recollections,* 64. J. F. Snyder notes that Ford was "destitute of the aggressive vigor necessary for success in worldly affairs" and that he served in a spy battalion during the 1831 Black Hawk scrimmage. See "Governor Ford and His Family," 47.

20. This definition of civil society is from Larry Diamond, *Developing Democracy: Toward Consolidation* (Baltimore: Johns Hopkins University Press, 1999), 221.
21. The consociational theory of democracy was developed by Arend Lijphart through close observation of the Dutch context. See *The Politics of Accommodation: Pluralism and Democracy in the Netherlands* (Berkeley: University of California Press, 1968). Lijphart later expanded the consociational idea into a model of "consensus democracy," which he contrasted with majoritarian democracies. See *Democracies: Patterns of Majoritarian and Consensus Government in Twenty-One Countries* (New Haven, CT: Yale University Press, 1984), xiii–xiv.
22. For Calhoun, see C. Gordon Post, ed., *A Disquisition on Government: And Selections from the Discourse* (New York: Liberal Arts Press, 1953).
23. Sue Donaldson and Will Kymlicka, *Zoopolis: A Political Theory of Animal Rights* (Oxford: Oxford University Press, 2011), 214.
24. For the story of Rajneeshpuram in Oregon, see Frances Fitzgerald, *Cities on a Hill* (New York: Simon & Schuster, 1986), 247–381. In 1984 the Rajneeshees imported homeless people to Antelope and registered them in the hope of reaching the seven thousand votes needed for a majority in Wasco County (347–50). Since the importation effort failed, the Immigration and Naturalization Service (INS) indictment, which ultimately led to the guru's demise, may not have been needed.
25. It is worth noting that what political scientists call an "exogenous shock"—that is, a pressure on the system exerted by an outside force—was present in the settler Illinois case in the form of the 1837 economic depression.
26. Because of developing democracies' stance in favor of popular justice, the claims of minorities have moral standing regardless of whether they are Indigenous. If, as William Carlos Williams intoned, "the pure products of America go crazy" so that minority group claims can frequently be characterized as irrational or nonrational, under democratic norms there will nevertheless be pressure to recognize them and treat them fairly. See Oscar Williams and Edwin Honig, eds., *The Mentor Book of Major American Poets* (New York: New American Library, 1962), 323–25.
27. For the case that local communities have a just claim against police practices, see Michelle Alexander, *The New Jim Crow: Mass Incarceration in the Age of Colorblindness* (New York: New Press, 2012).

28. Amy Gutmann lists such claims by majorities under the heading of "conscious social reproduction," which is essentially the capacity to reproduce any society with its particular social patterns into the future. See *Democratic Education,* 2nd ed. (Princeton, NJ: Princeton University Press, 1999), 39.
29. See Steven M. Nolt, *A History of the Amish* (Intercourse, PA: Good Books, 1992), 84–85, 115–19. Nolt makes clear that nineteenth-century Amish frequently participated in local politics by holding office and voting. Since then the Amish have gyrated between periods of political involvement and relative quietude. After the 1973 Supreme Court decision in *Wisconsin v. Yoder,* which granted the church the power to exempt their children from attending high school, relations between the Amish and their majority societal culture neighbors reached a period of mutual adjustment. It is a matter of debate whether this mutual adjustment was independent of state recognition or a "function" of it. For the latter claim, see Frank Way and Barbara J. Burt, "Religious Marginality and the Free Exercise Clause," *American Political Science Review* 77, no. 3 (September 1983): 652–65.
30. Leslie Pickering Francis and Anita Silvers, "Liberalism and Individually Scripted Ideas of the Good: Meeting the Challenge of Dependent Agency," *Social Theory and Practice* 33, no. 2 (April 2007): 311–34, quote at 31.
31. Producerism as a broad civic narrative should be distinguished from the ideology developed by 1830s and 1840s intellectuals and urban laborers, though the civic narrative clearly borrowed from the ideology. See Christopher Lasch, *The True and Only Heaven: Progress and Its Critics* (New York: W. W. Norton, 1991), and William R. Sutton, *Journeymen for Jesus: Evangelical Artisans Confront Capitalism in Jacksonian Baltimore* (University Park: Pennsylvania State University Press, 1998).
32. Rogers M. Smith, *Stories of Peoplehood: The Politics and Morals of Political Membership* (Cambridge: Cambridge University Press, 2003), 212.
33. In a similar vein, what makes scientific knowledge believable is not that scientists do not have biases but that they use double-blind peer review and other methods in a concerted effort to recognize and to control for their biases.
34. For the phrase "seeing like a state," see James C. Scott, *Seeing Like a State: How Certain Schemes to Improve the Human Condition Have Failed* (New Haven, CT: Yale University Press, 1998).

35. See the May 13, 1844, letter to Henry Clay in the appendix of B. H. Roberts, *The Rise and Fall of Nauvoo* (Salt Lake City: Deseret News, 1900), 380–88, quote at 388.
36. See Will Kymlicka's discussion of "accommodating non-liberal minorities" in *Multicultural Citizenship: A Liberal Theory of Minority Rights* (Oxford: Oxford University Press, 1995), 163–70.
37. Joseph Smith, quoted in Mervin B. Hogan, *Mormonism and Freemasonry: The Illinois Episode* (Richmond, VA: Macoy, 1977), 266.
38. See the ordinance quoted in Thomas Gregg, *History of Hancock County, Illinois* (Chicago: Chas C. Chapman, 1880), 367.
39. See the *Warsaw Signal,* September 30, 1845.
40. See Gary Gerstle, *Liberty and Coercion: The Paradox of American Government from the Founding to the Present* (Princeton, NJ: Princeton University Press, 2015), and Laura F. Edwards, *The People and Their Peace: Legal Culture and the Transformation of Inequality in the Post-revolutionary South* (Chapel Hill: University of North Carolina Press, 2009).
41. Robert Erlewine, *Monotheism and Tolerance: Recovering a Religion of Reason* (Bloomington: Indiana University Press, 2010), 27.
42. *Warsaw Signal,* December 29, 1841. Sharp learned of Smith's refusal to pay tax on Commerce, Illinois, land from Walter Bagby, the Hancock tax collector. He later conceded that Smith had paid the proper tax and the Commerce bill was a mistake.
43. Joseph Smith, quoted in Roberts, *The Rise and the Fall of Nauvoo,* 242–43.
44. On the role of the Methodists in the Illinois convention controversy of 1824, see James Simeone, *Democracy and Slavery in Frontier Illinois: The Bottomland Republic* (DeKalb: Northern Illinois University Press, 2000), 183.
45. Sundiata Keita Cha-Jua, *America's First Black Town: Brooklyn, Illinois 1830–1915* (Urbana: University of Illinois Press, 2000), 35.
46. George W. T. Davis in an article from the *Alton Telegraph* reprinted in the *Warsaw Signal,* July 17, 1844.
47. The tension between the first and second American regimes on this point is considerable. It has been overlooked, perhaps because influential first-regime thinkers like James Madison held that a plurality of memberships strengthened the civic nation. But those emphasizing Madison's pluralism sometimes forget that he viewed it as a means; the end was the public interest, which assumed an Aristotle-like common good. For Madison, the ultimate membership was the common good–based club of the state. Plural civil society clubs—Madison called them

"factions"—might proliferate, but it was implied that the single state, the Union, took priority. Madison argued that use of the national or federal level of representation was an innovation the Americans would add to what Hamilton called "the science of politics." See Alexander Hamilton, *The Federalist Papers,* ed. Clinton Rossiter (1788; repr., New York: New American Library, 1961), 72. The federal level would be so full of different interests that it would, by institutional design, lead to more public-spirited decisions inevitably respecting individual rights. Madison wrote of the design: "Extend the sphere, and you take in a greater variety or parties and interests; you make it less probable that a majority of the whole will have a common motive to invade the rights of other citizens." See *The Federalist Papers,* 83. The national interest was the public interest for Madison, and he pointedly differentiated the public from the mere majority interest, which he allowed would dominate state and local decision-making arenas.

48. Alexis de Tocqueville, *Democracy in America,* ed. J. P. Mayer, trans. George Lawrence (1832–36; repr., Garden City, NY: Doubleday, 1969), 525–28.
49. Alan Bloom, *The Closing of the American Mind: How Higher Education Has Failed Democracy and Impoverished the Souls of Today's Students* (New York: Simon & Schuster, 1987), 32. The challenge of identity politics took on a new and more pressing character by the dawn of the twentieth century, when the persistent exclusions based on race, sex, and gender were recognized by more and more voters as key obstacles to universal membership. The Mormons in Illinois make an intriguing case study because they were White, the women generally deferred to the men, and they were descendants of mainstream Protestantism; yet they were excluded by the independent-producer terms of the Illinois regime. By holding at least the complicating factor of race constant, the Mormon case allows us to explore the status order system and rules of exclusion not directly related to the regime's particularist biases about skin color.
50. The rejection of civic nationalism is forcefully argued in Bernard Yack, "The Myth of the Civic Nation," in *Theorizing Nationalism,* ed. Ronald Beiner (Albany: State University of New York Press, 1999), 103–18.
51. Mill, *On Liberty,* 102.
52. A recent article locates the assassination of the Smith brothers in the context of the repeated habeas episodes. See Alex D. Smith,

"Untouchable: Joseph Smith's Use of the Law as Catalyst for Assassination," *Journal of the Illinois State Historical Society* 112, no. 1 (Spring 2019): 8–42.

53. J. David Greenstone, *The Lincoln Persuasion: Remaking American Liberalism* (Princeton, NJ: Princeton University Press, 1993), 272.
54. As Susan Mendus writes, "We cannot, properly speaking, be said to tolerate things we welcome, or endorse, or find attractive." *Justifying Toleration: Conceptual and Historical Perspectives,* ed. Susan Mendus (Cambridge: Cambridge University Press, 2009), 3.
55. Ford, *History of Illinois,* 301.
56. Ford, 297n.
57. *Warsaw Signal,* July 10, 1844.
58. William J. Novak, *The People's Welfare: Law and Regulation in Nineteenth-Century America* (Chapel Hill: University of North Carolina Press, 1996), 3–6. The belief in "American exceptionalism" is premised on the weakness of the American state. Governance requires authoritative commands, and government authority in America, it is argued, whether federal, state, or local, has always been weak, checked, and contested. A weak state is celebrated by those who see it as evidence of American's classical liberal tradition committed to limiting governing power. This tradition of American liberalism has been contrasted with a European liberal tradition, which has been much more open to statist policies and which resulted in a comparatively more robust socialist tradition. Scholars of American political development have cautioned against the resultant understanding of the American state based on what it lacks. Thus, as Rick Halperin and Jonathan Morris put it, "a 'why didn't they do that' question" should become "a 'how did they do that' question." *American Exceptionalism? US Working-Class Formation in an International Context* (New York: St. Martin's, 1997), 5. While, for example, a labor party did not form in the United States or health care policy took a different form from many advanced industrial democracies, this is not the same as saying that labor interests or health care institutions play no role in American politics. The state was not missing in the American context, but its development did follow a set of dynamics different from those in Europe.
59. The capacity of electoral majorities to offer "an intelligible and determinate answer to the question why these particular people, rather than others perhaps equally well or better qualified,

should run the country" is a feature of free and fair democratic elections, emphasized by Brian Barry, "Is Democracy Special?," in *Philosophy, Politics and Society*, ed. Peter Laslett and James Fishkin, 5th ser. (New Haven, CT: Yale University Press, 1979), 155–96, quote at 193.

Bibliography

ARCHIVAL SOURCES

A.V. Pierson Papers, McLean County Historical Society, Bloomington, IL
Caroline Palmer Clarke Papers, Chicago Historical Society
Daniel Hitt Papers, Abraham Lincoln Presidential Library, Springfield, IL
Edward Warren Papers, Chicago Historical Society
The Joseph Smith Papers, http://josephsmithpapers.org.
Martin Van Buren Papers, Library of Congress, Washington, DC
Thomas Sharp Papers, Yale University, New Haven, CT
Walter Bagby Papers, University of Kentucky, Lexington
William Leggett Papers, New York Public Library

NEWSPAPERS

Alton Telegraph and Democratic Review
Baptist Almanac and Baptist Register
Belleville Advocate
Chicago American
Chicago Democrat
Elders' Journal
The Examiner
Illinois Advocate
Illinois Democrat
Illinois Mercury
Illinois State Register
Illinois Statesman
Iowa Patriot
Juliet Courier
Millennial Star
Missouri Republican
Nauvoo Expositor

Nauvoo Neighbor
Northwestern Gazetteer and Galena Advertiser
Peoria Democratic Press
Peoria Register and North-Western Gazetteer
The Plaindealer
The Politician
Quincy Argus
Quincy Whig
Representative and Belleville News
Sangamo Journal
Shawneetown Republican
Starved Rock Country
St. Clair Banner
Times and Seasons
Voice of the People
Warsaw Message
Warsaw Signal
The Wasp
Western World

PUBLISHED PRIMARY SOURCES

Abraham Lincoln's Great Speeches. New York: Dover, 1991.

Allen, James B., and Thomas G. Alexander, eds. *Manchester Mormons: The Journal of William Clayton, 1840–1842*. Santa Barbara, CA: Peregrine Smith, 1974.

Armstrong, James E. *Life of a Pioneer Woman, as Illustrated in the Life of Elsie Strawn Armstrong, 1789–1887*. Chicago: John F. Higgins, 1931.

Armstrong, Perry A. *The Sauks and the Black Hawk War with Biographical Sketches, Etc*. Springfield, IL: W. H. Rokker, 1887.

Austin, Emily M. *Mormonism; Or, Life among the Mormons*. 1882. Reprint, New York: Arno Press, 1971.

Baldwin, Elmer. *History of LaSalle County, Illinois*. Chicago: Rand McNally, 1877.

Ballance, Charles. *The History of Peoria, Illinois*. Peoria, IL: N. C. Nason, 1870.

Bean, George Washington. *Autobiography of George Washington Bean, a Utah Pioneer of 1847, and His Family Records*. Compiled by Flora Diana Bean Horne. Salt Lake City: Utah Printing, 1945.

Beebe, Henry S. *History of Peru*. Peru, IL: J. F. Linton, 1858.

Bonham, Jeriah. *Fifty Years Recollections with Observations and Reflections on Historical Events: Giving Sketches of Eminent Citizens Their Lives and Public Services*. Peoria, IL: J. W. Franks & Sons, 1883.

Bronson v. Kinzie, 42 US 311 (1843).

Brown, Everett Somerville, ed. *The Missouri Compromise and Presidential Politics, 1820–1825*. St. Louis: Missouri Historical Society, 1926.

Brown, Henry. *History of Illinois, from its First Discovery and Settlement to the Present Time*. New York: J. Winchester, New World Press, 1844.

Bryant, William Cullen, II, and Thomas G. Voss, eds. *The Letters of William Cullen Bryant*. Vol. 1, *1809–1836*. New York: Fordham University Press, 1975.

Burrows, J. M. D. *Fifty Years in Iowa: Being a Personal Reminiscence of J.M.D. Burrows, 1838–1888*. Davenport, IA: Glass, 1888.

Calhoun, John C. *A Disquisition on Government: And Selections from the Discourse*. 1851. Reprinted with introduction and notes by C. Gordon Post. New York: Liberal Arts Press, 1953.

Cappon, Lester J., ed. *The Adams-Jefferson Letters*. Chapel Hill: University of North Carolina Press, 1987.

Caswell, Henry. *The City of the Mormons; or Three Days at Nauvoo*. London: J. G. F. and J. Rivington, 1842.

Coffey, Achilles. *History of the Regular Baptists of Southern Illinois*. Paducah, KY: Martin, 1877.

Compendium of the Enumeration of the Inhabitants and Statistics of the United States. Washington, DC: Thomas Allen, 1841.

Daniels, William M. *A Correct Account of the Murder of Generals Joseph and Hyrum Smith, at Carthage, on the 27th Day of June, 1844*. Nauvoo, IL: John Taylor, 1845.

Davis, George T. M. *An Authentic Account of the Massacre of Joseph Smith, the Mormon Prophet, and Hyrum Smith, His Brother, Together with a Brief History of the Rise and Progress of Mormonism, and All the Circumstances Which Led to Their Death*. St. Louis: Chambers & Knapp, 1844.

———. *Autobiography of the Late Colonel George T. M. Davis*. New York: Jenkins and McCowan, 1891.

Davis, John. "A Diary of the Illinois-Michigan Canal, 1843–1844." In *Papers in Illinois History and Transactions for the Year of 1941*, edited by Gus A. Lee, 38–72 Springfield: Illinois State Historical Society, 1943.

Douglas, Stephen A. "The Dividing Line between Federal and Local Authority: Popular Sovereignty in the Territories." *Harpers' New Monthly Magazine*, September 1860, 517–37.

Farnham, Eliza W. *Life in Prairie Land*. 1846. Reprinted with introduction by John Hallwas. Urbana: University of Illinois Press, 2003.

Ford, Thomas. *A History of Illinois: From Its Commencement as a State in 1818 to 1847*. 1854. Reprinted with annotations and introduction by Rodney O. Davis. Urbana: University of Illinois Press, 1995.

———. *Message of the Governor of the State of Illinois, in Relation to the Disturbances in Hancock County*. Springfield, IL: Walters & Weber, 1844.

———. *Mormon Difficulties: Report of the Governor, in Relation to the Difficulties in Hancock County*. Springfield, IL: William Walters, Public Printer, 1846.

General Smith's Views on the Powers and Policy of the Government of the United States. Nauvoo, IL: John Taylor, 1844.

Gooding, William. 1838 report. In *Report of the Canal Commissioners of Illinois to Governor John R. Tanner, December 1, 1900*. Springfield, IL: Phillip Bros., 1901.

Greene, Evarts Boutell, and Charles Manfred Thompson, eds. *Governors' Letter-Books, 1840–1853*. Springfield: Illinois State Historical Library, 1911.

Greene, Evarts Boutell, and Clarence Walworth Alvord, eds. *Governors' Letter-Books, 1818–1834*. Springfield: Illinois State Historical Library, 1909.

Gregg, Thomas. *History of Hancock County, Illinois*. Chicago: Chas C. Chapman, 1880.

Hall, James. *Illinois Monthly Magazine*. Vandalia, IL: Robert Blackwell, 1831.

Hamilton, Alexander, James Madison, and John Jay. *The Federalist Papers*. 1788. Reprint, edited by Clinton Rossiter. New York: Penguin Books, 1961.

Harris, William. *Mormonism Portrayed: Its Errors and Absurdities Exposed. And the Spirit and Designs of Its Authors Made Manifest*. Warsaw, IL: Sharpe & Gamble Publishers, 1841.

Hedges, Andrew H., Alex D. Smith, and Richard Lloyd Anderson, eds. *Journals, Volume 2: December 1841–April 1843*. Volume 2 of the Journals series of *The Joseph Smith Papers*, edited by Dean C. Jessee, Ronald K. Esplin, and Richard Lyman Bushman. Salt Lake City: Church Historian's Press, 2011.

Hedges, Andrew H., Alex D. Smith, and Brent M. Rogers, eds. *Journals, Volume 3: May 1843–June 1844*. Volume 3 of the Journals series of *The Joseph Smith Papers*, edited by Ronald K. Esplin and Matthew J. Grow. Salt Lake City: Church Historian's Press, 2015.

Hendrick, Willene, and George Hendrick, eds. *On the Illinois Frontier: Dr. Hiram Rutherford*. Carbondale: Southern Illinois University Press, 1982.

Herndon, William H., and Jesse W. Weik. *Herndon's Life of Lincoln: The History and Personal Recollections of Abraham Lincoln as Originally Written by William H. Herndon and Jesse W. Weik.* 1888. Reprint, edited by Paul M. Angle. Greenwich, CT: Fawcett Publications, 1961.

The History of Livingston County, Illinois. Chicago: Wm. Le Baron Jr., 1878.

Jackson, Joseph H. *A Narrative of the Adventures and Experience of Joseph H. Jackson in Nauvoo.* Warsaw, IL: 1844.

Jacob, Udney Hay. *An Extract from a Manuscript Entitled The Peace Maker, or the Doctrines of the Millennium: Being a Treatise on Religion and Jurisprudence, or a New System of Religion and Politics.* Nauvoo, IL: J. Smith, 1842.

Jefferson, Thomas. *The Portable Thomas Jefferson,* edited by Merrill D. Peterson. New York: Penguin Books, 1975.

Johannsen, Robert W., ed. *The Letters of Stephen A. Douglas.* Urbana: University of Illinois Press, 1961.

———, ed. *The Lincoln-Douglas Debates of 1858.* New York: Oxford University Press, 1965.

Johnson, Richard Mentor. *Review of a Report of the Committee, to Whom Was Referred the Several Petitions on the Subject of Mails on the Sabbath, Presented to the Senate of the United States, January 16, 1829, by the Hon. Mr. Johnson, of Kentucky, Chairman of Said Committee.* N.p.: 1829.

Journal of the Senate of the Eighth General Assembly of the State of Illinois. Vandalia, IL: Greiner & Sherman, 1833.

Journal of the Senate of the Ninth General Assembly of the State of Illinois. Vandalia, IL: J. Y. Sawyer, 1835.

Journal of the Senate of the Twelfth General Assembly of the State of Illinois. Springfield, IL: 1841.

Kinzie, Mrs. John H. *Wau-Bun, the Early Day in the North-West.* New York: Derby & Jackson, 1856.

Launius, Roger D. "American Home Missionary Society Ministers and Mormon Nauvoo: Selected Letters." *Western Illinois Regional Studies* 8, no. 1 (Spring 1985): 16–45.

———. "Anti-Mormonism in Illinois: Thomas C. Sharp's Unfinished History of the Mormon War, 1845." *Journal of Mormon History* 15 (1989): 27–45.

Lee, John D. *Mormonism Unveiled: The Life and Confession of John D. Lee and the Complete Life of Brigham Young.* 1877. Reprint, Albuquerque: University of New Mexico Press, 2008.

———. *The Mormon Menace: Being the Confession of John Doyle Lee, Danite.* 1877. Reprint, edited by Alfred Henry Lewis. New York: Home Protection Publishing, 1905.

Leggett, William. *Democratic Editorials: Essays in Jacksonian Political Economy,* edited by Laurence H. White. New York: Liberty Press, 1984.

———. *Tales and Sketches by a Country Schoolmaster.* New York: Harper, 1829.

Lincoln, Abraham. *The Collected Works of Abraham Lincoln.* Edited by Roy P. Basler. 9 vols. New Brunswick, NJ: Rutgers University Press, 1959.

McCormick, Thomas J., ed. *Memoirs of Gustave Koerner, 1809–1896.* Cedar Rapids, IA: Torch Press, 1909.

Melville, Herman. *Typee: A Peep at Polynesian Life.* 1846. Reprint, New York: Penguin Books, 1996.

———. *White-Jacket.* 1850. Reprint, New York: Quality Paperback Book Club, 1995.

Middleton, Stephen. *The Black Laws in the Old Northwest: A Documentary History.* Westport, CT: Greenwood Press, 1993.

Muldur, William, and A. Russell Mortensen, eds. *Among the Mormons: Historical Accounts by Contemporary Observers.* New York: Knopf, 1958.

Newhall, John B. *Sketches of Iowa, or the Emigrant's Guide.* New York: J. H. Colton, 1841.

Partridge, George F. "'The Death of a Mormon Dictator': Letters of Massachusetts Mormons, 1843–1848." *The New England Quarterly* 9, no. 4 (December 1936): 583–617.

Pease, Theodore Calvin, ed. *Illinois Election Returns, 1818–1848.* Springfield: Illinois State Historical Library, 1923.

Peck, John Mason. *A Gazeteer of Illinois.* Jacksonville, IL: Goudy, 1834.

Post, C. Gordon, ed. *A Disquisition on Government: And Selections from the Discourse.* New York: Liberal Arts Press, 1953.

Pratt, Parley P. *Autobiography of Parley Parker Pratt.* 1874. Reprint. 8th ed. Salt Lake City: Deseret Book, 1970.

The Revised Code of Laws of Illinois. Vandalia, IL: Robert Blackwell, 1827.

The Revised Code of Laws of Illinois. Shawneetown, IL: Alexander Grant, 1829.

Revised Law of the Nauvoo Legion. Nauvoo, IL: John Taylor Printer, 1844.

Reynolds, John. *"The Balm of Gilead": An Inquiry into the Right of American Slavery.* Belleville, IL: printed by the author, 1860.

Roberts, B. H. *The Rise and Fall of Nauvoo.* Salt Lake City: Deseret News, 1900.

Scott, Jessup W. "Internal Trade No. 3." *Hesparian,* March 1839, 351.

Smith, Joseph. *History of the Church of Jesus Christ of Latter-day Saints.* Vol. 6, introduction and notes by B. H. Roberts. 2nd ed. Salt Lake City: Deseret Book, 1969.

Snow, Eliza R. *The Nauvoo Poems of Eliza R. Snow.* Mason County, IL: The Church of Jesus Christ of Latter-day Saints, 1989.

Steele, Eliza R. *A Summer Journey in the West.* 1841. Reprint, New York: Arno Press, 1975.

Turner, J. B. *Mormonism in All Ages: Or the Rise, Progress, and Causes of Mormonism; with the Biography of Its Author and Founder, Joseph Smith Junior.* New York: Platt & Peters, 1842.

Van Buren, Martin, "The Autobiography of Martin Van Buren." Volume 2, *Annual Report of the American Historical Association for the Year 1981,* edited by John C. Fitzpatrick. Washington, DC: Government Printing Office, 1920.

Verlie, Emil Joseph, ed. *Illinois Constitutions.* Springfield: Illinois State Historical Library, 1919.

Wootton, David, ed. *The Essential Federalist and Anti-Federalist Papers.* Indianapolis: Hackett Publishing, 2003.

SECONDARY SOURCES

Abzug, Robert H. *Cosmos Crumbling: American Reform and the Religious Imagination.* New York: Oxford University Press, 1994.

Alexander, Michelle. *The New Jim Crow: Mass Incarceration in the Age of Colorblindness.* New York: New Press, 2012.

Andreas, A. T. *History of Chicago: From the Earliest Period to the Present Time.* Vol. 1. Chicago: A. T. Andreas, 1884.

Arendt, Hannah. *On Revolution.* New York: Penguin Books, 1963.

Aristotle. *The Politics.* Translated by Carnes Lord. Chicago: University of Chicago Press, 1984.

Arrington, Leonard J., and Davis Bitton. *The Mormon Experience: A History of the Latter-day Saints.* 2nd ed. Urbana: University of Illinois Press, 1992.

Atkinson, R. F. *Knowledge and Explanation in History.* Ithaca, NY: Cornell University Press, 1978.

Balogh, Brian. *A Government Out of Sight: The Mystery of National Authority in Nineteenth-Century America.* Cambridge: Cambridge University Press, 2009.

Banner, Lois W. "Religious Benevolence as Social Control: A Critique of an Interpretation." *Journal of American History* 60, no. 1 (June 1973): 23–41.

Baron, Robert, and Nicholas R. Spitzer, eds. *Public Folklore.* Washington, DC: Smithsonian Institution Press, 1992.

Barry, Brian. "Is Democracy Special?" In *Philosophy, Politics and Society*, edited by Peter Laslett and James Fishkin. 5th ser. New Haven, CT: Yale University Press, 1979.

———. *Political Argument: A Reissue with a New Introduction*. Berkeley: University of California Press, 1990.

———. *Sociologists, Economists, and Democracy*. Chicago: University of Chicago Press, 1970.

Bates, Robert H., Avner Greif, Margaret Levi, Jean-Laurent Rosenthal, Barry R. Weingast, eds. *Analytic Narratives*. Princeton, NJ: Princeton University Press, 1998.

Baugh, Alexander L. "A Call to Arms: The 1838 Mormon Defense of Northern Missouri." PhD diss., Brigham Young University, 2000.

Baylor, Christopher. *First to the Party: The Group Origins of Political Transformation*. Philadelphia: University of Pennsylvania Press, 2018.

Bennett, Richard E., Susan Easton Black, and Donald Q. Cannon. *The Nauvoo Legion in Illinois: A History of the Mormon Militia, 1841–1846*. Norman, OK: Arthur H. Clark, 2010.

Bercovitch, Sacvan. *The American Jeremiad*. Madison: University of Wisconsin Press, 1978.

———. *The Puritan Origins of the American Self*. New Haven, CT: Yale University Press, 1975.

Berlin, Ira. *Many Thousands Gone: The First Two Centuries of Slavery in North America*. Cambridge, MA: Harvard University Press, 2000.

Berwanger, Eugene H. *The Frontier against Slavery: Western Anti-Negro Prejudice and the Slavery Extension Controversy*. 1967. Reprint, Urbana: University of Illinois Press, 2002.

Bestor, Arthur. "Patent-Office Models of the Good Society: Some Relationships between Social Reform and Westward Expansion." In *Backwoods Utopias: The Sectarian Origins and the Owenite Phase of Communitarian Socialism in America, 1663–1829*. 2nd ed. Philadelphia: University of Pennsylvania Press, 1970.

Black, Susan Easton. "How Large Was the Population of Nauvoo?" *Brigham Young University Studies* 35, no. 2 (1995): 91–94.

Black, Susan Easton, and Richard E. Bennett, eds. *A City of Refuge: Quincy, Illinois*. Salt Lake City: Millennial Press, 2000.

Blasi, Vincent, and Seana V. Schiffrin. "The Story of *West Virginia State Board of Education v. Barnette:* The Pledge of Allegiance and the Freedom of Thought." In *Constitutional Law Stories*, edited by Michael C. Dorf. 2nd ed. New York: Foundation Press, 2009.

Bloom, Alan. *The Closing of the American Mind: How Higher Education Has Failed Democracy and Impoverished the Souls of Today's Students*. New York: Simon & Schuster, 1987.

Bloom, Harold. *The American Religion: The Emergence of a Post-Christian Nation*. New York: Simon & Schuster, 1992.

Bourdieu, Pierre. "Rethinking the State: Genesis and Structure in the Bureaucratic Field." Translated by Loic J. D. Wacquant and Samar Farage. In *State/Culture: State-Formation after the Cultural Turn*. Edited by George Steinmetz. Ithaca, NY: Cornell University Press, 1999.

Brand, E. P. *Illinois Baptists: A History*. Bloomington, IL: Pantagraph Printing, 1930.

Brass, Paul. *The Production of Hindu-Muslim Violence in Contemporary India*. Seattle: University of Washington Press, 2003.

Bridges, Amy. *A City in the Republic: Antebellum New York and the Origins of Machine Politics*. Ithaca, NY: Cornell University Press, 1987.

Brinks, Daniel, and Sandra Botero. "Inequality and the Rule of Law: Ineffective Rights in Latin American Democracies." In *Reflections on Uneven Democracies: The Legacies of Guillermo O'Donnell*, edited by Daniel Brinks, Marcelo Leiras, and Scott Mainwaring, 214–39. Baltimore: Johns Hopkins University Press, 2014.

Brodie, Fawn. *No Man Knows My History: The Life of Joseph Smith*. 2nd ed. New York: Vintage Books, 1995.

Brooke, John L. *The Refiner's Fire: The Making of Mormon Cosmology, 1644–1844*. Cambridge: Cambridge University Press, 1994.

Brooks, Juanita, ed. *On the Mormon Frontier: The Diary of Hosea Stout 1844–1861*. Salt Lake City: University of Utah Press, 1964.

Brown, Richard Maxwell. *Strain of Violence: Historical Studies of American Violence and Vigilantism*. New York: Oxford University Press, 1975.

Brown, Robert E. *Jonathan Edwards and the Bible*. Bloomington: Indiana University Press, 2002.

Brumbaugh, Alice Louise. "The Regulator Movement in Illinois." Master's thesis, University of Illinois, 1927.

Buettinger, Craig. "Economic Inequality in Early Chicago, 1849–1850." *Journal of Social History* 11 (Spring 1978): 413–18.

Buruma, Ian. *Murder in Amsterdam: Liberal Europe, Islam, and the Limits of Toleration*. New York: Penguin Books, 2006.

Bushman, Richard L. *From Puritan to Yankee: Character and the Social Order in Connecticut, 1690–1765*. Cambridge, MA: Harvard University Press, 1967.

———. "The Inner Joseph Smith." *Journal of Mormon History* 32, no. 1 (Spring 2006): 65–81.

———. *Joseph Smith and the Beginnings of Mormonism*. Urbana: University of Illinois Press, 1984.

———. *Joseph Smith: Rough Stone Rolling*. New York: Vintage Books, 2005.

Calloway, Colin G. *The Shawnees and the War for America*. New York: Penguin Books, 2007.

Cavanagh, Helen M. *Funk of Funk's Grove: Farmer, Legislator, and Cattle King of the Old Northwest 1797–1865*. Bloomington, IL: Pantagraph Publishing, 1952.

Cayton, Andrew R. L., and Peter S. Onuf. *The Midwest and the Nation: Rethinking the History of an American Region*. Bloomington: Indiana University Press, 1990.

Cha-Jua, Sundiata Keita. *America's First Black Town: Brooklyn, Illinois 1830–1915*. Urbana: University of Illinois Press, 2000.

Chong, Dennis, and Raoul Rogers. "Reviving Group Consciousness." In *The Politics of Democratic Inclusion*, edited by Christina Wolbrecht and Rodney E. Hero, 45–74. Philadelphia: Temple University Press, 2005.

Christman, Henry. *Tin Horns and Calico: A Decisive Episode in the Emergence of Democracy*. New York: Henry Holt, 1945.

Clark, Christopher. "The Consequences of the Market Revolution in the American North." In *The Market Revolution in America: Social, Political, and Religious Expressions, 1800–1880*, edited by Melvyn Stokes and Stephen Conway, 23–42. Charlottesville: University of Virginia Press, 1996.

Clark, Walter Van Tilburg. *The Ox-Bow Incident*. New York: American Library, 1940.

Cohn, Norman. *The Pursuit of the Millennium*. Revised and expanded ed. New York: Oxford University Press, 1970.

Collingwood, R. G. *The Idea of History*. London: Oxford University Press, 1956.

Cox, Anna-Lisa. *The Bone and Sinew of the Land: America's Forgotten Black Pioneers and the Struggle for Equality*. New York: Public Affairs, 2018.

Dahl, Robert A., and Bruce Stinebrickner. *Modern Political Analysis*. 6th ed. Upper Saddle River, NJ: Prentice Hall, 2003.

Davis, David Brion. "Some Themes of Counter-Subversion: An Analysis of Anti-Masonic, Anti-Catholic, and Anti-Mormon Literature." *Mississippi Valley Historical Review* 47 (September 1960): 206–24.

Davis, Rodney O. "Judge Ford and the Regulators, 1841–1842." In *Selected Papers in Illinois History*, edited by Bruce D. Cody, 25–36. Springfield: Illinois State Historical Society, 1981.

de Tocqueville, Alexis. *Democracy in America.* 1832–36. Reprint, edited by J. P. Mayer and translated by George Lawrence. Garden City, NY: Doubleday, 1969.

Dexter, Darrel. *Bondage in Egypt: Slavery in Southern Illinois.* Cape Girardeau: Southeast Missouri State University, 2011.

Diamond, Larry. *Developing Democracy: Toward Consolidation.* Baltimore: Johns Hopkins University Press, 1999.

Donaldson, Sue, and Will Kymlicka. *Zoopolis: A Political Theory of Animal Rights.* Oxford: Oxford University Press, 2011.

Douglas, Mary. *Natural Symbols: Explorations in Cosmology.* New York: Pantheon Books, 1970.

———. *Purity and Danger: An Analysis of the Concepts of Pollution and Taboo.* London: Routledge, 1966.

DuBois, W. E. B. *Black Reconstruction in America 1860–1880.* 1935. Reprint, New York: Atheneum, 1979.

Dworkin, Ronald. *Taking Rights Seriously.* Cambridge, MA: Harvard University Press, 1977.

Eby, Cecil D. *"That Disgraceful Affair," the Black Hawk War.* New York: W. W. Norton, 1973.

Edwards, Laura F. *The People and Their Peace: Legal Culture and the Transformation of Inequality in the Post-revolutionary South.* Chapel Hill: University of North Carolina Press, 2009.

———. "Sarah Allingham's Sheet and Other Lessons from Legal History." *Journal of the Early Republic* 38 (Spring 2018): 121–47.

Elazar, Daniel J. *Cities of the Prairie: The Metropolitan Frontier and American Politics.* New York: Basic Books, 1970.

Elazar, Daniel J., with Rozann Rothman, Stephen Schechter, Maren Allan Stein, and Joseph Zikmund II. *Cities of the Prairie Revisited: The Closing of the Metropolitan Frontier.* Lincoln: University of Nebraska Press, 1986.

Ellikson, Robert C. *Order without Law: How Neighbors Settle Disputes.* Cambridge, MA: Harvard University Press, 1991.

Ellis, Richard J. *American Political Cultures.* New York: Oxford University Press, 1992.

———. *The Dark Side of the American Left: Illiberal Egalitarianism in America.* Lawrence: University of Kansas Press, 1998.

Elster, Jon. *Solomonic Judgements: Studies in the Limitations of Rationality.* Cambridge: Cambridge University Press, 1989.

Ericson, David F. *The Shaping of American Liberalism: The Debates of Ratification, Nullification, and Slavery.* Chicago: University of Chicago Press, 1993.

Erikson, Robert E., Gerald C. Wright, and John P. McIver. *Statehouse Democracy: Public Opinion and Policy in the American States.* Cambridge: Cambridge University Press, 1993.

Erlewine, Robert. *Monotheism and Tolerance: Recovering a Religion of Reason*. Bloomington: Indiana University Press, 2010.

Evans, Peter B., Dietrich Rueshemeyer, and Theda Skocpol, eds. *Bringing the State Back In*. Cambridge: Cambridge University Press, 1985.

Faragher, John Mack. "'More Motley Than Mackinaw': From Ethnic Mixing to Ethnic Cleansing on the Frontier of the Lower Missouri, 1783–1833." In *Contact Points: American Frontiers from the Mohawk Valley to the Mississippi, 1750–1830*, edited by Andrew R. L. Cayton and Fredrika J. Teute, 304–26. Chapel Hill: University of North Carolina Press, 1998.

Feinberg, Joel. *Social Philosophy*. Englewood Cliffs, NJ: Prentice Hall, 1973.

Feldberg, Michael. *The Turbulent Era: Riot and Disorder in Jacksonian America*. New York: Oxford University Press, 1980.

Fenn, Richard K. *The Persistence of Purgatory*. Cambridge: Cambridge University Press, 1995.

Fitzgerald, Frances. *Cities on a Hill*. New York: Simon & Schuster, 1986.

Flanders, Robert Bruce. "The Kingdom of God in Illinois: Politics in Utopia." *Dialogue: A Journal of Mormon Thought* 5, no. 1 (Spring 1970): 26–36.

———. *Nauvoo: Kingdom on the Mississippi*. Urbana: University of Illinois Press, 1965.

Foster, Lawrence. *Religion and Sexuality: The Shakers, the Mormons, and the Oneida Community*. Urbana: University of Illinois Press, 1984.

———. *Women, Family, and Utopia: Communal Experiments of the Shakers, the Oneida Community, and the Mormons*. Syracuse, NY: Syracuse University Press, 1991.

Francis, Leslie Pickering, and Anita Silvers. "Liberalism and Individually Scripted Ideas of the Good: Meeting the Challenge of Dependent Agency." *Social Theory and Practice* 33, no. 2 (April 2007): 311–34.

Frankfurt, Harry G. "Freedom of the Will and the Concept of a Person." *Journal of Philosophy* 68, no. 1 (January 1971): 5–20.

Franklin, Frank George. *The Legislative History of the Naturalization Laws in the United States*. 1906. Reprint, New York: Arno Press, 1968.

Fraser, Nancy, and Linda Gordon. "A Genealogy of 'Dependency': Tracing a Keyword of the US Welfare State." In *Fortunes of Feminism:*

From State-Managed Capitalism to Neoliberal Crisis, edited by Nancy Fraser, 83–110. London: Verso, 2013.

Fredrickson, George M. *White Supremacy: A Comparative Study in American and South African History.* Oxford: Oxford University Press, 1981.

Friedman, Lawrence J. *Gregarious Saints: Self and Community in American Abolitionism 1830–1870.* Cambridge: Cambridge University Press, 1982.

Friendly, Fred A. *Minnesota Rag: The Dramatic Story of the Landmark Supreme Court Case That Gave New Meaning to the Freedom of the Press.* New York: Vintage Books, 1982.

Gallie, W. B. "Essentially Contested Concepts." *Proceedings of the Aristotelian Society* 56 (1955–56): 167–98.

Galston, William A. *Liberal Purposes: Goods, Virtues, and Diversity in the Liberal State.* Cambridge: Cambridge University Press, 1991.

Gellner, Ernest. *Conditions of Liberty: Civil Society and Its Rivals.* New York: Penguin Press, 1994.

———. *Nations and Nationalism.* Ithaca, NY: Cornell University Press, 1983.

Gerstle, Gary. *Liberty and Coercion: The Paradox of American Government from the Founding to the Present.* Princeton, NJ: Princeton University Press, 2015.

———. "The Resilient Power of the States across the Long Nineteenth Century: An Inquiry into a Pattern of American Government." In *The Unsustainable American State,* edited by Lawrence Jacobs and Desmond King, 61–87. New York: Oxford University Press, 2009.

Gill, Emily R. *Becoming Free: Autonomy and Diversity in the Liberal Polity.* Lawrence: University of Kansas Press, 2001.

Givens, Terryl L. *The Book of Mormon: A Very Short Introduction.* Oxford: Oxford University Press, 2009.

———. *The Viper on the Hearth: Mormons, Myths, and the Construction of Heresy.* New York: Oxford University Press, 1997.

Goodman, Paul. *Toward a Christian Republic: Antimasonry and the Great Transition in New England, 1826–1836.* New York: Oxford University Press, 1988.

Gottschalk, Marie. *The Prison and the Gallows: The Politics of Mass Incarceration in America.* Cambridge: Cambridge University Press, 2006.

Gramsci, Antonio. "The Study of Philosophy." *Selections from the Prison Notebooks.* Edited and translated by Quintin Hoare and Geoffrey Nowell Smith. New York: International Publishers, 1971.

Green, Steven K. *The Second Disestablishment: Church and State in Nineteenth-Century America.* New York: Oxford University Press, 2010.

Greenstone, J. David. *The Lincoln Persuasion: Remaking American Liberalism.* Princeton, NJ: Princeton University Press, 1993.

Grover, Frank R. "Indian Treaties Affecting Lands in the Present State of Illinois." *Journal of the Illinois State Historical Society* 8 (October 1915): 379–419.

Guarneri, Carl J. *The Utopian Alternative: Fourierism in Nineteenth-Century America.* Ithaca, NY: Cornell University Press, 1991.

Gunnell, John G. "Louis Hartz and the Liberal Metaphor: A Half-Century Later." *Studies in American Political Development* 19, no. 2 (Fall 2005): 196–205.

Gutmann, Amy. *Democratic Education.* 2nd ed. Princeton, NJ: Princeton University Press, 1999.

Hall, Stuart. "Gramsci's Relevance for the Study of Race and Ethnicity." In *Stuart Hall: Critical Dialogues in Cultural Studies,* edited by David Morley and Kuan-Hsing Chen, 411–40. London: Routledge, 1996.

Hallwas, John E. *Western Illinois Heritage.* Macomb, IL: Illinois Heritage Press, 1983.

Hallwas, John E., and Roger D. Launius. *Cultures in Conflict: A Documentary History of the Mormon War in Illinois.* Logan: Utah State University Press, 1995.

Hammond, Bray. *Banks and Politics in America: From the Revolution to the Civil War.* Princeton, NJ: Princeton University Press, 1957.

Hampshire, Annette P. *Mormonism in Conflict: The Nauvoo Years.* New York: Edwin Mellen Press, 1985.

———. "Thomas Sharp and Anti-Mormon Sentiment in Illinois, 1842–1846." *Journal of the Illinois State Historical Society* 72, no. 2 (May 1979): 82–100.

Hansen, Klaus J. *Mormonism and the American Experience.* Chicago: University of Chicago Press, 1981.

———. "The Political Kingdom of God as a Cause for Mormon-Gentile Conflict." *Brigham Young University Studies* 2, no. 2 (1960): 241–60.

———. *Quest for Empire: The Political Kingdom of God and the Council of Fifty in Mormon History.* East Lansing: Michigan State University Press, 1967.

Harper, Steven C. "'Dictated by Christ': Joseph Smith and the Politics of Revelation." *Journal of the Early Republic* 26, no. 2 (Summer 2006): 275–304.

Harrison, John F. C. *Quest for a New Moral World: Robert Owen and the Owenites in Britain and America.* New York: Charles Scribners' Sons, 1969.

Harris-Perry, Melissa V. *Sister Citizen: Shame, Stereotypes, and Black Women in America.* New Haven, CT: Yale University Press, 2011.

Hart, H. L. A. *The Concept of Law.* Oxford: Oxford University Press, 1961.

Hartz, Louis. *The Liberal Tradition in America.* New York: Harcourt, Brace & World, 1955.

Hatch, Nathan O. *The Democratization of American Christianity.* New Haven, CT: Yale University Press, 1989.

Hatch, Nathan O., and Mark A. Noll, eds. *The Bible in America: Essays in Cultural History.* New York: Oxford University Press, 1982.

Hedges, Andrew H. "Extradition, the Mormons, and the Election of 1843." *Journal of the Illinois State Historical Society* 109, no. 2 (Summer 2016): 127–47.

Hegel, G. W. F. *Elements of the Philosophy of Right.* 1821. Reprint, edited by Allen W. Wood and translated by H. B. Nisbit. Cambridge: Cambridge University Press, 1991.

Herman, Barbara. "Pluralism and the Community of Moral Judgment." In *Toleration: An Elusive Virtue,* edited by David Heyd. Princeton, NJ: Princeton University Press, 1996.

Hiers, Wesley. "Party Matters: Racial Closure in the Nineteenth-Century United States." *Social Science History* 37, no. 2 (Summer 2013): 255–308.

Hill, Marvin S. *Quest for Refuge: The Mormon Flight from American Pluralism.* Salt Lake City: Signature Books, 1989.

Hinckley, Gordon B. *Truth Restored: A Short History of The Church of Jesus Christ of Latter-day Saints.* Salt Lake City: The Church of Jesus Christ of Latter-day Saints, 1979.

Hobbes, Thomas. *Leviathan with Selected Variants from the Latin Edition of 1668.* Edited with introduction by Edwin Curley. Indianapolis: Hackett Publishing, 1994.

Hofstadter, Robert. *The Paranoid Style in American Politics and Other Essays.* Chicago: University of Chicago Press, 1979.

Hogan, Mervin B. *Mormonism and Freemasonry: The Illinois Episode.* Richmond, VA: Macoy, 1977.

Holmes, Stephen. "Gag Rules or the Politics of Omission." In *Constitutionalism and Democracy,* edited by Jon Elster and Rune Slagstad, 19–58. Cambridge: Cambridge University Press, 1988.

Holt, Michael F. *Political Parties and American Political Development from the Age of Jackson to the Age of Lincoln.* Baton Rouge: Louisiana State University Press, 1992.

Homer, Michael W. *Joseph's Temples: The Dynamic Relationship between Freemasonry and Mormonism*. Salt Lake City: University of Utah Press, 2014.

Howe, Daniel Walker. *The Political Culture of the American Whigs*. Chicago: University of Chicago Press, 1979.

Hubbart, Henry Clyde. *The Older Middle West 1840–1880*. New York: D. Appleton-Century, 1936.

Huntington, Samuel. *Political Order in Changing Societies*. New Haven, CT: Yale University Press, 1968.

Hughes, Richard T., and C. Leonard Allen. *Illusions of Innocence: Protestant Primitivism in America, 1630–1875*. Chicago: University of Chicago Press, 1988.

James, William. *The Varieties of Religious Experience*. New York: Collier Books, 1902.

Jensen, Richard. *The Winning of the Midwest: Social and Political Conflict, 1888–1896*. Chicago: University of Chicago Press, 1971.

John, Richard R. *Spreading the News: The American Postal System from Franklin to Morse*. Cambridge, MA: Harvard University Press, 1995.

———. "The State *Is* Back In: Now What?" *Journal of the Early Republic* 38, no. 1 (Spring 2018): 105–18.

Johnson, Doug. *The Idea of a Liberal Theory*. Princeton, NJ: Princeton University Press, 1991.

Johnson, Paul E., and Sean Wilentz. *The Kingdom of Matthias: A Story of Sex and Salvation in 19th-Century America*. New York: Oxford University Press, 1994.

Kant, Immanuel. "What Is Enlightenment?" In *The Philosophy of Kant*. New York: The Modern Library, 1949. "What Is Enlightment?" originally published in 1784.

Katznelson, Ira. "Working Class Formation and American Exceptionalism, Yet Again." In *American Exceptionalism? US Working-Class Formation in an International Context*, edited by Rick Halpern and Jonathan Morris, 36–55. New York: St. Martin's, 1997.

Keane, John. *Civil Society: Old Ideals, New Visions*. Stanford, CA: Stanford University Press, 1998.

Kelly, Edith Packard. "Northern Illinois in the Great Whig Convention of 1840." In *Transactions of the Illinois State Historical Society*. Springfield: Illinois State Journal, 1915.

Key, V. O. *Southern Politics in State and Nation*. New York: Vintage Book, 1949.

Kimball, James L. "The Nauvoo Charter: A Reinterpretation." In *Kingdom on the Mississippi Revisited*, edited by Roger D. Launius and John E. Hallwas, 39–47. Urbana: University of Illinois Press, 1966.

Kimball, Stanley B. “The Mormons in Early Illinois: Introduction.” *Dialogue: A Journal of Mormon Thought* 5, no.1 (Spring 1970): 9–12.

King, Desmond. *In the Name of Liberalism: Illiberal Social Policy in the United States and Britain*. Oxford: Oxford University Press, 1999.

King, Desmond, and Rogers M. Smith. *Still a House Divided: Race and Politics in Obama's America*. Princeton, NJ: Princeton University Press, 2011.

Kohl, Lawrence Frederick. “The Concept of Social Control and the History of Jacksonian America.” *Journal of the Early Republic* 5, no. 1 (Spring 1985): 21–34.

———. *The Politics of Individualism: Parties and the American Character in the Jacksonian Era*. New York: Oxford University Press, 1989.

Koslofsky, Craig. “Explaining Change.” In *The Oxford Handbook of the Protestant Reformations*, edited by Ulinka Rublack, 585–600. Oxford: Oxford University Press, 2017.

Kramnick, Isaac, and R. Lawrence Moore. *The Godless Constitution: A Moral Defense of the Secular State*. New York: Norton, 2005.

Krenkel, John Henry. *Illinois Internal Improvements*. Cedar Rapids, IA: Torch Press, 1958.

Kymlicka, Will. *Contemporary Political Philosophy: An Introduction*.Oxford: Oxford University Press, 1990.

———. *Multicultural Citizenship: A Liberal Theory of Minority Rights*. Oxford: Oxford University Press, 1995.

Kymlicka, Will, and Wayne Norman. “Return of the Citizen: A Survey of Recent Work on Citizenship Theory.” In *Theorizing Citizenship*, edited by Ronald Beiner, 283–322. Albany: State University of New York Press, 1995.

Laats, Adam, and Harvey Siegel. *Teaching Evolution in a Creation Nation*. Chicago: University of Chicago Press, 2016.

Lamb, John M. *Historical Essays on the Illinois-Michigan Canal*. Romeoville, IL: Lewis University, 2009.

LaRoche, Cheryl Janifer. *The Geography of Resistance: Free Black Communities and the Underground Railroad*. Urbana: University of Illinois Press, 2014.

Larson, Scott. “‘Indescribable Being’: Theological Performances of Genderlessness in the Society of the Publick Universal Friend, 1776–1819.” *Early American Studies* 12, no. 3 (Fall 2014): 576–600.

Lasch, Christopher. *The True and Only Heaven: Progress and Its Critics*. New York: W. W. Norton, 1991.

Leonard, Gerald. *The Invention of Party Politics: Federalism, Popular Sovereignty, and Constitutional Development in Jacksonian Illinois*. Chapel Hill: University of North Carolina Press, 2002.

Levi, Edward H. *An Introduction to Legal Reasoning*. Chicago: University of Chicago Press, 1949.

Lewis, Jan. "The Problem of Slavery in Southern Political Discourse." In *Devising Liberty*, edited by David Thomas Konig, 265–97. Stanford, CA: Stanford University Press, 1993.

Lijphart, Arend. *Democracies: Patterns of Majoritarian and Consensus Government in Twenty-One Countries*. New Haven, CT: Yale University Press, 1984.

———. *The Politics of Accommodation: Pluralism and Democracy in the Netherlands*. Berkeley: University of California Press, 1968.

Locke, John. *The Second Treatise on Government and A Letter Concerning Toleration*. Mineola, NY: Dover Publications, 2002.

Lowi, Theodore J. "Four Systems of Politics, Policy, and Choice." *Public Administration Review* 32, no. 4 (July/August 1972): 298–310.

Maalouf, Amin. *In the Name of Identity*. Translated by Barbara Bray. 1996. Reprint, New York: Penguin Books, 2000.

Machiavelli, Niccolo. *The Discourses*. Edited by Bernard Crick. Translated by Leslie J. Walker. New York: Penguin Books, 1986.

Macpherson, C. B. *Democratic Theory: Essays in Retrieval*. Oxford: Clarendon Press, 1973.

———. *The Real World of Democracy*. Oxford: Clarendon Press, 1966.

Mahon, John K. *The War of 1812*. New York: Da Capo, 1991.

March, Eudocia Baldwin, Douglas L. Wilson, and Rodney O. Davis. "Mormons in Hancock County: A Reminiscence." *Journal of the Illinois State Historical Society* 64 (Spring 1971): 22–65.

Marcus, George E., Sandra L. Wood, and Elizabeth Theiss-Morse. "Linking Neuroscience to Political Intolerance and Political Judgment." *Politics and Life Sciences* 17, no. 1 (September 1998): 165–78.

Mardsen, George M. "Everyone One's Own Interpreter? The Bible, Science, and Authority in Mid-Nineteenth-Century America." In *The Bible in America: Essays in Cultural History*, edited by Nathan O. Hatch and Mark A. Noll, 79–100. New York: Oxford University Press, 1982.

Marx, Karl. *The Eighteenth Brumaire of Louis Bonaparte*. 1852. Reprint, New York: International Publishers, 1963.

Marx, Karl, and Frederick Engels. "Manifesto of the Communist Party." In *The Marx-Engels Reader*, edited by Robert C. Tucker, 469–500, 2nd ed. New York: W. W. Norton, 1978.

Mathews, Donald G. *Religion in the Old South*. Chicago: University of Chicago Press, 1977.

Mathews, Donald R., and James W. Prothro. "Social and Economic Factors and Negro Voter Registration in the South." *American Political Science Review* 57 (March 1963): 24–44.

McCloskey, Robert G. *The American Supreme Court.* Chicago: University of Chicago Press, 1960.

McConnell, Grant. *The Decline of Agrarian Democracy.* Berkeley: University of California Press, 1952.

———. *Private Power and American Democracy.* New York: Vintage, 1966.

McCormick, Richard P. *The Second American Party System: Party Formation in the Jacksonian Era.* Chapel Hill: University of North Carolina Press, 1966.

McFaul, John M. *The Politics of Jacksonian Finance.* Ithaca, NY: Cornell University Press, 1972.

McGrane, Reginald Charles. *The Panic of 1837: Some Financial Problems of the Jacksonian Era.* 1924. Reprint, Chicago: University of Chicago Press, 1965.

McLoughlin, William G., Jr. *Modern Revivalism: Charles Grandison Finney to Billy Graham.* New York: Ronald Press, 1959.

———. *Revivals, Awakenings, and Reform.* Chicago: University of Chicago Press, 1978.

Mendus, Susan, ed. *Justifying Toleration: Conceptual and Historical Perspectives.* Cambridge: Cambridge University Press, 2009.

Meyer, Douglas K. *Making the Heartland Quilt: A Geographical History of Settlement and Migration in Early-Nineteenth Century Illinois.* Carbondale: Southern Illinois University Press, 2000.

Mill, John Stuart. *On Liberty and Other Essays.* Edited by John Gray. Oxford: Oxford University Press, 1991.

Miller, Nicholas R. "Pluralism and Social Choice." *American Political Science Review* 77, no. 3 (September 1983): 734–47.

Miller, Perry. *Errand into the Wilderness.* Cambridge, MA: Harvard University Press, 1956.

Moore, R. Lawrence. *Religious Outsiders and the Making of Americans.* New York: Oxford University Press, 1986.

Morgan, Edmund S. *The Puritan Family Religion and Domestic Relations in Seventeenth-Century New England.* New York: Harper & Row, 1966.

Newell, Linda King, and Valeen Tippetts Avery. *Mormon Enigma: Emma Hale Smith: Prophet's Wife, "Elect Lady," Polygamy's Foe, 1804–1879.* Garden City, NY: Doubleday, 1984.

Niebuhr, H. Richard. *The Social Sources of Denominationalism.* 1929. Reprint, Cleveland: Meridian Books, 1957.

Nolt, Steven M. *A History of the Amish*. Intercourse, PA: Good Books, 1992.

Norgren, Jill. *The Cherokee Cases: The Confrontation of Law and Politics*. New York: McGraw-Hill, 1996.

Norton, Anne. *Alternative Americas: A Reading of Antebellum Political Culture*. Chicago: University of Chicago Press, 1986.

Novak, William J. "The Myth of the 'Weak' American State." *American Historical Review* 113, no. 3 (June 2008): 752–72.

———. *The People's Welfare: Law and Regulation in Nineteenth-Century America*. Chapel Hill: University of North Carolina Press, 1996.

Oaks, Dallin H. "The Suppression of the *Nauvoo Expositor*." *Utah Law Review* 9 (Winter 1965): 862–903.

Oaks, Dallin H., and Marvin S. Hill. *Carthage Conspiracy: The Trial of the Accused Assassins of Joseph Smith*. Urbana: University of Illinois Press, 1975.

Obert, Jonathan, and Eleonara Mattiacci. "Keeping Vigil: The Emergence of Vigilance Committees in Pre–Civil War America." *Perspectives on Politics* 16 (September 2018): 600–616.

O'Dea, Thomas. *The Mormons*. Chicago: University of Chicago Press, 1957.

Olson, Mancur, Jr. *The Logic of Collective Action: Public Goods and the Theory of Groups*. Cambridge, MA: Harvard University Press, 1965.

Onuf, Peter. *Statehood and Union: A History of the Northwest Ordinance*. Bloomington: Indiana University Press, 1987.

Opal, J. M. *Avenging the People: Andrew Jackson, the Rule of Law, and the American Nation*. New York: Oxford University Press, 2017.

Orrin, Karen, and Steven Skowronek. *The Search for American Political Development*. Cambridge: Cambridge University Press, 2004.

Osgood, Robert E., and Robert W. Tucker. *Force, Order, and Justice*. Baltimore: Johns Hopkins University Press, 1967.

Owens, Kenneth N. *Galena, Grant, and the Fortunes of War*. DeKalb: Northern Illinois University Press, 1964.

Pease, Theodore Calvin. *The Frontier State 1818–1848*. 1918. Reprint, Urbana: University of Illinois Press, 1987.

Peck, John Mason. *A Gazeteer of Illinois*. Jacksonville: Goudy, 1834.

Peirce, Charles S. *Essays in the Philosophy of Science*. Edited by Vincent Thomas. Indianapolis: Bobbs-Merrill, 1957.

Peterson, Jacqueline. "'Wild' Chicago: The Formation and Destruction of a Multiracial Community on the Midwestern Frontier, 1816–1837." In *The Ethnic Frontier: Essays in the History of Group Survival in Chicago and the Midwest*, edited by Melvin

G. Holli and Peter d'A. Jones, 25–71. Grand Rapids, MI: Eerdmans, 1977.

Pfeifer, Michael J. *Rough Justice: Lynching and American Society, 1874–1947*. Urbana: University of Illinois Press, 2004.

Pirtle, Carol. *Escape Betwixt Two Suns: A True Tale of the Underground Railroad in Illinois*. Carbondale: Southern Illinois University Press, 2000.

Plach, Casey. "Group Membership and Its Adverse Effects in *The Ox-Bow Incident*." Unpublished manuscript, October 11, 2011. https://www.iwu.edu/political-science/casey-plach-essay-pdf.pdf.

Plutarch. *Plutarch's Lives*. Translation by Bernadotte Perrin. 1914. Reprint, Cambridge, MA: Harvard University Press, 1967.

Pocock, J. G. A. *The Machiavellian Moment: Florentine Political Thought and the Atlantic Republican Tradition*. Princeton, NJ: Princeton University Press, 1975.

Poggi, Gianfranco. *The Development of the Modern State: A Sociological Introduction*. Stanford, CA: Stanford University Press, 1978.

Pope, Alexander. *Poetry and Prose of Alexander Pope*. Edited by Aubrey Williams. Boston: Houghton Mifflin, 1969.

Popper, Karl. "Toleration and Intellectual Responsibility." In *On Toleration*, edited by Susan Mendus and David Edwards, 17–34. Oxford: Clarendon Press, 1987.

Pratt, Harry E. *Lincoln 1809–1839*. Springfield, IL: Abraham Lincoln Association, 1941.

Putnam, Hilary. *The Many Faces of Realism*. LaSalle, IL: Open Court, 1987.

Putnam, James William. *The Illinois and Michigan Canal: A Study in Economic History*. Chicago: University of Chicago Press, 1918.

Ratcliffe, Donald J. "Antimasonry and Partisanship in Greater New England, 1826–1836." *Journal of the Early Republic* 15, no. 2 (Summer 1995): 199–239.

Rawls, John. *A Theory of Justice*. Cambridge, MA: Harvard University Press, 1971.

Reeve, W. Paul. *Religion of a Different Color: Race and the Mormon Struggle with Whiteness*. Oxford: Oxford University Press, 2015.

Richards, Leonard L. *"Gentlemen of Property and Standing": Anti-abolition Mobs in Jacksonian America*. London: Oxford University Press, 1970.

Robinson, Stacy M. *Hearts Beating for Liberty: Women Abolitionists in the Old Northwest*. Chapel Hill: University of North Carolina Press, 2010.

Rogers, Brent M. "Armed Men Are Coming from the State of Missouri." *Journal of the Illinois State Historical Society* 109, no. 2 (Summer 2016): 148–79.

Rohrbough, Malcolm J. *The Land Office Business: The Settlement and Administration of American Public Lands, 1789–1837*. London: Oxford University Press, 1968.

Ron, Ariel, and Gautham Rao. "Introduction: Taking Stock of the State in Nineteenth-Century America." *Journal of the Early Republic* 38, no. 1 (Spring 2018): 61–66.

Rosenbaum, H. Jon, and Peter C. Sederberg, eds. *Vigilante Politics*. Philadelphia: University of Pennsylvania Press, 1976.

Ross, Steven J. "The Transformation of Republican Ideology." *Journal of the New Republic* 10, no. 3 (Autumn 1990): 323–30.

Rousseau, Jean-Jacques. *Of the Social Contract*. 1762. Translated by Donald A. Cress. Introduction by Peter Gay. Indianapolis: Hackett Publishing, 1988.

Rugh, Susan Sessions. *Our Common Country: Family Farming, Culture, and Community in the Nineteenth-Century Midwest*. Bloomington: Indiana University Press, 2001.

———. "Saints and Old Settlers: The Conflict in Hancock County, Illinois, 1840–1846." Paper 91–3, Newberry Papers in Family and Community History, 1993, pp. 1–37. Chicago: Newberry Library, 1991.

Sandel, Michael. *Liberalism and the Limits of Justice*. Cambridge: Cambridge University Press, 1982.

Schattschneider, E. E. *The Semi-Sovereign People: A Realist View of Democracy in America*. Fort Worth, TX: Holt, Reinhart, and Winston, 1975.

Schelling, Thomas. *Micromotives and Macrobehavior*. New York. W. W. Norton, 1978.

Schweber, Howard. *The Creation of American Common Law, 1850–1880: Technology, Politics, and the Construction of Citizenship*. Cambridge: Cambridge University Press, 2004.

Scott, James C. *Seeing Like a State: How Certain Schemes to Improve the Human Condition Have Failed*. New Haven, CT: Yale University Press, 1998.

Sellars, Charles. *The Market Revolution: Jacksonian America, 1815–1846*. New York: Oxford University Press, 1991.

Sennett, Richard. *The Uses of Disorder: Personal Identity and City Life*. New York: Vintage Books, 1970.

Shackel, Paul A. *New Philadelphia: An Archaeology of Race in the Heartland*. Berkeley: University of California Press, 2011.

Shalope, Robert E. "Toward a Republican Synthesis: The Emergence of an Understanding of Republicanism in American

Historiography." *William & Mary Quarterly* 29, no. 1 (January 1970): 49–80.

Sherif, Muzafur. "Experiments in Group Conflict." *Scientific American* 195 (1956): 54–58.

Shermer, Michael. *Why People Believe Weird Things: Pseudoscience, Superstition, and Other Confusions of Our Time.* New York: Henry Holt, 1997.

Shipps, Jan. *Mormonism: The Story of a New Religious Tradition.* Urbana: University of Illinois Press, 1985.

Shklar, Judith N. "Jean-Jacques Rousseau and Equality." In *Rousseau's Political Writings,* edited by Alan Ritter and Julia Conway Bondanella, 260–74. New York: W. W. Norton, 1988.

Simeone, James. "The 1830 Contest for Governor and the Politics of Resentment." *Journal of the Illinois State Historical Society* 102, no. 3/4 (Fall–Winter 2009): 282–306.

———. *Democracy and Slavery in Frontier Illinois: The Bottomland Republic.* DeKalb: Northern Illinois University Press, 2000.

———. "Reassessing Jacksonian Political Culture: William Leggett's Egalitarianism." *American Political Thought* 4, no. 3 (Summer 2015): 359–90.

———. "William Kinney's Agrarian Dilemma." *Journal of Illinois History* 13 (Spring 2010): 2–32.

Singer, Peter. "All Animals Are Equal." *Philosophical Exchange* 1 (1974): 103–16.

Skinner, Quintin. *Foundations of Modern Political Thought.* Vol. 1. Cambridge: Cambridge University Press, 1978.

Skowronek, Stephen. *Building a New American State: The Expansion of National Administrative Capacities, 1877–1920.* Cambridge: Cambridge University Press, 1982.

———. *The Politics Presidents Make: Leadership from John Adams to Bill Clinton.* Cambridge, MA: Harvard University Press, 1997.

———. "Present at the Creation: The State in Early American Political History." *Journal of the Early Republic* 38, no. 1 (Spring 2018): 95–103.

Skowronek, Stephen, and Mathew Glassman, eds. *Formative Acts: American Politics in the Making.* Philadelphia: University of Pennsylvania Press, 2007.

Smith, Alex D. "Untouchable: Joseph Smith's Use of the Law as Catalyst for Assassination." *Journal of the Illinois State Historical Society* 112, no. 1 (Spring 2019): 8–42.

Smith, Andrew F. *Saintly Scoundrel: The Life and Times of John Cook Bennett.* Urbana: University of Illinois Press, 1997.

Smith, Nicholas Rush. *Contradictions of Democracy: Vigilantism and Rights in Post-apartheid South Africa*. Oxford: Oxford University Press, 2019.

Smith, Rogers M. *Civic Ideals: Conflicting Visions of Citizenship in U.S. History*. New Haven, CT: Yale University Press, 1997.

———. *Stories of Peoplehood: The Politics and Morals of Political Membership*. Cambridge: Cambridge University Press, 2003.

Smith, Rogers M., and Desmond King. "Racial Orders in American Political Development." *American Political Science Review* 99 (February 2005): 75–92.

Smith, Stephen D. *Foreordained Failure: The Quest for a Constitutional Principle of Religious Freedom*. New York: Oxford University Press, 1995.

Sniderman, Paul M., and Edward G. Carmines. *Reaching Beyond Race*. Cambridge, MA: Harvard University Press, 1997.

Snyder, John Francis. *Adam J. Snyder and His Period in Illinois History, 1817–1842*. Virginia, IL: E. Needham, 1906.

———. "Governor Ford and His Family." *Journal of the Illinois State Historical Society* 3, no. 2 (July 1910): 45–51.

Stegner, Wallace. *Mormon Country*. 1942. Reprinted with introduction by Richard W. Etulain. Lincoln: University of Nebraska Press, 2003.

Steinmetz, George, ed. *State/Culture: State Formation After the Cultural Turn*. Ithaca: Cornell University Press, 1999.

Steinmo, Sven, Frank Longstreth, and Kathleen Ann Thelen, eds. *Structuring Politics: Historical Institutionalism in Comparative Politics*. Cambridge: Cambridge University Press, 1992.

Stevens, Frank E. *The Black Hawk War*. Chicago: published by the author, 1903.

Stoll, Steven. *Larding the Lean Earth: Soil and Society in Nineteenth-Century America*. New York: Hill and Wang, 2002.

Stowell, Daniel, ed. *In Tender Consideration*. Urbana: University of Illinois Press, 2002.

Stuckey, Erma D. *Darnall, Spence, Steers, Spangler, Stuckey, Sill*. Henry, IL: M&D Printing, 1983.

Stuhlmacher, Peter. *Historical Criticism and Theological Interpretation of Scripture*. Philadelphia: Fortress Press, 1977.

Sunstein, Cass R. *Democracy and the Problem of Free Speech*. New York: Free Press, 1995.

———. "Incompletely Theorized Agreements in Constitutional Law." Working paper, University of Chicago Public Law and Theory, number 147, 2007.

———. *The Partial Constitution*. Cambridge, MA: Harvard University Press, 1993.

Sutton, William R. *Journeymen for Jesus: Evangelical Artisans Confront Capitalism in Jacksonian Baltimore*. University Park: Pennsylvania State University Press, 1998.

Swierenga, Robert P. *Pioneers and Profits: Land Speculation on the Iowa Frontier*. Ames: Iowa State University Press, 1968.

Tambiah, Stanley. *Leveling Crowds: Ethnonationalist Conflicts and Collective Violence in South Asia*. Berkeley: University of California Press, 1996.

Taylor, Samuel W. *Nightfall at Nauvoo*. New York: Avon Books, 1971.

Temin, Peter. *The Jacksonian Economy*. New York: W. W. Norton, 1969.

Thompson, Charles Manfred. "Attitude of the Western Whigs toward the Convention System." *Proceedings of the Mississippi Valley Historical Association* 5 (1912): 167–89.

———. *The Illinois Whigs before 1846*. Urbana: University of Illinois, 1915.

Thompson, Michael, Richard Ellis, and Aaron Wildavsky. *Cultural Theory*. Boulder, CO: Westview Press, 1990.

Tilly, Charles. *Democracy*. Cambridge: Cambridge University Press, 2007.

Tobin, Catharine. "The Lowly Muscular Digger: Irish Canal Workers in Nineteenth Century America." PhD diss., University of Notre Dame, 1987.

Toll, Robert C. *Blacking Up: The Minstrel Show in Nineteenth-Century America*. New York: Oxford University Press, 1974.

Troll, Millie. *Historical Account of the Origin, Growth, and Development of the Village of Tremont, Illinois*. Morton, IL: Johnson Printing, 1925.

Tuveson, Ernest Lee. *Redeemer Nation: The Idea of America's Millennial Role*. 1968. Reprint, Chicago: University of Chicago Press, 1980.

Underwood, Grant. *The Millenarian World of Early Mormonism*. Urbana: University of Illinois Press, 1993.

Valelly, Richard M., Susanne Mettler, and Robert C. Lieberman, eds. *The Oxford Handbook of American Political Development*. New York: Oxford University Press, 2016.

Van Doren, Carl. *Benjamin Franklin*. 1938. Reprint, New York: Penguin Books, 1991.

Van Dyke, Vernon. "The Individual, the State, and Ethnic Communities in Political Theory." *World Politics* 29, no. 3 (April 1977): 343–69.

Varshney, Ashutosh. *Ethnic Conflict and Civil Life: Hindus and Muslims in India*. New Haven: Yale University Press, 2002.

Von Clausewitz, Carl. *War, Politics, and Power.* Translated and edited by Edward M. Collins. South Bend, IN: Regency, 1962.

Voss-Hubbard, Mark. "The 'Third Party Tradition' Reconsidered: Third Parties and American Public Life, 1830–1900." *Journal of American History* 86, no. 1 (June 1999): 121–50.

Waldrep, Christopher. "Word and Deed: The Language of Lynching, 1820–1953." In *Lethal Imagination: Violence and Brutality in American History,* edited by Michael A. Bellesiles, 228–58. New York: New York University Press, 1999.

Waldsteicher, David. *Slavery's Constitution: From Revolution to Ratification.* New York: Hill & Wang, 2010.

Walker, Juliet E. K. *Free Frank: A Black Pioneer on the Antebellum Frontier.* Lexington: University Press of Kentucky, 1983.

Walzer, Michael. *Spheres of Justice: A Defense of Pluralism and Equality.* New York: Basic Books, 1983.

Way, Frank, and Barbara J. Burt. "Religious Marginality and the Free Exercise Clause." *American Political Science Review* 77, no. 3 (September 1983): 652–65.

Way, Peter. *Common Labour: Workers and the Digging of North American Canals: 1780–1860.* Cambridge: Cambridge University Press, 1993.

Weber, Max. *From Max Weber: Essays in Sociology.* Edited by H. H. Gerth and C. Wright Mills. Oxford: Oxford University Press, 1946.

———. *Economy and Society: An Outline of Interpretive Sociology.* Vol. 2, edited by Guenther Roth and Claus Wittich. New York: Bedminster Press, 1968.

Weiner, Dana E. "Anti-abolition Violence and Freedom of Speech in Peoria, Illinois, 1843–1848." *Journal of Illinois History* 11 (Autumn 2008): 179–204.

Wells, H. G. *The Future in America: A Search after Realities.* 1906. Reprint, New York: Arno Press, 1974.

Whitehead, Laurence. "Three International Dimensions of Democratization." In *The International Dimensions of Democratization: Europe and the Americas,* edited by Laurence Whitehead, 3–25. Oxford: Oxford University Press, 1996.

Williams, Oscar, and Edwin Honig, eds. *The Mentor Book of Major American Poets.* New York: New American Library, 1962.

Willis, John Randolph. *God's Frontiersmen: The Yale Band in Illinois.* Washington, DC: University Press of America, 1979.

Wilson, Major L. *Space, Time, and Freedom: The Quest for Nationality and the Irrepressible Conflict 1815–1861.* Westport, CT: Greenwood Press, 1974.

Winkle, Kenneth J. *The Politics of Community: Migration and Politics in Antebellum Ohio.* Cambridge: Cambridge University Press, 1988.

———. "The Voters of Lincoln's Springfield: Migration and Participation in an Antebellum City." *Journal of Social History* 25 (March 1992): 595–611.

Winn, Kenneth H. *Exiles in a Land of Liberty: Mormons in America, 1830–1846.* Chapel Hill: University of North Carolina Press, 1989.

Witgen, Michael. "Seeing Red: Race, Citizenship, and Indigeneity in the Old Northwest." *Journal of the Early Republic* 38, no. 4 (Winter 2018): 581–611.

Witte, John, Jr. "Blest Be the Ties That Bind: Covenant and Community in Puritan Thought." *Emory Law Journal* 36 (Spring 1987): 579–602.

Yack, Bernard. "The Myth of the Civic Nation." In *Theorizing Nationalism,* edited by Ronald Beiner, 103–18. Albany: State University of New York Press, 1999.

Young, Iris Marion. *Justice and the Politics of Difference.* Princeton, NJ: Princeton University Press, 1990.

Zinn, Howard. *Disobedience and Democracy: Nine Fallacies on Law and Order.* Cambridge, MA: South End Press, 2002.

Zoellick, Todd. "Daniel Elazar, Bogus or Brilliant? A Study of Political Culture across the American States." *Res Publica: Journal of Undergraduate Research* 5 (2000): 1–11.

Index

Page numbers in italics refer to figures and tables.